Gender, Work and Wages in the Soviet Union

Gender, Work and Wages in the Soviet Union

A Legacy of Discrimination

Katarina Katz
Research Fellow
Department of Economics
Stockholm University
Sweden

First published 2001 by
PALGRAVE
Houndmills, Basingstoke, Hampshire RG21 6XS and
175 Fifth Avenue, New York, N. Y. 10010
Companies and representatives throughout the world

PALGRAVE is the new global academic imprint of
St. Martin's Press LLC Scholarly and Reference Division and
Palgrave Publishers Ltd (formerly Macmillan Press Ltd).

ISBN 0–333–73414–9

A catalogue record for this book is available
from the British Library.

Library of Congress Cataloging-in-Publication Data
Katz, Katarina, 1953–
    Gender, work and wages in the Soviet Union : a legacy
of discrimination / Katarina Katz.
        p. cm.
    Presented as the author's thesis (doctoral—Gothenburg)
    Includes bibliographical references and index.
    ISBN 0–333–73414–9 (cloth)
    1. Wages—Women—Soviet Union. 2. Women—Employment–
–Soviet Union. 3. Sex discrimination in employment—Soviet
Union. I. Title.
    HD6166 .K34 2000
    331.4'2947—dc21
                                                    00–053095

10   9   8   7   6   5   4   3   2   1
10   09 08 07 06 05 04 03 02 01

Printed and bound in Great Britain by
Antony Rowe Ltd, Chippenham, Wiltshire

To my parents

Contents

List of Tables

List of Figures

List of Abbreviations

Goskomstat	*Goskomstat SSSR*, the Soviet Statistical Agency, *Goskomstat Rossii* (*Rossiiskoi Federatsii*), the Statistical Agency of the Russian Federation
ITD	*Individual'naia trudovaia deiatel'nost'*, individual labour activity
ITR	*Inzhenerno-tekhnicheskie rabotniki*, engineering-technical staff
MOP	*Mladshii obsluzhivaiushchii personal*, junior service staff
PTU	*Professional'no-tekhnicheskoe uchilishche*, technical-vocational school
RSFSR	Russian Soviet Federal Socialist Republic
SSUZ	*Spetsial'noe srednee uchebnoe zavedenie*, specialised secondary educational institution
USSR	Union of Soviet Socialist Republics, Soviet Union
VUZ	*Vysshchee uchebnoe zavedenie*, institution for higher education

Acknowledgements

A work that has been carried on over a number of years draws on the knowledge, advice and encouragement of a great number of people. As explained in chapter 1, my dissertation project of analysing Soviet wage data would have been impossible without the support of Anastasia Posadskaya and Natalia Rimashevskaya, Institute for Socio-Economic Population Studies (ISEPS), Ludmila Nivorozhkina, University of Rostov and my two thesis advisers, Johan Lönnroth and Anders Klevmarken. I also thank the Swedish Council for Social Research, the Swedish Institute and the Royal Swedish Academy of Sciences for the necessary funding.

With a thesis task as broad as this, I was lucky to have two advisers, with different fields of expertise but similar patience in reading and improving endless piles of manuscript. I am indebted also to so many other friends and colleagues in the Department of Econolmics at the University of Göteborg that I can only mention some. Wlodek Bursztyn and Björn Gustafsson provided advice and support through the whole venture, Lennart Flood filled in gaps in my econometrics.

I thank Alastair McAuley – who acted as faculty discussant for the thesis – and John Micklewright, Inga Persson, Elena Glinskaya, referees and editors of the *Cambridge Journal of Economics and Labour Economics* for many helpful comments and advice. Permission from Oxford University Press to use materials which have been published in the *Cambridge Journal of Economics*, vol. 21:4 (July 1997) in chapter 5 is gratefully acknowledged. Tables 2.1 and 2.2 are reprinted from *International Review of Comparative Public Policy*, vol. 3, S. L. Willborn, 'Women's Wages: Stability and Change in Six Industrialised Countries', p. 2. © 1991 with permission from Elsevier Science. Without the interest and encouragement of my friends I would probably have given up halfway from thesis to book. Special thanks go to Irene Bruegel and Kent Kjellgren.

I owe a lot to all the Russian friends and colleagues who have offered time, information, Russian tea and hospitality, among them Anastasia Posadskaya, Elena Mezentseva and Marina Baskakova at the Moscow Centre for Gender Studies, Professor Rimashevskaya, Olga Vershinskaya, Marina Pisklakova and others at the ISEPS and, above all, Ludmila Nivorozhkina, who has remained a source of advice and encouragement for many years. I learnt much from the late Dr Marina Mozhina and from the colleagues in her laboratory.

The Swedish Council for Social Research and the Swedish Collegium for Advanced Study in the Social Sciences provided the opportunity to write chapter 7. I thank Louise Grogan for a lot of valuable information and comments and Lena Barregård for excellent research assistance. I have made every effort to contact the copyright holders for permission to use their material.

It remains to say that none of those mentioned are responsible for remaining errors or for the views expressed in the book.

1
Introduction

1.1 The roots of the present in the past

The gigantic social and economic experiment carried out in post-USSR Russia has been accompanied by great and widespread hardship. The fate of women has, justly, raised particular concern. Accounts ranging from the anecdotal to scholarly case studies present us with two interrelated images – the polarisation between rich and poor, and the polarisation between women and men.

Obviously, women and men are found among both the rich and the poor. Yet, even at the level of media coverage there is a gender difference, which cannot be reduced to a general problem of poverty. When a Russian woman appears in the Western media, she is an unnamed representative of a group, an 'a': 'a teacher who hasn't been paid', 'a pensioner living in poverty', 'a single mother struggling to support her children', 'a prostitute', 'a "biznesmen"'s wife or mistress'. A man may also be introduced simply as 'a worker', 'a street vendor', 'a miner', but not necessarily. He can be a 'the', somebody – 'the minister', 'the head of the company', 'the mayor'; a woman hardly ever is.

Members of government, members of parliament (92 per cent of them), influential bankers and directors are male. Yet, the fact that the powerful are men is not new. True, there was a larger percentage of women in the Supreme Soviet and among People's deputies than in today's State Duma; power, however, did not rest with the deputies but with the leadership of the Communist Party of the Soviet Union (CPSU), and its highest body, the Politbureau. A woman appointed to the Politbureau under Gorbachev, but with one brief exception under Khrushchev, from Stalin's time to Chernenko's there was not a single woman in the leading body of the CPSU.

1

Thus in the Soviet period a certain level of political representation of women was maintained while in today's Russia it is not. But, this representation in the USSR was token rather than real. These facts have a bearing on the problems Russian women face today. They are not the same as the problems women faced in the USSR, but they are rooted in them. The collapse of the USSR did not signify a transition from gender equality to inequality, nor the reverse, but signified a transition from one form of inequality to another. This later form is conditioned by both the nature of the reforms and by the previous gender order. Not least, it is conditioned by the spurious belief that women were 'emancipated' in the Soviet Union. If they were, then, as the historian Marianne Liljeström puts it, they were 'emancipated to subordination' (Liljeström, 1995).

The present work was first conceived as a dissertation project in economics in 1990. At that time the USSR as a political entity was still in place. As a socio-economic system it had eroded, but was still alive. When preparations were finished and the work was about to start, we were held in breathless suspense by the August 1991 putsch, which ushered in the dissolution of the Union and the downfall of Gorbachev.

When the dissertation was completed three years later, the USSR and the Soviet economic system had been reduced to dust and ashes, defeated, discredited, dissolved. In the media, in politics and economics the consensus seemed to be that the Soviet era was a temporary aberration in history and was now of interest only to historians. The slate should be wiped clean for market reform with neoliberal characteristics.

A few years on it is clear that there are no clean slates and that history does not matter only to historians. Disregarding the legacies of the past – Soviet and even pre-Soviet – has backfired. To understand, predict or change the social and economic future of Russia it is necessary to understand its present, and the present cannot be understood or improved upon without understanding the past. That the Soviet system came to an end is not to be regretted, but that it ever existed cannot be ignored.

From this point of view, the present study of the labour and earnings of women and men in Russia and the USSR remains topical since the 'clean slate', shock therapy approach has proved over-simplistic. In the development of gender relations after the breakdown of the USSR, outlined in the final chapters of this book, change is seen to be interwoven with continuity.

For 70 years, the USSR was a major element in the shaping of history, of realities and ideas outside its own borders as well as within. From this point of view, it was always relevant for understanding the world we live in.

1.2 The history of the study

The condition of women in the USSR is a fascinating topic for a social scientist. It is an area where for a long time much was hidden by censorship and where some things remain obscured by ideological wishful thinking and taboos. The study of gender highlights the central power structures of a society whose gender system is both remarkably like and remarkably different from that in the West, making it an important subject for feminist theorising of the relationship between gender and other social structural dimensions.

For me, research on the situation of women in the USSR also honoured a commitment of many years standing to social and sexual equality and an equally longstanding awareness that this was not at all what the Soviet Union represented. In addition, it meant returning to a field I had studied at the Institute for Soviet and East European Studies in Glasgow, in 1980/81. With Hillel Ticktin and Alec Nove as tutors I learnt much about the underlying weakness of the apparently powerful Soviet system. I benefited from the theoretical discussions at the Institute and around the journal *Critique*, but my inclination was not to write one more abstract or abstruse treatise on 'the nature of the USSR'. Despite the vast literature, even at the most concrete empirical level, so much more needed to be known.

Before the *perestroika* period, it was out of the question for a Western researcher to get first hand micro-data from the USSR. But with *glasnost'*, suddenly, the impossible could happen. At the end of 1989, I met a pioneer of Russian feminism, Dr Anastasia Posadskaya, at a European Left Feminist meeting at Kvinnofolkhögskolan (Women's Folk High School) in Göteborg. Together with Professor Ludmila Nivorozhkina, Posadskaya had recently designed and led a household survey in the Russian city of Taganrog with an emphasis on gender issues, which in the USSR at that time was still unusual. Would they let me apply the multivariate statistical methods used in Western econometric studies of gender and discrimination to the data from this survey? The survey was conducted in one city but, with certain qualifications, results would apply to the Russian urban population generally. It would be the first time such methods were applied to primary data collected in the USSR. It is easy to forget, ten years on, how shocking such an idea was at that time. Nevertheless, the generous support of Posadskaya and Nivorozhkina, of Professor Natalia Rimashevskaya, Director of the Institute of Socio-economic Population Studies in Moscow, and Professors Anders Klevmarken and Johan Lönnroth at the University of Göteborg, enabled me to begin work in the autumn of 1991. Times had changed indeed, when it was an advantage for a Sovietologist to be a feminist.

This project resulted in a dissertation at the end of 1994, probably a low point of wider interest in studies of the Soviet system. The idea of a less technical version of the work occurred but was laid to rest. Developments in Russia and the situation of Russian women since then, however, seemed to me to call for a more comprehensive analysis of gender and social differentiation in the USSR. Since that time too, new survey data have become available from Taganrog, making a comparison of pre- and post-reform earnings differentials possible. In this book I have added a review of studies on gender and the Russian labour market and an analysis of post-reform data from Taganrog to the original dissertation research. The study cuts across the disciplines of labour economics, gender studies and Soviet studies and is intended for readers interested in each of these. It uses statistical methods and draws on elements from history and sociology, from critical, feminist and Marxist economic theory. To present it in a form that was suitable for both non-economists and economists has been something of a challenge. As far as practicable, I have followed Alfred Marshall's advice to economists to explain verbally and relegate the mathematics to footnotes and appendices. The argument and the evidence are presented so that the non-economist should be able to follow them, while the technical details are available to specialists.

Finally, a note on terminology: I have used quotation marks to indicate a quality ascribed to something by predominant social convention, as a convenient shorthand for saying that this is not inherent, inevitable or recommended by the author. For instance, occupations are not in themselves 'masculine' or 'feminine', but they are perceived and constructed as such. I speak of occupations as 'female-dominated' or even 'female' to state the empirical, contingent fact that their workforce is mostly female, without sharing the assumption that it must or should be so.

1.3   Underlying assumptions

Like any study of the USSR, or other society, this book is framed by an underlying, 'theorised' conception of the society and of its dynamics. This should be made explicit at the start, even if it is only implicit in the rest of the text, which is very much empirical.

It was evident that the USSR was not what it claimed to be. It was not socialist and not egalitarian. But what, then, was it? It was a very hierarchical society, very undemocratic, very oppressive and very unequal, in terms of both social strata and gender. It was also a very contradictory system and in many respects dysfunctional.

Women were not equal with men; workers were not a ruling class. They did not have power at the level of the party or the state, but did have it in a peculiar and constrained form at the workplace. Workers did not have control over production, only the means to set limits to the control that the ruling stratum had over it. Contrary to the propaganda, the USSR was not free from social conflict, but the conflict had resulted in a stalemate. With no power over what was produced or for whom, workers had no reason to exert themselves or to take an active interest in the efficiency of production. ('We pretend to work as long as they pretend to pay us.') With over-full employment there was no effective sanction against 'pretending to work'. Without active interest and exertion there was no way to escape waste and inefficiency, which further contributed to the lack of motivation.

The contradictions and waste imposed a disproportionate cost on women, through their double labour at work and at home. At another level of analysis, activities and values socially identified as 'feminine' were depreciated and neglected, to the detriment of the majority of women and men in the society. This was not *the* explanation of why the USSR was what it was, but it was certainly one important element of it.

The focus of this study is what workers are paid in wages. Wages are not the only determinant of economic well-being. This was particularly true in the USSR, with its plethora of non-monetary benefits and privileges and with the intricacies of differential access to scarce consumer goods. Soviet wages cannot be taken as a measure of the productivity of different kinds of labour, as is done in neoclassical theory for market economies. Yet, there are both theoretical and pragmatic reasons for choosing wages as a point of entry for the study of social differentiation in the USSR. In any society with wage labour, wages very much reflect the value and importance that are socially assigned to work of different kinds, and, therefore, to those who perform it and to the characteristics they bear. Soviet wages were highly correlated with the other forms of access to goods and status. An analysis of wages, which have the advantage of lending themselves to quantitative study, indicates the structure of social and value hierarchies in the USSR, even though it may underestimate the size of differentials. Hence, this book is a concrete, quantitative study of wage structure and wage discrimination in the USSR, which helps us understand the wider system of stratification in the Soviet system.

1.4   Western research on the employment and earnings of Soviet women

1.4.1   Problems of sources and data

There is general agreement that the gender wage gap in the USSR was large, but no one knows quite how large. Reliable data from the Soviet Union on men's and women's earnings have always been notoriously difficult to obtain. The claim of official propaganda that wages were fair – reflecting the individual's contribution to the economy – and that there was no inequality based on gender or race was important for the self-justification of the system. So was the ideology of the 'leading role of the working class'. When these claims were contradicted by the evidence of gender differences in pay and class differences in living standards, the evidence had to be suppressed.

Schroeder (1972, p. 312), noted that 'Soviet economists and Westerners alike must make heroic conclusions from indirect and excessively aggregated data. And nothing at all can be said as to whether equal pay for equal work prevails with respect to the earnings of males and females. One can merely observe that, as in market economies, there is a high inverse correlation between the percentage of women employed and the level of wages by sector of the economy.' As sections 5.6 and 7.6 will show, the inverse correlation remained up to and beyond the end of the USSR. With one exception (see section 1.4.2, below) the lack of data persisted until the dissolution of the Soviet Union and as far as Russian official statistics go, they are absent to the present day.

In the West, part of the gender gap in earnings can be attributed to differences in hours worked, in work experience and in education. These factors have less explanatory power in the USSR. Part-time work was always rare in the USSR. Even though men had second jobs and worked overtime more often than women, neither form of additional work was sufficiently widespread to make a substantial difference to the gender gap. With high rates of female employment, gender differences in work experience were also smaller in the USSR than in Western countries and the small difference in years of education was to women's advantage. According to the 1989 census, 78.1 per cent of employed women had secondary or higher education and 14.8 per cent had higher education as compared with 74.0 per cent and 13.8 per cent respectively of employed men.

Yet, there was a persistent gender gap in wages in the USSR, quite as large as in the West. The main object of this study is the factors and mechanisms that determined Soviet wages, and their differential impact on men's and women's earnings. For a Western study, first-hand access to survey data from the USSR is unique. An important aim has been to make models and results comparable, as far as is possible, with Western ones and with studies now undertaken in post-Soviet Russia.

1.4.2 Earlier Western studies

During the 1980s Western researchers studied aspects of the Soviet labour market, sometimes using econometric methods of estimation, and functional forms or lines of interpretation, borrowed from neoclassical microeconomic theory.[1] There is, however, relatively little published on the subject of 'women's work and wages in the USSR'. Alastair McAuley's monograph with this title (McAuley, 1981) is still one of the main non-Soviet sources in the field. Another from the same period is Atkinson et al. (1978), particularly Chapman (1978). Of more recent work, Ofer and Vinokur (1992) include substantial sections on women, as do Atkinson and Micklewright (1992) and Filtzer (1994).

The main sources available to Western researchers studying gender differences in the USSR have been (1) official statistics, including population censuses; (2) microeconomic data from surveys of emigrants; and (3) published results from Soviet sociological surveys.

Until 1989 the official statistical handbooks published no wage statistics disaggregated by gender, and even then what was published (*Nar. Khoz.*, 1989) was fragmentary.[2] (Katz, 1994, includes a graphical exposition of these data, which show that at each level of education, women's earnings were lower than men's.)

Data from the population censuses do not include information on incomes and earnings. The large-scale Soviet surveys of earnings (the March censuses and the Family Budget Surveys) have been criticised by both Western and Soviet researchers (Shenfield, 1983, Boldyreva, 1989, Micklewright and Atkinson, 1992). Above all, multivariate methods of analysis can be applied only to means for aggregates such as regions or republics, not to individuals or households. Econometric studies of fertility and labour supply have been made on the basis of regional census data (Berliner, 1983 and 1989, Kuniansky, 1983). These studies have produced some very interesting results, but certain of the findings are problematic (see section 4.4).

Surveys of emigrants from the USSR have been made in Israel and the United States. The most comprehensive such study is the multidisciplinary Soviet Interview Project (SIP). The SIP survey included 3,000 respondents who had emigrated from the USSR during the 1970s. Millar (1987) includes a selection of papers based on this survey. Ofer and Vinokur (1992) include analysis of data from SIP as well as from the Israeli émigré survey. The methods of analysis were chosen by some of the most prominent researchers in Western Soviet Studies. Still, the problem of selectivity remains and the answers are retrospective, referring to a period several years before the interviews.

Soviet sociologists and economists have collected large amounts of survey data. Results were presented as cross-tabulations of two or three variables; multivariate analysis was rare. Since little or no information on definitions and sampling frames was published it is hard to judge the validity of data and conclusions (Berliner, 1983, Shenfield, 1983, Gregory and Kohlhase, 1988). As mentioned, controversial findings such as social and gender inequalities were likely to be suppressed. For example, a survey carried out in the late 1970s in Taganrog included information on the gender wage gap, but the researchers were not allowed to publish it (Rimashevskaia, 1996).

Michael Swafford's study (1978) is unique. It is based on data from an unpublished dissertation by S. A. Karapetyan. Karapetyan used data from a survey made in Erevan in 1963, grouping 3,174 observations of employed men and women into 227 cells according to sex, age, education, branch of employment and type of occupation and calculating the average wage in each of them. Swafford used these 'cells' in a regression analysis of wages. This very interesting study was the closest anyone came to a multivariate analysis of men's and women's wages in the USSR, based on individual data collected in the USSR. Yet, it too is subject to some data problems.

Aggregation is only a minor disadvantage since estimates based on group averages are unbiased.[3] Unresolved issues of definition are more problematic. Swafford does not explain whether the 'mean earnings' estimated include tax, overtime pay or bonuses – in all likelihood because it is not reported in his source. Further, Swafford notes that in Armenia in 1963 birth-rates were higher and female labour force participation lower than the Soviet average, but considers that this does not make a major difference for a study of women who are in the labour force, particularly since he controls for education. It is possible that the women who actually worked in Armenia did not differ very much from other Soviet working women in terms of earnings potential. But it also possible that their potential earnings were equivalent to those of a similar percentage of women in republics with higher employment rates, those with the highest earnings. In this case, the gender ratio in Armenia would be higher than the Soviet average.

New possibilities for research and publications opened up first with *glasnost'*, then with the end of the Soviet system. Greater openness has, however, coincided with less funding for Russian academic institutions and the changes in attitude to gender issues have been mixed and ambiguous, to say the least.

1.5 Outline of the book

The preceding section has summarised previous Western research on Soviet gender wage differentials. Chapter 2 is an introduction to theories and empirical studies of wages and discrimination in economics. The application of mainstream economic theory to issues of gender differentials is discussed, from a critical perspective. The model for quantitative analysis of race and gender discrimination, which will be applied in chapter 5, is described and its interpretation discussed.

Chapter 3 is a description of the regulations and institutional framework of Soviet wage-setting, with particular emphasis on mechanisms that may have contributed to male/female differentials. An introductory section briefly presents the widely debated issues of the role of wages in the allocation of labour power and the role of supply and demand factors in the determination of wages. In section 3.2, I trace the changes in the wage system after 1953. Wage-setting for industrial blue-collar workers, white-collar staff and workers in the service sector is described in section 3.3. In section 3.4 evidence is presented on rewards to work other than official wages and salaries. These include non-monetary benefits from the workplace as well as legal, semi-legal and illegal opportunities for extra earnings, but also non-material rewards, including the pleasantness and intrinsic interest of the job, prestige and 'propriety' according to the stereotyped Soviet conceptions of 'masculinity' and 'femininity'.

In the first section of chapter 4, the sampling frame is described, and in the second, demographic characteristics of the sample are compared with regional and national statistics. The third describes education in the USSR, institutions, levels and gender differences. In section 4.4, I deal with rates of employment, in the sample and in the USSR, although in descriptive, not econometric form. The topic of section 4.5 is data and legislation on hours of work, which are essential for the analysis in chapter 5. The gender division of labour in the USSR, in paid work and housework, is treated briefly in sections 4.6 and 4.7, respectively, using mainly general sources since the sample does not provide detailed information on occupations. The last section is a short, descriptive introduction to gender differences in earnings in Taganrog and the USSR. The sections of chapter 4 can be read independently of each other.

The core of chapter 5 is an empirical analysis of men's and women's wages, based on the survey data. Wage functions are estimated separately for men and women, and the results analysed and compared with respect to age, experience, family situation, job level, economic sector and working conditions. (The main discussion of education is in chapter 6.) In section 5.4, the wage function is used to decompose the male/female wage differential and to determine the shares of this differential, which are attributable to different characteristics.

The last two sections of chapter 5 broaden the analysis to a wider Soviet population. In 5.5, a wage function estimated from the Taganrog data is applied to the sectoral distribution and education of Soviet workers and employees. The first part of section 5.6 shows how concepts from Marxist economic theory were distorted to provide an ideological justification for low wages in female-dominated sectors. In the second, the relation between average wages in different sectors and the gender composition of their workforce are analysed, using national statistics.

In chapter 6, the Taganrog data are used to explore the controversial issue of earnings and education in the USSR. Sections 6.1 and 6.2 introduce Soviet views on earnings differentials according to education: what they were and what they ought to have been. In section 6.3 some methodological issues in the study of earnings and education are raised. In section 6.4, wage functions are estimated in order to study the relation between education and wages under different assumptions about the choices available to Soviet women and men. The following sections return to the debates on wages, education and 'levelling' in the USSR, and their relation to the gender system.

Chapter 7 starts with a survey of studies of the emerging Russian labour market. The main content of the chapter is a new empirical analysis. Survey data from Taganrog 1993/4, comparable to those from 1989, as well as national aggregate statistics are used to compare male and female employment and unemployment, to study changes in the male/female earnings gap and changes in the impact of different labour force characteristics on the wages of women and men. Chapter 8 includes a summary of each chapter and the main conclusions from the study.

2
Gender, Discrimination and Western Economic Theory[1]

2.1 Gender wage differentials

Practically all studies from all countries show that women's average earnings are lower than those of men. The size of this gender gap varies across time and place and depends on what exactly the averages are taken of – of wages per year or per hour, all wages, or wages of full-time employed. If hours of work, or job, worker or enterprise characteristics are controlled for, the gap is reduced. But a gap there is, and it always has the same sign.

Studies using different samples and different definitions also come up with different estimates of the trend over time and of the portion of the gap which is attributable to discrimination (and the trend of that over time), even in the same reference population. Therefore, an international comparison would have to be more thorough than is possible in this context, and I will quote only a few figures (Tables 2.1–2.3) to indicate the order of magnitude.

Table 2.1 Female/male wage ratios in 1960 and 1988

Country	1960	1988	Increase
Australia	59	78	19
Britain	61	71	10
Canada	59	65	6
Japan[a]	45	58	13
Sweden[b]	72[c]	90	18
United States	61	65[d]	4

a. Firms with more than 30 employees.
b. In manufacturing only.
c. 1963.
d. Annual earnings. For weekly the ratio is 70 per cent.
Note: All figures for full-time workers, except for Sweden and Japan (for which hourly wages are used).
Source: Willborn (1991, p. 2).

Tables 2.1–2.2 show a range of female/male wage ratios in different OECD countries. Table 2.2 also indicates ratios of female to male labour force participation rates and an index of occupational segregation.

The figures in Table 2.2 indicate a positive relation between the ratio of female to male labour force participation and the ratio of female to male wages. (The Pearson correlation coefficient is significant at the 5 per cent level.) There are no statistically significant relationships between the measure of segregation and the wage or participation ratios.[2]

Table 2.2   Segregation, participation and wage ratios, OECD countries

Country	Participation ratio[a]	Wage ratio[b]	Segregation[c]
Australia	64.5	80	47.8**
Austria	60.7	—	44.4
Belgium	64.4*	—	39.2¤
Canada	73.2	66	40.2
Denmark	82.8	84	40.5**
Finland	83.6	77	43.0
France	72.0	79	38.3¤
FRG	59.9*	73	37.8¤
Greece	53.1**	78	24.4
Ireland	44.7	67	42.9**
Israel	64.3	—	—
Italy	54.2	—	24.6¤
Japan	64.2	48*	23.1
Luxembourg	51.7	61	48.9¤
Netherlands	60.9	75*	40.0¤
New Zealand	70.1*	72*	41.9¤
Norway	80.9	84	46.6
Portugal	67.4	—	25.1
Spain	45.8	—	36.9
Sweden	95.3	90	37.9
Switzerland	57.0	69	39.2¤
UK	58.7	68	44.4
USA	75.3	70	37.4

* 1986.
** 1985.
¤ Some year between 1980 and 1984.
[a] The ratio of women's to men's labour force participation rates.
[b] The ratio of female/male hourly earnings in manufacturing. The year is 1987, unless otherwise indicated. For the United States, weekly earnings of full-time workers. For Canada, yearly earnings of full-time workers.
[c] $S = 0.5\Sigma_i[M_i - F_i]$ where M_i and F_i are the shares of males and females in seven occupational categories. (Professional, technical, etc. workers; administrative, executive and managerial; clerical and related; sales workers; service workers; agricultural and related workers; production workers.)
Source: Calculations by Marianne Ferber in Ferber (1991) (based on ILO and OECD sources).

Table 2.1 shows that the gender gap in wages declined between 1960 and 1988, but to a varying extent in different countries. Table 2.2 shows that in the United States and the United Kingdom the differentials are larger than in Scandinavia, but smaller than in Japan. The female/male income ratio for full-time employed in 1980 was 0.60 in the United States and 0.77 in Sweden. In 1985 it was 0.70 in the Federal Republic of Germany and 0.77 in Denmark (Rosenfeld and Kalleberg, 1991). These overall figures do not show the within-gender dispersion of wages. A country with a relatively high female/male ratio could have very large differences between those with high and low pay within and across gender groups, but with many women among the high paid. It could also be one with fewer career opportunities for women, but not so low wages at the bottom of the scale, where women tend to be over-represented.

Blau and Kahn (1992) divide the male/female wage differential in a number of countries into different components to isolate the impact of overall wage differentiation on the gender pay gap. They show that when nine industrial countries are compared, those where the average woman has the highest position in the male wage ranking are not necessarily those with the highest average female/male wage ratio (Table 2.3). In all these countries, the median woman earns less than the median man. But the difference between their wages is determined both by how many percentiles down she is and by the distance between the percentiles (that is, by both how many rungs below the middle of the ladder she is and how far apart the rungs are).

They conclude that if the overall wage distribution is highly dispersed, or if the male wage distribution is, the female/male difference will be larger. If wage dispersion in the United States had been as small as that in Sweden or Austria, the gender gap would also have been of the same order.

In the United States, female/male wage ratios for whites showed almost no change at all in the period 1960–80, and remained below the 1939 level. Full-time working black women's annual earnings had increased by 15–20 percentage points relative to both black men and white women, but it was not until the 1980s that the wage ratio began to increase for whites, rising by 7 percentage points between 1981 and 1988[3] (Smith and Ward, 1989, O'Neill, 1991). O'Neill explains the increase by the rise in women's work experience and schooling from the 1960s onwards, a rise which, in the 1960s and 1970s, had been offset by the low levels of schooling and experience of the older cohorts of housewives entering the labour market. Yet, these factors alone do not determine wages. When O'Neill controls for schooling, age, experience, labour force commitment and number of children, the proportion of the wage difference which is

Table 2.3 Female/male earnings ratio adjusted for hours (in per cent) and percentile position of the female average in the male wage distribution

	Sweden	Austria	Australia	Norway	Germany	US	Switzerland	Hungary	UK
Year(s)	1984	1985–87	1986	1982	1985–88	1984	1987	1986–88	1985–88
Ratio	82.2	74.1	73.3	71.4	70.9	66.9	64.6	64.5	61.3
At percentile	29.9	30.5	32.3	26.4	27.5	29.6	27.6	21.2	23.6

Source: Blau and Kahn (1992), figures 2 and 3, Blau (1995), figures 1 and 2. Based on survey sample data.

unexplained by these so-called human capital variables diminished only from 96 per cent to 92 per cent of the gap from 1977 to 1987. Twenty per cent of the decrease in the gender wage differential was due to the decrease in lower relative wages for blue-collar workers.

As Blau and Ferber (1987) note, although the increase in women's experience and schooling no doubt contributed to the increase in their relative wages, this does not mean that anti-discriminatory measures or changes in attitudes were not important too.

Blau and Kahn (1992, 1997) find that the increase in North American women's education, experience and skills in the period 1971–88 reduced the wage gap but, according to their estimates, that reduction would have been one third larger if the overall wage distribution had not, at the same time, become more dispersed.

The tables include only rich, developed countries and regular employment. If Third World countries had been included, the relative position of women would probably have been worse. The same is true of women in marginal or non-standard employment, in the 'grey' sector of the economy or in domestic work or homeworking. This chapter will not cover these topics, nor that of the global 'feminisation of poverty', nor discuss the different degree to which women's work is organised as paid work (with much 'caring and curing' work performed in the public sector) and to what extent it is unwaged. (The last, in turn, requires a discussion of what is meant by 'work'.[4]) This is not intended to belittle these issues, but is rather a recognition that they are too essential and complex to be treated so briefly.

Women's wages must be analysed in the context of a complex gender division of labour, including paid as well as unpaid work. The division of unpaid tasks in the household (and the total time spent on housework), labour supply (to paid employment) and occupational choice, as well as the acquisition of new skills, are to a large extent decided simultaneously by male and female household members. Their earnings are determined by these decisions, but the decisions are influenced by prospective earnings. The way in which women and men have previously made their decisions affect the future range of choice available to themselves and others.

None of this can be determined by economic theory alone. An economic theory that takes its point of departure in individual utility maximisation, proceeds to investigate the economic aspects of it and subsumes all else under a black box heading of 'tastes' or 'preferences' which are taken as given, will leave unaddressed many of the most pertinent questions (Sen, 1984, Klamer et al., 1988, Ferber and Nelson, 1993, Duncan and Edwards, 1997).

2.2   Neoclassical and efficiency wage theory

The dominant theory in academic economics, the neoclassical, sees equilibrium wages as an equilibrium price for a quantity of labour.[5] In its simplest version, it predicts that at this equilibrium, the wage rate, the marginal productivity of labour and the marginal (dis)utility of work will be equal. The demand for labour power is determined by profit-maximising employers, who pay as much as it pays them to pay. The supply is determined by workers, who will work as much as they find it worthwhile to work, at each given wage level. If wages are below a certain minimum – the individual's reservation wage – he or she will not work. If they are above this minimum, the amount of labour power supplied depends on the wage. A higher wage rate may lead to either an increase or a decrease since it will, on the one hand, make work more worth the effort, but, on the other, enable workers to work less, since they can earn as much in fewer hours of work.

According to the theory of compensating (equalising) differentials, the more unpleasant the work, the greater the disutility and, hence, the higher the pay required to attract workers. (This idea goes back to Adam Smith. For a contemporary exposition see, for instance, Rosen, 1986.)

According to neoclassical theory, profit-maximisation on the part of the employer ensures that wages correspond to productivity. The qualities which endow a worker with a given productivity are known – with a reifying metaphor – as his or her 'human capital'.[6] People are perceived as 'investing' in themselves, or in their children, as if they were a piece of (their own/their parents') property. This imagery does have some common-sense truth, otherwise it would not be so powerful. Among the several factors that determine choices of education and occupation, the expectations of future wages are one, and are not unimportant. The sacrifice of current earnings in order to acquire an education depends on the relative pay in jobs that do and jobs that do not require it – and on other things such as their pleasantness, status, intrinsic interest, moral satisfaction and physical conditions of work, as well as social norms and expectations about what an individual of a given class, gender, age, family status and ethnicity should be doing. It can be worthwhile to choose the less well paid of two jobs if future career prospects are better in the job with the lower starting wage.

Yet the hold that this metaphor has over the minds of economists is strengthened by its power to confirm and reinforce a particular and conservative worldview, which focuses wholly on the instrumental aspects of human behaviour. It appears therefore – inappropriately – as more than a metaphor. Metaphors are legitimate and can be fruitful in scientific discourse, but they are not proofs, and the understandings they convey are necessarily partial. The imagery and metaphors of neoclassical economics consistently express a reified view of economic and social relations, which closely reflects and reproduces the commodity fetishism that Isaac Rubin (1972)[7] places at the core of a Marxist analysis of capitalist social relations.

Writers raised within mainstream economic thought as well as critics of it emphasise that the simple market model of purchase and sale is much too crude to describe the labour market. Sawyer (1995) summarises shortcomings of 'the orthodox neoclassical analysis' and calls for a more appropriate 'eclectic approach'. Solow (1990) describes the 'labour market as a social institution' and, thus, fundamentally different from other markets. Participation in the labour market is not a simple act of sale, but something that determines self-perception as well as one's relations to others. Too often the economist 'ignores the constraints arising from social norms' (ibid., p. 23). First, 'social status and self-esteem are strongly tied to both occupation and income', yet the occupation with the higher income is not always that with the higher status (ibid., p. 9). Second, issues such as whether to undercut the wage rate which is considered as 'fair' and 'normal' for a given job (or 'normal' for a worker of a particular race or gender, though Solow does not mention this) concern not only the individual, but also others and not only now, but also in the future. Solow appeals to efficiency wage theory (see below) as well as game theory and the perceived threat of a breakdown of society into 'Hobbesian competition' to explain that '[b]ehavior that has been found to be individually tempting but socially destructive is held to be socially unacceptable. Behavior that has been found to be collectively useful though at least mildly disadvantageous to the individual is held to be the right thing to do' (ibid., p. 43).

In principle, a neoclassical utility function could incorporate other people's wages as determinants of the worker's level of satisfaction This would agree with the observation that satisfaction with wages depends on comparisons, on whether employees consider their own and each others' pay to be 'fair'. Yet, although such models exist (Akerlof, 1982, Akerlof and Yellen, 1990), they are not standard. Usually, the model of the individual is atomistic.[8] Nor do the traditional approaches take into account that employers might find it profitable to adapt relative wages to prevalent ideas of what is 'fair' (Rees, 1993). To do so reduces tension and conflict in the workplace, increases satisfaction and motivation and, hence, productivity.

Within the framework of 'efficiency wage' theory it is shown that under certain conditions it may be profitable for employers to pay above-productivity wages to at least some of their employees.[9] In Akerlof's (1982) model above-'normal' (or market-clearing) wages and above-'normal' work effort go together as parts of a 'gift-exchange relationship' between employer and workers.

There is a two-way relationship between productivity and wages. A higher relative wage can reduce the number of quits, avert disaffection and discontent and may induce greater effort or deter shirking which could lead to dismissal or demotion. (For some empirical studies, see Rebitzer, 1993.) This is easily linked to an idea of 'fairness' of work demands, wages and wage differentials, as in Akerlof's model.[10] Another important and unusual trait of this model is that it takes into account worker solidarity (that is, that people are concerned that their fellow workers are not underpaid or overworked).

The authors cited do not explore any gender or race aspects of their models or assumptions, but their theories are highly relevant to such analysis. Psychologists have found that women tend to expect, and consider 'fair', a lower wage than men, even when doing the same work. (See Jackson et al., 1992, and references therein.) If men expect to have higher wages than women, they will be discontented, and possibly less productive, if they do not. If women accept that men 'should' have higher wages, they will not decrease their efforts for this reason. A wage above that in alternative employment enables the firm to pick and choose among job applicants. With such a 'queue' for the jobs, discrimination by race or gender becomes less costly. (See p. 28). The model developed by Layard et al. (1991) to explain different efficiency wages in different jobs, for workers with the same productivity, could easily be reformulated in terms of different workers in the same jobs instead.[11]

2.3   Why do women get lower pay?

On the surface, neoclassical theory appears to apply equally to men and women. Yet the position and behaviour of men and women in the labour market are easily seen to be very unequal. Can economic theory explain the pervasiveness and resilience of gender wage gaps? To do so it must both improve its theory of the labour market itself and look at conditions outside it.

Crudely speaking, within the conceptual framework of mainstream economic theory, explanations for the lower pay of women could follow two lines: to investigate why their work might be less productive or to investigate why they might be paid less than the productivity of their work would warrant. (Or, conversely, why men might be paid above productivity.) Orthodox neoclassical theory will only speak of 'discrimination' when equal productivity is unequally rewarded. The sympathies of this author are – as will be seen below – with the feminist, institutionalist, Marxist or other radical theories which apply a broader concept and with those of them that question the simple assumptions of standard economic theory about what productivity is and how it is measured.

In this chapter, the main arguments will be briefly outlined, and some of the empirical evidence cited: that is, why part of the gender wage gap might reflect lower productivity and why this is unlikely to be the whole explanation. An exposition is complicated by the distinction between unequal productivity in the same occupation and unequal productivity in different occupations.

Although the difference may be clear in principle, in practice, the issue of productivity will be entangled with that of occupational segregation. Note, however, that with a strict neoclassical approach, occupational segregation in itself does not explain wage differentials unless productivity can be shown to be lower in the lower-paid jobs. If work intensity and 'human capital' requirements are equal in a male- and a female-dominated field, then they ought to be 'separate but equal'. One explanation why male-dominated occupations, nevertheless, tend to be better paid could be that women choose jobs that require less 'human capital'. With the increase in female education and work experience over recent decades, these variables can hardly justify other than very small gender differentials. Further explanations are needed.

One explanation is that the social norms concerning household and family commitments restrict the occupational choices of women more than those of men. Discrimination restricts them further. According to the 'crowding hypothesis',[12] because women have fewer jobs to choose from, they 'crowd' into the available occupations. The resulting surplus labour supply depresses wages in these jobs.

Household and family commitments, the interaction between the household and the labour market, are also used to support the assumption that women both acquire less 'human capital' and apply what they have less energetically than men. According to human capital theory, since women interrupt employment or work part-time to care for children, it does not pay them to 'invest' in as long an education as men do, because this would need a longer career span to pay off. The same applies to 'investing' in further training and the commitments required for career advancement.

This does not explain why it is women whose careers are affected by housework and child-care, however. After all, men also marry. They live in cleaned houses and eat cooked meals. They even have children. To enter into a more extensive exposition and critique of the neoclassical theory of the household here would require too much space, and it has been done before. The archetypal neoclassical text is Becker (1991) and for feminist discussions of it, see, *inter alia*, Blau and Ferber (1986), Katz (1986, 1994), Folbre (1994) and Humphries (1995a, 1995b).

To summarise, according to neoclassical theory, households as well as single individuals divide their time between paid work, leisure and unpaid work ('household production') in such a way as to maximise utility.[13] Ignoring, in this case, its usual canon of methodological individualism, early neoclassical theory simply assumed that households jointly maximised joint utility. Once a joint utility function is introduced, issues of conflicts and unequal power within the household are by definition excluded from the analysis. More sophisticated models allow either the wife or the husband to make their choices separately, given those that the other has made, or apply a game-theoretic framework in which one can take unequal leverage into account. (Examples are Manser and Brown, 1979, McElroy and Horney, 1981, Ott, 1995.)

The outcome, according to the models, is that spouses specialise. The one who is relatively more productive in household activities will specialise in that and the one who is relatively more productive in market work (that is, earns more), will specialise in that. (Neoclassical authors tend to assume that the two are equivalent.) The strength of the theory is the vivid image it presents of a vicious circle, where an initial difference, be it ever so small, will induce a specialisation, which increases the difference and thus induces even further specialisation, and so on. One main weakness is that it ignores a number of motives for people not to specialise (such as non-monetary and non-transferable benefits of either activity or the risk of marriages splitting up.) Another is that it either does not explain why husbands nearly always have a comparative advantage in market work and wives in non-market work.[14] This is simply taken as given; at most a passing reference is made to pregnancy, childbirth and lactation.

More in-depth criticism focuses on the view of human behaviour and relations implicit in the theory. The critiques of the atomistic view of individuals, individual choice and individual motives raised against the neoclassical theory of the labour market apply equally to its theory of the household. (See pp. 32f below.)

Becker (1991, p. 77) claims – without citing empirical evidence – that 'married women spend less energy on each hour of market work than married men working the same number of hours' and that this 'is an important reason' for the difference in earnings and for occupational segregation.

Hakim (1991) agrees with Becker that the majority of women choose to work less intensely even though this, as she writes, 'is roundly rejected by sociologists as having no empirical basis'. Bielby and Bielby (1988) find the opposite, but their measure – self-reported effort – could suffer from a gender bias. Löfström (1993) cites research indicating that having children made little or no difference to women's productivity and/or wages. Her own study of university graduates working in a large Swedish enterprise found that men's basic salaries increased both with having children and working over-time, but neither had any effect on those of women. If having children has no effect on women's salaries, it means either that women with children spend as much effort on their job, or that a difference in effort makes no difference to women's salaries (or both).

Korenman and Neumark (1992) find that most of the negative effect of having children on women's wages, is mediated through experience and tenure. If wages are a good measure of effort and productivity, it appears that mothers work fewer hours, rather than less intensely.

One of the few studies that have explicitly included hours of housework per week (Hersch and Stratton, 1997) finds a substantial negative relation between wages and housework for married women. (Using panel data allows them to avoid the problems that some individuals might be very interested in child-care and domestic work and less interested in labour market-related activities.) This finding does indicate that housework competes with paid work. Yet, there is no such effect for men. Hence, not only do married men do a lot less housework, the time they do spend on it does not have the negative career effects that it has on women. This indicates that there is a complex interaction between household, worker and employer behaviour and attitudes, which requires closer study.

2.4 Occupational segregation

2.4.1 Segregation in the labour market

As section 2.1 has indicated, there is no necessary relation between aggregate measures of occupational segregation and male/female wage inequality across countries. Within countries, however, a large part of the gender wage gap can be ascribed to occupational segregation (Walby, 1986).

Women tend to be concentrated in a smaller number of occupations than men. In Sweden, it takes at least 57 out of the 282 occupations in the census to account for 75 per cent of the men, but 30 occupations include 75 per cent of women (SCB, 1986).[15] In Britain studies[16] show very little change in measures of occupational segregation from the beginning of the twentieth century to the 1970s. In 1979–89, however, Watts and Rich (1993) note a decline, mainly during the economic upturn of 1983–89. Partly, this is due to a shift of employment towards more integrated occupations, partly to integration within broad occupational groups. (For more detail on theories and measurement of occupational segregation, see Walby, 1988, Watts and Rich, 1993 and Jonung, 1997.)

Measures of occupational segregation and concentration are sensitive to the choice of occupational categories (Liff, 1986, SCB, 1986). For instance, occupations in manufacturing, where many men work, tend to be more finely disaggregated than those in the female-dominated services. Full-time unpaid housework is not included. Therefore a country with a high female labour force participation rate and many women employed to care for the young and the old, the ill and the disabled, may well appear more segregated than one in which more work is unpaid and performed by women 'outside the labour force'.

Women tend to be over-represented in low-paying sectors like caring and curing, teaching or retail trade, and men in science, engineering, metalworking and construction. But in each sphere of activity, the higher the position in the job hierarchy, the lower the proportion of women.

From a policy perspective it is useful to distinguish between segregation of occupation and of employer. Groshen (1991) quotes several US studies, which found that within occupations, wages were negatively related to the proportion of females in the job-cells (same occupation and same establishment). Both British and American studies have found that a majority of both women and men have no colleagues of the opposite sex in the same job and place of employment (Walby, 1988, Groshen, 1991). Watts and Rich (1993, p. 165) cite further studies indicating that firms segregate, in the sense of 'high-paying firms employing only males and low-paying firms employing only females, where both sexes did the same job'.

Where many women work, pay is on average lower. Why do women take these jobs? What choice do they have? And why are the wages so low?

2.4.2   Segregation: discrimination or preferences?

It is claimed, most prominently by Solomon Polachek, that women prefer traditionally female-dominated jobs – often with a job content close to that of housework – because in these jobs part-time work and interrupted employment have a relatively small impact on later earnings.

Yet, even if women do (or did in earlier generations) plan to be full-time home-makers for part of their lives, it would be quite a coincidence if all jobs with low attrition of skills were *traditionally* 'female' ones. Does a car mechanic or plumber have greater need of continuous 'investment in his human capital' than a hospital nurse or a librarian?

England (1982) objects that Polachek's argument assumes that women choose jobs with relatively high starting wages, as well as low rewards to experience. Planned career breaks do not, however, explain the choice of jobs with both low starting wages and low wage growth. Which female-dominated jobs have higher earnings at entry than male-dominated occupations requiring similar amounts of education? England et al. (1988) estimate an earnings model with fixed (time- and individual-) effects on US panel data to investigate the relationship between earnings and sex composition of occupations, for black and white men and women. They find significant negative effects of the female percentage in the occupation on starting wages, for full-time workers in all four race/gender groups.

To test the hypothesis of lower depreciation rates, England (1982) divides the 300 US Census occupational categories according to sex composition and then checks for a relationship between sex composition, on the one hand, and rewards to experience or 'penalties' for post-school years spent out of the labour force, on the other. Her conclusion is that 'women do not maximise lifetime earnings by working in traditionally female occupations; on the contrary, they earn less in such occupations at every level of experience' (p. 367).

Using an interaction term for gender composition and experience, England et al. (1988) find that for women[17] returns to experience/ penalties for home time are smaller in female-dominated jobs. This is as predicted by neoclassical theory, but could also be explained by discrimination. For men, however, the interaction term has a positive effect, which contradicts the explanation of low female wage growth as a feature of the occupations women choose.[18] The authors agree that 'human capital' explains a considerable part of the wage gap, but conclude that for occupational segregation, 'sociological explanations in terms of multiple feed-backs between gender-role socialisation, discrimination, and institutional practises' do better (ibid., p. 554).

Gronau (1988) simultaneously estimates earnings, planned labour force separations (spells out of the labour force), on-the-job training and job requirements. He finds that about a quarter of the gender difference in hourly earnings can be explained by differences in 'human capital', including on-the-job training, and two-fifths by job requirements.

Gronau also investigated whether the male–female difference in job requirements, in its turn, could be explained by differences in 'human capital', occupation and, above all, labour force separations. It turned out that, given the job and wage structure prevailing for women, they would have gained very little from having the same 'human capital' and the same labour force behaviour as men. Since many labour force characteristics are rewarded differently for men and women, it would, however, have led to a considerable loss in job quality and pay for men if they had done like women. Gronau's conclusion that those women who plan career breaks, choose jobs which require as much training, skill and experience as those who do not[19] is supported by other studies, cited by Blau and Ferber, (1991, p. 583), while England et al. (1988) quote mixed evidence as to whether young women who plan for continuous employment are more likely to choose untypical occupations.

Gronau does not find significant gender differences in wage gains from experience and tenure with employer, but women gain more than men from tenure in the job and lose *more* from time out of employment, which is contrary to what Polachek's hypothesis would predict.[20]

The seemingly lower return to tenure for men (replicated also in other studies) may stem from bias in the estimates. Men are more likely than women to increase their earnings by changing jobs. Sloane and Theodossiou (1993) indicate that women do not receive or do not take offers of favourable job changes as often as men do, particularly in the early years of their careers. Men have higher returns to experience than women, but their returns to tenure are masked by the wage increases connected with change of job.

The same conclusion can be drawn from a study of young American professionals (Loprest, 1992). The men and women in the sample obtain roughly similar wage increases when they do not change jobs, and the number of changes are approximately the same. The main reason why the young men earn more after four years in the labour market, is that job changes are connected with twice as big wage rises for them as for women.[21]

Indirect evidence on the existence of wage discrimination can be offered by studies of the impact of anti-discrimination measures (legislation or collective agreements between unions and employers). If, controlling for other relevant changes, these are found to reduce substantially the earnings gap or increase the probability that women will work in traditionally male-dominated jobs,[22] the implication is that there was gender discrimination in wages or employment.[23] Thus, Beller (1982) finds that the impact of the equal opportunities legislation introduced in the United States in 1967–74 increased women's entry into male-dominated occupations six times more than equality with men in respect of the 'human capital' variables would have.

According to Löfström (1989) laws and agreements made to promote gender equality in the Swedish labour market did reduce the gender wage gap in manufacturing, without detriment to the employment opportunities for women, relative to men, while according to Svensson (1995) the decreasing wage gap was the effect of structural changes. Löfström and Dex and Sewell (1995) cite British and Australian studies which find a positive impact of legislation, on its own or combined with income policies. The latter, however, also refer to British studies, which dispute this result.

Groshen (1991) tests for the importance of occupational versus establishment segregation in three service and two manufacturing branches. She finds that the contribution of the individual's sex to the wage gap within job-cell (the component against which anti-discrimination legislation is most effective) is small, the equivalent of around 1 per cent of women's wages. Occupational segregation, given establishment, contributes nearly half the total differential, that is, 11 per cent of female wages in manufacturing and 26 per cent in services. Job-cell and establishment segregation, within occupation, contribute about 6 per cent each. Including a set of 'human capital' variables and job characteristics made little difference to the estimated coefficients. Hence, her results tend to confirm that segregation, as a mechanism for discrimination by employers, is important for the male/female wage gap. Petersen et al. (1996) also find that within-firm/within-occupation differentials are a very small part of the gender wage gap.

This is also the tentative conclusion reached by Gronau (1988, p. 294). According to his estimates, job requirements account for nearly two-fifths of the wage gap. He finds it 'disturbing for traditional theory' that, at the same time, experience and tenure, as well as continuity of employment, have only a minor impact on the skill intensity of the jobs women get, irrespective of their marital status.

According to Filer (1986), women go into 'typically female' jobs simply because they like them. He estimates a logit model of a few occupational types on variables derived from a 'personality test' administered to job-seekers by a commercial employment agency (thus, it is not a random sample nor a questionnaire designed for research purposes). He concludes 'that gender differences in occupational structure are strongly linked to differences between men's and women's personalities and tastes' (ibid., p. 412). Since there are only five, very broad, occupational categories, each of these includes occupations with different proportions of women, different pay and different content. Filer assumes that it is always 'personality and taste factors' which determine occupation, not the other way around. (see pp. 32f below). He never asks why men and women have the 'tastes' they have.

Daymont and Andrisani (1984), using a more appropriate sampling frame than Filer, show that among young college graduates[24] attitudes to what are the most important qualities of a job have both direct and indirect effects on earnings. The young women – interviewed in high school – were more inclined to value relations with people at work and helping others, and put relatively less weight on earning a lot of money and on 'being a leader', compared to the young men. This attitude significantly increased the probability that they would choose an economically less rewarding college major, for instance in the humanities, and decreased the likelihood of taking a business studies course. Yet, even controlling for degree subject and for gender, the preferences that were more common among girls had a negative impact on earnings. Hence, in a sense, women do choose 'unprofitably'. Note, however, that after controlling for preferences, as well as college major and the usual 'human capital' variables, there is still an unexplained gender differential. If the women chose as men but continued to be paid as women, it would make only a small difference to their earnings. (Men who value helping and human relations suffer a greater penalty.) Second, as the authors point out, this 'leads to difficult questions about the reasons for the greater payoff to the traditionally male objectives of being a leader and making a lot of money than to the traditionally female objectives of helping others and working with people' (ibid., p. 423).

According to Hakim (1991) only a minority of women are career-oriented, while the majority prioritise home-making and care little about job content, pay, working conditions or job security. She emphasises that one reason for this is the 'all-pervading influence of the husband's traditional views and homeworkers' acceptance of his right to control her labour' (ibid., p. 111, which includes further references). As Hakim notes, that would tend to increase the tendency for women to appreciate low-paid work, which can be performed with only a minimal impact on their roles in the household.

The priority given to home-making is taken to explain the high levels of satisfaction expressed by women workers in sociological surveys. Another interpretation is, of course, that the women express satisfaction with these jobs relative to what they perceive as the relevant alternative – which may be only other 'typical women's jobs'. Major and Forcey (1985) in an experiment find support for this answer to the 'paradox of the contented female worker' (F. Crosby, quoted in ibid.): men and women all performing the same task – but told that there were three different jobs – were much more likely to compare their wages with only same-sex individuals said to be in the same occupation as themselves than with all participants in this occupation. (For references to other psychologists reaching similar conclusions, see ibid.) Jackson et al. (1992) find, as do other studies (cited in ibid.), that women students have lower estimates both of what is 'fair pay' for given occupations and of what they themselves will earn than male students in the same field, even when both receive the same information about actual salaries.

The importance of including conditions of work, when analysing male/female wage differences, is emphasised by Filer (1985). In his study, depending on specification, compensating differentials account for 12–17 per cent of the wage gap. le Grand (1991) and Palme and Wright (1992) find that, in Sweden, differences in working condition account for a gender differential of less than 1 per cent. (They use the same data, but slightly different specifications.) When England et al. (1988) include working conditions and work requirements in the wage function, the negative impact of the percentage of females in the occupation is reduced, but only by a third for white women and a fifth for black. (In both cases it remains significant.) For white men, the effect of gender composition of the occupation becomes more pronounced when these variables are included. Only for black men do compensating differentials appear to explain a major part of the wage difference between male- and female-dominated occupations.

Compensating differentials, like differentials for skill, depend on the evaluation of different kinds of strain, either informally or through formal systems of evaluation, used in collective bargaining. As an example, Ericsson (1991) finds in a study of Swedish food factories that the system of evaluation used did not include monotony and gave little weight to repetitive movements and to being tied to one's place of work, characteristics typical of many women's jobs. Independence and initiative, which were more common in men's jobs, were 'compensated for', as they often are. It is ironic that the concept of compensating differentials originated with Adam Smith, whose account of the ills of performing repetitive and uncreative labour is so vivid and forceful.

2.5   Discrimination

2.5.1   The neoclassical view of discrimination

According to the neoclassical theory of race or gender discrimination, women (or some other group) could be discriminated against because employers and/or employees and/or customers do not want them to do particular jobs, or have prejudices about their ability. In a model, which assumes perfect competition, however, it would be profitable for the less prejudiced to discriminate less.[25] Hence, such models do not readily explain persistent discrimination in a competitive market. It would tend to be eroded and replaced by occupational segregation. (For erosion to take place, there would, however, have to be enough non-discriminating employers, in the case of employer discrimination and enough jobs where the worker's race or gender are unimportant to the customer, in the case of customer discrimination.) The models are certainly consistent with occupational segregation, but have more difficulty explaining that segregation results in different wage levels in jobs with equivalent requirements.

A study by Ragan and Horton Tremblay (1988) tested the evidence of discriminatory preferences among young North American full-time employees. If members of one group had a 'taste for discrimination' against another, then it would require higher wage rates to get members of the first group to work in an integrated than in a segregated workplace (controlling for other relevant variables). For race, the data offered some support for the theory, but not for gender. On the contrary, irrespective of race, both men and women had lower pay in female-dominated workplaces. Since attempts to control for amenities and working conditions did not appreciably alter the results, the authors turn to the crowding hypothesis or to institutional factors (see below) for an explanation.[26]

Beller (1982) compares data from the 1967 and 1974 US censuses and finds that in 1967 men earned 50 per cent more in male-dominated[27] occupations than in others, women 33 per cent more. In 1974 the difference was reduced to 30 per cent for both. The residual difference when controlling for a number of other variables (experience, hours, education, region, race, etc.) was 12 per cent for women and did not decline perceptibly over this period. For men it decreased from 14 to 10 per cent. In Sweden, le Grand (1991) finds that the negative effects on wages of the percentage of women in an occupation are significant for women, but not for men.

Relaxing the assumption of competitive markets, economists have argued that discrimination can be upheld by employers with some degree of monopoly power (monopsony) in the labour market. The ability of the monopsonist to discriminate against women rests, however, on the assumption that since women have fewer options in the labour market, they have a lower elasticity of labour supply. Cain (1986) objects to this that most empirical studies find a higher elasticity of labour supply for women than for men and is therefore sceptical about the realism of these models. There is a distinction, however, between how overall female labour supply is affected by changes in pay, *ceteris paribus*, and the supply curve faced by a particular employer who is alone in offering some other advantage.

Another class of models of discrimination are the stochastic. If employers know that women on average have lower labour force participation over their life-time and fulfil more of their family responsibilities than men do, they can practise 'statistical discrimination' by treating all women as if they had the average amount of career breaks and career impediments. Women with a high commitment to paid work will be paid less than they would be if the employer had correct information about them individually, while those who spend very little time in market work will gain. If the employer is risk-averse, the over- and under-payment will not even out and women in the aggregate will lose.

It seems intuitively plausible that in the absence of reliable information about each individual, statistical discrimination based on 'true stereotypes' (Schwab, 1986), though unfair to individuals would increase the probability of getting the right person in the right job at the right wage rate. This does not, however, take into account the social cost if members of one sex or ethnic or social group refrain from realising their potential because they know that they will be discriminated against on the basis of the stereotype.[28] Further, Schwab shows that, even disregarding this long-run effect, statistical discrimination may imply a socio-economic loss, depending on how skills are distributed within groups and on their reservation wages under different circumstances.

The above presupposes that the information about group productivity is correct, at least on average. Given how prejudices work, it seems psychologically and sociologically credible that the stereotypes will exaggerate the real differences. Impressions are subconsciously selected and modified so as to confirm pre-existing beliefs.[29] In the case of women, the fact that earlier generations had less labour force attachment and professional training than the younger would increase the likelihood of 'untrue stereotypes' which reflect images from the past.

2.5.2   A broader concept of discrimination

2.5.2.1   *How free are 'free choices'?*

In pure theory, the differentials between male and female, black and white, natives and immigrants, people of different social class origins, could derive wholly from differences in productivity. In reality, however, this is unlikely, for two reasons. First, it is hardly credible (unless one believes that women, blacks or working-class children are born biologically inferior) that these differences in productivity would be so systematic. Second, the deep sense and many recorded instances of injustice or exclusion experienced by women, ethnic minorities or people of working-class origin, indicate that this concept of discrimination is very narrow.[30] The dividing line between earnings differentials attributable to differences in capacity and differentials due to unequal rewards for the same capacity is not at all as clear cut as it might sound.

The greater part of the variables usually taken to determine productivity is the result of choices, but choices made within certain social parameters. The implications of choosing a certain level of education within a particular field, or looking for a job within a given branch, are not the same for men and women. The same tasks may be assigned a different job label, depending on whether they are performed by a man or by a woman. Even with rules of 'equal pay for equal work', the chance of getting a job or a promotion is unequal. (Winter-Ebmer and Zweimüller, 1997, p. 42, find that women 'have to fulfil higher ability standards to be promoted'.) This in its turn may be due to statistical discrimination, to tradition or to preferences on the part of employers or colleagues. Women may not choose the same jobs as men because they do not expect to be equally rewarded and it is possible to reward them unequally because they do not have the same range of options as men.

If women are discriminated against (formally or informally) in hiring and in access to higher education, then variables taken to explain differentiation, such as skill and responsibility and even education levels, for example, in themselves reflect discrimination.

Both firm and industry of employment are important for wage levels, even when skills are the same. As Horrell et al. (1989, p. 176) point out, it is only in a textbook model of the perfectly competitive market that 'workers of similar productivity level could be expected to face similar options in the labour market, reflecting their potential productivity level'. In actual firms, 'pay may be determined more by the characteristics of the firm or industry in which the worker is employed than by either their own qualities or the demands of the job'. Hence discriminatory hiring practices will result in lower wages for women relative to men with equal ability – but in the estimated wage functions for the firm no wage discrimination will be detectable. In a national sample, the difference may appear in the guise of a set of industry coefficients, if employers in high-paying branches discriminate more when they hire (which they well may do if discrimination is correlated with job rationing).[31]

Nor is it only a matter of pay. Women may forgo a career in which they expect to meet distrust, hostility or harassment, or to be – intentionally or unintentionally – excluded from informal networks. In early socialisation, men and women (as well as ethnic groups or social classes) are taught different ways to speak and to listen, different body language and self-presentation. Therefore it can be discriminatory if women are required to 'behave like the boys'. To sense low or negative expectations of one's ability is a barrier in itself, particularly if it is combined with lack of self-confidence and absence of positive role models. Jackson et al. (1992, p. 652) summarise research in social psychology: 'Across a wide variety of tasks and domains, women have lower performance expectations, evaluate their performance less favorably and attribute their successful performance more to external causes than do men.'

As many writers have pointed out, large numbers of jobs tend to be typecast as 'male' or 'female'.[32] Taking a long historical view, or comparing different cultures, one may find that an occupation or task which is 'typically male' in one setting could be performed only by women in another. But within a specific environment, the boundaries between what it is appropriate for men and women to do are often rigid. Sometimes the 'gender' of a job is derived from its association with psychological or physical or geographical characteristics, which are otherwise perceived as 'masculine' or 'feminine'. Sometimes it derives from traditions and historical contingencies to do with that particular occupation. Sometimes it is consciously established or reinforced by employers or by employees.

Once the sex typing is there, it is self-sustaining and self-reinforcing. (which is not to say that it never changes – for some examples see p. 34 below). There are gains from sticking to custom, both in terms of self-perception and because men and women who choose an unconventional career may be made to pay a price, inside and outside the workplace – men to an even greater extent than women perhaps, again reflecting the lower status of 'women's work'. Strong tradition may make it impossible for a person even to imagine that he or she could do a job 'appropriate to' the other sex.

The role of male workers and male-dominated worker organisations in restricting women's wages has been the subject of much research in recent years. In particular, early craft unions often excluded women from skilled jobs. It remains to be explained, however, why it was the men who were organised (and this has not always been true). It is notoriously difficult to make *ceteris paribus* estimates of the effect of union membership on wages. However, as Blau and Kahn (1992) note, centralised wage-setting, which decreases inter-branch and inter-firm differentials, tends to reduce gender differentials as well. Since one would expect a high level of overall unionisation to make for such a system, it would contribute to reducing the male/female wage gap. An EU cross-country study (cited in Dex and Sewell, (1995)), found that fewer women had low pay in countries with collective, centralised wage bargaining.

2.5.2.2   Endogenous preferences

Social science cannot take 'preferences' as given or as immutable. They are developed in a process of interaction with others and with social institutions, in an interplay of propensities with the environment. This makes the idea of a well-defined, self-contained utility-maximising 'self' problematic, particularly in those normative modes into which neoclassical economics regularly slips. In neoclassical labour economics, autonomous, consistent, self-interested, rational optimisers choose to make 'investments in human capital' according to their unambiguous and stable preferences.[33] But crucial 'investment' decisions were made for them by their parents – who helped form their preferences by doing so.[34] Over what range of alternatives can the individual be said to optimise?

As McCrate (1988) points out, since gender is socially constructed and experiences internalised, men and women make 'large and long-term investments in sex-typed preferences or identities, developing very different capacities for tastes' which make untraditional choices costly and unlikely.

If we are, as Feuerbach said, what we eat, we are to a much larger extent what we do, and in particular what we do in interaction with others. Since 'tastes' are influenced by experiences and observations of the labour market, they are not only changeable, but also endogenous in models of labour supply, wages and occupational choice.

Economists have not always considered personalities, capacities or preferences as given and fixed at the time of labour market entry. 'The difference of natural talents in different men is, in reality, much less than we are aware of; and the very different genius which appears to distinguish men of different professions, when grown up to maturity, is not upon many occasions so much the cause as the effect of the division of labour', wrote Adam Smith in *Wealth of Nations*. Experience at work, relations to others, expectations of others and the character of the work activity itself shape propensities and options.

If women earn less because they choose less productive work, this choice is influenced by seeing that women do work in female-dominated jobs with low wages, and by the conclusion that this must be what they should do and should want and because women and men have been socialised into being good at as well as enjoying different kinds of work (McCrate, 1988).

Choices of occupation and of domestic life-style are made according to a very deep sense of who we are and who we should be. The outcomes of the choices become part of the environment that affects identities and desires that determine choices. Women and men are, simultaneously, subjected to prevalent gender structures and sex typing, and recreating them, for themselves and for each other. The narrow rationalism of neoclassical theories of choice sits uneasily with issues of identity, which reflect an interplay between conscious and subconscious mental processes. As Sigmund Freud pointed out, a characteristic feature of the human subconscious is the coexistence of opposites. The logic of the subconscious does not satisfy the consistency and differentiability requirements for a well-behaved utility function.

2.5.2.3 *The measurement of productivity*

According to standard neoclassical theory, employers set wage rates equal to marginal productivity. This is not correct. At most, employers may set wage rates equal to what they believe marginal productivity to be. In order for wages to reflect productivity, these beliefs must be accurate. This raises the questions of who believes and of how beliefs are transformed into wage rates.

Skill and experience are assumed to increase productivity. Yet, it is often not self-evident which skills and experiences are relevant. Economic historians and industrial sociologists, studying the labour process, emphasise that recognition of skill is a social and historical process, involving traditions, interactions and conflicts between workers and employers and between categories of employees as well as a history of gendering of jobs and individuals.

A study by social psychologists found that 'job applicants who communicated lower pay expectations were actually offered less pay than identically qualified applicants, despite the fact that prospective employers correctly perceived that the applicants were similarly qualified'

(Major, Vanderslice and McFarlin, 1984, quoted in Jackson et al., 1992, p. 651). Thus, women's well-documented lower pay expectations will translate into lower actual wages.

Acker (1989) describes a comparable worth scheme, in which she was involved, and how suggestions from feminist participants were consistently stalled by management consultants and management representatives, because a higher evaluation of skills in traditionally female, low-paid jobs conflicted with established class hierarchies and differentials. These skills were made 'invisible'. Male employee representatives could not believe the accounts that female, mainly clerical, workers gave of the variety and complexity of their work. Acker comments that, although the re-evaluation would affect relative earnings, this was not what mattered most. Male professionals and skilled workers 'were concerned with respect, getting their due. Admitting that certain female jobs might be worthy of a similar respect seemed to be demeaning to them'. Their gender identity hinged crucially on the sense of being skilled – and being 'skilled' meant, consciously or not, being more skilled than women.

Feminists have pointed to many historical examples when traditionally female skilled work has been redefined as unskilled or taken over by men. Cases in point are obstetricians/midwives (Witz, 1988), dairy work (Lindberg, 1993, Olsson, 1993, Sommestad, 1992) and secondary school-teaching (Florin and Johansson, 1990). Conversely, some occupations have simultaneously come to be regarded as less skilled, experienced decrease in relative pay and seen a shift from male to female labour. Classical examples are clerical workers, primary schoolteachers and pattern and cutting work in the textile industry.

Acker (1989, p. 69) points out that despite 'the high probability that *a priori* job evaluation methods contain an inbuilt cultural devaluation of women's work, these systems have consistently demonstrated … that female-dominated jobs are underpaid when compared with male-dominated jobs with similar point scores'.

Phillips and Taylor (1980, p. 85) conclude, after summarising several case studies, that 'skill has become saturated with sex. It is not that skill categories have been totally subjectified. … But the equations – men/skilled, women/unskilled – are so powerful that the identification of a particular job with women, ensured that the skill content of the work would be downgraded.'

In a British study of the relation between (self-reported) job content and wages, Horrell et al. (1989) asked respondents about a range of detailed job characteristics and requirements. When an index based on these responses is compared with respondents' general assessment of the skill level of their job, women turn out to have a lower evaluation of their skill than men who score equally on the index. Women also turn out to be more likely to be overqualified for their jobs, and less likely to be underqualified than the men. The authors suggest that the evaluation of many female-dominated jobs – service and part-time jobs in particular – as unskilled could be a result as well as a cause of their traditionally low pay. (On the other hand, being overqualified could make women more likely to underestimate the skills required by the job.)

Studies of women in administrative and caring work have found that qualities identified as feminine – for example, social and nurturing skills – are not perceived as skills that make the work more highly qualified. In a study of administrative staff in health-care, Davies and Rosser (1986) found occupations where the complexity of the job content was not matched by its low grading. For these jobs, the abilities women had acquired through socialisation, and through home and family responsibilities, were essential but because 'there was no formal training involved and because these skills were not clearly *acquired* from experience within the workplace, these qualities and capabilities were not acknowledged as skills; they were unrewarded in financial terms . . .' (ibid., p. 103, emphasis in the original). Acker (1989, pp. 69 and 213) makes the same point. Dexterity and patience may be as necessary to one job as physical strength is to another, yet the latter tends to be more highly valued in wage terms.

Many of the studies referred to above are made within paradigms different from that of neoclassical economics. Are the results compatible? To some extent, they are. When employees share these gender-biased perceptions of skill and productivity, women will demand less for their labour, have lower reservation wages and supply more labour at a given wage. This will depress equilibrium wages. Wage differentials perceived as legitimate will not have the disruptive effect on motivation and production that those seen as unfair have. Akerlof's (1982) gift-exchange model (p. 18 above) provides an illuminating formalised approach.

Yet that a theory is logically compatible with certain empirical evidence does not necessarily mean that the evidence proves the theory, if those findings could be explained in terms of alternative theories as well. Also, most of the mechanisms suggested work through the tastes – the supply curves or the effort functions – of male and female employees. The role of the employer is reduced to passively surfing these pre-existing conditions, or at most to behaving in a way that reinforces an already prevalent ideology.

Finally, any measure of productivity depends on how valuable the product is considered to be. If gender bias leads to a lower evaluation of the output of 'female' activities, then the work that goes into it will appear less productive. (Take, for example, the low value assigned to work with young children.) This applies also to markets, but when dealing with a public sector or with a non-market economy the subjectivity of evaluations behind the measure of productivity becomes even more obvious – and hence its dependence on whose preferences have most impact. (See p. 145.)

2.5.3   Alternative theories: segmented labour markets

In the 1970s, institutional and radical economists presented an alternative approach to labour market inequalities. The earlier of these theories describe the labour market as *dual*, divided into two segments with small opportunities for passage from one to the other. In the primary labour market, wages are relatively high, jobs are secure and opportunities for careers, enhancing of skills and promotion are good. In the secondary labour market, wages are lower, benefits like pension or health-care schemes are poorer, jobs are temporary and insecure, working conditions worse, health and safety standards often neglected, and jobs offer little or no prospect of advancement. The theory can be modified to recognise a more complex stratification; that labour markets are segmented, rather than simply dual. (See for instance, Nilsson, 1988.)

While neoclassical economics focuses on individual behaviour, the theories of segmentation reason in terms of structures and of collectives (e.g. employers or workers or particular categories of workers). In some versions, the perspective approaches a Marxist one. The dualism of the labour market is seen as corresponding to the employers' interest in a 'divide-and-rule' strategy. Some of the proponents of segmentation theories, such as Piore (1983), see them as an alternative to, and incompatible with, the neoclassical, above all because they depart from methodological individualism. Other writers (e.g. Smith, 1989) see the two as complementary. Studies made in the neoclassical tradition sometimes incorporate elements of theories of segmentation.

Akerlof (1982, p. 544) also writes in terms of 'primary' and 'secondary' labour markets, defining the first as those where 'the gift component of labor input and wages is sizeable, and therefore wages are not market clearing. Secondary labor markets are those in which wages are market clearing.'

Given gender inequality in the household, and given the existence of a secondary labour market, it is not difficult to see why women would be more likely than (white) men to work in it. But those 'givens' would, of course, still remain to be explained.

Beechey (1978) criticises the application of dual labour market theories to the position of women. First, according to Beechey, the theory does not distinguish between female/male-dominated branches and occupations (horizontal segregation) on the one hand, and lower positions for women in mixed work settings (vertical segregation) on the other. All kinds of female-dominated work are lumped together under the heading 'secondary jobs'. Second, a large proportion of employed women work in the public sector and it is not made clear how these jobs relate to the primary/ secondary distinction and whether the same mechanisms of gender differentiation operate there as in the private sector.

Dual labour market theories provide analytical concepts for describing stratification and inequality in the labour market, and how the subordinate position of women in the labour market and in the household mutually reinforce each other, but they do not explain the origins of these conditions.

2.6   Modelling wages and wage discrimination

2.6.1   Estimation of wage functions

In empirical studies of wages, the wage of an individual is supposed to be determined by a number of factors. To estimate the relation between wages and these variables quantitatively, one must assume some particular mathematical form for the relationship (the wage function). The most general form for such a wage function for individual i is:

$$w_i = f(X_i, u_i)$$

where w is a wage rate (hourly, monthly or yearly earnings), X is a vector of characteristics of the individual or of the job and u a (random) error term for which some probability distribution is assumed. Usually, to facilitate empirical estimation, the function f is assumed to be linear or log-linear[35] (since the components of X can be functions of observed variables this assumption is not very restrictive). In most of what follows we will, as is standard in the literature, assume that w is a semi-logarithmic function of X and that u is normally distributed with zero mean.

The characteristics that go into X can, crudely, be grouped as follows:

1. Variables that have to do with the capacity and ability ('productivity') of the individual, such as education, age, experience and talent. Experience, or on-the-job training, can be general or firm-specific. Therefore, a distinction is made between overall work experience and

seniority (tenure) in the firm or job. Productivity is expected to increase with age and with experience, but at a diminishing pace. Above a certain age, productivity may actually begin to decline. To capture this, the squares of age, general work experience and seniority are often included, as well as the variables themselves.

Innate talent cannot be measured, but sometimes education is seen not only as skill-enhancing, but also (or even primarily) as a 'signal' to employers of an unobservable, underlying potential. (See Willis, 1986.) A model may include total years of study or distinguish different types of schooling.

2. Job characteristics, which may require compensating differentials.
3. Level, type, sector or field of occupation.
4. Institutional or social factors. Ethnicity, unionisation, place of residence and type of employer (large/small, public/private) make a difference to wages. Marital status,[36] number and age of children, availability of child-care and housework can be included because they affect the time, energy, interest and commitment available for work, or because they are linked with social norms and constraints or with differential treatment by employers. Cohort variables may reflect changes in attitudes and cultural patterns, among them gender roles. The effect of social class background (position or education of parents) on wages can reflect abilities fostered in the home, encouragement, 'cultural capital' or 'contacts'. For cross-country or longitudinal data, business-cycle variables or years when institutions or legislation have been altered can be pertinent. What all these variables have in common is that if they have significant parameters in a wage equation, there are a number of possible explanations for it.

A neoclassical economist sees such a wage equation as an expression of marginal productivity and marginal utility, deriving from a production function for the firm and a utility function for the worker. The approach taken in this study is, however, to see it as a tool of multivariate statistical analysis, to investigate whether certain variables are correlated with earnings. The nature of the relationships remains for economic, psychological and sociological interpretation.

2.6.2   Quantifying discrimination

2.6.2.1   *Decomposing the gender gap*

The simplest way of measuring to what extent the gender wage gap reflects different rewards for similar work, is to estimate a parameter for 'sex' in a wage equation on a mixed sample. This, however, amounts to making the restrictive assumption that the same characteristics have the same effect on the wages of men and women, and that the effect of discrimination (and possible unobserved characteristics) is equally large for all women.

Since the 1970s it has instead been standard practice to decompose wage differentials between gender or ethnic groups into parts attributable to different factors (Blinder, 1973, Oaxaca, 1973). The basic distinction is between that part of the differential due to difference in the variable values (the X's, characteristics or 'endowments') for the two groups and the part measured by differences in parameters when a wage equation of the same form is estimated for each of them separately.

As mentioned above, US studies tend to find that only about half the wage gap is 'explained by human capital factors'. In Britain, Horell et al. (1989) found that for full-time workers 20 per cent of the gender gap in hourly wages was attributable to skills while 76 per cent resulted from differential rewards. In Paci et al.'s (1995) model, schooling and experience account for less than a tenth of the 20 per cent wage difference between full-time working women and men born in 1958. As job and employer characteristics are introduced, the 'explained' share increases to 23 per cent. In Sweden, le Grand (1991) found a gap in hourly wages of 19.5 per cent. A few 'human capital' variables accounted for a fifth of the wage gap. Family situation and career interruptions added little to the 'explained part', but housework somewhat more. When further variables reflecting occupational segregation and working conditions were included, 57 per cent of the wage gap was attributable to difference in characteristics. This implies that if Swedish women had personal and professional characteristics similar to those of men, their hourly wages would still be 8 per cent lower.

Formally, the procedure is as follows:[37] Starting from a linear equation for the logarithm of the wage rate, ln(w), and from an error term with zero mean, and using the subscript m for variables referring to men and f for women we can write the equation for the average of the logarithm of the wage as

$$\ln w_i = \beta_i X_i \qquad i = m, f$$

where X_i is the vector of means of the independent variables for sex i. The first element of X is taken to be equal to one for every individual. Hence β_m^1 and β_f^1 are the intercepts of the male and female wage equations.

The difference between the male and female averages[38] can then be written as

$$\Delta = \ln w_m - \ln w_f = \beta_m X_m - \beta_f X_f \qquad (1)$$

Adding and subtracting a term $\beta_f X_m$ or $\beta_m X_f$ we get either

$$\Delta = [\beta_m - \beta_f] X_m + \beta_f [X_m - X_f] \qquad (2)$$

or

$$\Delta = [\beta_m - \beta_f] X_f + \beta_m [X_m - X_f] \qquad (3)$$

In equation (2) the second term shows how much larger women's wages would be if their wage function remained the same, but their average values for all variables were equal to those of men. This is described as the difference attributable to the X's – differences in endowments or characteristics – evaluated by the female wage function. The first term, analogously, is the difference attributable to differences in parameters, including the intercept. (The term equals the difference in parameters weighted by the men's endowments.). If we consider the female function as, in some sense, 'correct', then this term shows the 'extra' that the men get because they are paid more than this for the same things. This component of the wage differential is often referred to as the 'unexplained part' or the 'discrimination term'.[39]

In equation (3) we do the same thing, using the male wage function as the benchmark. The choice between the two is an index number problem and there is no 'right' or 'wrong' answer to it.[40] Whether the difference this choice makes is large or small, varies from sample to sample. To show this, the differential can be decomposed into three terms:

$$\beta_m X_m - \beta_f X_f = \beta_f(X_m - X_f) + (\beta_m - \beta_f)X_f + (\beta_m - \beta_f)(X_m - X_f) \qquad (4)$$

The first term on the right-hand side indicates how much women's wages would increase if, without changing their wage function, their characteristics had instead been the same as those of men. The second represents the wage difference due to unequal rewards to equal characteristics, given women's present endowments. The third is equal to the difference between the 'discrimination terms' in equations (2) and (3), respectively. Hence, it measures how much our appreciation of what is explained by endowments differs according to which wage function we use to evaluate it. (Or, in other words, how much more men are paid for the things that they are, do, choose or value.) It is sometimes called an 'interaction term'. If it is large, this implies that it means a relatively small improvement in women's pay if they choose untypical careers. Daymont and Andrisani (1984), aptly, describe this as a 'chilling effect', by which women are deterred by observed or past discrimination from acquiring those labour market characteristics which according to human capital theory would raise their wages.

It is standard to point out that equations (2) and (3) are special cases of a more general decomposition:

$$\ln(w_m) - \ln(w_f) = (\beta_m - \beta_*)X_m + (\beta_* - \beta_f)X_f + \beta_*(X_m - X_f) \qquad (5)$$

In equation (5), β_* stands for the wage structure that would prevail if no discrimination existed. The first of the three terms shows by how much men's earnings deviate from what they would have received in the absence of discriminatory treatment ('nepotism'). The second is the amount by which women's pay differs from the non-discrimination level ('discrimination'). The third term stands for the difference due to endowments, weighted by the non-discriminatory wage function. (Equation (2) is a special case of equation (5) with $\beta_* = \beta_f$, equation (3) with $\beta_* = \beta_m$.)

β_* can also be chosen as an average of β_m and β_f weighted by scalar weights or by a weighting matrix.[41] One possibility is to weight the male and female parameter vectors by the proportions male and female in the sample (Cotton, 1988). Using μ for the proportion of men in the sample we have:

$$\beta_* = \mu\,\beta_m + (I - \mu)\beta_f \qquad (6)$$

Generalising from scalar weights to a weighting matrix Ω we have:

$$\beta_* = \Omega\,\beta_m + (I - \Omega)\beta_f \qquad (7)$$

In this case the proportions of the differential that are explained and unexplained need no longer fall in between the cases given by equations (2) and (3), as is the case with scalar weights. Oaxaca and Ransom (1994) suggest a choice of matrix which is equivalent to assuming that the non-discriminatory wage function is equal to that which would be obtained from estimating the wage equation on the pooled sample of men and women.[42]

Neumark (1988) derives a method of decomposition from a Beckerian discrimination model in which discrimination can be derived from an 'employer's utility function'. The employer's utility or disutility depends on how many men and women are employed in each of a number of different job categories. Neumark uses the assumption that the employer's utility depends on the proportion of male/female employees in a given category, but not on the absolute numbers,[43] to construct an estimator for the 'non-discriminatory wage function' which coincides with that proposed by Oaxaca and Ransom.

Although the weights for ΔX in *any* decomposition present themselves as 'no-discrimination wage structures', they share the crucial assumption that, as Neumark writes, 'labor supply and individual characteristics are fixed and would not respond to the changes in wages that would result from the elimination of discrimination' (ibid., p. 281). It is important not to interpret them as predictions or proposals of what wages would be in a discrimination-free society. They are illustrations of the unequal present, 'as if' rather than 'if' there was no discrimination.

It is true that the scenarios implied by equations (2) and (3) – that both men and women would do exactly the same as men do now or exactly as women do now – are wholly unrealistic. Yet, those of Cotton, Neumark or Oaxaca and Ransom are just as much 'as if'. If men and women had equal power, possibilities and access, equal responsibilities and equal rewards in all spheres of life, it is most unlikely that jobs would be exactly the same as now, require and reward exactly the same skills and characteristics in exactly the same way and that the overall distribution of time and energy between different activities would be the same – yet this is what is implicitly assumed.

The Neumark/Oaxaca and Ransom decomposition, in addition to this general objection, has two shortcomings, which incline to an under-estimate of discrimination. The first is a narrowness in conception. It is said to be an advantage of the method that the parameters estimated for the whole labour force reflect 'the market's evaluation' of the corresponding characteristics. This assumes that this market evaluation is in itself objective and discrimination-free. The Neumark/Oaxaca and Ransom method thus disregards that the evaluation of a characteristic by participants in this market is consistently biased according to how strongly it is associated with 'masculinity' or 'femininity'.[44]

Secondly, if all women are discriminated against because they are women, a wage equation estimated for men and women jointly, without a variable for gender, is mis-specified. Suppose the variable 'male' had had a positive significant parameter, if it was included. If it is omitted, the parameters estimated on the pooled sample will be upward-biased for variables positively correlated with being male, and downward-biased for those correlated with being female. If these parameters are used to construct an endowment term, this will include an effect actually due to discrimination. (Chapter 5 provides an illustrative example.) Under such circumstances, to call the pooled OLS estimates 'the non-discriminatory wage' is not appropriate, and there is no reason to prefer this weighting to the traditional male and female equations. These give a clearer picture of actual options for men and women.

A different critique of the traditional decomposition is presented by Jenkins (1994). Instead of focusing on and decomposing the difference between the sample means for men/women or black/white, Jenkins suggests use of the entire distribution of 'discrimination experiences', that is, of the percentage difference between an estimated non-discriminatory wage and the actual for each person in the discriminated group. This adds information on which groups of women are more and which are less exposed to gender discrimination. (The issue of what the non-discriminatory wage would be remains, however.)[45]

The endowment terms in equations (2)–(5) can be further decomposed to quantify the part of the wage gap attributable to the difference between the average levels for a particular variable for men and women. Let X^k refer to, say, years of experience, and X^j to having a university degree. Then $\beta_f^k[X_m^k - X_f^k]$ measures the wage difference due to the fact that men and women have different amounts of work experience, evaluated by the female wage function, and $\beta_m^j[X_m^j - X_f^j]$ measures the difference due to the different proportions of men and women who have degrees, evaluated by the wage function for men. It is tempting make a similar decomposition of the 'discrimination term'. A number of studies do this to obtain the 'total difference' attributable to one variable or group of variables, adding the respective endowment and parameter terms. In particular, many studies have wanted to separate the difference between the intercepts of the male and female functions as an effect of group membership *per se*.

The problem with this is that the part of the 'discrimination term' attributed to a particular variable depends on rather arbitrary choices of how to measure this variable. For instance, the size of the part of the wage difference which is attributed to differential effects of marital status on women's and men's wages, would be different depending on whether the variable was equal to 1 for 'married' and to zero for 'single', or the other way around. Using 1 and 2 instead of zero and one would produce yet another 'discrimination effect due to marital status'. The same would happen if 'years of school' was exchanged for 'years of school beyond the compulsory'. (Formally, this decomposition is invariant under changes of scale, but not under parallel shifts. This is illustrated by pedagogical examples in Jones and Kelley (1984), while a general algebraic demonstration is provided in Katz (1994, p. 72f) and available from the author.)[46]

2.6.2.2 Interpretation

The term attributable to difference in the wage equation is often simply identified with 'discrimination'. This is too simple. Since there can never be a perfect model, one can always suspect that some part of the discrimination term in equations (2)–(5) would disappear if more variables were added to the equations or if those included were more specific.

Taking this to its logical conclusion nevertheless leads to absurdity. It means that discrimination is, *a priori*, impossible to prove. There are no two identical individuals in the world and for any number of observations we could propose an equal number of variables.

Kim and Polachek (1994) estimate wage equations from US panel data, with a range of model specifications, to investigate the effects of introducing individual-specific intercept and individual-specific slopes into the model.[47] They find that these individual-specific effects reduce the gender coefficient, in some cases by about a quarter, in others by nearly a half. Their verbal interpretation that this reduction is due to 'controlling for unmeasured differences in work motivation' (ibid., p. 37) rather begs the question.

First, no reason is given why the unmeasured effects are in fact a matter of work motivation. The same econometric story could well be told with 'being subject to discriminatory treatment' cast in the leading role – or any other factor which we cannot measure. Second, a crucial assumption is that the hidden factor, which reveals itself in the individual-specific effect, is uncorrelated with gender. That remains to be shown.[48]

By definition, the 'missing variables' explanation of the discrimination term cannot be proved or disproved. It is logically possible that there are some factors that affect women's and men's productivity differently, which are perceptible to employers, but not to econometricians. Proof and refutation are both impossible, but it is also logically possible that the systematic bias is in the perceptions of employers. Prejudice may lead to downward-biased perceptions of women's productivity or to better chances for men to advance within occupations.

With a broader concept of discrimination and subordination nearly all the 'endowments' can be seen to be the results of choices conditioned by existing inequalities. If custom, social norms and socialisation make women believe that their work is less important and their skills are less useful, and they therefore accept lower wages than men, then 'women's work' will be less well paid. It is restrictive not to include this in discrimination. If the existing wages contribute to this acceptance, all estimates are subject to what statisticians call an endogeneity problem and, therefore, are biased. Another aspect of endogeneity is the 'chilling effect' of past discrimination mentioned above.

There is no unique measure of discrimination, because variables are partly exogenous, partly endogenous. Should seniority be included? Yes, because without any discrimination by employers, but rewards to experience in the company, irrespective of sex, this could explain a differential. But what if women are the first to be made redundant? Or if the choice of who makes a career-break to care for a baby is not free and equal? Or if it is taken for granted that wives move with husbands' jobs, but not vice versa? Then seniority reflects other forms of discrimination. Experience improves ability and, therefore, we would expect employers to pay for it. Yet, if women expect wage discrimination, their labour force participation may be lower than if they believed that they would get the same wages as men, and, hence, experience is endogenous in wage estimation.[49]

Should only years of education be included or field *and* years of study? A midwife and an engineer may need an equally long period of training. But they are not equally rewarded. Is that discrimination? Or do too many women 'crowd' into midwifery and depress the wages? Do they do this because female engineers experience discrimination? Or is the midwife's work less demanding or less important? Or could that be an androcentric evaluation?

Wages vary with occupation. But, as noted above, choice of occupation is conditioned by existing inequalities in a number of ways. Occupational segregation is an essential and logical outcome of a discriminatory system and to control for it in the model means defining away a large part of the problem under study.

As Blau and Ferber (1987) note, 'in the not implausible case that both discrimination and choice play a role, neither procedure will be unbiased.' D'Amico (1987) further discusses the methodological problems of isolating discrimination from a 'productivity gap' between blacks and whites, part of which can 'be traced to the presence of labor market discrimination'.

A further distinction is whether a variable is exogenous to the labour market or exogenous to an individual employer. Factors that are endogenous in a study of wage discrimination in a country may be properly considered exogenous in a court case involving a specific firm (but may, yet again, be relevant in an affirmative action program for an individual employer).

It is a misguided effort to search for a single number or percentage as the measure of discrimination. Decomposition of wage differentials 'explains' wage inequality only in a very limited sense, but tells us something about the form and the mechanisms of it. The indications of discrimination we get from different model specifications differ according to the different assumptions implicit in the models, and can, thus, enable us to place these assumptions under scrutiny. This helps us draw conclusions about the importance of different variables (and the forces that affect them, in their turn) for male/female differentials.

Both wider and narrower concepts of discrimination have their place – so long as the definition used is made clear and the values ascribed to particular characteristics are not taken for granted.

Appendix

A.1   Linear functions, vector notation and linear regression

w is a linear function of the n variables $x_1, x_2, x_3, \ldots x_n$ if

$$w = \alpha + \beta_1 x_1 + \beta_2 x_2 + \beta_3 x_3 + \ldots + \beta_n x_n = \alpha + \Sigma \beta_k x_k \qquad \text{(A1)}$$

where α and each β_i are given, fixed numbers (parameters), while each variable x_k can take on different values. α is called the intercept and the β's are coefficients. The x-variables can be continuous, such as age, or discrete such as having/not having a university degree. A discrete variable which takes only two different values is called a dummy variable.

Hence, given a set of values for the n x_k variables, the value of w is known. In order to have to write as little as possible, it is usual in statistical analysis to have a first variable, x_1, which is equal to one for all observations. The coefficient for x_1, β_1 is then the intercept and replaces α. The equation becomes:

$$w = \beta_1 x_1 + \beta_2 x_2 + \beta_3 x_3 + \ldots + \beta_n x_n = \Sigma \beta_k x_k \qquad \text{(A2)}$$

Using the terminology of linear algebra, the β_k's and the x_k's are called components of the n-element vectors β and X. In this notation $w = \beta X$ where βX is a short-hand notation for the sum of the products of each parameter β_k with the value of the corresponding variable x_k.

If for a number of observations we know the value that each explanatory x_k-variable takes and the value of w, we can try to find out what the underlying β_k's are. (Assume, for instance, that w is the wage and the x's are personal or job-characteristics – age, education, etc.) Usually, there is no set of β_k's that satisfies (A2) exactly for all individuals. We have to conclude that for individual i,

$$w^i = \beta_1 x_1^i + \beta_2 x_2^i + \beta_3 x_3^i + \ldots + \beta_n x_n^i + u^i \qquad \text{(A3)}$$

where w^i, and x_k^i are specific for this person, while the β_k's are the same for everyone. That is, the wage is equal to the 'predicted value' given by (A2) plus an individual residual, or error term, u^i. The purpose of an ordinary linear regression estimate is to find out what values of $\beta_1, \beta_2, ..., \beta_n$ would make the u^i's as small as possible for all the observations. More precisely, the β_k are chosen so as to make the sum of the squares of all the u^i's as small as possible. Crudely, β_k shows how a particular value of x_k contributes to w, when the other x's are held constant.

A.2 Linear and log-linear wage functions: interpretation of parameters

Assume that w (measured in, say, pounds) is a linear function, that is to say is of the form (A1). The parameter for an explanatory variable x, estimated by ordinary least squares (OLS) regression, shows the addition to wages, in pounds, connected with a marginal increase in x. If x is continuous this increase is the derivative of w with respect to x, if x is a non-continuous (discrete) variable it is the effect of a one unit increase in x.

This form of the wage equation amounts to assuming that a certain qualification or characteristic will bring about, on average, a particular money addition (or diminution) of the wage, all else equal. If wages depend only on years of schooling (s) and gender (g) the equation is:

$$w_i = a + bs_i + dg_i + u_i \qquad (A4)$$

A person with one year more of schooling can expect to earn b pounds more than a person of the same gender with one year less of schooling.

In many cases, a higher level of education may be rewarded by so many per cent increase in wages, rather than so many pounds. To capture this one needs a 'semi-logarithmic' or 'log-linear' wage equation – instead of placing the wage on the left side of the equation one uses its logarithm. In empirical estimates this form has tended to produce the best fits of estimated function (equation) to actual wage data and it is therefore the most common in the literature.

Mathematically a semi-logarithmic wage function with schooling and gender as the explanatory variables is:

$$\ln w_i = a + bs_i + dg_i + u_i \qquad (A5)$$

and thus $w = e^{(a+bs_i+dg_i+u_i)} = e^a e^{bs_i} e^{dg_i} e^{u_i}$ is an exponential function of s and g.

Given gender and experience, the effect of more education on wages can be expressed as the derivative of w with respect to s:

$$\frac{\partial w}{\partial s} = bw \qquad (A6)$$

The percentage change in w, due to a change in s is equal to $\frac{\frac{\delta w}{\delta s}}{w} = b$, that is, to the estimated parameter for s in the equation.

For a non-continuous variable, we do not need (and cannot take) derivatives. Assume that we code female gender as $g = 0$ and male as $g = 1$. Then, if person m and person f have the same amounts of schooling, but person f is a woman and m is a man, then the woman's wage is $w_f = e^a e^{bs} e^0 e^u$ and the man's wage $w_m = e^a e^{bs} e^d e^u$ respectively. Thus, $w_m = e^d w_f$ and $\ln w_m = d + \ln w_f$. The relative difference (the wage increase in percentage terms due to being male) is

$$\frac{w_m - w_f}{w_f} = \frac{e^d w_f - w_f}{w_f} = e^d - 1$$

If d is small, $e^d - 1 \approx d$. (The approximation is good enough for most purposes if $d < 0.1$.)

3
Soviet Wages and Salaries

3.1 Issues in Soviet wage formation

3.1.1 Purpose of the chapter

The institutional context of Soviet wage formation is obviously very different from that which is envisaged by neoclassical economic theory, as well as from the capitalist mode of production that Marx analysed. The assumption, discussed in the preceding chapter – that at the margin, wages should equal productivity – is deduced from an assumption that firms maximise profits. Irrespective of whether one accepts this theory, as applied to capitalist firms, or not, profit-maximisation was clearly not a good approximation of the behaviour of Soviet enterprises. In the USSR, there were centrally determined wage rates. Implicit 'wage-bargaining' took place when these were applied locally. Bonuses, which were a substantial part of earnings, were determined at enterprise level, albeit subject to official regulations. Hence, as will be discussed here and in chapter 6, wage formation was the outcome of a complex interplay of local and central forces, regulations and demand and supply pressures.

To analyse the results presented in chapters 5 and 6, it is necessary to look at these regulations, at the social forces involved (planning authorities, enterprise management, male and female workers and employees) and at the social and ideological context. In this chapter, attention is restricted to earnings and benefits from, or dependent on, employment in the state sector. Since the study is of an urban sample, agriculture is not considered.

I will rely mainly on some well-researched Western studies and turn to Soviet handbooks for the 'official' Soviet definitions.[1] I have been considerably helped by interviews with Russian researchers with long experience in the study of earnings.[2] The main aim is to describe the situation in 1989, the year in which the data used in chapters 4–6 were collected. I briefly describe developments from the end of the Stalin period up to 1989, but not after the dissolution of the USSR. There is a difficulty in that a number of reforms were decided in 1986–88 and supposed to be gradually implemented over the following years, but to what extent they actually had been by 1989 is impossible to tell. Furthermore, disintegration had begun to make itself felt at this time. Earlier data would have described 'the Soviet system' in a purer form – but precisely because the Soviet system was what it was, earlier data are not available.

Five themes will recur in chapters 3 and 6. These are the effect of demand and supply on relative pay; local (enterprise) influence; mechanisms that regulate the change of earnings over a person's career; wage dispersion and, finally, mechanisms that cement the gender gap and discriminate against women.

3.1.2   Labour legislation, labour allocation and wage policies

In 1956 three years after the death of Stalin laws according to which workers could be assigned jobs by the authorities and workers and employees could not change their employment without permission, were repealed. Able-bodied adults who were not students or mothers of young children were still legally obliged to work, however, and there were exceptions to the right to choose one's job.

Until the late 1970s, *kolkhoz* peasants needed the consent of the local authorities to obtain the internal passports without which they could not leave the farms. There was still forced labour in prisons and labour camps, although the scale cannot be compared to that of the Terror. Graduates from specialised secondary schools and higher education were assigned posts for the first three years. There is, however, evidence that a considerable number of youngsters either did not take up these jobs or left them before the close of the term (DiFranceisco and Gitelman, 1984, Malle, 1987, Oxenstierna, 1990).[3] The *propiska* system of internal residence permits indirectly restricted what jobs people could take. Permits to settle in Moscow and Leningrad were especially difficult to obtain. In these two cities, the so-called '*limitchiki*' had residence permits linked to work in a particular enterprise or institution. According to Malle (1987, p. 360), by 1980 the share of *limitchiki* in industrial employment in Moscow had risen to almost one third. For them, change of jobs meant leaving town or facing the problems of illegal residence. There was also certain 'protective legislation' restricting the employment of women.

Yet, generally speaking, in post-Stalin USSR individuals were allowed to seek, choose and change jobs among those available,[4] and sectors, enterprises and institutions had to compete to attract workers.

People were not allowed to try to improve their conditions through collective action, collective self-organisation or collective bargaining. Soviet trade unions were not supposed to have a wage-bargaining role. Individual workers could turn to the trade union when they were not paid the right amount or when health and safety standards were violated. Trade union consent was required for dismissals and unions were represented on norm-setting and certification committees (see below). The writ of the trade unions included the conflicting goals of defending workers' rights and ensuring productivity and plan fulfilment. Therefore, in many cases they did protect individual workers, but in many others they did not. They also functioned as an agency for the distribution of benefits and goods (see p. 73). They were no organs for collective action or for protection against political victimisation. When strikes (or threats of strikes) or go-slows occurred, they were independent of the official union structures. Although all action of this kind was cloaked in deep official secrecy, there is evidence that it occurred and could be successful,[5] but it was also punished by victimisation, and strikes were certainly not frequent.

Soviet workers were, however, allowed to vote with their feet and did so, to the dismay of the authorities. Malle (1987, 1990) describes the efforts to tighten discipline and discourage quits in the 1970s and early 1980s. Although the rate of mobility never was very high by Western standards (Granick, 1987, Oxenstierna, 1990) it was higher than the authorities wished.

Shortage of, or excess demand for, labour power was endemic in the USSR. The terms in which this phenomenon is analysed depend on the writer's theoretical framework and view of the nature and dynamics of the Soviet economic system. Such an analysis is beyond the scope of the present study. For our purposes it is enough to state that shortage of labour power, unfilled vacancies, labour hoarding by enterprises and institutions, overstaffing and low productivity of labour were among the 'stylised facts' of the Soviet economy and keys to understanding many issues of behaviour and policies. (For three different theoretical perspectives, see Arnot, 1988, Oxenstierna, 1990, Marnie, 1992.)

Granick (1987) claims that workers' 'job rights', that is, the restrictions on management's discretion to move or fire staff, caused over-staffing and undermined labour discipline. Yet, this view, as well as Blair Ruble's (quoted in Godson, 1981, p. 117) that 'it has become virtually impossible to dismiss a Soviet industrial worker for other than political reasons' are highly disputable.

Enterprise management had the right to dismiss workers because of reductions in the workforce or technological change, but had to offer them alternative employment. If the offer was rejected, the worker could be dismissed (but had the right to appeal to a tribunal if the alternative job was considered 'unsuitable'). Dismissals were also allowed because of 'unsuitability for the job' and for disciplinary reasons. Such dismissals had to be approved by the union, but this was often neglected or a mere formality (Godson, 1981, Lampert, 1986). Tribunal appeals, however, were not a formality. According to Malle (1990) few of the dismissed went to a tribunal, but two-fifths of those who did were reinstated.[6]

Hanson (1986) concludes that people were sacked 'for persistent drunkenness, absenteeism, political dissent, exit-visa applications and annoying the boss', but that nevertheless 'the typical Soviet enterprise's insatiable demand for additional labour is sufficient to ensure both a general regime of job security and aggregate full employment'.

Malle (1987, p. 372) reports evidence from the early 1980s that managers did move workers to other jobs without their consent and that a substantial number of 'voluntary' quits may in practice have been forced. Marnie (1992, p. 177) also concludes from a detailed study of labour shortage in the USSR that Soviet laws 'certainly did not encourage redundancy dismissals, but neither were they ever a significant restraint'. The real obstacle to dismissals was the difficulty of finding a replacement.

This indicates that the main systemic causes for excess demand for labour are to be sought elsewhere, among the reasons why production could not be organised efficiently and was so badly planned and co-ordinated that management had to hoard any resources it needed, including labour, against contingencies (such as irregularity of supplies, breakdowns of equipment, sudden orders from the planning authorities to use less labour or produce more, or requisitioning of labour power from the local authorities for such purposes as road-building, harvesting or construction). There was, to use Lampert's term (1986, p. 260), an 'informal bargain' according to which management accepted a certain amount of shoddy work, drunkenness and shirking, so long as the plan target was met – if necessary through overtime and storming. ('Storming', or *sturmovshchina*, means a great increase in speed and quantity of work just before the end of a plan period – usually at the expense of quality – to meet the plan target.)

Malle (1987, p. 359) refers to 'influential Gosplan officials' who wanted to ban hirings 'at the gate' and even advertisements for vacancies at the enterprise, so that all hirings would be through the labour allocation authorities and unattractive jobs be filled 'without wage inflation'. In other words, it was clearly recognised that labour shortages increased workers' bargaining power and led to higher wages, in particular for unpopular jobs. In branches with high rates of job turnover and limited possibilities of promotion, workers' skills were often highly graded relative to the job, while they were underrated in more favoured branches such as engineering (ibid., p. 375). This increased wages in unattractive jobs more than the official rates allowed.

3.1.3 The discretion of the enterprise and rewards for seniority

In theory, wages were set according to centrally determined rules. In fact, the shortage of labour power, and the need for and low cost to the enterprise of labour hoarding, meant that managers had to, could and did adjust wages so as to attract labour. Granick's (1987, p. 67) conclusion that 'by using its power to manipulate bonuses, wage-rate supplements, and piece-rate norms, enterprise management in the Soviet Union can enjoy the same freedom of choice as does the non-unionised capitalist firm' is definitely exaggerated. Yet, these and other means could be used – legally or semi-legally – to adjust the price of labour to supply.

One way to encourage workers to stay is to reward seniority (tenure). Soviet wages and salaries were not supposed automatically to increase with age, experience or seniority. Nevertheless, both cross-section studies and retrospective work-histories (Prokofeva, 1988, 1991) indicate growth in earnings over people's working life. Ofer and Vinokur (1992) found returns to years of experience that were higher than in most Western studies, particularly for men.

Komozin (1991, p. 59), describing the problems of young workers, complains that managers favoured 'old-timers' by 'adjusting wage grades and giving promotions as a function of number of years on the job and not on the basis of final results'.

On the other hand, people are less inclined to quit relatively well-paid jobs. Managers may have paid 'extras' to the staff they least wanted to lose. If the strategy – which agrees with efficiency wage or transaction cost theory – was successful, these workers would stay longer, and a standard wage regression would show 'returns to seniority'.

Rewards to seniority could affect male:female differentials in either direction. On the one hand, if women had left paid work to care for young children, this would reduce their seniority relative to that of men. On the other, Soviet women are said to have had lower quit rates than men (Baranenkova, 1983, Clayton and Millar, 1991).[7] This would increase their seniority and pay, all else being equal. (In fact, all else was not equal, since men and women did not work in the same jobs and branches, and the reward to seniority varied between these.)

We will return to the issue of seniority, promotion and bonuses dependent on seniority below.

3.1.4   Were wage differences too small?

Overall earnings dispersion in the USSR is a subject of much dispute. The myth that 'levelling' minimised differentials is still widespread but not well founded. Atkinson and Micklewright (1992) estimate decile ratios for the Soviet wage distribution which are at least as high as those of the United Kingdom for the whole post-war period.[8] This is in line with earlier research, which found earnings dispersion in the USSR in the 1960s and 1970s smaller, but not drastically so, than in the United States and similar to or greater than in Western Europe. This is the conclusion Bergson (1984) reached, and is supported by Ofer and Vinokur (1992, p. 36f.). See also Chapman (1979).

The United States and United Kingdom are more inegalitarian than most developed Western countries and the Scandinavian countries less inegalitarian. Redor (1992) compares Western and Soviet-type economies and finds that, in terms of overall wage and income dispersion and gender equality, intra-systemic differences dominate over the inter-systemic. In particular, in several respects the difference between the Scandinavian and other Western countries are greater than between the latter and the Eastern European. Yet, in the Soviet-type economies, he finds smaller wage differentials between manual and non-manual labour, but larger dispersion within the blue-collar category. The inter-branch pattern also differs, since the priority accorded certain 'key' sectors in Soviet-type economies is reflected in higher wage levels.

Gustafsson and Nivorozhkina (1996), using the same sample as in this study, find levels of earnings dispersion in the Soviet city of Taganrog to be similar to those in Sweden. Note, however, that the Swedish are of a national probability sample, while the Soviet sample is local. Income distribution in Taganrog must be more equal than in the USSR, or in Russia.[9]

Measurement of inequality of earnings, and of total benefits from work, becomes even more complicated given that a very large part of work-related benefits are non-monetary. This is discussed in sections 3.4.1–3.4.2.

Male/female difference is one element of wage dispersion. The existence of 'women's jobs' with pay below what men would accept increases the total spread of wages. Conversely, male/female wage differences tend to be larger when the overall wage dispersion is greater. (See section 2.1.)

In the USSR women have been entitled, by law, to equal pay for equal work since the first years after the October Revolution. As in many other countries with such legislation, the actual wages showed that women's work was considered very unequal. Ofer and Vinokur (1992) conclude that the most forceful drive towards equalisation of wages came from the 'rapid expansion of the educational system and the establishment of higher levels of minimum wages', while the main force in the opposite direction was the persistent 'gap between male and female pay scales'. The sectors of the economy accorded the lowest priority were also the most female-dominated, as we will see in chapter 5.

3.2   The post-war Soviet wage system

3.2.1   The system under Stalin

From the time of the first five-year plan, the policy of those in power was to increase wage differentiation. 'Petty bourgeois levelling' (*uravnilovka*), which Stalin denounced in 1931, became a standing philippic in Soviet writings.

In a given industry, a skilled worker could earn up to 12 times as much as the junior service staff (*'mladshii obsluzhivaiushchii personal'*, MOP) – that is, cleaners, caretakers, etc. (Nove, 1977). Mandel (1969) quotes a British delegation which found, in Moscow in 1952, that a roadsweeper earned 300 roubles per month, a lorry-driver 700–800, while the head of a large enterprise got 7,000–8,000 (including bonuses).

Differentials between rates of pay in priority and non-priority branches of the economy increased and a huge increase in piece-rate work further added to differentiation (Nove, 1977). Piecework was said to be the appropriate form of wages under 'socialism'. Time-rates were considered too egalitarian and, therefore, ideologically inferior. Often the rates were 'progressive', which further increased the advantage of Stakhanovite 'record workers' over the others. (With 'progressive' piece-rates, rate per unit increases with the number of units produced.) There were, of course, those who saw that Stalinism had little to do with socialism, and Stalinist wage policy little to do with Marxist theory. In this respect, Trotsky probably spoke for all the currents of Left critics of the USSR when he wrote of 'the furious insistence with which the bureaucracy is applying the maxim . . . "Divide and rule!"'. Moreover, to console the workers, this forced piecework labor is called "socialist competition". The name sounds like a mockery' (Trotsky, 1973, p. 128).

Each sector of the economy and each major branch of industry created its own wage scales. After 1946, the pre-war wage scales became increasingly incongruous, but there was no broad attempt to make them more consistent. According to Soviet authors quoted by Kirsch (1972), by 1956, nearly 2,000 different skill scales were in force in industry alone.

To some extent, the large differentials between skilled and unskilled labour in the 1930s can be explained as incentives for the millions of unskilled workers attracted, or driven, to industry from the countryside, to acquire the skills industrialisation required. But although the supply of qualified labour (both blue- and white-collar) had increased considerably from 1931 to 1956 there had been no decrease in the differentials – officially, that is. In reality, managers bent the rules to be able to recruit workers to jobs, far down on the official pay scales.

One way of doing this was to 'adjust' the norms. Wage rates for a normal amount of work could be set centrally, but what a 'normal' amount – the appropriate 'norm' – was had to be worked out locally. Low norms meant high wages, which would attract labour power. By 1958 *average* norm overfulfilment in industry was 169 per cent, with a corresponding gap between basic rates and actual earnings (Kirsch, 1972). Another method was to rename jobs in order to increase pay. Nove (1977, p. 205) quotes the Soviet magazine *Krokodil*, famous for its satirical cartoons: 'My secretary is so good, I hired her as a turner of the 5th grade'. 'Re-naming' was used both for white- and blue-collar workers – by the mid-1950s hardly any manual workers were graded as 'unskilled' (Nove, 1977, Kirsch, 1972).

3.2.2   Wage reforms, 1956–89

In 1955 a new government body was established, the State Committee on Labour and Wages (*Goskomtrud*), which was supposed to reform wages. Power struggles and opposition from the branch ministries made the start slow and feeble, but in 1958–59, the work gathered pace. By 1960, wages had been reformed for all industrial workers (Kirsch, 1972) and during the following 2–4 years analogous reforms were carried through in the rest of the state sector.

Piece-rates were no longer automatically preferred to time-rates. Kirsch quotes Soviet criticisms, such as the story of a plant said to have spent so much on calculating piece-rates that it increased the cost of the parts produced three-fold. Another put its repair workers on piece-rates, which made it profitable for them to have as many breakdowns of machinery as possible (Kirsch, 1972, p. 32). Straight piece-rates were increasingly replaced by various bonus systems, combined with either piece-rates or time-rates (see Kirsch, 1972, chart 2.1). Collective piece-rate systems increased at the expense of individual ones and 'progressive piece-rates' all but disappeared.

The wage reform made the system more uniform and consistent. After the 1972 wage round, there were three tariff scales for industrial workers as compared with approximately 1,900 in 1956 (McAuley, 1979). Nevertheless, the wage reform created anomalies of its own and it was still possible for enterprises to manipulate wages (for examples, see Filtzer, 1989). The actual outcome inevitably depended on relations of power between workers and management and between management and central planners.

The effect of the reform on overall wage differentiation is difficult to estimate – the range of the wage scales generally decreased, but if, as several Soviet economists claim, the two bottom grades in the scales were not actually used before the reform, then the effective range was greater after it. Tightening of norms, increased standardisation and decrease of piece-rates, on the other hand, would have worked in the direction of more equal take-home pay. Kirsch (1972) and McAuley (1979) cautiously conclude that interpersonal differentials in earnings probably fell after 1957. According to McAuley, inter-industrial earnings differentials increased, while intra-industrial differentiation decreased.

Wage reform entailed a redefinition of all occupations in all branches and a re-evaluation of their relative pay. Such a task could not be undertaken very frequently. After the 1958–62 reform there were two general reforms, that of the 1970s (implemented piecemeal, sector by sector, over the period 1972–79) and Gorbachev's wage reform of 1986–89. The economic reforms of the mid-1960s (Kosygin's reforms) did not affect basic rates, but increased the weight of bonuses in total remuneration and gave the enterprises greater freedom in their distribution. In 1990 the system of centralised wage-setting was abolished.

All three wage reforms increased the weight of basic pay in total earnings – thus attempting to strengthen the centralised element in wage-setting. They were all said to improve incentives to work harder and increase skills, as well as to 'eliminate tendencies to levelling'. They also attempted to improve wages in services, particularly the 'social-cultural sphere', relative to those in material production. Between wage reforms, however, there was an unplanned 'wage drift', working in the opposite direction. Since wage reforms took years and always started in industry, by the time wages in health-care, schools, etc. had been raised to levels considered 'appropriate' relative to those in industry (as set in the same round of reforms) the latter had already run on ahead.

The reform of the 1970s was less thoroughgoing than the previous one and less has been published in the West about it. The short-lived Gorbachev reform of 1986–89 entailed significant changes in the size of wage differentials, but not in the method of determining them. The reform encouraged enterprises to increase differentiation, between groups and individuals. There was a strong emphasis on incentives for managerial and highly qualified staff, engineers and technicians, as well as skilled workers. In early 1989, when the new system covered three-quarters of those scheduled to be transferred to it, average earnings of workers had increased by 10 per cent and those of salaried staff by 24 per cent (Chapman, 1988, 1991).

According to Rzhanitsyna (1991), managerial staff in industry benefited more from the reform than lower categories of engineering-technical staff. In enterprises applying the new tariffs, monthly wages increased between 1987 and 1989 by 75 roubles for managerial staff, 43 roubles for all 'specialists' and 36 roubles for workers. Bonuses added a slightly higher percentage to the pay of managerial staff, and hence considerably more in roubles.

Wages in the socio-cultural sphere were to be increased, absolutely and relatively. Nevertheless, relative to the national average, wages in health-care and education were almost unchanged from 1985 to 1988, while in art and culture they decreased by several percentage points (*Nar. obr.*, 1989, pp. 24–7). Only the science sector improved its position, though university teachers slipped from 94 per cent of the national average to 85 per cent.

An important novelty was that enterprises had to finance wage and salary increases demanded by the reform themselves, by raising their revenue or decreasing their costs – the reform gave them increased possibilities of making staff redundant.[10] However, the basic features of Soviet wage setting remained intact.[11]

In 1956–57 a minimum monthly wage ranging from 27 to 35 roubles was established (the variation depended on branch and region). From 1959 to 1965 it was raised to 40–45 roubles[12] (McAuley, 1979, p. 200, *Trud v SSSR*, 1988, p. 225), in January 1968 to 60 roubles, and in the course of the 1970s to 70 roubles. According to the eleventh five-year plan, it should have been raised to 80 roubles between 1981 and 1985, but the increase was later postponed (*Trud v SSSR*, 1988, p. 228f). It is unclear whether it had taken place by 1989 (Chapman, 1991).

Rises in the minimum wage compressed wage scales, particularly in low-income branches. They had a considerable impact on the earnings of the low paid and on the level of differentiation. According to Chapman (1983), the increase in the minimum wage in 1968 eliminated the first three skill grades in most consumer goods industries. The effect in the service sectors must have been equally drastic. To maintain the desired relative wages, the authorities would, no doubt, have preferred to increase all wages proportionally, but if the minimum wage was to cover what was considered minimum subsistence, then this would have implied a larger increase in aggregate wages than the economy could afford. This is probably a main reason why the decile ratio for earnings reached its post-war minimum of 2.83 in 1968, after a gradual decrease from 4.44 in 1956, through 3.26 in 1966. It then increased, until the mid-1970s (Ellman, 1980).[13] Another period of decrease followed after 1976, due, according to Chapman (1983), to the wage reform of the 1970s and the introduction of the 70 rouble minimum. From around 1980, a steady upward trend in differentiation was resumed (Atkinson and Micklewright, 1992, table UE1).

Increases in the minimum wage raised the potential wages for many women who were not in the labour force and encouraged them to seek employment. An inflow of previously non-employed workers into the lowest paid jobs increases differentiation within the labour force, while the higher minimum in itself tends to decrease it. The end-effect on earnings dispersion depends on the absolute and relative size of the increase, on the numbers of new entrants into employment, and on the shape of the earnings distribution. The gender gap in income in the total population decreases since higher minimum wages benefit women, both as potential entrants into the labour force and as the workers most likely to be paid the minimum rate. The direction of change in the gender wage ratio, for employed women and men, is indeterminate, however.[14]

3.2.3   The post-Stalin Soviet system of wages and salaries

Formally, wage-setting was supposed to ensure payment 'according to the quantity and quality' of labour. This implies, among other things, 'equal pay for equal work'. In the Stalinist period there was a marked tension between this principle and the use of wage policy to enforce regime priorities in labour allocation (as well as a glaring contradiction between the official ideology and what had until then been known as Marxism or socialism). These contradictions remained through the whole Soviet period.

Each enterprise was assigned a wage fund to cover all money payments for labour, except certain bonuses paid from the Material Incentive Fund (*Fond Material'nogo Pooshreniia*, see below). The Wage Fund, like output and supplies of inputs, were assigned to the enterprise by the planning authorities, and like those, the outcome of a bargaining process. Through the Wage Fund, planning authorities were supposed both to control relative wage levels in different enterprises and sectors and to ensure a macro-economic balance between the supply of consumer goods and disposable household income. Enterprises had strong incentives not to exceed the Wage Fund, but very weak incentives to spend less than the allotted maximum (Kirsch, 1972, Chapman, 1983).[15]

Basic wages bore no relation to enterprise output, income or profitability. The Material Incentive Fund and the Social Development Fund (*Fond Sotsial'nogo Razvitiia*), however, depended on enterprise profits. The MIF was used for money payments to employees, the SDF for social and cultural amenities for them. (See, further, section 3.4.)

As concerns the so-called 'non-productive sphere', all *Kratkii* ... (1989, p. 353) has to say is that usually 'the planned Wage Fund is determined proceeding from the number of staff and the average wage'. Here, there were no profits and, hence, no Material Incentive Funds.

To summarise, the basic wages and salaries of employees were subject to centralised grading schemes, but the form of wage payment as well as work norms and the distribution of bonuses between employees were decided at the enterprise level. This gave management (and the groups of employees that had clout in relation to management) substantial influence.

3.3   Wages by occupation and sector

3.3.1   The wages of industrial blue-collar workers

Both the Soviet and the Western literature on wages in the USSR tend to focus attention on industrial blue-collar workers. In this chapter, their wages will be the point of reference in the sections on other categories of workers and employees.[16]

'Worker' can be used to mean the Russian '*rabochii*', or blue-collar worker, but also '*rabotnik*', a person hired to work.[17] I have tried to make sure that the meaning is always clear from the context. To avoid repetition, I use 'manual worker' and 'non-manual worker/staff' 'interchangeably with 'blue-collar workers' and 'white-collar workers'. Thus, 'manual work' should not be confused with the Russian '*ruchnaia rabota*', literally 'work by hand', meaning 'non-mechanised work'. 'Employee' when used alone includes all categories, while in the expression 'workers and employees', 'workers' are, of course, blue-collar and 'employees' white-collar.

Strictly speaking, '*rabochii*' should not include the 'junior service staff' (MOP), doing unqualified work not directly linked to material production. According to the definition of '*rabochie*' in *Kratkii* ... it does not include anyone working in the service sector. My impression is that in common usage, *'rabochii'* includes both MOP and blue-collar worker in the service sector, and that is how I use 'blue-collar worker'.

Following Soviet terminology (Kirsh, 1972, p. 21), 'industry' includes manufacturing and mining and is divided into 'light' and 'heavy' industry. In Soviet terminology, the food industry is a separate category, but I will, for simplicity, include it in 'light industry'.[18]

Since too little information is available, I will not distinguish between civilian and military production, even though wages and fringe benefits were better in the latter. In any case, 'the military-industrial complex' will generally be included in heavy industry and make up quite a large part of it, since any factory that produced anything at all for the armed forces was considered a part of this 'complex'.

The basic pay (*tarifnaia stavka*) of most industrial workers was set as an hourly or daily rate, according to the job.[19] The first criterion was the 'skill grade' (*razriad*). All blue-collar jobs were listed in handbooks, one for 'general professions' (*skvoznye professii*, that is those that exist in several branches of industry) and sector handbooks for occupations specific to one sector. The handbooks detailed the characteristics a job should have, as well as the knowledge and skill it should require, to count as a specific occupation with a specific skill grade.

For workers in higher grades the basic rate was equal to that for a worker in grade I in the relevant scale, multiplied by the tariff coefficient of the worker's skill grade. The set of coefficients was known as a skill scale (*tarifnaia setka*). Junior service personnel were usually paid as workers in the first skill grade. From 1979 a worker could receive an 'addition for skill' (*nadbavka za masterstvo*). (See Table 3.1.)

Most skill scales included six grades, though some included eight. After the 1970s reform, scales with proportions of wages in grade I and VI of 1:1.58, 1:1.7 and 1:1.86 were common (*Kratkii . . .*, 1989, Chapman, 1988). Table 3.1 shows the scale that was most widespread after the Gorbachev reform.

There were different scales, with different rates for *razriad* I, both within and between branches. Therefore, the ratio of average wages in the different

Table 3.1 Relative basic wage under normal working conditions

Skill grade	I	II	III	IV	V	VI
Tariff coefficient	1	1.09	1.20	1.36	1.55	1.80
Maximum addition for skill (%)	—	—	12	16	20	24

Source: Rofe et al. (1991, pp. 108–9).

skill grades could differ from the proportions indicated by the scales. Granick (1987, p. 47) cites two studies, which indicate that workers who were in the lower grades were more likely to be assigned lower scales as well. According to Chapman (1988, p. 343) the maximum rate for the highest skill grade was nearly six times higher than the lowest rate for skill grade I in 1962, about three times higher in 1975 and four times higher in 1988.

Men, on average, had higher skill grades than women in the same branch. According to *Vestnik Statistiki* (1/90) some of the industries with particularly large differences were paper and pulp (average grade of 2.75 for women and 4.10 for men) and light industry (2.91 and 4.17). Also, the average skill grades were higher in male-dominated heavy industries than in the predominantly female light and food industries.

To qualify for a higher *'razriad'*, a worker would appear before a commission with representatives of management and of the local trade union as well as 'specialists', to prove that he or she had the necessary knowledge and ability. Graduates from vocational-technical schools (*professional'no-technicheskoe uchilishche*, or PTU, see p. 87) were graded by a board within the school. It was hard, if not impossible, to reach the highest skill grades without vocational school education. This tended to exclude women. Further advancement could be made through training programmes. Since these were often run outside working hours, the practical possibilities for women with children to participate were much smaller than those for men.

To get the wage corresponding to a particular skill grade, the worker needed both to get the certificate qualifying him or her for it and find a job that required this level of skills. While in the 1930s and 1940s the great problem was to train a labour force with very low levels of schooling and industrial experience, by the 1960s Soviet authors had begun to write of skilled manual workers who had difficulty finding a job corresponding to their qualifications. We will return to this issue in sections 6.6.2 and 6.8, and note only, first, that in a situation where there are not enough highly graded jobs to go around for those qualified for them, seniority is likely to become important for promotion and, hence, for wages; and second, scarcity of good jobs makes any inclination to discriminate against women (or others) easier to indulge.

Piece-work was assumed to lead to higher intensity of work than work on time-rates and was, therefore, paid according to a higher scale. In the late 1980s basic rates for piece-work were 7 per cent above time-rates (Chapman, 1988, p. 45).[20]

Workers with unpleasant or dangerous working conditions were entitled to extra payments, as well as to certain non-monetary benefits (longer paid holidays, free or subsidised milk or other food-stuffs, free medication, shorter working days, lower retirement age).[21] Supplements for 'heavy work or harmful conditions of work' were 4–12 per cent of the worker's basic rate. For 'especially heavy or harmful' conditions they were 16–24 per cent. (Rofe et al., 1991). According to Goskomstat statistics from 1991, 14.5 million, or 45 per cent, of all industrial workers received some kind of compensation for unpleasant working conditions. Of these, 5.7 million were women. This is a lower percentage of women than the 44 per cent reported in *Vestnik Statistiki* 1/90. The latter figure is close to their share of the industrial blue-collar workforce.

There were also additions for night-work, shift-work and work on assembly lines. In the far north and a few other areas with particularly inhospitable conditions or climates, wages were multiplied by a 'regional coefficient', ranging from 1.1 to 2.0.

For blue-collar and most white-collar workers overtime was supposed to be paid at 150 per cent of the normal hourly basic rate for up to two hours a day and, after that, at 200 per cent. The exception was a minor percentage of jobs (usually managerial positions) where working hours were not regulated (*nenormirovannye*) and no compensation for overtime was paid. Kirsch (1972) quotes a source from the 1960s claiming that overtime constituted 0.5 per cent of total working time. Given the anecdotal evidence of irregular supplies and work rhythm ('storming') in the USSR this low figure is surprising. One might suspect, with Nove (1977), that a substantial amount of overtime was unpaid and unreported. McAuley (1981, p. 28f) also reports some surveys that indicate a substantial amount of unreported overtime. (If overtime at the end of the plan period was necessary for plan fulfilment, which, in its turn, was required for bonuses, then 'unpaid' overtime may have paid quite well.)

The work expected of an industrial worker was the 'work norm'. For piece-workers, rates were set so that those who produced 100 per cent of the norm received the appropriate hourly rate for their job, skill and work conditions. For time-rate workers, norm fulfilment did not determine the basic wage, but did affect bonuses.

As mentioned, managers could use norm-setting to manipulate the centrally determined wage levels, or as one Soviet economist wrote, 'the existing system of payments makes not norms of work, but norms for wages'.[22] In 1983, the average level of norm fulfilment in industry was 124 per cent. (Malle, 1987, p. 372).

Norms were an important locus of class conflicts in the USSR. Official commentators saw work norms as a necessary means of control over the workforce, and therefore wanted to increase the percentage of employees whose work was normed (Arnot, 1988). For industrial workers the increase was from 50 to 79 per cent from 1974 to 1978, and for white-collar workers from 14 to 58 per cent (ibid., p. 83).

Workers could adjust their work pace in order to influence norms. Komozin (1991, p. 56) writes that according to a survey study 'roughly two-thirds of workers share the view that it is disadvantageous for them to overfulfil the norm substantially, for this leads to an automatic decrease in piece rates' (see also Kirsch, 1972, and Arnot, 1988).

Workers could express their discontent and put pressure on planners and enterprises by low intensity of work and by quitting. Two ways for management to attract and keep labour power was to manipulate pay scales and permit low labour discipline. Low norms could serve both these ends. On the aggregate level, this practice worsened the shortage of labour power that gave rise to it. For the individual enterprise, however, low norms made it easier for management to hoard labour power. Thus, norm-setting could be both a point of collision between workers and management and a ground for collusion between them in a tug-of-war with central planners. It is not surprising that central authorities wished to increase centrally set norms as opposed to local ones, and that norming was an essential battleground in the struggle for power over labour and over the social surplus.

When norms were negotiated between workers, management and unions, women were likely to be under-represented and the general disregard for women in the society was quite likely to be to their disadvantage.

In addition to basic pay staff received bonuses, which were usually paid monthly, quarterly or yearly. These bonuses could be paid for norm fulfilment and overfulfilment, for increasing productivity, for savings on tools and raw materials, for quality of products, and so on. (There were also one-off or *edinovremmennye* bonuses designed to stimulate increases in productivity, technological innovations and export undertakings.)

Enterprises that achieved their targets could pay a bonus 'according to the results of the enterprise'. The distribution of this bonus was influenced by the wages of the workers and by seniority. A specific yearly seniority bonus (*voznagrazhdenie za vyslugu let*) was paid in certain occupations and sectors. This bonus ranged from 0.6 to 3.6 monthly (basic) wages (*Kratkii* . . ., 1989, p. 44, Oxenstierna, 1990, p. 132).

How the share of bonuses in industrial workers' wages developed over time can be seen in Table 3.2.

Enterprises had more autonomy in determining the size and distribution of bonus payments than of basic wages. Therefore, bonuses were the

Table 3.2   Bonuses as a percentage of industrial workers' wages

Year	1950	1960	1970	1980	1987
Bonus share	9.2	8.4	14.2	19.9	22.5

Source: Trud v SSSR (1988, p. 213).

second main vehicle for unplanned wage drift. McAuley (1979, p. 250) estimates that if bonuses had increased only in line with productivity since 1961, wages by 1972 would have been some 11 per cent lower.

If enterprise autonomy in setting bonuses was large enough to increase overall wages above the level desired by central planning organs, then it must have been large enough to influence relative wages within the enterprise, including those of women and men, if management chose to do so.

The majority of industrial workers worked in the 'general professions' which had a uniform skill classification, across branches. According to the principle of equal pay for equal work, one might have expected the basic wage rate for workers in these jobs not to depend on branch of employment. 'The uniformity of tariff rates for workers of the same professions carrying out work of equal complexity in different branches is ensured,' write Rofe et al. (1991, p. 108).

In fact, 'equal pay for equal work' often gave way to the priority enforcement of the regime. With a general shortage of labour power it was vital to attract enough of it to what those in power considered most important. Wage policies were used to keep up employment in high-priority sectors, letting the low-priority ones bear the worst of the shortage.[23] Priority was strongly inversely correlated with the share of women in the workforce. (See section 5.6.2.) If the priorities of ordinary consumers, housewives in particular, could have been measured, they would probably also have been inversely correlated with the official ones.

Inter-industry differentials were also affected by skill grading for industry-specific professions. We would, however, require much more detailed information to investigate gender bias in these.

Actual differences in pay could be smaller or larger than the differences in basic rates, since branches differed in the skill composition of the workforce, in work conditions and in the frequency of piece-rate work. (Table 3.3 shows average wages in different branches of industry.) They would depend on bonuses, which in their turn depended on the tautness of plans and on centrally set prices for inputs and outputs – both of which depended on priorities and power relations.

Table 3.3 Relative monthly earnings by branch of industry (as per cent of average industrial wage)

Branch	1970	1980	1988
All industry	100	100	100
Heavy industry	106	104	104
Fuel-energy Complex	137	133	132
Electric energy	104	103	104
Fuel	151	147	146
Metallurgy	126	125	123
Machine building	101	101	100
Chemicals & wood	102	101	101
Chemicals & petrochemicals	103	99	98
Wood, paper, pulp	102	103	103
Building materials	104	97	99
Light industry	77	81	81
Textiles	81	86	86
Garment	71	74	74
Leather, fur & shoes	85	87	88
Food industry	89	90	91
Food processing	77	78	79
Meat and dairy products	84	85	84
Fish	167	160	166

Source: *Nar. Khoz. v 1988 g.*, pp. 377–8.

According to the Soviet economist Rakoti (quoted in Oxenstierna, 1990, p. 136), the share of bonuses in average wages differed substantially between branches and, even more, between enterprises. The highest shares of bonuses were found in the machine-building industry,[24] the energy producing branches and in pharmaceuticals.

3.3.2 White-collar industrial staff

In industry, in 1987, blue-collar workers and MOP constituted 82 per cent of the workforce. The remainder can be divided either into engineering-technical staff (*inzhenerno-teknicheskiie rabotniki*, ITR) and clerical staff, or into managerial staff, specialists and clerical workers. With the former division, managers are normally included in ITR, together with foremen, engineers, technicians, etc. In 1985, ITR made up 14.6 per cent of the workforce in industry.

The average wage of white-collar workers (*sluzhashchie*) in industry in 1989 was 301 roubles per month, while that of blue-collar workers was

255 roubles. The relative differential had increased from the mid-1980s, but was smaller than in earlier periods (see section 6.1.2). These averages do not necessarily tell us much about the differentials between individual professions. As Pravda (1982) emphasises, the divisions of blue-collar workers into skilled and unskilled and of white-collar workers into professional, semi-professional and clerical, could be as important as those between workers and employees in the USSR.

White-collar jobs (*dolzhnosti*) were also defined in handbooks and characterised in terms of responsibility, complexity and the education, experience and skill required. Monthly salary rates (*oklady*) depended not only on these characteristics, but also on the 'significance of the branch', conditions of work, the volume and 'complexity' of the product of the enterprise (Rofe et al., 1991, p. 112). For each *dolzhnost'* a highest and a lowest salary were decided centrally. The range (*vilka*) between them could be substantial. Hence staff in well-endowed or successful enterprises, or employees with a good bargaining position in relation to management, could get more.

Although there was no automatic increase in salaries with experience or seniority, specified experience could be required for a job. Also, a committee periodically revised the level of qualification of employees. If the committee agreed, the employee could apply for a higher position.

The salaries of ITR had the salary of a foreman as their reference point, and that, in its turn, stood in a particular proportion to the tariffs for skilled workers. According to the 1986–89 wage reform a foreman's (basic) salary should exceed that of a worker in skill group VI by 20–35 per cent (ibid., p. 112) and that of the head of a shop or section by 60–90 per cent (Chapman, 1988). Further, the reform entitled management to give substantial 'individual' additions to salaries of ITR and managerial staff. For clerical staff, technicians and MOP 'unitary salaries were established for all enterprises' (*Kratkii*, p. 75f). (Earlier they had been higher in heavy industry than in food or light industry. See Chapman, 1991, p. 181.) If the enterprise made savings on its Wage Fund, these could be used to add up to 50 per cent to the basic pay of salaried staff, on an individual basis.

The reform granted managers 'quite large increments' (Chapman, 1991, p. 181), but inter-branch differences between them were reduced. For managerial and supervisory staff, salaries depended on the number of subordinates and the size of the plant, department or workshop they were in charge of. The examples of directors' salaries in manufacturing, given in Chapman (1991), range from 310 to 450 roubles per month (that is, about six and a half times the minimum wage).

As for workers, there were additions for working conditions, regional coefficients and bonuses. Bonuses made up a larger share of earnings for white-collar than for blue-collar workers. Chapman (1988) concludes that, following the Gorbachev reform, for 'top managers', current bonuses could be as much as 108 per cent of the salary rate.

3.3.3   The 'non-productive sphere'

Soviet statistical yearbooks proudly present figures on health centres (known in Russia as 'polyclinics'), nurseries and kinder-gartens,[25] numbers of doctors and hospital beds per 1,000 inhabitants, and so on. Yet, the quarter of the employed that provided these services were described as 'non-productive' (see pp. 176f) and remained worse paid than those in the 'productive' sphere.

Much less is published on wages in this sector than on those in industry. Both McAuley (1979) and Oxenstierna (1990), after extensive searches of the Soviet literature, have little more to say on the wage and salary scales than that they are 'determined by comparisons to similar jobs in the productive sector'. Veretennikov (1991, p. 225) adds that salaries in the service sector, especially in the social and cultural areas, lagged behind because 'an ill-conceived policy equalises skill-grading scales and salaries there with those in light industries and food production'.[26] Rimashevskaia and Onikov (1991, p. 27) conclude that 'the existence of low-paid staff, whose labour is valued below their qualifications, is above all, a consequence of the relatively low wages in the non-productive sphere, the existence of a certain disproportion in the wages of those employed in the basic branches of the economy.'

Table 3.4 shows that in 1975 relative wages in the socio-cultural sphere were even lower than they had been in 1960, and remained so up to the end of the Soviet period, despite large wage increases in education and health-care, in both 1964 and 1972 (McAuley, 1979, p. 200f).

The proportion of staff given longer paid holidays as a compensation for poor working conditions was 56 per cent in health-care, which is higher than in any other sector: the figure was 39 per cent in industry, in housing, municipal and consumer services, and 37 per cent in construction; in education it was only 3 per cent (but 18 per cent in science!) (*Trud* ..., 1988, p. 138. The figures are for 1987). Health-care staff also received pay increments if they worked with patients with contagious diseases, in psychiatric care or in work that was physically heavy.

It is difficult to compare skills and qualifications across sectors with work of a very different nature. Figure 3.1 shows the percentages of employees with secondary and higher education in different sectors.[27]

Table 3.4 Relative average monthly wages for workers and employees in different sectors (average for the economy as a whole = 100)

Branch	1960	1965	1975	1986	1988	1990
Industry	114	108	111	110	110	108
Agriculture*	68	78	87	98	96	101
Construction	115	116	121	125	131	128
Transport	108	110	119	117	118	114
Communications	78	77	85	84	89	87
Trade & catering		78	75	78	75	86
Information, etc.				81	84	95
Municipal services		75	75	76	76	76
Education	90	100	87	80	78	69
Culture	61	70	63	60	58	60
Art	79	81	71	76	71	72
Science	137	121	107	106	113	123
Credit & insurance	88	89	92	98	94	141
Healthcare	73	82	70	69	69	68
Administration	107	110	90	90	93	123

* In state agriculture, i.e. not including *kolkhozniki*.
Sources: For 1960, 1965 and 1975, Oxenstierna (1990), for 1986, 1988 and 1990, *Nar. Khoz. v 1990 g.*, p. 36.

Figure 3.1 Education of the workforce in different branches. Numbers with higher, secondary specialist or PTU education per 1,000 employed

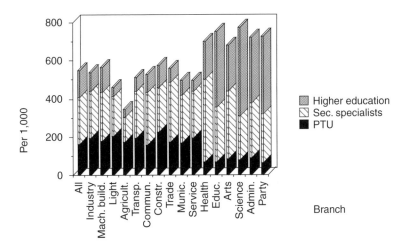

Source: 1989 census, table 3, vol. X.

These proportions were considerably higher in the socio-cultural sphere (health, education, science and culture) than in industry, while in other services, trade, catering, housing and municipal services they were slightly lower than in industry. Since 'skills and qualifications' also include skills acquired in professional schools and on-the-job training and experience, no direct estimate can be made from these percentages of what the level of salaries should have been without 'sector discrimination'. They do indicate, however, that the education of (the mainly female) employees of the socio-cultural sphere does not compensate factors depressing their wages, including the low priority of the sector and the 'disadvantage' of being women.

Within sectors, a doctor earned more than a nurse, a schoolteacher less than a university lecturer. A shop manager earned more than a sales assistant, a *vospitatel'* (nursery teacher) more than a *niania* (nursery nurse). Within professions, teachers and medical staff with postgraduate degrees received a supplement to their salaries. There were supplements for well-qualified doctors and middle-level medical staff. There were also differences within job categories. A physician in a hospital earned more than one in an outpatient clinic. Sales assistants in food-shops had 10 per cent higher basic rates than in non-food shops (Danilov, 1982, p. 82).

Organisations in services like trade and catering, repairs or utilities could have bonus schemes similar to those in industry. This was not the case in the socio-cultural sphere, but there staff could earn premia for quality of work and extra work. School teachers received supplements to they pay basic for additional duties such as, administrative work in the school or for being form teacher, a librarian for organising cultural activities like public lectures, a general practitioner for organising prophylactic work such as preventive care in her district, and so on.

In 1986 bonuses made up 21 per cent of wages in industry (17 per cent in the 'productive sector' as a whole), but only 7.3 per cent in the 'non-productive' – and a paltry 1.4 per cent in health-care and 2.4 per cent in education (Gendler, 1988, p. 82). In retail trade, in 1980, bonuses made up 17 per cent of wages and salaries, and in catering 11 per cent (Danilov, 1982).

Employees in services, as in industry, could have their qualifications upgraded every few years. In the socio-cultural sectors this took place more or less automatically.

3.4   Not just the money wage

Besides the (money) wage or salary, work offered other material rewards. These could be goods or services, or opportunities for acquiring goods or services ranging from company cars to subsidised child-care. Old-age pensions depended on previous work-record and earnings, and hence these had significance as an incentive.[28]

Some kinds of earnings on the side were dependent on having a particular job or profession. (Although a plumber's or a doctor's earnings on the side come from having the skills of the profession rather than the employment, with a legal requirement to be employed, they were conditional on having a job. A Soviet doctor could legally have private practice alongside work in the state sector, but not instead of it.) But there are also non-tangible rewards – job satisfaction, self-esteem, enjoyment, prestige in the community. Psychological satisfaction or dissatisfaction, as well as working conditions, affect the wage that needs to be paid for a person to take a certain job, as do advantages connected with the location of the workplace.

Free or subsidised services unconnected to occupation or place of work will not be dealt with here. Publicly provided health-care, education, child-care, subsidised cultural and sports amenities, or children's clothes and toys must be taken into account in an analysis of real income and income dispersion within the USSR, in any cross-country comparison or comparison between living standards in Soviet and post-Soviet periods. But they fall outside the scope of this study.

3.4.1 The importance of goods and services provided by the employer

Fringe benefits provided by the employer are very important for a study of rewards from work and job choice in the USSR. Unfortunately, this is a subject on which quantitative data are lacking. Therefore, much of this section is imprecise and is based on conversations with social scientists and other Russians.

Non-monetary, or fringe, benefits are not, of course, a phenomenon restricted to Soviet-type economies. How important such benefits are depends on the social and institutional setting. For example, the importance of medical care provided by or paid for by the employer depends on the quality, price and accessibility of public health-care and would, therefore, be smaller in countries like Sweden or the United Kingdom than in the United States. In the USSR public health-care was free, but its quality could be very low. Better health-care was a highly appreciated fringe benefit and a good reason for choosing a profession that increased one's chances of working for a 'strong' employer or in a large city. It is, however, not measurable in money terms.

In the Soviet system, some fringe benefits were more important than their money value would indicate. It would therefore be very difficult to calculate the value of this component of the wage, even if we had known the exact 'in kind' extent of it. Many things that were bought at work were not only more expensive in ordinary shops, they were impossible to get! The rent for a municipally owned apartment was the same per square metre as for an enterprise-owned one, but getting a company flat could reduce time on the housing waiting list by a number of years. (The same was true of vegetable allotments.) Company stores offered a greater variety of foods with less queuing than in the state shops. The price of a car or TV set bought at work may have been the same as in a shop, but the shop might have a 10- or 20-year waiting list. For the more privileged echelons, differential access could be to goods of a quality never seen in shops open to the general public.

This is not to say that money never mattered. Many essential goods were very cheap in the state distribution network, but the more expensive goods, including clothes and shoes, could be *very* expensive. Although stories of people unable to find goods to spend their money on were legion, this was far from being the experience of the whole population. For a low-paid nurse or cleaner, a subsidised lunch did matter, even in pure money terms.

3.4.2   Fringe benefits to workers, employees – and the *nomenklatura*

In the USSR as in the West, what the idea of 'fringe benefits' first brings to mind are those enjoyed by the top tier in society. Everybody knew that the very highest echelon in Soviet society – the party leadership, military commanders, academicians, top artists or performers – enjoyed tremendous[29] privileges, but the full extent was a carefully kept secret. Eye witnesses have given occasional glimpses (Smith, 1976, du Plessix Gray, 1990, chapter 12) of luxurious villas, large, chauffeur-driven cars, of domestic servants and imported foods, drinks and *haute couture*.

A somewhat larger, but still small, tier enjoyed cars, country houses (*dachi*), access to 'special shops' and high quality health-care. Davis (1988) estimates that 0.4 per cent of the population (one million) enjoyed 'elite' health-care in 1975. Enterprise managers, local party secretaries, professors, heads of departments, military officers, less prominent artists, would belong to another stratum, still privileged but less than the very top. They would probably still get a car or a *dacha*, the size and quality of which would vary according to their position on the hierarchical ladder. Institutions could have several dining rooms, where the best food and service were reserved for those of the highest rank. In the Academic City at Novosibirsk, a professor's family of four was allotted an apartment nearly twice as large as a construction worker's (Bergson, 1984, p. 1059).

Not the least of privileges was the influence that a high position gave, in a system based so much on contacts and mutual services. It could give access to medical specialists, to good flats and – very important indeed – to the most prestigious universities for one's children and good jobs for them when they graduated. A study, carried out in Leningrad in 1968, found that children who achieved good grades but had blue-collar parents were less likely to do well in gaining admission to higher education than others with poorer grades and white-collar or professional parents. In this sense, membership of the privileged elite had a hereditary element, which makes it possible to speak of it as a class *in statu nascendi*.

The top couple of per cent of the population were mainly concentrated in the largest cities. The probability of 'catching' them in a sample of 1,200 provincial households is small. But, although of a far more modest kind, non-monetary benefits were also important for the great majority of workers and employees.

Sick pay and maternity benefits were paid from the state budget and, thus, were not dependent on the employer. But the ability to subsidise housing, consumer goods, health-care, child-care[30] or holiday travel – or simply to make these available to employees at any price – varied a lot between employers.

The importance of these benefits for an ordinary Soviet household must not be underestimated. According to Davis (1988), 33 per cent of the population gained access to medical care through the departmental (*vedomstvennyi*) or industrial health-care system. Holiday travel and holiday homes, places in children's summer camps and consumer durables were paid by the employer and distributed by the trade unions. The opportunity to spend a few weeks in the countryside or by the sea, or send the children there, was widespread and considered very important.

One survey in the Taganrog-III project found that just over 40 per cent of the households surveyed lived in employer-owned housing.[31] The ability to provide housing depended on profitability, on influence with building companies and suppliers of building materials, and were greatest in organisations which could build themselves (usually enterprises in construction and large industrial complexes). An earlier study in Taganrog found that it was not uncommon for men with young families to change jobs in order to obtain housing – even if it meant accepting a lower wage (Prokofeva, 1991, p. 128). (Note, however, that one did not have to give up the apartment when quitting the job.)

If the husband was mainly responsible for obtaining housing, the wife was mainly responsible for shopping, housework and looking after the children. Her choice of employment had to take this into account. A survey conducted in August 1990[32] asked men and women which factors were 'absolutely necessary' and which were 'desirable but not mandatory' for a job to be considered 'suitable' for them. Figure 3.2 indicates that characteristics that make it easier to combine work with household responsibilities played a relatively greater role for women.

According to one survey,[33] 80 per cent of the female respondents used 'everyday services' (*bytovye obslushchivanie*) at their workplace, 70 per cent shopped there, 60 per cent used cultural facilities, 86 per cent sports or gym facilities, and 30 per cent canteens. (One might add that more than half of the users were dissatisfied with the everyday services, especially the canteens.)

The actual distribution of these benefits between employers and between categories of staff does not seem to have been the topic of much research; I have not found any study of it from the Soviet period. There is a general impression that within the enterprise or institution those in leading positions got more of these benefits, and that there were more benefits available in material production – in particular in mining and heavy industry – than in services or in the socio-cultural sphere.[34] A striking detail from Taganrog II is that low-income families paid one and a half times as much per kilo of meat as high-income families (Rimashevskaia and Onikov, 1991, p. 16).[35] Professor Leonid Kunel'skii estimated that in the late 1980s money wages constituted 90–93 per cent

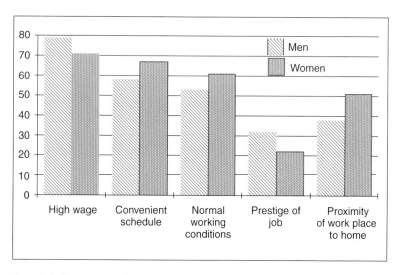

Figure 3.2   Percentage who consider a given factor 'absolutely necessary' for a job to be suitable

of labour costs in industry, but 97–98 per cent in the socio-cultural sphere (personal conversation, June 1992).

Both a correlation with rank and relative advantages for material production would tend to link larger non-monetary benefits to higher monetary income and would benefit men more than women. According to Pravda (1982), 'higher income non-manual groups' tended to benefit most from subsidised goods and services at work, while ITR staff had better housing than workers (and managers and professionals better still).

Yet, there were some advantages in the service sector, which partly offset the low pay. Some were legal. For instance, mothers who worked in nurseries could obtain a place there for their own children, and personally see to it that they were well cared for. Since professionals with higher education were reluctant to work in the countryside, rural teachers and medical staff were offered benefits such as a rent-free apartment.

An important benefit to overburdened women in 'the socio-cultural sphere' was that the normal working week was often less than the standard 41 hours. (We shall return to this in chapters 5 and 6.) Opportunities to attend to personal affairs during working hours would also be attractive to women who had to run a never-ending race between work, shops, nurseries, home, launderettes. Almost anyone in the former USSR can tell anecdotes about people who were absent from work without permission or about shirking and drunkenness on the job. Quantitative evidence is, for obvious reasons, difficult to obtain. The Soviet Interview Project found that men and women spent approximately the same amount of 'working time' on personal business, but women did 64 per cent more shopping during working hours (Clayton and Millar, 1991, p. 16. See also Gregory, 1987).

Some idleness at work was involuntary, due to machinery breakdowns or lack of materials or instruments. Yet, it is generally agreed that poor labour discipline contributed to low productivity in Soviet industry and to consumer frustration with Soviet services. (If these services had been more plentiful and functioned better, workers, and particularly women, in all sectors would have had more time to spend on their jobs.)[36]

The length of paid holidays varied between jobs and branches. The minimum was 15 working days per year, but in 1987, 81 per cent had longer holidays than that. Hazardous or harmful working conditions gave rights to additional holidays, as did unregulated working hours, work in the far north and – in some branches – seniority. Minors (under 18 years) had longer holidays.

On average, those working in consumer services had short holidays, while those in the social-cultural sphere had holidays even longer than those in 'the productive sphere'. In this respect, teachers, medical staff and the *intelligentsia* in science, art and culture, do not appear to have been discriminated against (*Nar. Khoz.*, 1988, pp. 60–1).

The problem of measuring non-monetary rewards means that the present study of male/female differentials can only analyse the differentials that are quantifiable, even though these are only a part of the total work-related benefits we would ideally want to include.

3.4.3   Private earnings on the side

Private practice was legal for physicians and dentists (and paid very well) provided it was declared to the tax authorities. Teachers and university students could supplement their income by private tuition. For example, a 1974 survey of first-year students in Kharkov found that 11 per cent of those from worker families, 20 per cent of the children of white-collar workers and 69 per cent of those with parents belonging to the *intelligentsia* had employed private tutors to prepare for their entrance examinations.[37] Pravda (1982) quotes a Soviet author who estimated that 'white-collar and professional families' spent 1.5 billion roubles per year on private tutors for their children – equivalent to one fifth of state spending on general secondary schools!

Ofer and Vinokur (1992) note that there was a fine line between legal and illegal 'individual economic activity'. Many kinds of such work, which were in principle legal, could in fact be a part of the shadow economy, either because taxes were not paid or because materials and equipment from the state sector workplace were used without permission. So even though a survey of emigrants is probably one of the best opportunities for eliciting truthful answers to sensitive questions like these, Ofer and Vinokur conclude that private incomes are likely to be seriously under-reported in their data. This, and the problems of representativeness, mean that the results must be treated with caution.

According to Ofer and Vinokur's study, 8 per cent of the gainfully employed had some income from private work.[38] The vast majority of these worked full-time in the state sector. It was twice as common for men to do private work as for women. Average (state sector) wages for those who also did private work were higher than for those who did not.

Hourly earnings in private work were nearly four times as high as those in the state sector (for the same individuals) for men, 3.2 times as high for women.[39] Those most likely to engage in private work were employed in health-care, education and 'everyday and municipal services'. Dentists had a very high incidence of private practice, more so than nurses; and nurses more than doctors. Technicians, engineers and administrative staff did not often do private work. Overall, the proportion doing private work was higher among workers than employees.

Granick (1987, p. 286) goes so far as to claim that taking 'the second economy' and second jobs into account 'perhaps eliminates ... the health sector from those of low earnings'. This would definitely require quantitative evidence (which Granick does not present) to be convincing. In addition, the amount of extra income must have varied a lot with position and gender.

Since Ofer and Vinokur's emigrant sample had an over-representation of service professions and of large-city dwellers, my guess is that the percentage doing private work was larger than in the average Soviet population.[40]

3.4.4 Theft, fraud and corruption

Certain kinds of job-related incomes were very clearly illegal – but here the evidence, of course, becomes almost entirely anecdotal. Hospital and child-care staff are accused of stealing food intended for patients or children, of providing medical services only if given a 'gift'. The municipally employed plumber or electrician was said to do a better job if offered a bottle of vodka. Secretaries and typists could take on 'extra work', but, in fact, do it in their ordinary working hours Administrative authority officials could extract bribes. Teachers and headmasters could accept money or 'favours' in return for better grades or admission to popular schools.[41]

According to *Vestnik Statistiki* (1/90) 16 per cent of women who had given birth in lying-in clinics complained that it was impossible to get the necessary assistance from staff without 'material encouragement' (two-thirds complained of lack of bed linen, about a third of the uncaring attitude of both doctors and other staff).[42]

This was not a marginal phenomenon. Even though their emigrant sample[43] may not be fully representative, the findings of DiFranceisco and Gitelman (1984) are interesting. Three-quarters of their respondents believed that at least half of Soviet officials 'derive material benefit from citizens who approach them for help', the majority felt that a bribe could induce a policeman to overlook a minor breach of traffic regulations and 46 per cent considered that 'a gift' was the appropriate response if an official refused to fulfil his/her obligations towards them. Three-quarters would use bribes or connections to influence the admissions committee of an institution of higher education.

DiFranceisco and Gitelman conclude that the highly educated were more than twice as likely as workers to be able use 'connections', whether it was a question of admission to university, military assignment or job placement for a graduate, and almost twice as likely if it was housing. They were less likely to resort to bribery and very much less likely passively to wait for an answer. Hence, on the one hand, nepotism and corruption opened up sources of income to officials (probably the more so the more highly placed); on the other hand, those in a good position and with a higher education (that is, professionals) could avoid the expense of bribes by using connections and influence instead.

In 1989, the statistical yearbook reported that incomes from 'illegal operations' in the service sphere (fraud, bribes, gifts given as tips) amounted to 17.1 billion roubles. There were 32 million people employed in the 'unproductive sector'. Average annual incomes in the service sector were approximately 2,000 roubles. Hence, these estimates imply that illegal incomes added about a quarter to average earnings in these sectors. Theft and pilfering from the state sector were estimated at 4.9 billion, equivalent to 1 per cent of the production of consumer goods. (*Nar. Khoz. v 1990 g.*, p. 50).[44]

Granick (1987, p. 28) considers work in the 'second economy' as complementary to employment in the state sector, rather than as a substitute for it, since the materials and equipment usually belonged to the state.

Shop assistants and restaurant staff had very low salaries. But the widespread shortages of goods placed them in a strategic position. They could let certain customers know if sought-after goods had been delivered to the shop and keep them 'under the counter' for them, either as a part of the informal network of mutual assistance, or directly for a money bribe.

According to Kagarlitskii (1991), the scarcity of good quality goods and services made employees in trade and services 'the most privileged part of the middle layers in Russia, as opposed to the West'. A similar point is made by Ovsiannikov (1985): 'in our sample the families of employees engaged in trade, everyday services and organs of administration ... whose pay and income level in general were relatively low, still own a fairly significant amount of property in value terms (double the average indicator)'. According to the Taganrog survey of the late 1970s, 'staff in trade and public catering, despite the relatively low level of wages and official incomes, gave the highest assessment of the quality of food in their families ...' (Rimashevskaia and Onikov, 1991, p. 17).

In Professor Shubkin's studies undertaken in 1963–73 on how young people assessed the prestige of different professions,[45] working as a shop assistant or waiter came consistently at the very bottom of the list, (irrespective of whether the question was put to secondary school students or to young workers and employees, to boys or to girls, to urban or rural youth). Low-paid work in the socio-cultural sphere was considered not nearly as unprestigious as work in trade, catering and 'everyday services'. The latter saw, however, some improvement in 1973 compared to 1963, at least among the girls. In a similar survey made ten years later, in 1983, the 'points' (on a ten-point scale) given to being a shop assistant had increased by more than 50 per cent among boys and 75 per cent among girls in Novosibirsk (and even more in the surrounding country-side). It appears that work in trade became more attractive during the 'stagnation period', when shops became increasingly empty of goods for ordinary customers. It is tempting to see a connection.

3.4.5 Job satisfaction, prestige and gender roles

Some low-paid caring and teaching jobs get relatively good evaluations from girls, and 'middling' evaluations from boys. 'Physician' is a very popular profession for young women, and not as unpopular among boys as it would have been if pay had been all that mattered. It would be wrong to discount appreciation of the content of the work and of the prestige connected with high skills and high education.

For girls, 'caring and curing' work would have a value in itself and would go well with the gender role they were socialised into, making it possible to unite professional pride and skill with a 'motherly', 'womanly' role. Liljeström (1993) analyses Soviet texts on gender role socialisation and demonstrates that what is typical of it is that, at one and the same time, these traditional gender roles are described as 'natural' and inevitable *and* women are severely criticised for deviating from them – not least for 'feminising' their poor, hen-pecked husbands. She quotes the prominent Soviet sociologist Z. Iankova who writes that 'many traits of the woman-mother are transferred to the woman's relationship with the man, form the basis for attraction, for the charm of the bride and wife. Beside that, many of these traits *appear and are expressed in her professional and political activity*' ('Sovietskaia Zhenshchina', 1978, quoted in Liljeström, 1993, p. 168, my emphasis).

'School successfully copes with the training of girls as good workers and actively involved citizens …. But has not the time come to pay more attention at school to instilling in girls such qualities as femininity, gentleness, kindness, housewifeliness and neatness …. Girls must be brought up to be aware of their natural destiny as mothers, nurturers of children and keepers of the family,' wrote *Literaturnaia Gazeta*, in a typical article from 1977.[46]

Different qualities were required from boys:

> The only thing to be noticed in male behaviour, besides the expressions of activity, is his capability and aptitude for reasoning, thought and consideration. Already a long time ago it was noticed that 'woman loves it when man reasons'. ... We combine the fact that man speaks and woman listens with the division of roles between them, with male activity and female receptiveness. Here the man demonstrates his capability for logic and abstract reasoning, which expresses the distinctive features of his sex. (Khripkova and Kolesov, 'Devochka – podrostok – devushka', 1981, quoted in Liljeström, 1993, p. 170)

The self-images Soviet girls were socialised into wanting were ambiguous. On the one hand, the belief that Soviet women could do untraditional jobs and that they had the same opportunities for a career as men was an object of self-congratulation in certain contexts. On the other, from a very early age, girls and boys were formed by highly traditional, stereotyped and rigid expectations of what constitutes 'masculine' and 'feminine' behaviour, from parents, nursery staff and teachers, which were reinforced by children's books, textbooks, psychologists and educators[47] and the media. Being good at a good job was important – but it must come second to being a good wife and mother (not husband and father). Women were expected to have an income of their own – but the husband was expected to earn more![48]

Besides self-respect, it is important to be respected by others. Following the conventional gender roles is more likely to promote respect than to challenge them. Yet, although boys and girls sought recognition in different spheres of activity, a high level of education was prestigious across both gender and social group lines. Pravda (1982) notes that unskilled workers enjoyed as little prestige in the USSR as in the West, while respect for highly skilled workers and craftsmen was higher in the Soviet Union. But the prestige of professionals, according to Pravda, was even higher, and higher than that of equivalent groups in the West. On the basis of this he concludes that 'education and work complexity provide a surer guide than earnings to the relative prestige of workers and professionals' (ibid., p. 14).

Malle (1987, p. 370) observes that the decrease in pay of ITR staff relative to manual workers did not diminish the demand for higher education. The generation of working-class women who swept the streets, carried bricks or sorted pellets at the mines wanted a better life for their daughters. They wanted them to work, certainly, but with an education which protected them from this gruelling physical toil.

Pravda, Malle and many other authors write of the official 'glorification' of manual work. There was, however, also glorification of studying and rising from unskilled to skilled manual work or from manual work into technical or professional work. What was positive about the positive 'worker-hero' of Soviet fiction was, as often as not, that he ceased to be a worker, having educated and 'bettered' himself into being a 'specialist'![49]

The official view, that for children from all social backgrounds access to education was equal and depended only on talent, though contradicted by the statistics, easily takes on an undertone of contempt for those who don't make it. (This contempt can be quite open when Soviet/ex-Soviet intellectuals speak or write of workers, or – with the standard euphemisms for 'working class' – of 'untaught people' or 'people of low cultural level'.) Marnie (1986) quotes Soviet sources from as late as 1983, to the effect that school teachers threatened lazy pupils with the terrible fate of going to a technical-vocational school – and hence ending up with only a (skilled) worker's job.

A number of studies find that the correlation between prestige and education was much stronger than between income and education. Aage (1984, p. 92) concludes that the 'Soviet information does not at any rate give much support to mechanical conceptions of education as investment in human capital'. A theory of choice of profession, which disregarded job content, self-image and respect from the community, would be very unsatisfactory in any society, and in the Soviet case this is underlined by how public opinion ranked different jobs. On the other hand, one would assume that earnings play some part, as would other material benefits from work.

Hence, as will be discussed more extensively in chapter 6, earnings differentials between the more and the less educated were under pressure from two quarters in the USSR. First, widespread access to education provided a greater supply of skilled workers, as well as of professionals with higher education, than the economy could absorb. Second, the importance of non-monetary material benefits and of prestige should reduce the sensitivity of labour supply and job choices to wage rewards.

4
Women and Men in Taganrog and in the USSR

4.1 The data

4.1.1 Why Taganrog was chosen

This study is based on a survey carried out in the southern Russian city of Taganrog. Taganrog is a port on the Azov Sea, which is linked to the Black Sea by a narrow strait. It is in the Rostov region (*oblast'*) and thus not far from the Ukrainian border. Soviet Taganrog was an industrial city, dominated by a few large industries linked to the so-called 'military industrial complex'. In 1989 it had a population of approximately 300,000. The region is among the richer agricultural districts of the USSR, and this was reflected in better availability and quality of foodstuffs than in most of Russia.

This city, which was founded by Peter the Great, has a predominantly Russian population, as well as Greek, Armenian, Ukrainian and Jewish minorities, and a strong Cossack tradition. Taganrog is known historically as the place where Tsar Alexander I died, an event that triggered the Decembrist uprising in 1825. It is known in literature as the birthplace of Anton Chekhov and in sociology as, probably, the best researched town in the USSR.

In the 1960s Taganrog was chosen by a team of Soviet researchers as a 'typical Soviet middle-sized town' (see Rimashevskaya, 1992). A number of surveys covering different fields were carried out in 1967–68.[1] Similar projects were undertaken in 1977–78 and 1988–89 (Taganrog I, II and III).[2] The most comprehensive accounts are Onikov (1977), Rimashevskaia (1988a), Rimashevskaia and Onikov (1990) and Rimashevskaia and Patsiorkovskii (1992a). The data used in the following are from one survey included in Taganrog III called 'Way of Life' (*Obraz zhizni*), which focused particularly on gender issues.[3] The interviews were carried out February–April 1989.

What generalisations is it legitimate to make from this sample? It is always hazardous to generalise about the Soviet Union. The USSR was the size of a continent in itself and even within Russia there were large differences, between regions, between urban and rural life and between province and metropolis. The degree of centralisation, on the other hand, helps to make inferences from a local sample more general. Excluding the additions for work in the far north, wage scales and wage regulations were the same in the whole Union.

Compared to Russia as a whole, Taganrog had an unusually large heavy industry sector. The level of education was somewhat higher than at the national level. Keeping these characteristics in mind, I consider it legitimate to make inferences from Taganrog to the urban population of the European regions of the USSR.

The highest average wages in the USSR were found in the three Baltic republics, and the lowest in Moldavia, Azerbaidzhan and Central Asia (excluding Kazakhstan). The Russian average was 7 per cent above the Soviet average in 1987. According to Taganrog I and II, the average wage in Taganrog was higher than in the USSR, because of the well-paying military industries. By 1989, this was no longer the case, since the arms industry had gone into decline.

In the following section the sampling is briefly described. More information is available in Katz (1994), Prokofeva (1992) and Rimashevskaya (1988a, pp. 111–16). The rest of this chapter contains descriptive accounts of topics that are relevant for the employment and wages of women. The accounts will present information on the USSR generally and from the sample. In section 4.2 the demographic composition of the sample is summarised. Section 4.3 begins with a short history of education in Russia and a description of the system of education in the later Soviet period, with section 4.3.3 focusing on the gender aspects of this institutional set-up. Section 4.3.4 summarises statistics on the education of the Soviet population and the sample in 1989. In section 4.4 possible determinants of and some earlier research on female labour force participation rates in the USSR are discussed. Section 4.5 is also devoted to labour supply, but to hours of work of the employed, legal and institutional aspects and basic data from the sample. The subject of section 4.6 is the jobs men and women have. Different aspects of occupational segregation in the USSR are discussed. Section 4.7 introduces the other side of the gender division of labour – in bringing up children and housework. In section 4.8, descriptive data on earnings of respondents and in the country are presented, to prepare for the econometric analysis in chapter 5.

4.1.2   The sampling frame

For the 1988–89 surveys a sample of 10,000 households was selected in Taganrog. As in 1978, the selection was made from a register of dwellings, classified according to type and size, in such a way that each Taganrog household should have an equal probability of being selected. 'Household' excludes those living in students' or workers' hostels.[4] Those excluded from the sample were therefore probably mainly young, single people – students and workers.

The households were then divided into four sub-groups, each of which formed the sample for one of four separate surveys. The 'Way of Life' survey includes 1,187 households from an original sample of 1,200, a very high rate of response. In each household one person was chosen as 'the respondent'. Counting all household members, our sample includes 3,722 individuals, of whom 2,020 were female (1,562 adults, that is 18 years or older) and 1,644 male (l,259 adults).[5]

Much more information is available about the main respondents than about other household members, but they were not chosen according to any precise mechanism which would have allowed calculation of sampling probabilities. Hence, they do not form a strictly random sample of the population of Taganrog. Interviewers were instructed to try to obtain a variation in sex, age, etc. of respondents, but to choose when possible an employed person. In practice, the choice had to depend on who happened to be at home and was willing to be interviewed. (No advance notice of interviews was given.) In the following, 'respondents' or 'the sample' are the subset of 'one per household', unless otherwise specifically stated. The appendix to this chapter compares characteristics between the two sets, and chapter 5 includes tests for systematic differences between their wage structures.[6] The biggest difference is that there is an over-representation of the employed and of women among the respondents. In multivariate analysis, deviation of the sample from the Taganrog average *in terms of the variables controlled for* does not affect the results.

4.2   Gender and age composition of the sample

Even if historians could agree on the numbers of lives lost in the two world wars and one civil war, in the massacres committed under Stalin and Hitler, and in the famine caused by war and forced collectivisation, the result would defy human comprehension. Both men and women suffered, but men were more likely to die in battle and more likely to be heads of peasant households or party members – the two categories most likely to be slaughtered in the terror of the 1930s. Thus, at the end of the Second World War the female/male ratio was 4 to 3. After the Second World War, the percentage of men increased, but did not catch up. Nearly 53 per cent of the Soviet population in 1989 was female, even though the effects of the war would be felt only in the oldest cohorts. The main reason is the higher male mortality in all adult age groups (*Demograficheskii ezhegodnik*, 1990). The most common explanations for the large gender difference are alcoholism and work accidents (explained, in their turn, by low health and safety standards, and by drunkenness). Table 4.1 indicates a larger gap in life expectancy between men and women in the USSR than in Western Europe.

The percentage of women in the sample of all household members is 56 per cent. This is 1.5 percentage points higher than the census figure for Taganrog as a whole, which in turn is higher than the Soviet and Russian averages of 53 per cent. The deviation is not statistically significant. Figure 4.1

Table 4.1   Life expectancy at birth

	USSR	RSFSR	UK	FRG	Sweden
Men	65	64	72	72	74
Women	74	75	78	78	80

Source: *Narodnoe Khoziaistvo* (1989 pp. 43 and 678), USSR, 1989, UK 1985–87, FRG, 1985–87, Sweden, 1988.

Figure 4.1   The proportion of women to men in the sample and according to census data for Taganrog and the RSFSR urban population

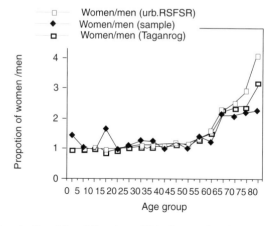

Sources: Sample, *Dem. Ezhegodnik* and unpublished census data for Rostov *oblast'*.

shows how the proportion of women to men increases with age, for the sample and according to census figures for Taganrog. It also indicates that the sample reflects Soviet demography well in this respect. The exceptions are the 16–19 age-group and the very oldest. There is a 'deficit' of young men in the sample, probably because many of them live in hostels or are doing their military service. It is harder to explain that there are relatively few old women in the sample, since this does not agree with census figures for Taganrog. (For a more detailed comparison of the age and gender composition of the sample with Soviet and Taganrog census data, see Table A4.2 and Katz, 1994, figures 4.1–4.4.)

4.3   Education

4.3.1   An historical digression

After a brief historical background based mainly on Stites (1978), the Soviet system of education will be described in section 4.3.2, gender differences in education in section 4.3.3 and, education of the sample in section 4.3.4.

The ideological importance attached to female education in the USSR has its roots in pre-revolutionary Russia. Despite the very patriarchal culture, society and policies of tsarist Russia, the country has an impressive history of female education and of female aspirations for education. The state schools for girls founded by Catherine II served a very small proportion of the female population, but were nevertheless an unusual and progressive phenomenon in Europe in 1784. From then on, women's access to education varied with the political climate. In periods of reaction, such as under Nikolai I, it was suppressed. In 1861, the year of the abolition of serfdom, universities were opened to women, only to be closed again two years later, as the regime of Alexander II became less and less liberal.

Among the radical youth of the nineteenth century were large numbers of young women, eager to learn and to contribute to social and political change. They often had to study abroad, since they were not allowed to do so in Russia. (In 1889 two-thirds of female students at the Sorbonne were from the Russian Empire.) Many sought a socially useful occupation as doctors or teachers in the villages.

In the early twentieth century access to schooling for girls increased. Education was still mainly for the socially privileged, but some working-class and peasant girls made it into the classroom. In 1914 one third of Russian schoolchildren were girls. In 1920, just under a third of Soviet women were literate and just under three-fifths of men.[7]

In the 1920s, the Soviet regime started a large-scale literacy campaign, and education was gradually expanded. The schooling of the population increased drastically and the difference between men and women narrowed. By 1939, more than 80 per cent of women and 93 per cent of men were literate. The proportion of men and women with secondary and higher education also increased. While the opportunity for each child to obtain more education than its parents increased enormously, the children of the well-educated – to say nothing of the *nomenklatura* – were much more likely to make their way into higher education than working-class children, and urban children more so than rural. This was particularly the case with the more prestigious institutions. (This was acknowledged in Soviet sociological literature. For an English-language account, see Yanowitch, 1986).

4.3.2   Education in the Soviet Union

In the USSR the first four years of school were 'primary education'. 'Incomplete secondary education' was achieved after eight years of school (before 1963, after seven years). The duration of a 'complete general secondary education' was ten years.[8] Those who did not go on to year 9 could either start work or go to a technical-vocational school, a PTU. A person with PTU schooling could have less than secondary schooling plus one-year training in an industrial skill or (from 1969 onwards) incomplete secondary plus a three-year programme which gave both a vocational training and a full secondary education.

Those who continued into year 9 could either go to general secondary school (for two years), or to a specialised secondary educational institution (*spetsial'noe srednee uchebnoe zavedenie*,[9] SSUZ), or continue into specialised education after year 10. Specialised secondary education qualified graduates for semi-professional work (medical nurses, nursery teachers and technicians). In principle, any full secondary education qualified for higher education at a VUZ (*vysshchee uchebnoe zavedenie*),[10] but the usual route to it was general secondary school.

Specialised secondary and higher education could also be acquired through evening or correspondence courses. In 1970/71 just under half the students in higher education were on day courses; in 1980/81 the figure was 57 per cent (*Nar. Khoz.*, 1988, p. 195). Among all working household members in the sample with complete higher education, 22 per cent of the men and 14 per cent of the women had obtained their degrees in evening or correspondence courses.

4.3.3   Gender and the school system

In terms of years of schooling, or of numbers who achieved secondary or higher education, there was little difference between girls and boys. Yet, in

Table 4.2   The percentage of women among students in higher education

	1940/41	1960/61	1980/81	1988/89
Total	58	43	52	54
Industry, transport, construction	40	30	42	40
Agriculture	46	27	34	35
Economics and law	64	49	67	70
Health-care and sports	74	56	58	63
Education, arts, cinematography	66	63	69	71

Source: Narodnoe Obrazovanie v SSSR (1989).

the early 1980s, although women comprised just over 50 per cent of under-graduates, only 28 per cent of Candidates of Sciences, 14 per cent of Doctors of Sciences and 11 per cent of professors and members of the Academy of Sciences were female (Rimashevskaia and Zakharova, 1989). Further, as Table 4.2 shows, female university students were under-represented in institutions training for the high-paying sectors of the economy, while they formed the overwhelming majority of those becoming low-paid school teachers, accountants and general practitioners. This segregation is even more marked in specialised secondary institutions (*Narodnoe Obrazovanie*, 1989, Katz, 1994). Of SSUZ students training for health-care and physical education occupations, 88 per cent were women.

This gender polarisation owes a lot, as Rimashevskaia and Zakharova (1989 p. 12) write, to the 'traditional attitudes of parents, teachers and girls themselves towards the role of women in the social division of labour'. But it was also entrenched by the school system. Schwartz Rosenhan (1978) surveys the highly stereotyped images of women and men in Soviet primary school textbooks. The 'labour training', which was compulsory in the first eight grades, steered boys into metal- or woodwork, and girls into domestic skills (Swafford, 1979).

After year 8, girls were more likely to end up with general secondary education, and boys more likely to go to a vocational school. PTU were linked with enterprises, mostly in heavy industry and construction, less in light industry and service trades. Students could usually expect a job with this enterprise, and according to McAuley (1981), this was a route into relatively well paid, skilled blue-collar work, mostly for young men.

In the late 1970s, 600 of the 1,200 subjects taught in PTUs were closed to women (Swafford, 1979). In the courses which admitted girls, the associated enterprises had some influence over who was admitted. McAuley (1981), among others, cites this enterprise influence as a mechanism of discrimination against women.[11] In the Taganrog I study,

Figure 4.2 The education of employed men and women in the USSR, 1989

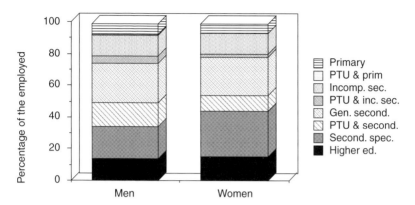

Source: 1989 census, vol. X, table 3.

researchers criticised the system of vocational education for its bias against girls, and suggested reform of the PTU in order to overcome the low level of qualification of women in manual jobs (Onikov, 1977, p. 106).

The career paths of both workers and employees depended on further education and training to improve and widen skills. Women were much less likely to participate in such training than men, both because it often took place outside working hours and conflicted with their household and child-rearing work, and because of employers' negative attitudes. A 1979 law granted mothers of children under eight the right to further professional training on full pay, to improve their qualifications, but it appears to have had little practical impact (Zakharova et al., 1989).

More qualifications did not necessarily result in better jobs. In a survey of 93,000 women, carried out by Goskomstat, two-thirds of the women who had upgraded their skills or qualifications said that 'nothing had changed' for them at work and 81.5 per cent that their pay had not increased. Only one in ten were moved to a higher '*razriad*' (skill grade of worker), or '*dolzhnost*' (job-level of employee) (*Vestnik Statistiki*, 1991, p. 55). This finding is supported by a case study, cited by Rimashevskaia and Zakharova (1989).

Since corresponding figures for men are not published, it is impossible to tell to what extent this is a general failure to use the qualifications of the workforce and to what extent it is discrimination against women.[12] But the second Taganrog study (1977–78) surveyed the work histories of married couples and found both that twice as many husbands as wives had continued their education after marriage and that in the first ten years of marriage women's earnings increased less than those of men.

4.3.4   Education in Taganrog and in the sample

The education levels of men and women in the sample of all household members are very similar. Of working age men, 30 per cent have complete or incomplete higher education and 29 per cent of the women; 29 per cent of each sex have specialised secondary education. Men are considerably more likely to have PTU training (13 per cent of men as compared with 5 per cent of women) and women more often have general secondary education (25 per cent as opposed to 18 per cent for the men). The appendix to this chapter compares the education of the sample to census figures for the Russian and Taganrog workforce (Table A4.2). Education levels in Taganrog are higher than the Russian average. Yet the difference is not very large: it consists mainly in a higher percentage with specialised secondary education in Taganrog, and a smaller percentage with general or incomplete education. For these three levels, sample and census data for Taganrog agree well, but there is an over-representation in the sample of higher education – or over-reporting. Respondents may exaggerate their educational achievements.

In the sample of all household members 20 per cent of males aged 10 and over have (complete) higher education and 18 per cent of the females.[13] Of the men, just under 8 per cent have primary education only or less, but nearly 13 per cent of women do. The census data, both local and national, also show larger gender differences in the total population than in the labour force. The proportion of elderly is larger among women and, for both sexes, education is less the older the cohort. Further, in the oldest cohorts the difference between men and women is larger, reflecting reduced female access to education in the past. The longer life expectancy of women explains the seeming paradox that after some decades of improved educational access for girls, the difference between the percentages of men and women with at least secondary education was larger in the 1970s than in 1939.

4.4   Female labour force participation

Female labour force participation in the USSR increased dramatically in the 1960s, both in older cohorts who had previously not been employed outside the home, and in the new generations, who were better educated and more employment-oriented than their mothers. Or, to be precise, participation increased in the 20–54 age group. In the whole adult female population (15 years and older) participation was lower in 1990 than in 1926. With increased length of schooling and better pensions, there was a drastic decrease in employment of women under 20 and over 54 (see Ofer and Vinokur, 1992, table 8.1).

Yet, the stereotype that 'the state forced all women to work outside the home' is oversimplified. The 'parasitism laws', in principle, obliged able-bodied, adult non-pensioners to work or study, but there was a choice of work and study and of time between jobs[14] and whether to postpone retirement, and there was the option of private subsidiary agriculture. In practice, the parasitism laws were never generally applied to pregnant women, mothers of children under 12 or to married female homemakers. In 1984 this was codified in law (*Raissi Bysiewicz* and Shelley, 1987, p. 67f). (It is another matter that the law could be used to harass individuals of whom the regime disapproved.)

Because of the high proportion of women in the population, they constituted just over 50 per cent of the workforce from 1970, despite a somewhat higher male participation rate. Oxenstierna (1990) considers the increase in wage levels and income-related pensions as one of the most important causes of the increased labour supply. The younger, better-educated cohorts of women had higher potential earnings. Also, the increases in the minimum wage (p. 58) increased the potential earnings of women with limited professional qualifications. Another economic reason was the measures directed against private subsidiary agriculture (*lichnoe podsobnoe khoziaistvo* – the famous 'private plots'). In 1959 this was still the main source of subsistence for 8 per cent of all Soviet women. By 1979 the figure was down to 0.5 per cent. (For more on changes over time, see Oxenstierna, 1990, Mashika, 1989, McAuley, 1981, or Buckley, 1981.)

Oxenstierna's conclusion is in agreement with Ofer and Vinokur's estimates (1983) from émigré data. It is at variance, however, with studies of female labour force participation based on 1970 census statistics.

Since there is a two-way relationship between the number of children women have and their decision to work outside the home, econometric models often estimate the factors that influence number of children (fertility) and probability of labour force participation in a simultaneous system of equations. As micro-data were not available, Kuniansky (1983) uses *oblast'* (regional) data from the RSFSR to estimate female labour force participation, birth rates and marital stability (marriage to divorce rates). Berliner (1983) estimates fertility rates separately for the urban and rural populations of Soviet regions. In Berliner (1989) he makes a simultaneous estimate of labour force participation and fertility from Soviet regional data (aggregating the urban and rural population). Kuniansky finds that the higher women's education levels, the lower the participation rate. Berliner (1983) finds that a variable for 'frequency of higher education among women in the region' (HIED)[15] has a significant positive impact on the birth rate for the urban population. (It is not significant for the rural population.) Yet, in a more complex model of birth rates, where female labour force participation is controlled for, the coefficient for HIED is insignificant for the urban population as well. (In both models the participation rate has a significant negative effect on birth rates.)

This implies that higher education in itself does not affect the number of children women want to have, but it does make them less likely to be employed outside the home, and working women have fewer children.

Both authors treat education as a proxy for wage (or potential wage). Therefore they interpret their findings as signs of an underlying negatively sloped labour supply curve – that is, the higher the potential earnings, the less the women are willing to work. Economic theory does not predict whether the labour supply will increase or decrease with a rise in wage rates (see p. 16). In this case, however, the interpretation appears to be straining a point, to force observations into a neoclassical framework, at the cost of realism. What we observe are not 'hours of work', but the decision to participate. The participation rate can fall when wage rates rise, only if some individuals leave the labour force. This option of not working was, however, open to them before the wage increase too, and was then rejected in favour of work at a lower wage. The only way to make this consistent with the standard neoclassical assumption of strictly positive marginal utility of income is to assume that women with higher earnings work for fewer years and save to spread the additional income over their lifetime. Kuniansky's appeal to the standard model of choice of individual labour supply at one point in time is therefore misleading. Berliner does mention the possibility of a lifetime framework. Yet, it is odd that neither investigates the simpler explanation, that when more women have higher education, more will spend more years studying, and will therefore be out of the workforce, so decreasing the regional participation rate.

Among the group with the largest variation in participation rates – pensioners – those with little education were likely to have very small pensions and would need to work, unless their relatives supported them. On the other hand, pensioners with more education would usually have higher potential earnings and more interesting jobs. My guess is that, on balance, the less educated pensioners would be more likely to work, but the sample includes too few working pensioners to help resolve the issue.

Ofer and Vinokur who have micro-data from an émigré sample estimate labour supply, both as a model for the likelihood that a woman will be employed, and for the number of hours she works, if she is employed.[16] They find significant positive effects of years of schooling as well as of expected wage on participation and a negative effect of having children under three years of age (older children have no significant impact). For number of hours worked, the 'child parameters' are all insignificant, whereas the hourly wage has a significant negative coefficient. Rather than seeing this as a decision to work fewer hours because of the income effect of a higher hourly wage-rate, I would propose an alternative interpretation, which is also suggested by Ofer and Vinokur: that given the job, the opportunities for choosing one's hours of work were limited, but many women choose jobs with shorter than average working weeks.

In the West, economists and sociologists would expect women with higher education to be more oriented towards employment (because of higher earnings or more interesting jobs). Could it have been otherwise in the USSR? If the conclusions of Berliner and Kuniansky are correct – and it would require better data to settle the issue – one would want a more sociological explanation of why women with higher education might be less likely to be employed, when number of children is controlled for. It is worth noting that, according to Soviet researchers, at about the same time various 'studies testify to the fact that the level of labour activity of women is directly dependent on the level of education' (Onikov, 1977, p. 165). According to this account of Taganrog I (1967–68), among families with pre-school children, mothers with less than secondary education were five times as likely to be at home as those with higher or specialised secondary education. More generally, 'non-working' women were found three times as often in workers' families compared with families of the *intelligentsia* (ibid., p. 167).[17]

In 1991–92, I interviewed a number of Russian experts on female employment. The quality of the evidence varied from sociological surveys of some hundreds of women to the anecdotal, but they all agreed that highly educated women were more critical of public child-care and tended to stay home longer after the birth of a child. In Taganrog I, however, when parents with children in nurseries were asked why they had chosen public child-care, 24 per cent of *intelligentsia* families said that they considered public child-care to be better than care in the home compared to 12 per cent of the other parents (Onikov, 1977, 168f). The 1989 Taganrog survey did not ask what respondents thought about public child-care, only whether they used it. There was no statistical relation between that and the mothers' education.

According to the scholars I interviewed, although women with highly qualified non-manual work might find the job itself more interesting and rewarding, the workplace and work-mates seemed to play a larger role in the social life of Soviet working-class women. It would be interesting to know more about class-specific attitudes to work among Soviet women, and whether it was more common for the *intelligentsia* than among workers to wish to live as a full-time housewife of a high-income husband. (This was believed to be 'how married women live in the West'.)

In the Taganrog sample (of all household members),[18] the overall labour force participation rate for the able-bodied working-age population is 85 per cent as compared to 82 per cent for the USSR in 1987. (*Trud v SSSR*, p. 9. 'Working age' is from 16 to the usual pension age: 54 for women, 59 for men.) Of the men, 86 per cent state their primary occupation to be 'working' compared with 79 per cent of the women. Labour force statistics, however, include employees on leave of absence, including maternity leave, among the employed. Therefore, I will distinguish between 'employed' which includes those who have a job, but are on leave, and 'working' or 'at work', which does not. This brings the employment rate for Taganrog women, aged 16–54, to 84 per cent, only 3 percentage points below men of the same age. Fifty-one per cent of the employed are women, equal to the Soviet average for workers and employees.

Table 4.3 compares the sample with Swedish and US figures. Note that because of the low age of retirement for Soviet women the participation rate in the 16–64 age band is lower than in Sweden.

Of the 13 per cent of men of working age who are not presently working, nearly two-thirds are students. Nearly half the rest are doing military service, and about 0.5 per cent are disabled, or retired or 'temporarily not working' respectively. Of the women, 21 per cent are not working. About a half of them are students and a quarter are on maternity leave. Less than 2 per cent define themselves as 'housewives'. (See also Table 7.1.)

Table 4.3   Female and male labour force participation rates, 16–64 years of age, 1989

Country	Male %	Female %	Female/male ratio
USA	85.9	67.8	78.9
Sweden	86.8	82.2	94.7
Taganrog sample	84.9	76.1	89.6

Source: Jonung and Persson (1993, p. 270) and sample.

4.5 Working hours

4.5.1 Working hours in the USSR

Even with high female participation rates, employed women may work fewer hours per week than employed men. This is the case in Sweden, Britain and the Netherlands, which have high rates of part-time work. Average hours of work per week can be measured in different ways – as agreed (contractual) hours, as answers to the question 'how many hours do you usually work?' or computed from time-use studies which measure amount of time used for various activities during a particular day (days). Comparisons show that respondents often report contractual hours as the 'usual' without allowing for days of absence (Carlin and Flood, 1997). The best measure of how long people actually work is therefore time-use studies.

Ofer and Vinokur (1981) asked for 'usual hours' and found a gender difference in total hours worked of 5.5 hours per week, of which nearly half is due to a difference in regular hours. The sample, however, consisted of emigrants and had an over-representation of teachers, who may have reported only teaching hours, and nurses, who had a reduced full-time working week (see below). They also found that, among the full-time employed, it was twice as common for men to do private sector work as for women. In addition, 13 per cent of men and 4 per cent of women had a second job in the public sector. This is probably untypical – according to Malle (1990, p. 34), in 1988 only about 2 per cent of the state employed had a second job.

4.5.2 Legislation on working hours[19]

From 1967 the normal working week in the USSR was five days, or 41 hours. Schools, however, kept a six-day week. Also, staff on 'unnormed' time were excluded (p. 63).

For a number of occupations, Soviet labour legislation stipulated shorter working days or weeks. This is known as 'not full' (*nepol'noe*) or 'shortened' (*sokrashchennoe*) working time. It applied to both work under hazardous conditions and certain non-manual jobs considered to involve 'heightened intellectual and mental strain'. For example, nursery school teachers did 36 hours, primary school teachers 24 hours and teachers in specialised secondary schools 18 hours. For teachers, this includes only hours spent in the classroom. The working hours of medical staff varied, but working days of 5.5, 6 or 6.5 hours were common.[20]

Given that there were few opportunities for part-time work (Moskoff, 1982) it is reasonable to assume that many women chose jobs in teaching or the health sector as a kind of undeclared part-time job, to facilitate the combination of paid work and housework.

4.5.3   Respondents' hours of work

The data include 'usual working hours per week' only for main respondents, not for all household members. For most sectors, average working hours for men and for women are in the range 39–43 hours. Men in co-operatives[21] work very long hours, women in culture and education report short hours, and women in health-care relatively short hours. Both women and men in trade and catering work somewhat longer hours than in other sectors. The difference between the hours men and women work is significant at the 5 per cent level in industry, education and co-operatives.

Excluding those working in schools,[22] the average working week for men in the sample is 42.4 hours at the primary place of work (including overtime) and 43.4 including second jobs. For women the figures are 40.2 and 40.3 hours respectively. (See also Table A7.3.)

Two-thirds work 40–42 hours. The majority of the others say that they work more. Deviation from the standard 41 hours is larger than in the official statistics, which presumably state contractual hours. According to these, 90 per cent of Soviet workers and employees worked 41 hours per week and 8 per cent worked 36 hours or less (*Trud v SSSR*, 1988, p. 135). This difference, and the very long average basic working hours reported by some respondents (Table A7.3), are probably due to some including usual overtime at their primary place of work, despite being asked not to. Therefore, it is difficult to measure overtime from these data. Nine per cent say that they work overtime every week, 23 per cent that they work overtime at least a few times per month, but only 16 per cent report some amount of 'usual' overtime per week at their primary place of work.[23] For those who report usual overtime, the average is 6.6 hours/week. More men than women work overtime, but the average amount for those women who do work overtime is slightly more than for the men.

4.5.4   Reduced time and part-time work

The survey asks whether respondents work 'a full working week', 'not a full working week' or 'not a full working day'. The idea that part-time work and homeworking for women, in particular for mothers of young children, were the best solutions to 'the problem of motherhood and work' and to 'the demographic question' had been discussed since the 1970s and in the late 1980s received strong official support.[24] (Posadskaia, 1989, section 2.3, summarises the arguments and makes a balanced assessment of advantages and disadvantages for women. See also p. 101, below.)

In the Taganrog sample, more than 7 per cent answered that they worked less than a full working day or less than a full working week. Yet, according to the official statistics, only 1.2 per cent of women in the USSR worked part-time in 1990! The likeliest explanation is that the majority meant that they had a reduced working week, as defined above. (Another 7 per cent, who state that they work full-time, usually worked 27–39 hours.) We will return to this topic in chapters 5 and 6.

4.6 Segregation by gender

Occupational segregation in the USSR has been documented in earlier English-language sources. Chapman (1978, p. 238) wrote in the 1970s of a 'dual labor market divided along sex lines'. McAuley (1981) carefully extracts the available information on gender segregation from the 1939, 1959 and 1970 censuses. Since the sample is too small for a study of detailed occupational structure, the treatment here will be brief. It is based mainly on chapters 4 and 5 of McAuley (1981), adding a few more recent figures (see also Atkinson et al. 1978, and Lapidus, 1978).

4.6.1 Horizontal segregation

It is usual to distinguish between 'vertical' and 'horizontal' segregation. In the Soviet context, the horizontal dimension includes segregation between sectors controlled by 'ministerial' or 'departmental' authorities with very different degrees of power. As in the West, in the Soviet Union women were much more likely than men to work in the child-care, schools and health-care sectors. All these sectors had lower wages, lower priority in allocation of resources and less influence with central decision-making bodies than material production did.

Table 4.4 shows the proportion of women in different sectors. Columns 1 and 2 represent the USSR, 1940 and 1968, columns 3 and 4, the USSR, 1989. Column 5 represents the Taganrog sample. In the 1980s, neither the census nor the statistical yearbooks reported the proportion of women for all the main sectors. The figures in column 4 are therefore imputed from census data. (See p. 147.)

Within manufacturing, women dominated light industry – textiles, garments and leather. They were less likely than men to work in high-priority branches like metallurgy, fuels, mining or energy. No information was published about the military-industrial complex, but it is likely that it was male-dominated, as was most of heavy industry.

In the Taganrog sample, information on sector of occupation is available for respondents, but not for other household members. Two-fifths of the

Table 4.4 Percentages of women in different sectors

	(1) USSR 1940	(2) USSR 1968	(3) USSR 1989	(4) USSR, 1989 (estimated)	(5) Taganrog sample
Industry[a]	38	47		44	56
of which light industry				71	66
Construction	23	27		25	51
Transport & communications	24	30		29[b]	42
Housing and municipal services				48	
Consumer services				67	
Housing, municipal & construction services	43	51			64
Trade and catering	44	75	76	76	83
Health-care	76	85	81	80	80
Culture and art			67	67	62
Education[c]	59	72	75	75	77
Science	42	46	51	50	55
Public administration				39	
Party & social organisations				50	
Publ. administration & social organisation	34	58			82
Agriculture (excl. kolkhoz)	34	43		39	0
All workers and employees	39	50	51	49	60
Thousands of women[d]	13,190	42,650	58,729	62,560	0.564

[a] In columns 1–3 this includes only industrial-production staff.
[b] Transport and communications weighted with number employed 1987 (*Trud v SSSR*).
[c] For 1940 and 1968, this includes culture.
[d] Figures in columns 1–3 are averages over the years. Col. 4, as of 12 January (census).
Sources: Columns 1 and 2: *Nar. Khoz.* (1968, pp. 548 and 552), col. 3: *Nar. Khoz.* (1989, pp. 48 and 53), col. 4: Estimated from 1989 census, table 3, vol. X. (For method of imputation, see p. 261, n. 23).

female respondents and just over half of the male respondents work in heavy industry. The share of industry in Soviet employment was large, but not as large as this (40 per cent of the urban workforce). The employment of women is more varied than that of men. While there is a substantial number of women in the male-dominated sectors (heavy industry, transport and construction), very few men work in the female dominated 'socio-cultural sphere' (see Table A7.1).

Occupational segregation is intrinsically difficult to measure. Some arbitrariness in choice of index and definition of 'occupation' is inevitable. In the case of the USSR, the problem is aggravated by the characteristically Soviet way in which the statistics were organised. The 1989 census has one table of the numbers of people employed in different occupations, and another of the numbers and percentage of women. The problem is that in the second table, a number of occupations included in the first table, comprising several million workers and employees, are omitted. These are jobs one would expect to be male-dominated, such as 'workers in metallurgy and foundries' or 'machinist'. For these, consequently, we do not know the proportion of women.

In 1939 three-fifths of employed Soviet women were engaged in manual agricultural labour; by 1989 the figure was down to one in ten. Men have left 'the village' too, in the last half-century, but they have taken a different route. In 1939, one in five employed men was a white-collar worker, but only one in seven women. In 1989, 43 per cent of employed women were non-manual workers, but only 29 per cent of men.

Among manual workers, McAuley finds an increase in gender segregation over the 1939–70 period, while among non-manual workers the evidence is ambiguous. It appears that more men came to work in mixed occupations, while a larger share of female employment was concentrated to female-dominated jobs. (Part of the reason, however, is that the growth in female employment has made a larger number of occupations female-dominated.)

According to the 1989 census, among professionals, the probability is larger for a physician to be female (67 per cent) than for legal staff (49 per cent). Among workers, 88 per cent of hairdressers were women, but only 1 per cent of car and bus-drivers; 92 per cent of cloakroom attendants were women, while their share of night watchmen isn't even reported.

In the Taganrog sample, jobs are divided into six broad categories. These are further discussed in connection with the wage estimates in chapter 5. Of the employed male respondents, 69 per cent have manual jobs, or jobs with elements of manual work, compared with 55 per cent of the female respondents. Among the Soviet urban employed in the state sector, 72 per cent of the men and 51 per cent of the women were manual workers. In this respect, therefore, the sample is typical of the USSR as a whole.

According to Figure 4.3 women have either unskilled manual work or white-collar work more often than men, while among the men, skilled blue-collar jobs predominate. The job composition varies sharply between sectors. In the female-dominated socio-cultural sphere, the proportion of non-manual employees is larger than in material production. The majority of both male and female staff in this sector have higher education. In material production about three-fifths of women and four-fifths of men are manual workers. The proportion of skilled to unskilled manual workers is higher than in the socio-cultural sphere. Among male manual workers in material production only about one in ten is unskilled; among the female it is nearly one in three.

4.6.2   Vertical segregation

'Vertical segregation' refers to the level of jobs. There is, of course, no universally accepted measure of this. If pay is taken as the measure of level, then clearly women's jobs in the USSR were below those of men. If we use the number of years of schooling required it was not so. If job satisfaction, intrinsic merit or working conditions define the level, we cannot really know, particularly since men and women often appear to value different aspects of work. (For the status of occupations in the USSR, see pp. 79ff.)

Figure 4.3   Job types of male and female respondents

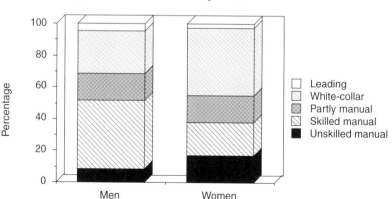

Note: 'Leading' jobs include both managerial and highly qualified creative jobs. The 'partly manual' jobs are highly skilled.

Table 4.5   Percentages of women in selected non-manual occupations

ITR and clerical		Teachers	
Heads of enterprises	23	Heads of teaching institutions	46
Heads of departments, sectors, etc.	31	University lecturers	44
Chief engineers	18	Teachers in primary and secondary schools	73
Engineers	56	Nursery teachers	98
Technicians	82		
Foremen	32	**Medicine**	
Norm-setters	83	Doctors	67
Typists, stenographers	98	Nurses	98
		Orderlies, nursing auxiliaries	97

Source: 1989 census, table 3, volume XI, part 1.

Table 4.5 illustrates that the higher up the occupational hierarchy, the fewer the women, in particular where positions of authority are concerned. (Hence the low numbers of women among managers and foremen, compared with engineers and norm-setters who have little control over the work of others.)

Within industry, manual workers in the branches in which women are concentrated have lower average skill grades, and within each branch women have lower skill grades than men, as noted above (p. 62). Yet, while in 1990 *Zhenshchiny v SSSR* claims that the gender difference was particularly great in the female-dominated textiles industry, McAuley (1981) and Granick (1987) cite Soviet studies from the early 1970s which show that women had higher skills, both absolutely and relative to men, in textiles than in the more 'mixed' food industry, and higher skills in the food industry than in male-dominated engineering. This may be because not even the better-paid jobs in these industries were attractive to men, thus leaving more openings for women. We would thus have the reverse of a 'crowding effect'.

4.7   Children, housework and employment

4.7.1   'The demographic problem'

In the USSR, as everywhere else, gender relations and gender roles in paid work interacted with those outside work. This section will, very briefly, treat issues of household structure, child birth and unpaid work.

Starting in the 1960s, low birth rates were a constant topic of concern among Soviet policy-makers and in the Soviet literature. (For English-language summaries, see Lapidus, 1978, McAuley, 1981, Buckley, 1981 and Gregory, 1982 for Eastern Europe in general.) Proposals for tackling the low birth rates included lower employment rates or part-time work for mothers, more household services and equipment to ease the 'double burden', more and better public child-care, longer maternity leave and more emphasis on 'femininity' and on the importance of motherhood in the socialisation of little girls. From the *nomenklatura* point of view, reducing women's labour force participation to improve the future labour power supply was a problematic choice, not, I believe, because of a high commitment to gender equality in itself, but because there were already severe labour shortages, which would be exacerbated by mothers with-drawing from employment. Yet, proposing an equal role of parents in the care of children and in housework was beyond the pale, ideologically (Posadskaia, 1989).

The total number of births reached its minimum in 1968, but the number of expected births per woman continued to decrease to the end of the 1970s, with a figure of 2.2 in 1980–81 (1.9 in the RSFSR). In 1986–87 the total fertility rate was 2.5 (2.2 in the RSFSR) (Naselenie SSSR, 1988, pp. 56–8 and 328). The population was increasing in Central Asia, and declining in the European part of the USSR and this was considered worrying. With underemployment in Central Asia and labour shortages in the Western regions there would be difficulties – neither millions of people nor millions of jobs can be moved simply and costlessly. To this were added nationalist, supremacist overtones at the prospect of Russians becoming a minority in the Union.

4.7.2 Maternity leave

The Labour Code of 1922 granted paid pregnancy leave of 6 weeks (8 weeks for manual workers) and a further 6 weeks after giving birth. In the Stalinist period, the leave was alternately shortened and increased several times, and only in 1956 were the 1922 levels reached again, together with the option of a further three months' unpaid leave with the right to return to the same or an equivalent job, and up to a year with unbroken work record.[25] In 1968 unpaid leave, without loss of job or work record, was extended until the child's first birthday, and in 1982 to 18 months.

In 1982, also, the leave was fully paid for 8 weeks before giving birth and 8 weeks after giving birth. (The leave was extended by an additional two weeks in the event of multiple births or medical complications.) The mother received a small benefit for one year, about half the minimum wage. These rights applied to mothers, only, though either parent, in theory, could stay at home on sickness benefit to care for a sick child. This was the situation at the time of the survey (McAuley, 1981, pp. 168ff, Mashika, 1989, pp. 155, 266–78).

I have found no data on the length of actual work interruptions, in connection with child birth and child-raising. McAuley (1981) uses census data to calculate the average time women would have been home after each birth if the whole difference between male and female participation rates in each republic were attributed to this. However, since the census defines women on leave as 'employed',[26] it is impossible to infer anything from these data about women who stayed home for less than 12 months. Nevertheless, McAuley's findings indicate that most women returned to work after one year, or not much longer.

Using the official statistics for the regions, Kuniansky (1983) did not find that education had a significant effect on birth rates (see p. 91f, above.) Berliner (1983), on the other hand, finds (in a multivariate estimate) that having only primary schooling is associated with lower birth rates compared with incomplete secondary education, but with higher birth rates compared with complete secondary education. These relations are statistically significant. The proportion of women with university education has no significant impact on fertility levels, if labour force participation is taken into account. When the urban and rural populations are aggregated, however, Berliner (1989) finds that higher education for women has a significant negative impact on fertility. Again, the absence of micro-data makes itself felt. Since the proportion of women with higher education is larger in the urban population (18 per cent) than in the rural population (11 per cent) the parameter for 'women with higher education' may partly reflect the negative impact of urban life-styles as urbanisation is usually accompanied by lower birth rates.

Berliner (1989) finds that, where more women were employed, fewer children were born, but higher birth rates did not imply lower female employment rates. He does not mention, however, that the census statistics used do not reflect work interruptions of less than one year. This would bias estimates of the effect of child-birth on the actual work of women. The only conclusion that really can be drawn from the estimates is that mothers did not drop out of work significantly more than the maximum one-year maternity leave.

4.7.3   Employment of mothers in Taganrog

In the Taganrog sample, a small majority (53 per cent) of households include children. In more than 60 per cent of cases, there is just one child. Households with two or more children are few, even compared with the average for Russian urban households. The maximum number of children is four, but there are very few such families in the sample.[27] Most women though become mothers. Of female respondents aged 25–60 about 90 per cent have had children, though very few have more than two.

All the women in the sample with children less than one year old were at home, but only about a quarter of those whose youngest child was between 12 months and three years. Less than 5 per cent are still at home by the time the youngest child is 3–7 years old. Of the 324 pre-school children in the sample, 44 per cent attend public child-care and 28 per cent have a mother who is at home. Three quarters of the children whose mothers are not working or studying either are, or have a sibling who is, no more than 18 months old.

According to the official statistics, in 1988, 76 per cent of urban children in the RSFSR had a place in a child-care institution. (*Nar. obrazovanie*, 1989, p. 38). In the sample the figure is much lower: 63 per cent for 4–6 year olds. If the official figures are correct, this is surprising, since many women in Taganrog worked in large industrial enterprises, which could afford to offer their staff subsidised child-care.

In the USSR, households were much more likely than in Western Europe to include adults of two generations. In the sample, more than two fifths of households have more than two adult members. This partly reflects a culture with strong inter-generational ties, and partly the shortage of housing, which made it very hard for young couples, let alone young single adults, to find a place of their own. Elderly parents, particularly if they were widowed, often moved in with their children.

For all the strain and discomfort that lack of space and involuntary closeness between generations brings, the extended family was also a support for economically vulnerable groups. For elderly women, often subsisting on a very low pension, and for lone mothers, this was essential, and it was also important for students and young couples with children.

Did the extended family affect female employment? For mothers of young children, financial assistance from their own parents or parents-in-law could make it possible to extend maternity leave beyond the fully paid weeks. The '*babushka* factor', that is, the help of older female relatives in caring for children, would tend to increase the employment of mothers, but perhaps decrease that of grandmothers. Some pensioners would be able to leave the labour force if they were supported by their children, while some, mainly the younger, might continue working precisely to help their children financially. In the sample of all household members, 30 per cent of men over 60 years, and 17 per cent of women over 55 work.

The great majority of working pensioners are less than five years over the standard pension age.

Sternheimer (1987) concludes from surveys made in the 1970s that although elderly Soviet women were becoming less willing to assume the traditional role of full-time *babushka*, and preferred to live independently, one pre-school child in three or four was still cared for by a grandmother.

In another sub-project of Taganrog III, employed men aged 55–59 and women age 50–54 were asked what they wanted to do in retirement. In reply 57 per cent of men and 73 per cent of women said they wanted to occupy themselves with their 'homes and grandchildren'.[28]

One child in seven in the sample lives with only one parent (in all cases but one, the mother) which is about the same proportion as in Sweden. In Taganrog, however, approximately half of the lone mothers live with their own parents or mothers.

4.7.4 Housework

The seminal study of time-use in 12 countries, headed by Szalai in the mid-1960s, indicated that total labour time – paid and domestic – in the USSR was higher than in all the others, except Poland.[29] The time spent on housework in the USSR was near the average, but that in paid labour was higher than in any other country. The difference between the total working hours of men and women was 2.3 hours per day – 0.1 hours less than in record-holding Poland and West Germany. In Norway the gender difference was 0.4 hours per day, and in Belgium and the GDR, 1.1 hours (Lingsom, 1978, pp. 56–7).

There is some information on time-use in the Taganrog survey, but it must be considered very approximate.[30] Respondents were asked how much time they had spent on each of a number of activities during the most recent working day and the most recent non-working day. To get weekly averages, I have multiplied the working day figures by five and added two times the non-working day figures, except for people working 24-hour shifts (*dezhurnye*). For the latter I have used the most common schedule – 24 hours on work, 72 hours off work – for weighting.[31]

In total, male respondents spent 21 hours a week on housework, and female 36 hours. Among those who are working, the men spend three hours more working, or travelling to and from work, than women, but they spend 13 hours less on housework (including activities with children, gardening and household repairs). Repairs are the only predominantly male task – women spend 1.9 hours at it per week and men 2.4. Men spend 5 hours a week on housework in the more narrow sense of cooking, cleaning and laundry, women 15 hours. Shopping is shared, more equally with 7 hours for men and 10 hours for women. Men spend 5 hours a week caring for or bringing up children and women 6 hours. Men have 29 hours a week for leisure activities (sports, reading, watching TV, etc.) women 22 hours. This is somewhat more than in other Soviet data, but the male/female differences are of a similar order. For workers and employees in industry, *Narodnoe Khoziaistvo* (1989) reports that women spend 28 hours and 40 minutes per week on housework, of which 6 hours and 40 minutes are spent on shopping. Men spend 11 hours on housework, of which three hours are spent on shopping and have one and a half times as much leisure (not counting sleeping, eating, bathing, etc., on which the sexes spend about the same amount of time).

The burden of housework and the degree of inequality vary much over the life-cycle. Yet, even among non-married youngsters, girls do considerably more housework than boys (Gordon and Klopov, 1975, table 4, p. 266). Tables 4.6–4.8 show the amount of housework performed by men and women, in Taganrog, in a sample of large cities from the late 1960s (Gordon and Klopov, 1975) and in the Russian town Pskov in 1986 (Niemi et al., 1991).

Table 4.6   Housework done by men and women in Russian cities, 1965–68 (hours and minutes per week)

	Women	Men
Unmarried youths	17.07	5.40
Young spouses	24.25	12.10
Couple with minor children	32.40	12.10
Parents in extended family	30.50	12.15
Single parents	26.15	n.a.
Elderly	29.15	18.00

Source: Gordon and Klopov (1975).

Table 4.7   Housework and paid work done by men and women in Pskov, 1986 (hours per week)

	Single, childless		Married, childless		Married with children of pre-school age	
	Men	Women	Men	Women	Men	Women
Paid work	37.1	28.0	42.2	34.7	50.4	29.5
House-work	12.5	23.3	16.0	32.4	18.7	45.2

Note: Paid work includes travel to and from work and housework includes child-care.
Source: Niemi et al. (1991)

Table 4.8 Housework and paid work done by working men and women in Taganrog, 1989 (hours per week)

	Single, childless		Married, no children		Married with children		Single parent	
	Men	Women	Men	Women	Men	Women	Men	Women
Paid work	48	41	48	45	47	45	48	44
Housework	15	27	16	30	23	36	27	35
of which, child-care	0.25	0.4	0.8	0.5	9	10	16	9
N	53	187	132	141	187	247	1	70

Note: Paid work includes travel to and from the workplace, and housework includes child-care and repair and maintenance. 'Children' means that there are children aged 16 or younger in the household.

Table 4.9 compares time-use in Pskov and in Finland, from a co-ordinated Soviet–Finnish study. We see that the amount of housework performed by each sex is a little larger in Pskov than in Finland, but not dramatically so. Russian fathers put more time into child-care than Finnish fathers. The greatest difference between the countries is that the Russian women devote much more time to paid work than the Finnish, without less time spent doing housework. The anecdotal evidence of shopping in the USSR would have led one to expect a greater difference in time spent on purchases. (In Sweden in 1990/1 women aged 20–64 spent three and a half hours per week on purchasing goods and services, according to SCB (1992). The methodology is, however, not exactly the same.)

In other respects comparisons with time-use data from other countries are not straightforward. In Soviet studies the respondent was asked about time spent during the most recent day she or he actually worked and the most recent free day, whereas Western studies randomise the days of the week. This means that the Soviet time-budgets ignore all days when the respondent was absent from work and overestimate actual average hours worked per week,[32] not least for mothers who are at home caring for sick children. If more housework and child-care are performed on days off (excluding for illness or with permission) than on working days, these will be underestimated, but the sum of housework and paid work will be somewhat less affected. Married, working mothers in Pskov worked a total of 75 hours per week and their husbands 69 hours, while, full-time working mothers in Sweden worked about 69 hours per week and their husbands 73 hours if the children were below school-age, otherwise 69 hours (SCB, 1992).

Table 4.8 for Taganrog includes working respondents only. Therefore the difference between time spent on housework for women and men is less than in Tables 4.6–4.7. It is nevertheless very large, and although men

Table 4.9   Housework and paid work done by urban, employed men and women aged 18 and above in Pskov and Finland

	Finland		Pskov	
	Men	**Women**	**Men**	**Women**
Paid work	44.1	33.3	50.6	45.5
Housekeeping	7.5	15.3	7.2	16.2
Care of children	2.6	4.3	3.7	5.3
Purchasing goods and services	3.6	5.4	4.1	6.2
Domestic work load, total	13.7	25.0	15.1	27.7
Workload, total	57.8	58.4	65.7	73.2

spend more time in paid work, the total is considerably larger for women in all household types. Comparing Tables 4.6 and 4.7, we see that men have increased their share of housework over the 20-year period, but not by very much. What has disappeared is the striking feature of Table 4.6 that the amount of housework done by married men did not increase when they had children. According to the Taganrog data, working fathers spend almost as much time with their children as working mothers, but the difference in total hours spent on housework is the same for couples with and without children. Further, if mothers stay at home when their child is ill and the fathers do not, this would not show in these data. It is also worth noting that married mothers have to spend as much time on housework as single-mothers.[33] Working women with only a husband expecting to be cared for still do a 75-hour week, according to the Taganrog data. Married women with no children at home in Pskov did 67 hours, their husbands 58 hours, even though this includes people outside the labour force.

To sum up, households', working hours – particularly women's working hours – are long. Increased labour force participation has been at the expense of free time – cooking, cleaning, laundry and shopping still have to be done. Goods and services to make domestic life easier were not a priority in Soviet planning. According to an all-Union survey in 1989, 9 per cent of urban households lacked running water, 22 per cent lacked hot water and only 39 per cent had a telephone (*Sostav Sem'i* ..., pp. 383 and 386), (In the Taganrog sample, 15 per cent lacked running water, only a third of households had hot water and 29 per cent had telephones.)

Second, according to the old, rural patriarchal division of labour each gender had certain tasks which were not done by the other. In the cities, most of the traditional 'men's tasks', like chopping wood, fetching water from the well, repairing the small wooden house, had largely disappeared. Despite this, and even though women's labour force participation rates are almost equal to those of men, they remain responsible for the traditional 'women's tasks'. The only activity men seem to have entered fully is 'bringing up children' (*vospitanie detei*). This includes going for walks, reading stories and, helping with homework, but not 'caring' for them (*ukhod za det'm'i*), that is, they don't do the 'menial' tasks such as feeding, washing and dressing or taking them to or from the nursery.

4.8 The wages of Soviet women and men: a first look

Using census data and other Soviet statistics, as well as the published results from Soviet sociological surveys, McAuley (1981) found that working women earned about 60–70 per cent of what men earned. The Armenian data analysed by Swafford (1978) indicate mean earnings for women at 65 per cent of those of men, with only 5 per cent of the women earning as much as the average man. The earlier Taganrog surveys found female/male wage ratios of 67 per cent in 1968 and 68 per cent in 1977–78 (Migranova and Mozhina, 1991). This is a smaller difference than in most Western countries at that time, but larger than in Scandinavia.

Atkinson and Micklewright (1992, table U6) estimate average wages for men and women by republic.[34] Three very poor republics (two of them with predominantly Muslim populations) had the highest ratio of female to male wages, while Georgia, Kazakhstan and Turkmenia clustered with Russia, Ukraine and Lithuania at the bottom of the list. Women in the Asian republics had less education and were in a generally more subordinate position. Atkinson and Micklewright point out that when the wage level is very low, the legal minimum wage raises women's wages relative to those of men. I would also suspect that with lower female participation rates in Central Asia and the Caucasus than in the Slav and Baltic republics, there was a selection effect, so that urban, more highly educated women with the highest potential earnings were more likely to be employed.

The Taganrog data include information about wages from the state sector. These are what I refer to as 'wages' in the following. Respondents also report income from self-employment and co-operatives. These, together with wages, make up 'earnings' or 'total labour income'. Unless otherwise stated, all wages and incomes derived from the survey are after tax, in accordance with the design of the questionnaire. When comparability with the official statistics, which are of gross wages, was important I have, however, imputed pre-tax wages from the data.[35] The wage measure, and possible measurement errors, are discussed in chapter 5.

A little was said about the distribution of household income and of wages in the USSR in section 3.1.4. Household income distribution in the Taganrog sample is the subject of a separate study (Gustafsson and Nivorozhkina, 1996, 1998) to which I refer the reader. (See also Mozhina et al., 1992.)

The average take-home wage for men is 235 roubles per month and for women 155 roubles. If we include income from co-operatives and self-employment, this rises to 245 and 159 roubles, respectively. (The difference is small, since only a small number of people report income from the private sector.) Women's average wage is 66 per cent that of men. The median wage for men is equal to the highest decile wage for women.

Average monthly earnings for male and female working pensioners are 160 and 106 roubles, respectively.

Table 4.10 shows the relationship between schooling and wages. According to the first row, the wages of respondents with vocational school (PTU) education are as high as those of university graduates. This agrees with the view that (skilled) workers were highly valued and the *intelligentsia* depreciated, which was widely held at least among the Soviet *intelligentsia*. Cross-tabulation of wages according to education *and* gender modifies this picture. For men, general and specialised secondary school and PTU result in equal wages, but less than university graduates and more than low education. For women, wages slowly but steadily increase with schooling, except that women with PTU and with secondary specialised earn about the same. (The difference in length of schooling between these is small.) The striking differences are between men and women with the same education, at every level. Indeed, each group of men, including those with eight years or less of school, earn more than every group of women, including university graduates!

In this respect, the Taganrog data seem to agree with the tables published by Goskomstat in 1989 (*Nar. Khoz.*, 1989). According to these, at any given level of education, the median wage for women is in a lower band than for men. What is more, the median for university-educated women and for men with only primary education are in the same 181–200 roubles/month band, while the medians for all other groups of men are in higher bands and those for all other groups of women are in lower bands. The median for men with higher education is in the 221–250 roubles/month band.

Male skilled workers were more highly valued than *female* professionals in the USSR. Thus, Table 4.10 anticipates the topic of chapter 6: an analysis of social stratification in the USSR requires a gender perspective.

Table 4.10 refers to all household members. If we want to take sector, type of job or working hours into account, we are restricted to the sub-sample of respondents, as in Table 4.11. The table indicates a hierarchy between job categories, in the sense that skilled workers earn one and half times as much as unskilled, and managerial staff one and half times as much as 'ordinary' white-collar workers. Since the two better-paid groups are male dominated, the differentials are somewhat smaller within gender groups. The wage advantage of skilled manual over white-collar workers is roughly halved when men and women are separated. Note that unskilled male manual workers earn more than skilled female workers.

Table 4.12 shows average wages in different sectors of the Taganrog sample, and compares them with the national statistics. Wages in

Table 4.10 Average monthly wage (after tax) by type of education (all household members with non-zero wage the previous month)

Education	Total	Low education	General secondary	Special secondary	Vocational	Higher (VUZ)
Total	**195.1**	**163.4**	**180.4**	**195.9**	**213.4**	**213.0**
	78.9	*71.3*	*74.5*	*80.2*	*77.0*	*78.7*
	(2,012)	(195)	(404)	(682)	(193)	(505)
Men	**234.6**	**195.8**	**236.8**	**234.2**	**235.1**	**248.5**
	81.6	*75.8*	*75.3*	*85.0*	*72.5*	*83.7*
	(1,009)	(91)	(157)	(353)	(139)	(258)
Women	**155.4**	**135.0**	**144.6**	**154.8**	**156.5**	**176.1**
	51.5	*53.0*	*46.8*	*48.4*	*58.2*	*51.8*
	(996)	(104)	(247)	(325)	(53)	(245)

Note: The difference between male and female wages is significant at the 1 per cent level at every level of education.
'Low education' is eight years or less.
'Specialised secondary' includes incomplete higher
'Vocational' school may or may not include full secondary education.
'Higher education' includes both full-time (day)-study and evening and corespondence courses.
Observations with partial non-response have been included when possible. Therefore rows and columns may not add up to the 'totals'.
* Standard deviations in italics and number of observations in brackets

113

Table 4.11 Average monthly wage (after tax), by job level

	1 Unskilled manual	2 Skilled manual	3 Skilled, partly manual	4 Non-manual	5 Management position	6 Highly qualified & creative
Total	145	216	194	181	275	250
	59.9	*80.7*	*69.7*	*70.9*	*103.4*	*102.2*
	(129)	(279)	(157)	(329)	(18)	(12)
Men	193	247	238	234	331	299
	67.3	*81.7*	*69.7*	*89.2*	*107.0*	*116.9*
	(33)	(165)	(68)	(99)	(10)	(5)
Women	129	172	161	158	205	214
	47.5	*54.8*	*47.8*	*45.2*	*32.2*	*80.6*
	(96)	(114)	(89)	(230)	(8)	(7)

Standard deviations in italics and number of observations in brackets.
All respondents reporting a non-zero wage the preceding month.

Table 4.12   Average monthly pre-tax wages[a] for workers and employees in different branches of the state sector (roubles)

Branch	USSR 1988	USSR 1989	Sample (unweighted)	Sample (weighted)[b]
Industry	240.8	263.7	230	242
of which manual	235.0	255.4	239	n.a.
non-manual	267.3	301.0	208	n.a.
Construction	288.9	316.2	223	242
Transport & communications	251.8	268.9	229	242
Trade and catering	165.1	187.1	144	144
Service	168.0	180.6	182	n.a.
Health-care	152.5	163.3	179	179
Education	171.4	175.5	203	206
Science	248,4	303.1	224	228
Culture & art	134.5	143.1	167	160
Administration	203.9	235.4	203	n.a.
All	219.8	240.4	216	219

Note: The survey in Taganrog was done in Spring 1989 and should be somewhere 'in between' the yearly averages for 1988 and 1989. The average monthly wage for workers and employees in 1988 in the RSFSR was 235.2, that is 7 per cent higher than the Union average.
[a] For the RSFSR and USSR these are average gross wages over the year, including bonuses. For the sample, gross wages have been imputed, but the wage measure is wage and monthly bonuses paid the preceding month.
[b] Male and female average wages for sample, weighted by proportions men and women in the USSR (as estimated in Table 4.4).
Source: *Nar. Khoz. 1989 g.* pp 76–7.

Taganrog are considerably lower than the national average for certain sectors. The discrepancy is reduced when the over-representation of women in the sample is corrected for, by weighting the male and female average wages for Taganrog by the proportions of men and women in the sector nationally (Table 4.12, column 4). One reason for the difference may be that yearly and quarterly bonuses are not included in the wages reported by the sample.

There were no official statistics on male and female average wages in different sectors, but in the sample, women earn less than men in each sector and the difference between male and female earnings is significant at the 1 per cent level in nine out of 14 sectors, and at the 5 per cent level in another two. Of the remaining three sectors, two include less than a dozen observations each.[36]

Average pay is lower in female-dominated sectors, but there is no immediately obvious correlation between the proportion of women in a sector and its *ratio* of male to female wages. Unfortunately, this sample includes so few men in female-dominated sectors that no reliable conclusions can be drawn. For instance, in health-care, the sample includes only eight male respondents and they earn twice as much as the women, but in another sub-project of Taganrog III the ratio of women's wages to men's in health-care was 67 per cent. (Rimashevskaia, 1992, p. 18).

Appendix

This appendix reports data on age, eduation and employment of the sample. Its purpose is to indicate the degree of representativity of the sample of (main) respondents relative to that of all household members, and of the sample to reference populations. (Education is compared with the population of Taganrog to check for bias in the sample selection; age and education to that of the RSFR/USSR populations to explore the representativity of a local sample relative to that of the country.)

The interviewers were instructed to try to recruit equal numbers of male and female respondents. When the household included both working and non-working adults, the former were preferred as respondents. Certain information, such as age, employment status, education and income, was requested for each member of the household. This is used in Tables A4.1–A4.3 and in chapter 5 to check for bias in selection of respondents.

Women are over-represented relative to men. The proportion of women is 55 per cent among the whole sample of adults but 62 per cent among the respondents. The middle age-groups are over-represented as compared with the young and the elderly. In addition to what can be seen from the table, about 4 per cent of household members are 18–19 years old, but less than 0.5 per cent of respondents.

Among respondents there is an over-representation of the employed, and an under-representation of pensioners and students and, to a smaller extent, of housewives and women on maternity leave: 87.5 of male household members of working age are working, 97.2 per cent of respondents. For women, the figures are 79.4 per cent among all household members and 90.7 among respondents. (This does not include those on maternity leave.) For data on employment status, see also chapter 7.

The differences in education, between all employed household members and employed respondents, are small. There is, however, a marked difference relative to the Russian workforce. This could be because Taganrog differs from the average or because the sample is not typical of Taganrog. Table A4.3 shows that the proportion of men and women claiming to have higher education in the sample is considerably larger than census data for Taganrog, even though they are larger in Taganrog than in Russia as a whole. Similarly, the share with only primary education is smaller in Taganrog than in Russia generally, but much smaller still in the sample. The low proportions of men with general or incomplete secondary education in the sample, compared to the RSFSR, deviate less from the census data for Taganrog, and those with incomplete higher or specialised secondary, very little.

Table A4.1 Age distribution in percentages of adult (aged 20+) men and women among all household members (All), among respondents (Resp.), in Taganrog and in the Russian urban population

Agegroup	Men (Resp.)	Men (All)	Men Taganr.	Men RSFSR	Women (Resp.)	Women (All)	Women Taganr.	Women RSFSR
20–29 years	14.7	21.9	22.4	24.7	17.1	18.5	18.2	20.0
30–39 years	24.3	22.5	23.1	27.3	30.0	23.3	19.9	23.0
40–49 years	29.0	24.4	18.2	17.0	22.9	21.0	16.2	15.1
50–59 years	18.1	16.8	18.2	16.8	14.7	16.3	16.9	16.8
60–69 years	8.0	9.0	10.9	9.5	10.2	11.4	14.7	13.6
70–79 years	4.2	4.1	5.5	3.7	4.7	7.2	10.1	8.1
80 upwards	1.6	1.2	1.7	1.0	0.4	2.3	4.1	3.3
N	448	1217			735	1478		

Sources: For RSFSR, *Demograficheskii Ezhegodnik SSSR* (1990, p. 31) for Taganrog, unpublished regional census data.

Table A4.2 Education of employed men and women among all household members (All), among respondents (Resp.) and according to census data for Taganrog and the RSFSR (%)

	1 Men (All)	2 Men (Resp.)	3 Men (Taganrog)	4 Men RSFSR	5 Women (Resp.)	6 Women (All)	7 Women (Taganrog)	8 Women RSFSR
1. Higher education	25.8	29.5	17.2	13.8	25.2	25.9	16.4	15.4
2. Incomplete higher or specialised secondary	35.4	32.6	32.4	20.5	33.4	33.3	35.7	31.1
3. General secondary	24.4	22.1	29.7	36.6	29.5	28.6	27.9	30.5
of which with PTU	*8.7*	*6.6*	*n.a.*	*15.1*	*4.1*	*4.4*	*n.a.*	*10.3*
4. Incomplete secondary	12.6	14.8	15.1	20.8	9.6	9.6	14.5	15.9
of which with PTU[a]	*5.2*	*6.6*	*n.a.*	*7.0*	*1.3*	*0.9*	*n.a.*	*2.7*
5. Primary[b]	1.4	1.1	5.2	7.3	2.0	2.2	4.7	6.1
N	998	380			974	541		

[a] The coding of the sample did not distinguish between PTU with incomplete secondary and PTU with primary education. Therefore, both are included in this row, for the RSFSR. Since less than 1 per cent of the RSFSR workforce had PTU with primary education, the oversimplification is small.

[b] The columns do not add up to 100 per cent. The residual consists partly of those with less than primary school, partly of rounding error. Since I could not separate these two in the census figures, I have followed Soviet usage, omitting those (very few) with less than four years schooling.

Source: For RSFSR, 1989 census vol. X, table 3. In the sample, those reporting a wage for the previous month are included.

Table A4.3 Wages from the state sector and total labour income (including income from co-operatives and self-employment) of the sample of all household members and of respondents (roubles/month, after tax)

1. Average wages	Total	Men	Women	Male pensioners	Female pensioners
All	195	235	155	158	107
Resp.	191	232	152	164	107
2. Average labour income	**Total**	**Men**	**Women**	**Male pensioners**	**Female pensioners**
All	202	246	159	160	106
Resp.	203	261	163	169	112

5
The Wages of Soviet Women and Men

5.1 The raw materials of analysis – sample and variables

5.1.1 Sample selection

In the first part of this section the sub-sample available for wage estimations is presented. Since the wage and wage rate variables are the foundation for the subsequent analysis and conclusions, some problems with their measurement are stated in section 5.1.2 (and treated in more detail in the appendix). Section 5.1.3 describes the explanatory variables used. Section 5.1 is important for assessing the validity of the study. It is possible, however, for the reader to proceed directly to section 5.2 with the help of the list of variables in Table A5.1.

In section 5.2, two models for hourly wage rates are introduced and in section 5.3 these are compared with estimates for monthly wages. This leads to interesting conclusions about the gender dimension of Soviet working hours legislation. Analysis of education parameters is largely deferred to chapter 6. In section 5.4, decomposition of the gender wage differential is analysed, drawing on the theories and methods outlined in chapter 2. Sections 5.5 and 5.6 represent attempts to generalise beyond Taganrog. In section 5.5 a wage function estimated from Taganrog data is applied to all-union workforce characteristics and in section 5.6 the importance of sectoral priorities for the Soviet gender wage gap is discussed from empirical and theoretical perspectives.

The data are always those of the sub-project '*Obraz zhizni*' of Taganrog-III, but in the appendix data from another sub-project is used to test the validity of the wage variable derived from the '*Obraz zhizni*' data. The relevance of the Taganrog data for the USSR in general was discussed in chapter 4.

The full set of all working household members in the whole sample would have been a good random sample of the employed population of

Taganrog. Yet, as explained in chapter 4, in each household one member ('the respondent') was chosen, in a non-randomised way, for an extensive interview, while only a little information was obtained about 'other household members'. Therefore, the estimates were made from only these main respondents. Respondents differ from other household members in certain respects: 59 per cent are of women, which is much higher than the 50 per cent of women among those presently working in the random sample of all household members. An over-representation of women in the sub-sample used for estimates is not a problem in itself, since we will estimate wage equations for men and women separately, but reflects the non-randomness of the sub-sample. There may be a selectivity bias in other respects too.

To check for bias in the selection of respondents, one regression model, using only those variables that were available for all household members, was run on the entire sample and on the subset of respondents. The results, for male and female wages, are shown in Table A5.3 and do not indicate any grave selectivity bias. Only two parameters for individual variables differed significantly at the 5 per cent level,[1] and few did even at the 20 per cent level.[2] A so-called Chow-test applied separately to the 'male' and 'female' equations did not lead to rejection of the hypothesis of equality of the full set of parameters for respondents and other household members, at the 5 per cent level, for either men or women.[3] The selection of 'main respondents' cannot be shown to distort wage estimates.

To conclude, the set of respondents is not an ideal sample of Soviet citizens, and average values of variables in the sample differ from the national. Yet, results from multivariate analysis are more reliable than crude averages since important factors, which differentiate the sample from the Soviet average, have been controlled for. The estimates depend on the impact that characteristics have on wages, not on the proportions of people who have these characteristics.

The data set included 935 respondents, working in the state sector during the month preceding the survey. Of these, 890 (367 men and 523 women) had answered all the questions necessary to include them in the estimates. This 5 per cent partial non-response rate is not high.

If those people who participate in paid work systematically differ in their earning capacity from those who do not, wage equations may be biased (Heckman, 1979). In our case this was less of a problem than in Western studies of female wages, since such a large percentage are working. Even for the mothers of pre-school children, the pattern of return to work after having a baby is fairly uniform, as shown in section 4.7.3. I have therefore not made any attempt at a (Heckman-) correction of such potential selectivity.

5.1.2 What are the 'wages'?

The dependent variables used in the wage equations to be estimated were alternately the net-of-tax wage from the state sector, reported by the respondent for the previous month, ('wage') and an hourly wage rate ('w') imputed from it, and the natural logarithms of these ('lwage' and 'lw'). In the econometric analysis, semi-logarithmic equations were preferred to linear,[4] for the pragmatic reason that the residuals from them were much closer to a normal distribution. In the sample of all working household members, the average net-of-tax wage for women was 155 roubles per month and for men 235 roubles. The female/male ratio is thus 66 per cent.[5]

The hourly wage rates were calculated from the wage of the preceding month and answers to the question 'how many hours do you usually work each week?' (see section A5.1.2). For respondents whose main job was in the state sector, normal hours in primary job, overtime in primary job and second job in the state sector were added to an 'hours of work' variable 'h', after consistency and plausibility checks.

It is not easy to estimate one's 'usual' hours, in particular one's 'usual overtime'. Under Soviet conditions, the irregularity of workloads must have made estimation even more difficult. As mentioned above (p. 96) many respondents consider working hours well in excess of the legal maximum (41 hours) as part of their normal work week, not as overtime. (See p. 63.)

I compared the imputed working week measure 'h' with answers to time-use questions. How this was done, and how these time-use data underestimate actual working hours by ignoring absence from work, was explained above (p. 108). On the other hand, answers concerning 'usual' working hours would also be likely to disregard absence, thus making the two measures correspond relatively well to each other, although the time-use estimate could still be expected to be somewhat higher. Table 5.1 shows that the difference between the averages is small and has the expected sign.

There is, inevitably, an error involved in combining 'usual' hours of work with wages for a particular month when hours may have differed from the 'usual'. This would be avoided by analysing models for monthly wages only. It can be argued that this is the appropriate variable anyway because monthly wages are the pay unit in terms of which wage-earners as well as wage-setters were thinking. The hourly rate, however, is more standard in Western studies and therefore more useful for comparisons.

Table 5.1 Comparison of average working hours reported as 'normal' hours and calculated from time-use data* (standard deviations in brackets)

Regular hours	Men	Women	Total hours***	Men	Women
Time-use**	41.26	39.98	Time-use	42.29	40.35
	(5.74)	(5.86)		(6.91)	(6.07)
'Usual time'	42.67	40.83	'Usual time'	43.50	40.99
	(4.42)	(5.41)		(5.75)	(5.44)
Coefficient of correlation (Pearson)	0.39	0.46	Coefficient of correlation (Pearson)	0.50	0.44
N	343	472			

* For those working in the state sector and not on 24-hour shifts.
** Calculated as five times working hours the previous day of work plus twice hours worked the previous non-working day except for those on 24-hour shifts.
*** 'Usual' hours per week in primary job (regular + overtime) and in secondary job.

Analysis of both monthly and hourly wages indicates how much of the gender difference in pay can be attributed to difference in hours worked. Therefore, estimates are reported here for both. The average hourly wage rate for women was 97 kopecks and for men 1 rouble, 32 kopecks. Hence, the female/male ratio was 73 per cent.[6]

This data set was not originally designed for a study of wages and there are a number of measurement problems. Respondents may not remember how much they have received or report it in 'round figures'. (Nearly 80 per cent report after-tax wages of even tens of roubles.) Further, the only instruction given to interviewers was that they should report the wage received 'in the hand'. It is therefore possible that sickness benefits (paid through the enterprise together with wages) were included. This is not bad in itself since it brings us closer to a 'usual' monthly wage to match the 'usual' hours of work per week (which respondents are not likely to have reduced by an average amount of sick leave). The problem is that some may have included benefits and some not.

The potentially most serious measurement error, however, concerns bonuses. According to the survey design, bonuses paid the preceding month should be included. This is quite acceptable for monthly bonuses, which were part of monthly income and had only a limited, random variation from month to month. Quarterly and yearly bonuses are a different matter. If quarterly or yearly bonuses are counted as part of the month's wage for some respondents the precision of estimates and the explanatory power of the model are reduced. Worse, if these bonuses are unevenly distributed in the sense that their incidence and size are correlated with explanatory variables in the models, the parameters in the wage model will be biased.

It is not at all certain whether respondents did include these bonuses in the reported wage, even if they received them during that month.[7] Yet, if they did, the error in estimates could be large. Therefore, the effect was investigated, using another sub-sample of Taganrog III in which the most recent monthly, yearly and quarterly bonuses were reported separately from the wage, excluding bonuses. Section A5.1.3 includes an account of how the probability of receiving a bonus was analysed, as well as the effect an erroneous inclusion of it in the wage measure would have on estimated wage models. The results were reassuring. In the 'worst' case – if all respondents receiving bonuses included them in the reported wage – the parameters for sectors may be downward biased by 3–12 percentage points, relative to heavy industry, but other coefficients are more or less unaffected.

5.1.3 Explanatory variables

The means of independent variables are reported in Table A5.1, for men and women separately. They can be grouped in seven categories. Age and experience variables include age, *stazh* (years of work-record, as defined by Soviet legislation), seniority (years in the enterprise), their squares and agecube. The average age of the men is two years more than that of the women, reflecting the higher pension age for men. The proportion of pensioners among the women is 7.1 per cent, among the men 7.6 per cent.

According to Soviet regulations, age, years of work experience or seniority in themselves were not wage-setting criteria. Yet, there were mechanisms through which seniority and experience could affect wages. (See chapter 3.)

The average work-record (*stazh*) is 23 years for men, 19 for women. This measure of work experience is not perfect since it may include periods of adult education, maternity leave or military service.[8] In neoclassical models, an increase of wages with seniority is interpreted as increased productivity. With labour shortage, however, managers and planners, are likely to reward 'stayers', as an incentive for reduced labour turnover. Years spent in the enterprise can also allow the employee to establish good relations with foremen or management, which give an advantage in promotions, job reclassification or norm-setting. (The same point has been made in a Western context in institutionalist analysis such as England, 1982, p. 360. In the USSR, with a much weaker link between productivity and enterprise performance, the argument is reinforced.)

Average seniority for women is 11 years, for men 13 years. The difference is very small in the younger cohorts.

Clayton and Millar (1991) emphasise that low turnover rates made it attractive to employ women in the USSR. Their only empirical evidence is a study according to which a larger percentage of women employees had been in the firm for at least two years. In the Taganrog data, however, the same percentages of men and women have been at least two and at least five years in their present firm. Kirsch (1972) quotes a study of 11,000 Leningrad workers, which found higher than average turnover rates among women, low-paid workers and workers in 'general professions'

The models control for pensioner status, party (or Komsomol) membership, marital status, a measure of hours of housework ('house'), number of children born to the respondent and the number of children aged 0–6 ('presch') or 7–16 ('school') in the household, whether they are the respondent's own children or not.

The variable 'pens' for 'pensioner' is used alongside age. It could reflect selectivity – people with interesting or well-paid jobs may be more likely to want to continue to work or, conversely, the low-paid may need to continue working because their pensions are too small. It is also possible that pensioners did not take or get the same jobs as non-pensioners with similar characteristics.

'Party' indicates membership of the Communist Party or its youth organisation. The holders of certain jobs were expected to be party members. Twenty per cent of women and 32 per cent of the men in our sample were CPSU/Komsomol members – but two thirds of those in the two highest job categories. The working class, particularly women workers, were the people least likely to be party members.

Section 4.7.4 explains how the variable 'house' was constructed from time-use questions, by weighting time spent on housework in the previous working day and non-working day, respectively. It includes time spent shopping, acquiring household services (laundry, repairs, etc.), cleaning, shopping, cooking, taking care of the children, sewing or mending, and repair and maintenance work.

For those whose usual working hours were less than 40, variables describing different work regimes were introduced. As explained in section 4.5.4, of those respondents who indicated that they worked 'not a full working week', few worked 'part-time' in the sense of 'less than the normal hours in the job'. First, there were jobs for which a reduced working week was legislated. Second, there were jobs for which it was very difficult to recruit staff at the low official wage rates. As with other illegal practices, there is no 'hard' proof, only anecdotal evidence that employees could be officially employed full-time, and paid full-time, but work much less. Typical examples are typists, secretaries, cleaners and caretakers. To model this, new variables were created: official part-time ('offpart') for those working a part of the normal time for the job (*na nepolnuiu stavku*); unofficial part-time ('unoff') for those who are hired for a full week but, in reality work much less; and shortened working week ('short') for those in jobs where full-time means less than 41 hours.[9] Some models of monthly wages also included the work-time variable 'h', defined above.[10]

Finally, 'short' was made continuous and divided into two. The variables 'reduc' and 'reduc-ed' measure the number of hours by which a reduced working week falls short of 41 – 'reduc-ed' for those working in public education and 'reduc' for others. The average weekly working hours for those with reduced working weeks (including overtime and second jobs in the state sector) were 30 hours in the education sector. Outside the school system it was 36 hours for men and 32 hours for women.

Schooling was measured by dummy variables for education levels:

1. Higher education acquired in full-time study (Highed1) or from evening or correspondence courses (Highed2).
2. Incomplete higher education (this means having a full secondary education plus the greater part of a higher education programme) (Inchigh).
3. Specialised secondary education (Specsec).
4. General secondary education (Gensec).
5. Vocational school with (PTU1) or without (PTU2) full secondary education.
6. Eight years or less of school (Less8).

Among working respondents, almost as many females as males have university education, but more female than male respondents have general secondary school, and men are more likely to have been to PTU. General secondary education was often followed by low-paid white-collar work, while certain vocational school courses could lead to relatively well-paid work.

The coding made by the Russian researchers distinguished six job types ('qualification levels'). The first (qual1) included manual workers in skill grades I–III and junior service staff (MOP) and the second (qual2) skilled workers with predominantly manual labour. (For industrial workers this includes skill grades IV–VI.) Qual3 implied 'highly skilled work with elements of physical labour' (for examples, see Table A5.1). In principle, these three correspond to blue-collar workers ('*rabochie*' including MOP) in the official statistics. (see p. 60). Qual4 is very broad. It ranges from clerical workers to professionals, from typists and nursery teachers (*vospitateli*) to physicians and engineers. Qual5 consists of managerial staff, including hospital consultants, chief engineers, etc. Qual6 is also made up of higher-level employees, in jobs described as 'linked with the creative process' (university teachers, researchers, artists). Qual1 was used as the reference group in estimations.

The proportion doing unskilled manual work is twice as high among female respondents as among male. The proportion doing skilled blue-collar work is twice as high among men as among women. Women are much more likely to do non-managerial[11] white-collar work than men (see Figure 4.3). The two highest levels include few observations, but the proportion of men holding such jobs is almost one and a half times that of women. The difference is greatest among managerial staff.

There were dummy variables for each of the main sectors of the economy. Because of the small number of observations, I have included the food industry in 'light industry'. I have followed the Soviet statistical practice of including schools in 'education', but institutions of higher education in 'science'.

Sector differentials in pay, holding personal characteristics such as education constant, reflect Soviet priorities and serve as a mechanism for gender differentiation. In this sample, several sector parameters are estimated from a very small number of observations and therefore have low precision.[12] Given the untypical gender and sector composition of the sample, it is nevertheless important to control for sector of employment.

The Taganrog survey included questions about ten different types of unpleasant or harmful working environment. Dummy variables were included for these, to control for compensating wage differentials and because hazardous or arduous conditions of work were a determinant of Soviet wage tariffs.

Since respondents classify their working environment and working conditions themselves classification is to some extent subjective. Perceptions of what are 'abnormally' heavy, dirty, stressful jobs are socially conditioned, influenced by what is publicly recognised. Monotonous work and repetitive movements did not qualify for additional pay in the USSR, nor were they included in the questionnaire.

5.2 Wage functions for hourly wage rates

5.2.1 Model A for hourly wage rates

Model A was estimated separately for men and women. Chow-tests showed that the 'male' and 'female' equations were significantly different, even at the 1 per cent level, for both monthly and hourly wages. When Model A of hourly wages was estimated for both sexes jointly, adding the variable 'sex' increased the adjusted R^2 by 0.07. The coefficient –0.29 (with a t-value of –10.5) indicates a 25 per cent negative wage effect of being a woman.[13] For monthly wages, the wage effect of being a woman was –27 per cent (with a t-value of –13) and including the sex variable increased the adjusted R^2 by 0.1.

The model contains a large number of variables. Some were suggested by socio-economic or institutional facts, some have been debated in the Soviet Studies literature and some have been shown to be important for the gender gap in wages in other countries. A detailed model was also desirable for the decomposition in section 5.4, since it decreases the inevitable 'unmeasured characteristics', which could be held to increase unduly the 'discrimination component' of the gender wage differential. The drawback, besides long, ugly tables, is that with a sample as small as this and such a large number of variables, many of them correlated with each other, many coefficients are not significantly different from zero. In addition, several dummies for sectors and education and qualification levels have few non-zero observations. The adjusted R^2 is 32 per cent for men and 49 per cent for women; this is reasonably high for a cross-section sample.

In some cases, models where several related variables were replaced by one joint dummy variable resulted in estimates with greater precision. This will be pointed out, since it indicates that a non-significant estimate is likely to represent more than just 'noise'. In chapter 6, some smaller models will be estimated, but here the object is to include as full a range of variables as possible.

The wage–age profile has a much more pronounced downward turn in the higher age-brackets than the smooth quadratic form predicted by neoclassical theory and usually found in Western studies. Two different ways of modelling this were tried: to include the cube of age to get a more flexible functional form and to include a dummy variable (pens) for being above standard pension age, or receiving a pension. Agecube was significant when pens was not included; but insignificant when it was. Therefore, I concluded that a discrete drop at pension age was the most accurate model. Nevertheless, agecube was retained in the model to illustrate this. The estimates show that for a 25-year-old man the rate of wage increase as a function of age was 1.2 per cent per year and for a 50-year-old it was –0.65 per cent. For women the corresponding figures are 0.56 per cent and –0.74 per cent.[14]

The parameters for experience and seniority are positive, and those of their squares negative, as is usual. The derivatives range from about 0.5 to

Table 5.2 Model A: hourly wages of men and women

	Definition	Men		Women	
		Param. estimate	t-value	Param. estimate	t-value
INTERC	Intercept	-0.606	-0.94	-0.039	-0.06
	Age and experience				
AGE	Age	0.037	0.79	-0.046	-0.99
AGESQ	Age squared	-0.001	-1.05	0.001	1.29
AGECUB	Age cubed	0.000	1.10	0.000¤	-1.66
STAZH	Work-record	0.017	1.31	0.008	0.85
STAZHSQ	*Stazh* squared	0.000	-0.80	0.000	-0.16
SENIOR	Years in enterprise	0.015*	2.33	0.017**	3.02
SENSQ	Senior squared	0.000¤	-1.79	0.000*	-2.30
	Institutional				
PENS	Pensioner	-0.322**	-3.97	-0.273**	-3.57
PARTY	Party member	0.052	1.33		0.027
0.72					
	Family				
MTS	Married	0.079	1.49	0.033	1.06
SCHOOL	Children 7–16 yrs in household	-0.029	-0.81	0.042	1.47
PRESCH	Children 0–6 yrs in household	-0.041	-0.87	0.005	0.14
CHILD	No. of own children	-0.003	-0.10	-0.013	-0.51
HOUSE	Hrs of housework/week	0.001	0.79	-0.001	-0.80
	Short working weeks				
OFFPART	Part-time	0.544*	2.53	0.350**	4.66
UNOFF	'Unofficial' part-time			1.218**	10.13
REDUC	Statutory reduction in working hours	0.055**	7.46	0.030**	6.10
REDUCED	As REDUC, for teachers	0.027*	2.58	0.039**	8.98

Table 5.2 (continued)

	Definition	Men Param. estimate	Men t-value estimate	Women Param.	Women t-value
	Job type				
QUAL1	Unskilled manual	0	–	0	–
QUAL2	Skilled manual	0.118□	1.85	0.134**	2.85
QUAL3	Skilled partly manual	0.089	1.22	0.092□	1.84
QUAL4	White-collar	0.026	0.33	0.043	0.91
QUAL5	Managerial	0.318*	2.41	0.301**	2.62
QUAL6	Highly qual., 'creative'	0.220	1.24	0.442**	2.93
	Education				
HIGHED1	Full-time higher ed.	0.216*	2.53	0.280**	4.40
HIGHED2	Part-time higher ed.	-0.029	-0.28	0.264**	3.22
INCHIGH	Incomplete higher ed.	0.064	0.62	0.241**	2.57
SPECSEC	Specialised secondary	0.058	0.85	0.108*	1.98
GENSEC	General secondary ed.	0.060	0.86	0.064	1.23
LESS8	Incompl. secondary or less	0	–	0	–
PTU1	PTU + secondary ed.	0.115	1.34	0.206**	2.59
PTU2	PTU but not secondary	0.133	1.56	-0.055	-0.34
	Sector				
HEAVY	Heavy industry	0	–	0	–
TRANSP	Transport	-0.063	-1.03	-0.086	-1.24
CONSTR	Construction	-0.073	-1.10	-0.072	-1.09
LIGHT	Light and food industry	-0.013	-0.17	0.012	0.21
SERVICE	Consumer services	-0.219**	-2.89	-0.005	-0.10
TRADE	Trade and catering	-0.416**	-3.07	-0.354**	-6.35
TEACH	Education (not university)	-0.069	-0.75	-0.107*	-1.97

Table 5.2 (continued)

	Definition	Men		Women	
		Param. estimate	t-value estimate	Param.	t-value
HEALTH	Health-care	−0.141	−1.19	−0.151*	−2.51
ART	Art and culture	−0.123	−0.85	−0.219*	−2.00
SCIENCE	Science	−0.086	−1.10	−0.226**	−3.27
ADMIN	Administrative bodies	−0.237	−1.08	−0.043	−0.42
OTHER	Other sectors	−0.122	−1.64	0.106	1.50
	Conditions of work				
HEAT	Heat	0.163*	2.53	0.180*	2.00
HAZARD	Hazardous work	0.027	0.52	0.105α	1.76
DUST	Dust, fumes, gas	0.001	0.01	−0.008	−0.12
HARDTE	Hard tempo	0.031	0.49	0.091α	1.73
HEAVY	Heavy work	0.019	0.34	0.145*	2.52
DIRT	Dirt	0.017	0.36	−0.041*	−0.79
NOISE	Noise	−0.013	−0.25	0.029	0.47
TEMPCH	Abrupt changes of temperature	0.007	0.12	−0.064	−1.31
NERVOUS	Nervous strain	−0.129**	−3.30	−0.092**	−2.59
NOSPACE	Lack of space or light	−0.091	−1.27	−0.020	−0.34
N		367		523	
Adj. R2		0.32		0.49	

α Significant at 10% level   * Significant at 5% level   ** Significant at 1% level

2 per cent per year, but the parameters for seniority have greater precision. This agrees with the hypothesis that Soviet managers used wage increases to discourage labour turnover. Rewards for general work experience are higher for men, while there is very little gender difference in the parameters for seniority. In a model where separate *stazh* parameters were allowed for manual and non-manual staff, the coefficient was about twice as high for white-collar employees as for blue-collar, for both men and women. Obviously, age, *stazh* and seniority are correlated[15] and swallow each other. Any one of the three is significant when the other two are omitted from the model.

The variable 'pens' has large negative parameters and high precision, despite the inclusion of age, aged squared and even agecube, in the regressions. In Model A, it corresponds to a loss of 28 per cent in wages for men and 24 per cent for women. This could indicate that the minority who continue working after retirement age are those who were earning least to begin with. However, it could also imply that many pensioners are either offered only low-paying jobs relative to their qualifications or seek easier, but lower paid occupations.

Taking age minus seniority and age minus time in present job, respectively, I found that quite a large proportion of working pensioners had changed jobs or firm at around the standard year of retirement. Turnover was not nearly as high at any other age.

Average monthly wages are lower among male and female pensioners who have changed jobs at, or after, retirement age than among those who retain the same job. In order to control for other factors, I replaced 'pens' by two other dummies in the regression. One represented pensioners who had changed jobs at or after retirement age and the other pensioners who were still in the job they had before retirement age.[16] For women, being a 'pensioner who had changed job' still implies a significantly greater pay disadvantage, while for men the opposite is true. Changing to a lower-paid job is probably one cause of low pensioner wage rates, but not the only one.

Neither marital status, number of children nor housework is significant for either male or female wages! They remain insignificant even if introduced one at the time, with the others omitted.

The reward for full-time higher education over incomplete secondary is 32 per cent for women, 24 per cent for men. For women, part-time and incomplete higher education are almost as good as full-time, but for men in this sample they entail no wage premium. This is probably not typical – an issue we will return to in chapter 6. Neither general nor specialised secondary education brings a significant wage advantage for men, and only specialised secondary does for women. Most coefficients for PTU have low precision – but if the two forms of PTU are combined, the parameter for women (of 17 per cent) becomes significant at the 5 per cent level and that for men (of 13 per cent) at the 10 per cent level.

This agrees with the results in Ofer and Vinokur (1981, 1992), that university education makes a bigger difference to women's earnings than to men's, whereas the reverse is true for vocational schools. As in our estimates, they too found that experience had a higher 'rate of return' for men. Swafford's (1978) estimate produces the opposite result. Whether this is attributable to chance, to region or to time is a matter for conjecture (Swafford's data are from 1963, Ofer and Vinokur's refer to the mid-1970s).

For skilled workers (qual2), the wage premium of about 13 per cent has high precision for women and is significant at the 10 per cent level for men, whereas that for qual3, with fewer observations, is lower and has less precision. Considering the sample size and the correlation between skilled manual work and PTU or secondary specialised (occasionally university) education, these results do indicate that, even controlling for gender, skilled workers earned more than unskilled.

Qual4 does not show a significant difference from qual1. Yet, when the model was re-estimated with an interaction term for qual4 and university education, the parameters for highed1, qual4 and the interaction term together add up to 28 per cent, for men and 41 per cent for women.[17] Thus, there is a wage premium for professionals, but it takes the form of an education premium. The two most qualified groups, qual5 and qual6, earn wage premia ranging from 25 per cent to 55 per cent.

When all ten working condition variables are included, only a few are significant – 'working in high temperatures' stands out for both sexes, and 'heavy work' does for women. When the separate variables for hazards, noise and fumes were replaced with a dummy for being exposed to at least one of these three, this had a parameter in the order of 19 per cent for both sexes, with probability values below 12 per cent for men and 2 per cent for women. No doubt, compensating differentials did play a role, not only in the rule books for Soviet wage-setting, but also in fact. Note, though, the negative and significant coefficient for 'nervous strain' for which the regulations did not stipulate any compensation!

5.2.2 Working weeks and Model B
Reduced working weeks in full-time positions were not supposed to result in lower monthly pay, and therefore those who have them receive higher pay per hour. The parameter estimates for 'reduc' indicate that for each

hour the normal working week is reduced, the remaining hours worked are paid at 3 per cent more for women and 6 per cent more for men. For teachers, the parameters are 3–4 per cent for both men and women.

The label 'offpart' was assigned whenever a person working less than 40 hours did not obviously fit into the other three categories. These observations are very few – two men and 18 women. Thus, the positive coefficient for 'offpart' may reflect particular skills or unusual jobs. Also, some observations, which should have been in 'unoff' or 'reduc', may have fallen into 'offpart', thus raising its coefficients. Note that if t-values are corrected for heteroskedasticity, the coefficient for offpart is no longer significant. (This is the only variable for which such a correction makes the difference between being significant and insignificant.)

The eleven individuals who, according to my judgement, work part-time 'unofficially', earn about three times as much as would be expected from their other characteristics. Nine of them are cleaners. The shortage of labour power made it necessary to pay unpopular jobs like cleaning relatively well – or allow cleaners to work fewer hours. This was not an ideological preference for egalitarianism, but an expedient to fill the vacancies.

The inclusion of these three variables complicates the interpretation of other parameters. If, say, those working in health-care tend to have reduced working weeks which increases their hourly wages, and our model includes a variable for reduced working weeks, the parameter for 'working in health-care' is too low. Therefore, a model (Model B) was estimated which excluded the part-time variables from Model A. This reduces the explanatory power of the model dramatically. (Estimates are reported in Table A5.4.) For hourly wages, R^2 is halved, for both men and women, while for monthly wages it decreases very little. For the specific purpose of describing choice of occupations (or planners' priorities), Model B gives a more accurate picture of options. The issue is not one of statistical fit, but of socio-economic interpretation.

The majority of those with reduced working time are white-collar employees, usually with higher education – not blue-collar workers doing heavy or hazardous work. Comparison of Models A and B show that, for men, the group least advantaged by reduced working hours are skilled manual workers. The parameters for education, health-care and art are higher in Model B. For women, wages in these sectors differ significantly from those in heavy industry in Model A, but not in Model B. Hence, the disadvantage of working in these sectors is partly offset by the advantage (in terms of *hourly* rates) of having the reduced hours which are common in them.

Since shorter working hours may be a reason for choosing an education or occupation or, conversely, the automatic consequence of a choice of professional role, they should be seen as part of a 'package'. It is this package which explains the negative relation between wage rates and working hours found by Ofer and Vinokur. (see p. 93). We will return, in chapter 6, to the importance of this for choice of occupation.

Few sector coefficients are significant. One reason for this is that such a large part of the sample is in the reference category heavy industry. (However, Ofer and Vinokur (1981), with a larger and more varied sample, also find very few significant sector parameters.) Since the estimates have such low precision, I will make only a few comments on them.

First, the sector that stands out is 'trade and catering'. The parameter has high precision and implies a wage disadvantage of 38 per cent for men, when compared with heavy industry, and 24 per cent for women. Opportunities for staff to compensate for the low wages in this sector were discussed above (p. 78).

Second, 'art and culture' and 'science' have large negative parameters. One in seven of the staff in these sectors are in the smallest qualification category, qual6 (highly qualified and creative work), which includes 1 per cent of all respondents. The positive parameters for qual6 outweigh the negative sector-coefficients by far.

Third, Soviet teachers had low monthly pay, yet in Model B of hourly wages 'working in education' has a significant parameter of 18 per cent for women, because of the short working week. On the other hand, hourly wages in this sector are exaggerated if teachers have not reported hours of work outside the classroom. Making the opposite extreme assumption, I set working hours for each teacher equal to 41 (in Model B). The parameter for the sector decreased and was insignificant (negative) for both men and women. The 'true' sector effect must be somewhere in between, if the 'true' input of work is somewhere between hours in class and 41 hours.

5.3   Monthly wages

The regression results for Model A, applied to monthly wages, are reported in table 5.3 and for Model B in Table A5.4. An 'hours per week' variable 'h' was added to both models. 'Offpart' was excluded, since it too reflects a difference in hours.

As can be seen, for Model A, the parameters for hourly and monthly wages are very similar, except, of course, for the working time variables. Almost identically the same parameters are significant at the 1, 5 and 10 per cent levels, respectively. My conclusion is that the elaborate

Table 5.3 Model A of monthly wages

	Definition	Men		Women	
		Parameter Estimate	t-value	Parameter Estimate	t-value
INTERC	Intercept	4.594	7.13	4.084	7.09
H	Hours of work/week	0.005	1.39	0.004□	1.87
	Age and experience				
AGE		0.028	0.62	0.027	0.66
AGESQ	Age squared	−0.001	−0.98	−0.000	−0.50
AGECUBE	Age cubed	0.000	1.06	0.000	0.21
STAZH	Work-record	0.022□	1.70	0.011	1.32
STSQ	*Stazh* squared	−0.000	−0.95	−0.000	−0.88
SENIOR	Years in enterprise	0.013*	2.05	0.016**	3.16
SENSQ	Senior squared	−0.000	−1.43	−0.000*	−2.06
	Institutional				
PENS	Pensioner	−0.360**	−4.57	−0.238**	−3.53
PARTY	Party member	0.033	0.88	0.036	1.08
	Family				
MTS	Married	0.064	1.25	0.021	0.77
SCHOOL	Children 7—16 yrs in household	−0.034	−0.99	0.014	0.56
PRESCH	Children 0–6 yrs in household	−0.048	−1.07	−0.029	−0.81
CHILDREN	No. of own children	0.015	0.52	−0.006	−0.26
HOUSE	Hrs of housework/week	0.000	0.21	−0.002	−1.45
	Short working weeks				
UNOFF	'Unofficial' part-time	–	–	0.207□	1.75
REDUC	Statutory reduction in working hours	0.035**	4.56	−0.001	−0.15
REDUC-ED	As REDUC, for teachers	−0.001	−0.13	0.014**	3.10

137

Table 5.3 (continued)

	Definition	Men		Women	
		Parameter Estimate	t-value	Parameter Estimate	t-value
	Job type				
QUAL1	Unskilled manual	0	–	0	–
QUAL2	Skilled manual	0.117◻	1.91	0.140**	3.35
QUAL3	Skilled partly manual	0.093	1.32	0.078◻	1.75
QUAL4	White-collar	0.036	0.46	0.015	0.34
QUAL5	Managerial	0.386**	3.00	0.313**	3.08
QUAL6	Highly qual., 'creative'	0.248	1.45	0.411**	3.08
	Education				
HIGHED1	Full-time higher ed.	0.219**	2.67	0.268**	4.73
HIGHED2	Part-time higher ed.	-0.002	-0.02	0.194**	2.67
INCHIGH	Incomplete higher ed.	0.048	0.48	0.217**	2.61
SPECSEC	Specialised secondary	0.072	1.09	0.093◻	1.93
GENSEC	General secondary ed.	0.059	0.87	0.027	0.58
LESS8	Incomplete secondary or less	0	0	0	0
PTU1	PTU + secondary ed.	0.105	1.27	0.156*	2.21
PTU2	PTU but not secondary	0.138◻	1.68	-0.140	-1.00
	Sector				
HEAVIND	Heavy industry	0	–	0	–
TRANSP	Transport	-0.017	-0.29	-0.047	-0.77
CONSTR	Construction	-0.089	-1.38	-0.036	-0.62
LIGHT	Light and food industry	-0.023	-0.30	0.055	1.09
SERV	Consumer services	-0.216**	-2.95	0.027	0.55
TRADE	Trade and catering	-0.421**	-3.22	-0.307**	-6.18
TEACH	Education (not university)	-0.054	-0.61	-0.062	-1.28

Table 5.3 (continued)

	Definition	Men		Women	
		Parameter Estimate	t-value	Parameter Estimate	t-value
HEALTH	Health-care	-0.117	-1.02	-0.109*	-2.04
ART	Art and culture	-0.157	-1.12	-0.336**	-3.45
SCIENCE	Science	-0.080	-1.06	-0.166**	-2.70
ADMIN	Administrative bodies	-0.076	-0.35	-0.032	-0.36
OTHER	Other sectors	-0.152*	-2.12	0.025	0.40
	Conditions of work				
HEAT	Heat	0.176**	2.83	0.159*	1.99
HAZARD	Hazardous work	0.021	0.42	0.061	1.15
DUST	Dust, fumes, gas	0.007	0.12	0.038	0.65
HARDTE	Hard tempo	0.047	0.76	0.098*	2.08
HEAVY	Heavy work	0.011	0.21	0.116*	2.29
DIRT	Dirt	-0.006	-0.13	-0.007	-0.15
NOISE	Noise	0.000	0.00	0.026	0.49
TEMP	Abrupt changes of temperature	-0.006	-0.10	-0.056	-1.29
NERVOUS	Nervous strain	-0.104**	-2.73	-0.046	-1.43
NOSPACE	Lack of space or light	-0.051	-0.73	-0.022	-0.42
Adj. R^2		**0.29**		**0.40**	
Prob < W		**0.70**		**0.17**	

□ Significant at 10 per cent level   * Significant 5 per cent level   ** Significant at 1 per cent level
W is the Shapiro-Wilks statistic.

modelling of part-time structure leaves relatively 'pure' sector, education, qualification and working conditions parameters in the function for hourly wages.

For men, the coefficient for hours per week was only about 0.5 per cent and was not significant, even at the 10 per cent level. Reduction in the work schedule for teachers does not significantly affect monthly wages. Jobs other than teaching, with shorter than normal hours, have a significant wage advantage of 4 per cent. Returns to managerial jobs are larger in terms of monthly wages, and pay in the transport sector somewhat higher. Otherwise, the differences between the equations are minimal.[18]

For women, the time variable is significant at 10 per cent, even though its parameter is smaller than that for men. (It was insignificant in all models estimated that did not include the part-time variables.) 'Reduc' is close to zero, as expected, but 'reduc-ed' is positive and significant, although less than for hourly wages. This might pick up that teachers at higher levels of education have fewer teaching hours as well as higher pay. It is more surprising that 'unoff' has a near-significant (positive) parameter. It is 23 per cent – far less, of course, than for hourly wages. Yet, though wages for cleaning jobs were low, they were not low for a woman with low education, doing unskilled work.

Rewards for all types of education above elementary are of a similar order for monthly and for hourly wages. Health and education come out worse for monthly wages compared with hourly wages in Model B.

5.4 Results from the decomposition

Men and women differ in terms of personal characteristics that are correlated with the size of the wage (wage rate), but the estimates also show that men and women do not have the same wage functions. Section 2.6.2.1 described how differences between the average wages of groups can be decomposed to distinguish between these two phenomena.

Such decompositions of the gender difference in lw and lwage were performed with Models A and B. They are summarised in Tables 5.4 and 5.5. (For a full decomposition of the endowment term for Model A of hourly and monthly wages, see Katz (1994, pp. 256–7). If either the male or the female wage function is used as a weight, Model A can account for only 27 per cent of the gender difference between the logarithms of monthly wages and less than 16 per cent for hourly rates. The discrimination index, D_f, as defined in p. 252, n. 31, is 31 per cent for hourly wages and 36 per cent for monthly wages. This is a strong

Table 5.4   Decomposition of the gender wage gap according to Model A (per cent)

Weights[1]	For hourly wages			For monthly wages		
	Male	Female	Pooled	Male	Female	Pooled
Hours/week				3.3	3.1	5.3
'Family' variables	0.5	3.7	15.3	2.4	5.0	14.9
Pensioner	0.8	0.7	0.8	0.7	0.4	0.6
Short week variables	−14.7	−20.9	−20.0	−1.8	−3.1	−3.8
Party	2.0	1.0	3.1	1.0	1.1	2.5
Age	−4.6	−1.4	−3.2	−5.2	−2.4	−3.1
Experience	9.1	8.1	13.4	9.9	4.3	9.4
Job types	8.4	8.6	14.1	6.2	8.1	11.8
Education	2.7	1.8	6.0	2.2	0.4	4.6
Sectors	9.1	8.0	11.8	6.5	4.6	8.2
Working conditions	2.2	6.5	6.4	1.8	5.9	5.7
Total due to endowments	15.4	15.9	47.7	26.8	27.4	56.2
Due to wage function	84.6	84.1	52.3	73.2	72.6	43.9

[1] See section 2.6.2.1. The 'male' and 'female' weights are the coefficients found in estimates with only male and female respondents, respectively, and the 'pooled' those estimated on the sample of both men and women.

Table 5.5   Decomposition of the gender wage gap according to Model B (per cent)

Weights	For hourly wages			For monthly wages		
	Male	Female	Pooled	Male	Female	Pooled
Hours/week				−0.1	0.6	2.2
'Family' variables	−2.6	−15.1	5.0	1.0	3.4	14.5
Pensioner	0.7	0.8	0.8	0.7	0.5	0.6
Short week variables						
Party	1.9	1.9	3.7	1.1	1.4	2.6
Age	−5.1	2.5	−0.5	−6.2	−2.2	−3.1
Experience	9.9	2.4	8.2	12.1	3.5	9.6
Job types	4.0	5.9	11.1	4.7	7.9	11.7
Education	2.3	10.2	7.1	2.1	1.1	4.6
Sectors	7.4	0.8	6.2	6.9	3.5	6.8
Work conditions	2.2	8.6	7.7	1.7	6.4	6.1
Total due to endowments	20.7	18.2	49.3	24.0	26.1	55.6
Due to wage function	79.3	81.8	50.7	76.0	73.9	44.4

indication of discrimination. As should be clear from chapters 3 and 4, many of the segregating and subordinating mechanisms described in chapter 2 apply also to the USSR. Much of the 'explained'[19] part of the wage gap must be due to discrimination and patriarchal structures, both at work and in the household, and to those differences between men and women which are – to paraphrase Adam Smith – 'not so much the cause as the effect of the division of labour'.

In Ofer and Vinokur's (1992) study on émigré data, the unexplained part of the differences in log (monthly wage) was smaller than in this study, 51 per cent using the male equation and 61 per cent using the female. However, separate estimates, made by them for groups with different levels of education and by me for manual and non-manual workers, indicate that the more homogeneous the group, the more of the gender gap is accounted for by endowments. Further, among such sub-groups, the unexplained part is smaller, the higher the education and smaller for white-collar than for blue-collar workers. For both these reasons, the over-representation of white-collar workers and people with higher education in the émigré sample could account for some of the difference in results.

Another way of using the decomposition is to ask how big the difference between men's and women's wages would be if they and their jobs had the same characteristics, but the respective wage functions remained the same, irrespective of whether the average characteristics of both sexes are set equal to those that men have in the sample or set equal to women's, given the estimated unequal wage functions, men's hourly wages (in this sample) would still have been 32 per cent higher than those of women and their monthly wages 36 per cent higher.[20]

Because of the differences in definitions and models, it is difficult to make a straight comparison with results from Western studies. A model fairly closely resembling that used here, and used for decomposition of the gender wage gap, is found in le Grand's (1991) Swedish study which found a corresponding difference of 8 per cent in hourly wage.

Note that, even though the parameters were not significant when taken singly, marriage, children and housework together account for 4 per cent of the monthly and hourly wage differences, when weighted by the female equation. They have much less importance, using the male equation. Having families is a career impediment only for women!

Table 5.4 shows that, given the Soviet wage structure which was in itself male-biased, differences in experience, education, qualification level, sector and working conditions account for roughly one third of the difference in hourly wages. Different forms of reduction in working hours, however, decrease the endowment term by 15–21 percentage points (depending on the weighting). Reduced working hours and 'unofficial part-time' work increased hourly wages and were more available to women than to men. It may be seen as anomalous that the indicator of discrimination is increased because women had the benefit of short working weeks. Therefore, decomposition was made using Model B, without the part-time variables. Yet, this only marginally increases the 'endowment term' except when the parameters for the pooled sample are used.

The most striking change, as can be seen in Table 5.5, is that when 'female' parameters are used for weighting, the endowment term due to 'family' variables becomes large and negative. Closer inspection reveals that the variable that accounts for this is hours of housework per week. Usually, the fact that women do more housework would be expected to add to, not detract from, the 'explained' part of the wage gap (Hersch and Stratton, 1997). In this Soviet sample, however, the amount of housework done by women is strongly correlated with having a reduced working week. Therefore, when the part-time variables are omitted, 'house' catches some of their effect and gets a significant positive coefficient in the female wage equation! (see Table A5.2).

Decomposition according to the pooled equation consistently produces 'endowment terms' 2–3 times larger than with the male or female. A variable-by- variable decomposition shows that it is variables which are strongly correlated with gender, such as the predominantly female quality of doing housework and the predominantly male characteristics of being a skilled manual worker or a party member, which appear to 'explain' more of the wage-gap, using this weighting.

This nicely illustrates the argument made in section 2.6.2.1 that the 'pooled' estimates, proposed by Neumark (1988) and Oaxaca and Ransom (1994), are biased because of existing discrimination and therefore not suitable as a 'non-discriminatory wage function'. Models A and B were estimated on the pooled sample of men and women, for both hourly and monthly wages. When a variable for sex was added, the parameter for 'qual2' dropped by a third. That for 'house' changes from significantly negative at the 1 per cent level to insignificant at the 10 per cent level, except in Model B for hourly wages where it becomes significantly positive!

How can we interpret the fact that the wage gap was decreased by shorter working weeks for (some) women? It seems that women's attempts to combine the demands of work and family by working fewer hours were encouraged by wage policies. This was apparently preferred to a change in gender roles and gender division of labour (including that in the household) which would have signified more genuine equality between the sexes.

That women work fewer hours and earn less is far from unique to the USSR. Roughly 20 per cent of women in Taganrog have reduced working weeks. There are Western countries where part-time work is more common (e.g. Britain, the Netherlands and Sweden, the last with a very high employment rate), yet this institutional set-up is specifically Soviet.

Model A showed that those who had reduced working hours earned rather more than less per month. Yet, this is by comparison with other women. A female doctor or teacher got a 'not so bad' wage for a woman, while being low-paid compared with men!

Ultimately, the Soviet arrangement reinforced tradition and inequality in the household. It also reinforced the widely held view that women were a 'second-rate' labour force and this restricted their options. Further, this division of labour was hidden behind a screen of officially proclaimed 'equal participation in the national economy', which made it hard to challenge.

Formally, the Soviet wage system was based on productivity. Yet, there appears to be a systematic undervaluation of work considered 'feminine'. Despite the broad range of factors controlled for in the analysis, we are still left with the simple answer that Soviet women were paid less because they were women.

5.5   Beyond Taganrog

The endowment terms in the decompositions use not only parameters, but also averages. This makes generalisations to the reference population of Soviet, urban workers and employees problematic.

For example, sectoral segregation may contribute less to the wage gap in the heavy industry town of Taganrog than it would have done in an all-Russian or all- Soviet sample. Of the female working respondents, 57 per cent work in industry, transport and communications or construction, as opposed to 37 per cent of the Soviet female workforce in 1989 (*Vestnik Statistiki*, 2/91).

Therefore, a model was estimated on the Taganrog sample, including only variables for which reasonably accurate average values could be imputed for the Soviet workforce. These imputations were made from data in statistical yearbooks (*Narodnoe Khoziaistvo* and *Trud v SSSR*) and the 1989 census. Details are available in Katz (1994) or on request from the author. The variables included and their means for the sample and for the USSR are listed in Table A5.6. The parameters estimated for this 'all-Union model' (reported in Katz, 1994) were multiplied by these all-Union variable averages to 'predict' average male and female wages for the USSR.

Finally, the coefficients from the 'male equation' were multiplied by the averages for women, and vice versa.

The model included seven levels of education, age, being a blue-collar worker, having a managerial or highly qualified creative job, being a worker in industry, construction or transport with bad working conditions, and the usual sector dummies (except that the light and food industries were separated). When this model is estimated for the Taganrog sample, adjusted R^2's are 14 per cent for men and 25 per cent for women. (The working condition and education coefficients have high precision in this model, and so do those for some service sectors.) For hourly wages, the adjusted R^2 is only 9 per cent for men and 18 per cent for women.

Using Soviet variable means, this model 'predicts' an average after-tax wage of 213 roubles for men and 134 roubles for women and, thus, a gender ratio of 63 per cent. Applying the wage function estimated for men in Taganrog to national average endowments for women indicates that if Soviet women had been rewarded in the same way as men, they would have earned 48 per cent more. This estimate is tentative, since the sector parameters for the socio-cultural sphere in the 'male equation' are based on such a small number of observations.[21] On the other hand, if men had been rewarded according to the wage function for women – which is more reliable in this respect – their endowments would have earned them only 138 roubles per month after tax.

The predicted average hourly wage rate for men was 1.16 roubles and that for women 0.82. Hence the ratio was 70 per cent. Women's endowments combined with the 'male' wage function produced a wage rate of 1.10 roubles, not very far from that of men. Conversely, if men were paid according to the 'female' wage function, the model predicts an average rate of 0.84 roubles.

Not too much should be made of the failure of the model to explain more than a minimal part of the gender wage gap, since it has so little success in explaining variation within gender groups. The crudity of the model and of the assumptions made to obtain 'Soviet averages' make all results in this section tentative. Yet, it does suggest that the gender inequality in the sample does not differ dramatically from that in the reference population and that it is more likely to be smaller than larger.

The gender ratio is similar to what was found in the more affluent market economies some 20–30 years ago, but less than it is today. Soviet women had achieved participation rates and educational levels almost equal to those of men far earlier than Western women. Yet, when the women's movement and gender equality gained ground in the West, the Soviet Union, with its inflexible economic structures and its repression of independent social and political movements and criticisms, remained inert.

5.6 'Productive' and 'non-productive work'

5.6.1 Chicken-and-egg *à la Russe*

We are not likely ever to solve the chicken-and-egg problem: Do women have low earnings because they have jobs with low pay, or is the pay for those jobs low because it is women who do them? Yet, we can probe some way into it. Chapter 2 discussed occupational segregation and how the gendering of jobs affects their prestige and remuneration. In the Soviet context, sector of employment is very important for earnings, because of the difference in priority accorded to different spheres of activity. Comparative worth studies indicate that 'women's work' is undervalued in Western economies, but in a market economy the mechanisms of evaluation are much less transparent. The next step in this investigation is to relate earnings to gender and to sector on a macro level, using all-Soviet data.

Such a study was made by Redor (1992), who estimated a semi-logarithmic wage equation for 19 sectors in five Western European and three Soviet-type economies. The sectors were mainly branches of manufacturing, plus mining, construction and civil engineering. The only services were wholesaling and retail trade, thus excluding the 'reproductive' sector. The models included the percentages of women and of managerial staff, measures of capital intensity, of concentration of firms and of formal education and professional training of the workforce.

The percentage of women in each sector turned out to be one of the two most important variables in all the countries, except Denmark. Redor concludes that if 'we were to consider "a Scandinavian system" as a distinct entity, we might find greater differences within the W[estern] S[ystem] than between the WS and the S[oviet] T[ype] S[ystem]'.

One thing that did differ between systems, however, was that in the Soviet-type economies, mining and certain sectors of heavy industry stood out as 'priority' sectors with high earnings. These sectors employ few women. It is obvious that there are strong correlations: low priority – low earnings; low priority – many women; and many women – low earnings. Yet, correlations do no tell us which is the reason for what.

One criterion for inter-branch differentials in Soviet basic wages was 'importance for the national economy'. No precise way of quantifying this 'importance' was specified. (cf. McAuley, 1979, p. 192). By including it in the 'quality of labour', a choice of evaluation, corresponding to the interests of a specific ruling layer, was made to appear objective and necessary. Thus, overwhelmingly male Soviet decision-makers were free to decide that both 'intensity of work' and 'importance for the economy' were greatest in sectors with a male-dominated workforce which did not produce goods or services for immediate, civilian consumption – to the detriment of women workers and of consumers of both sexes (and of many female and male workers whose health and safety were sacrificed to the crash industrialisation of the Stalin period).

Another official Soviet justification for low wages in the female-dominated sectors was the notion that some work is 'productive' and some 'unproductive'. These terms provide a neat example of how concepts were defined and justified in Soviet ideology and of the very tenuous relation between the 'Marxism' of the USSR and that of Marx. They have created some confusion, both among former Soviet and Western writers, including Western feminists. According to a recent article 'the patriarchal approach quite remarkably coincided with the principles of Marxist political economy, according to which the production of means of production is superior to the production of consumer goods, and the so-called "non-productive sphere" (health-care, education, personal services) has the lowest priority' (Ogloblin, 1999, p. 604).

'Productive' work, Soviet-style, was essentially the work that produced, moved, preserved, or sorted things – visible, tangible objects. (For a detailed definition, see *Kratkii* . . ., p. 318.) Services were not included in the Soviet equivalent of GNP. Originally, the distinction between productive and non-productive economic activity comes from the eighteenth-century physiocrats who considered only agriculture to be 'productive'. It was taken over from them, but broadened to other forms of material production by Adam Smith. Marx took the term from Smith, but changed the content profoundly. When it is introduced in *Capital* (Marx, 1976, pp. 1038–49), it explicitly refers to social relations in a capitalist society (which is what the book is intended to analyse – Marx wrote very little on what he called 'recipes for the kitchens of the future'). For Marx, a fundamental characteristic of capitalism is that the capitalist class has the power to impose its interests on society, and another that, from the perspective of the capitalist, labour is deemed to be 'productive' if, and only if, it produces surplus value for the capitalist. Marx emphasises that this has nothing to do with the concrete content of the work, its usefulness or its relation to human needs.

To exemplify, Marx chooses a teacher. A teacher can work in the public sector or in a private school where 'in addition to belabouring the heads of his pupils . . . [he] works himself into the ground to enrich the owner of the school'. Even though the teacher performs the same concrete work in both cases, he does it under different social relations. Hence, in the former it is non-productive labour and in the latter productive – from the point of view of capital accumulation (in the Marxist sense of the term) – because it gives a return to the capital that has been invested 'in a teaching factory, instead of a sausage factory' (ibid., p. 644).[22]

In the hands of Soviet theorists, this somehow became a justification for paying (female) teachers, doctors, nurses and child-care workers less than engineers, bookkeepers or workers in metallurgy or construction.

'When *I* use a word', Humpty-Dumpty said in a rather scornful tone, 'it means just what I choose it to mean ...' (Lewis Carroll, *Alice Through the Looking Glass*)

5.6.2 Soviet practice

To make estimates similar to Redor's, for the USSR, we have to know the proportion of women in different sectors of the economy. In the 1980s, this figure was published for selected sectors only. However, for each of seven types of education and of a number of sectors, the census reports how many per 1,000 employed in this sector have that level of education, as well as the numbers per 1,000 men and per 1,000 women. From this one can calculate the proportion of women in the sector, using the proportions with any one type of education.[23]

The dependent variable in the estimates was the logarithm of the average monthly wage in 1988, and the regression weights were the square roots of numbers employed in 1989.[24] Data were available for the basic sectors of the economy, except municipal, housing and consumer services. 'Industry' was replaced by ten sub-sectors, covering 92 per cent of industrial employment. All in all, the sectors included account for 93 per cent of workers and employees outside forestry and agriculture. The explanatory variables included the proportions with higher education ('HED'), with secondary specialist education ('SSED'), with vocational-technical education ('PTU') and of women ('FEM'), plus a dummy for 'material production', 'PROD'. The results from some regressions are reported in Table 5.6.[25]

When the wage was regressed on the share of women in the sector or branch alone, the adjusted R^2 was 0.77. PROD also had high precision and considerable explanatory power, although not as much as FEM or the joint set of education parameters. PTU had the largest coefficient and highest precision of the education variables, but both decrease substan-

148

Table 5.6 Estimates of models of average monthly wages in branches of the economy

	(1) Par.	Prob	(2) Par.	Prob	(3) Par.	Prob	(4) Par.	Prob	(5) Par.	Prob	(6) Par.	Prob
INTERC	5.90		5.18		3.81		5.77		4.81		3.82	
HED					1.93	0.005			1.08	0.05	1.93	0.003
SSED					0.77	0.38			0.70	0.30	1.09	0.19
PTU					6.59	0.0005			3.45	0.03	5.04	0.006
FEM	-1.01	0.0001					-0.86	0.003	-0.68	0.003		
PROD			0.36	0.0001			0.08	0.30			0.24	0.05
adj. R2	0.77		0.54		0.66		0.77		0.80		0.72	

Dependent variable = logarithm of average monthly wage 1988.
Number of branches = 21.
Regressions weighted by (the square root of) the number employed in the branch in 1989.
Sources: Average wages in 1988 from *Nar. Khoz.* (1989, pp. 76 and 373).
Number employed 1989 in branches of industry imputed from *Trud v SSSR* (1988, pp. 49–50) in other sectors from *Nar. Khoz* (1989, pp 47–9).
Education variables and estimated proportion female from 1989 census, vol. X, table 3.
HED = percentage of workforce with higher education.
SSED = percentage of workforce with secondary education.
PTU = percentage of workforce with PTU education.
FEM = percentage female in workforce
PROD = dummy for material production branch

tially when FEM is included. Part of the higher wage level of sectors with many skilled workers is due to the fact that most of them are male.

When female and PROD are combined, only FEM is significant, and the adjusted R^2 is no higher than for FEM alone. It seems that 'material production' and gender are closely connected, but if one must be chosen, 'FEM' has more explanatory power.

It is clearly impossible to explain the Soviet wage structure without taking into account a pervasive devaluation of what is identified as 'feminine' or as having qualities similar to those ascribed to women. Although the priorities that the USSR was locked into since the 1930s are not reducible to sexism, they are strongly interwoven with it. The ideological use of the concept of 'productive' work was used as a smoke screen.

> 'When I make a word do a lot of work like that,' said Humpty-Dumpty. 'I always pay it extra.' (Lewis Carroll, *Alice Through the Looking Glass*)

Appendix

A5.1   Non-response, definitions, imputations and measurement error

A5.1.1   *Partial non-response*

When individuals earning their primary income as co-operators or self-employed are excluded, 934 working respondents remain. Data on wages, age and sex were missing in one case each. In 21 cases data on one or more of education, sector of employment and job-type (qualification) were missing. Twelve respondents did not report hours of work per week. Six respondents had not answered the time-use questions necessary for the variable 'house'. One further observation was excluded because, for this person, whose occupation was coded as 'student' and who probably worked irregularly, usual hours and wage of preceding month did not 'match' at all. 890 observations could be used to estimate Model A and somewhat more for models excluding variables for which there was partial non-response.

Another 39 observations had missing values replaced by imputed ones. First, in the judgement of the researcher responsible for carrying out the survey the large number of non-answers to the question on party membership was not due to a reluctance to answer; it was much more likely that the interviewers simply did not record the 'non-answer' 'no'. The risk of miscoding a few genuinely non-responding party members seemed less grave than omitting 28 observations, so I coded non-response as non-membership. (Generally, even when the questionnaire provided the alternative 'difficult to say' – *zatrudniaius' otvetit'* – there were much more blanks than such answers. Recording non-response or distinguishing between a zero and a missing value, was apparently not usual.)

Second, a further 11 respondents did not state their '*stazh*' (work-record). Since regression of *stazh* on a number of variables produced an R^2 above 0.9 for men and 0.8 for women, the predicted values from these regressions were used to impute where there was non-response.

A5.1.2   The wage measure

Respondents were asked to report both income from and hours of work in co-operatives or self-employment separately. There could be a measurement error if people report income from private professional practice in their usual profession as 'wage' rather than as self-employment income. Twenty-six respondents answered 'yes' to the question whether they participated in private labour activity. Half of them did not report any income from it for the preceding month, at least not separately from their wage.

To impute hourly wage rates I have assumed that the yearly wage is 12 times that of the preceding month and divided that by hours of work per year. Hence $w = \dfrac{(\text{wage}*12)}{\dfrac{365*h}{7}}$ where 'h' is reported 'usual hours of work per week' (both wage and h include overtime and second jobs if these are in the state sector). Obviously, there is a discrepancy in combining the wage of a particular month with 'usual' hours. The more untypical the preceding month, the worse the error. As an absolute number, w is on the high side, since I did not take holidays into account. I have no information on the length of holidays of individual respondents. Also, w is an average rate. To calculate a strictly marginal wage rate is impossible, considering the discontinuities of 'storming' and overtime to get the premium for plan fulfilment, etc.

'h' was calculated as the sum of normal hours (excluding overtime) in primary job, usual overtime in primary place of work and extra work in the state sector (i.e. excluding self-employment and work in co-operatives). In 19 cases another value was imputed: four had stated a number of hours of overtime per week as well as a 'basic' time equal to this number plus 40. Since their wages were not particularly high I assumed that the overtime had been 'counted twice'. Fifteen individuals reported the same usual hours per week as they had worked the

Table A5.1 Definition and means of variables

Name	Definition	Male mean	Female mean
wage	Wage *from the state sector* (including overtime and second jobs) received the previous month	240.2	157.7
w	Hourly wage rate imputed from 'wage' and 'h'	1.33	0.97
lwage	Natural logarithm of 'wage'	5.42	5.01
lw	Natural logarithm of 'w'	0.21	−0.11
h	Usual hours of work per week in state sector, reported by respondent (including overtime and second jobs)	42.6	39.5
Age	Age in years	41.57	39.78
Agesq	Age squared	1845	1687
Agecube	Age raised to three	86612	75953
Stazh	Work-record (*Obshchii stazh.*)	22.64	19.10
Stazhsq	*Stazh* squared	636	459
Senior	Seniority, i.e. years at present place of employment (*Stazh na predpriiatie*)	13.11	11.28
Sensq	Seniority squared	272	196
Pens	= 1 if respondent states his/her occupation as pensioner/ working pensioner or if he/she is above normal retirement age, otherwise = 0	0.08	0.09
Party	= 1 if respondent is member of the CPSU or Komsomol, otherwise = 0	0.32	0.19
Mts	Marital status = 1 if respondent has spouse living in the household, otherwise = 0	0.86	0.72
School	Number of school-age children (7–16 yrs) *living in the household*	0.45	0.54
Presch	Number of preschool children (0–6 yrs) *living in the household*	0.23	0.23
Children	Number of children born *to respondent*	1.33	1.29
House	Hours spent on housework the preceding week, imputed from time-use data (see below for details)	19.40	32.38
Short	= 1 if the full time work-week is < 40 hours, otherwise = 0	0.08	0.15
Offpart	= 1 if the respondent says that s/he works 'not a full' working week or day, and the hours stated are below the standard, and the wage appears too low for a fulltimer in this job, otherwise = 0	0.01	0.04
Unoff	Working hours too low for full-time in the job and wage too high for part-time	0.00	0.02
Reduc	Reduction in work-time (41 minus 'h') if respondent states usual working hours below 40 and respondent is not a white-collar employee in the education sector, otherwise = 0	0.49	0.72
Reduced	Defined as 'reduce' but only for those working in the education sector as a non-managerial white-collar employees (i.e. probably teachers)	0.20	0.87
Qual1	Blue-collar worker in unskilled work (drivers in the 3rd class, cleaners, caretakers, loaders/dockers, workers in skill-grade I–III, laundry workers, postmen, sorters, ironers, nurses auxiliaries) (Reference)	0.09	0.18
Qual2	Blue-collar workers in highly skilled, predominantly physical work (drivers in class 1 and 2, workers in skill-grade IV–VI, shop assistants)	0.44	0.21

Table A5.1 (*continued*)

Name	Definition	Male mean	Female mean
Qual3	Highly skilled work with elements of physical labour (machine repairers, brigade leaders, tailors, cutters, those repairing household goods and machines, medical nurses)	0.18	0.16
Qual4	Economists of low–middle grade (bookkeepers. enterprise planners), teachers, doctors, engineers, technicians, laboratory staff, nursery teachers	0.26	0.42
Qual5	Heads of enterprises and institutions and their deputies, head specialists, (medical consultant, chief engineer, etc.)	0.03	0.01
Qual6	Researchers in scientific institutions, teachers in higher education, workers in cultural or artistic institutions linked with the creative process	0.01	0.01
Highqual	Highly qualified non-manual work. Equals qual5+qual6	0.04	0.03
Physqual	Skilled physical/partly physical work. Equals qual2+qual3	0.61	0.37
Highed1	Higher education, accquired in full-time programme	0.24	0.22
Highed2	Higher education from night or correspondence courses	0.06	0.04
Highed	Higher education (sum of highed1 and highed2)	0.30	0.26
Inchigh	Incomplete higher education	0.03	0.03
Parthigh	Highed2+Inchigh	0.09	0.07
Specsec	Specialised secondary education	0.29	0.30
Gensec	General secondary education	0.16	0.24
PTU1	PTU with secondary education	0.07	0.04
PTU2	PTU without secondary education	0.07	0.01
Incsec	Incomplete secondary education. (Ref. in Models C–L)	0.08	0.09
Lowed	Less than incomplete secondary (i.e. < 8 years of school)	0.01	0.03
Less8	8 years or less of school (Incsec+Lowed. Ref. in Models A–B).	0.09	0.11
High4	Interaction (product) of qual4 and full-time higher education (highed1)	0.15	0.19
Mid4	Interaction of qual4 and part-time or incomplete higher education (highed2+inchigh)	0.05	0.05
Sec4	Interaction of qual4 and general or specialised secondary school (Specsec+gensec).	0.06	0.18
Edyrs	Imputed years of schooling (according to level)	11.93	11.70
Heavind	Heavy industry (Reference)	0.54	0.43
Transp	Transport and communications	0.08	0.04
Constr	Construction	0.06	0.04
Light	Light industry (including food)	0.04	0.07
Service	Services in utilities, consumption and housing	0.05	0.06
Trade	Trade and catering	0.02	0.07
Teach	Schools (not institutes of higher education)	0.05	0.12
Health	Health-care and physical education	0.02	0.06
Art	Art and culture	0.01	0.01
Science	Research institutes and higher education	0.06	0.04
Admin	Economic administration, government and social organisations	0.01	0.02
Other	Other branch	0.06	0.04
Heat	Hot workplace	0.08	0.02
Hazard	Hazardous work	0.14	0.07
Dust	Dust, fumes, gas	0.15	0.07
Hardtemp	Hard work tempo	0.09	0.07

Table A5.1 (*continued*)

Name	Definition	Male mean	Female mean
Heavy	Physically heavy work	0.15	0.08
Dirt	Dirt	0.20	0.09
Noise	Noises, vibrations	0.15	0.07
Tempch	Abrupt changes of temperature	0.14	0.11
Nervous	Nervous strain	0.27	0.21
Nospace	Lack of space or light	0.06	0.05
Othcond	'Other working conditions'. Sum of Hazard, Dust and Noise	0.45	0.21

Table A5.2 Imputed years of schooling (edyrs) for different levels of education

Type	Highed 1	Highed 2	Inc-high	Spec-sec	Gensec	PTU1	PTU2	Incsec	Lowed
edyrs	15	15	13	12	10	11	9	8	4

previous day (according to the time-use data). Twelve of these stated – in reply to another question – that they worked 'a full working week'. After checking their wages for plausibility, I multiplied the working hours by five (except for *dezhurnye* on 24 hour-shifts whose working hours were set at 42).

A5.1.3 The bonus problem

The survey was carried out in February and March 1989. Quarterly bonuses were usually paid in January, April, July and October. Yearly bonuses were normally paid in February or March.

Thus, in principle, the wages that might include quarterly bonuses are those from interviews made in February and these were only 5 per cent of the total. Hence, 5 per cent of the sample wages may be overestimated by two-thirds of a quarterly bonus, for 95 per cent they are underestimated by one third of it since the average of monthly earnings over the year include a third of an average quarterly bonus. I estimate the probability that a respondent who received a yearly bonus for 1988 did so in the month referred to in the interview to be nearer 45 per cent than 50 per cent.[26] If so, in 45 per cent of cases wages were overestimated by eleven-twelfths of a yearly bonus while in 55 per cent they were underestimated by one-twelfth of it.

Far from all Soviet workers and employees received yearly or quarterly bonuses. This reduces the average error in under- or overestimating

Table A5.3 Comparison of main respondents with other household members

	Male resp. Param	Std dev.	Other men in household Param	Std dev.	Female resp. Param	Std dev.	Other women in household Param	Std dev.
INTERC	4.4797	0.5626	4.0740	0.3940	4.3038	0.5542	5.0436	0.4853
AGE	0.0438	0.0416	0.0749	0.0292	0.0222	0.0402	-0.0417	0.0428
AGE^2	-0.0005	0.0010	-0.0014	0.0007	0.0001	0.0009	0.0019	0.0012
AGE^3	5E-7	7E-6	9E-6	5E-6	5E-6*	7E-6	-2E-5	1E-5
PENS	-0.3366	0.0827	-0.4243	0.0733	-0.3084*	0.0772	-0.0403	0.1017
MTS	0.0489	0.0501	0.0885	0.0444	0.0341	0.0302	0.0364	0.0440
PRESCH	0.0011	0.0380	0.0155	0.0254	-0.0342	0.0330	-0.0406	0.0327
HIGHED1	0.0822	0.0461	0.0492	0.0373	0.1621	0.0368	0.1568	0.0433
HIGHED2	-0.1749#	0.0738	-0.0257	0.0598	-0.00023□	0.0676	0.2066	0.0970
INCHIGH	-0.1653	0.0886	-0.0543	0.0637	0.0907#	0.0797	-0.0921	0.1067
SECSPEC	0		0		0		0	
GENSEC	-0.0288	0.0518	0.0115	0.0395	-0.0426	0.0356	-0.0673	0.0401
PTU1	0.0394	0.0716	0.0539	0.0482	0.1155	0.0668	0.0863	0.0879
PTU2	0.0429	0.0749	0.0213	0.0667#	-0.2124	0.1393	0.0671	0.1135
INCSEC	-0.1484	0.0670	-0.1483	0.0559	-0.0532	0.0533	-0.0705	0.0629
PRIMARY	-0.0075	0.1652	-0.2017	0.1072	-0.0751	0.1026	-0.1638	0.1471
<PRIMARY	–		-0.4563	0.1840	-0.1089	0.2222	0.1494	0.2417
N	380		605		542		411	
Adj R^2	0.15		0.19		0.22		0.16	
Prob < W	1.00		0.86		0.29		0.06[a]	

W is Wilks-Shapiro's test statistic for normal distribution of residuals.
[a] When the model is estimated for all women in the household, Prob < W is 0.87. Prob. values for difference between respondents and other household members: #0.1 < p < 0.2   □ 0.05 < p < 0.1   * 0.01 < p < 0.05

bonuses. Yet, since both the probability of getting yearly and quarterly bonuses and their size are likely to be correlated with variables used in the models, the estimated coefficients might be distorted.

Given the emphasis on bonus rewards to ITR in general and managers in particular during the Gorbachev period, it is unlikely that bonuses should have had no differentiating effects in 1989, but it is hard to quantify these. Chapter 3 also presented evidence that staff in services, above all in the socio-cultural sphere, received less in bonuses than staff in material production, but again it is hard to quantify. As to the distribution of different types of bonuses according to period of payment (monthly, quarterly or yearly), I have no evidence at all.

All the estimates of wage equations in this study are based on the sub-sample '*Obraz zhizni*' of Taganrog III and were made on the assumption that the wages measured included only monthly bonuses. To check the consequences if that assumption was incorrect, data from another sub-project (*Sem'ia, trud, dokhody*) were used as a 'control group' to estimate the impact of such an error. The questionnaire for that survey included separate questions on wages (including monthly bonuses for the preceding month) the previous quarterly bonus, and the previous yearly bonus.

These data indicate that about half the wage earners received a yearly bonus and one fifth received quarterly bonuses. For those who received bonuses, average yearly bonus was 122 roubles and the quarterly was 94 roubles.

If the figures are similar in the '*Obraz*' sample, the expected proportion of respondents having received a quarterly bonus the preceding month is only about 1 per cent (a fifth of the 5 per cent interviewed in February). This error I consider negligible. Yearly bonuses, however, are likely to have been received by about a quarter of the respondents. For those who received yearly bonuses, they made up 5 per cent of annual income (for both men and women). Added to one month's wage, this is an increase of 60 per cent. A larger proportion of men than of women receive yearly bonuses. For each sex separately a probit-model was run to see how the probability of receiving a bonus depended on variables included in wage equations.

Neither level of education nor job type (skilled and unskilled blue-collar, managerial and other white-collar) had a significant impact on the probability of receiving a yearly bonus for either sex. Age, experience and seniority had positive significant parameters. Compared to heavy industry the parameters for all other branches were negative. For the socio-cultural sphere the coefficients were significant and quite large for both men and women. For women other services and construction had smaller, but also significant, negative parameters, for men only construction.

The next step was an attempt to simulate the effect on the estimated wage parameters. The same model was estimated for both a 'normal' definition of monthly wage[27] (equation 1) and for this plus the yearly bonus for 45 per cent of those who had received one[28] (equation 2). The difference between the means of the two wage measures was about 10 per cent both for men and women. As expected, the coefficient of variation was larger when the wage measure was 'distorted' by yearly bonuses. However, not one of the differences between coefficients for the same variable in the two equations, was significant even at the 10 per cent level. A closer look at the numerical values of the differences showed that for age and experience and, particularly, for seniority the parameters were larger in equation (2), as expected. For nearly all job type and education parameters the changes were minimal, in most cases less than 2 percentage points and never more than 5. Hence, there is no indication that the parameters for these variables (including returns to education) estimated from the sample '*Obraz zhizni*' are substantially biased. For sector variables, the difference was larger. If this set-up correctly reflects the structure of the data in '*Obraz zhizni*', the estimates made in this study exaggerate the difference between heavy industry and other branches. For women, the parameters for the socio-cultural branches, light industry and trade (relative to heavy industry) should be some 7–9 percentage points larger ('smaller negative') and 5–6 percentage points for transport and construction. For men, the coefficients for all service branches and light industry should be revised some 6–12 percentage points upwards, those for transport and construction 3–4 percentage points upwards.

Given the low precision of these estimates, my conclusion is that if yearly bonuses have inadvertently, been included in some respondents' monthly wages, wages in heavy industry could be overestimated by some 6–10 per cent, and those in other branches outside the socio-cultural sphere by less than this, and the effect of seniority on earnings may be exaggerated. Estimates of returns to education and of differentiation according to job category are not substantially affected.

A5.1.4   *Tests of the model specification*

Tests of the specification of models are, for reasons of space, only summarised here. They are more fully reported in Katz (1994).

In chapters 5 and 6, *Wilks-Shapiro's test-statistic for normal distribution of residuals* are reported for the estimated wage-equations, as are adjusted R^2's and standard deviations or t-values for parameter estimates. Generally, normality is accepted for models of monthly wages, and for male hourly wages. For monthly wages, in particular the male, probability values are very high. For female hourly wages, normality is resoundingly rejected in models that do not include the 'working week variables'. (For models that do include them, on the other hand, probability values for the male hourly wage are low, though above 5 per cent.)

Rejection means that tests will have to be considered as large sample tests and that probability values, etc. are not known in small samples. However, for each case where normality of the residuals is rejected, there is a rather similar model for the same dependent variable, for which residuals fit the normal distribution reasonably well, and with very similar parameter values and with very similar t-statistics.[29] Therefore, I will speak of 'significance' even when it is not strictly legitimate to do so.

For Model A for hourly wages, White's adjusted covariance matrix was calculated to check for *heteroskedasticity* (White, 1980). Comparison of adjusted and unadjusted t-statistics led to the conclusion that although there is some heteroskedasticity, its impact is very limited and the unadjusted t-values and confidence levels are acceptable.

Chow-tests led to rejection of the hypothesis of *equality between the wage equations for men and women*, for both monthly and hourly wages, for respondents, for all household members and within sub-samples (manual/non-manual workers, specialists/non-specialists, material production/services). For some of these three divisions, *equality of wage equations within gender groups* was rejected, but the sample was considered too small for separate wage equations to be estimated.

The DFFITS-statistic for influence of individual observations on predicted values indicated some *sensitivity of results to outliers*, but this concerned mostly coefficients of dummies for very small sub-groups.

Table A5.4 Model B (without part-time variables)

| | Hourly wages | | | | Monthly wages | | | |
| | Men | | Women | | Men | | Women | |
	Parameter	t-value	Parameter	t-value	Parameter	t-value	Parameter	t-value
INTERC	-0.853	-1.21	-0.546	-0.71	4.736	7.17	4.180	7.27
H		–		–	0.000	-0.07	0.001	0.48
AGE	0.059	1.15	-0.004	-0.08	0.036	0.78	0.029	0.70
AGESQ	-0.002	-1.48	0.000	0.03	-0.001	-1.24	-0.001	-0.58
AGECUBE	0.000	1.58	0.000	0.09	0.000	1.36	0.000	0.35
STAZH	0.026	1.78	0.006	0.55	0.029	2.19	0.013	1.62
STSQ	0.000	-1.20	0.000	-0.30	0.000	-1.24	0.000	-1.30
SENIOR	0.011	1.54	0.014	2.13	0.009	1.47	0.015	2.99
SENSQ	0.000	-1.31	0.000	-1.85	0.000	-1.02	0.000	-1.85
PENS	-0.311	-3.50	-0.349	-3.77	-0.378	-4.67	-0.250	-3.68
MTS	0.053	0.92	0.040	1.06	0.030	0.58	0.022	0.78
SCHOOL	-0.035	-0.89	0.022	0.62	-0.035	-0.97	0.008	0.32
PRESCH	-0.012	-0.23	0.018	0.37	-0.032	-0.69	-0.032	-0.90
CHILDREN	-0.007	-0.22	-0.020	-0.65	0.016	0.55	-0.005	-0.20
HOUSE	0.002	1.09	0.004	2.90	0.000	0.26	-0.001	-0.88
PARTY	0.050	1.18	0.049	1.09	0.038	0.98	0.047	1.42
QUAL1	0	–	0	–	0	–	0	–
QUAL2	0.055	0.79	0.098	1.71	0.084	1.35	0.133	3.18
QUAL3	0.044	0.56	0.050	0.81	0.060	0.83	0.067	1.51
QUAL4	0.013	0.15	0.032	0.55	0.025	0.31	0.006	0.14
QUAL5	0.205	1.43	0.151	1.08	0.369	2.79	0.279	2.72
QUAL6	0.277	1.43	0.672	4.00	0.306	1.74	0.326	2.62
HIGHED1	0.268	2.87	0.309	3.97	0.236	2.79	0.288	5.05
HIGHED2	-0.066	-0.59	0.232	2.31	0.005	0.05	0.191	2.60
INCHIGH	0.076	0.67	0.230	2.01	0.061	0.59	0.231	2.75
SPECSEC	0.089	1.18	0.103	1.55	0.098	1.45	0.102	2.10
GENSEC	0.091	1.19	0.074	1.16	0.073	1.05	0.035	0.73

Table A5.4 continued

	Hourly wages				Monthly wages			
	Men		Women		Men		Women	
	Parameter	t-value	Parameter	t-value	Parameter	t-value	Parameter	t-value
PTU1	0.135	1.44	0.197	2.03	0.119	1.40	0.156	2.20
PTU2	0.147	1.57	0.431	2.42	0.145	1.70	-0.089	-0.67
LESS8	0	–	0	–	0	–	0	–
HEAVIND	0	–	0	–	0	–	0	–
TRANSP	-0.030	-0.44	-0.065	-0.77	0.002	0.03	-0.041	-0.67
CONSTR	-0.077	-1.05	-0.081	-1.00	-0.096	-1.45	-0.035	-0.59
LIGHT	-0.035	-0.39	0.008	0.12	-0.037	-0.46	0.061	1.21
SERV	-0.208	-2.51	0.017	0.25	-0.202	-2.68	0.030	0.60
TRADE	-0.476	-3.21	-0.280	-4.13	-0.462	-3.44	-0.298	-6.01
TEACH	0.006	0.07	0.165	2.94	-0.096	-1.19	0.010	0.24
HEALTH	-0.008	-0.06	-0.079	-1.11	-0.021	-0.18	-0.122	-2.34
ART	0.054	0.34	-0.185	-1.38	-0.069	-0.49	-0.348	-3.54
SCIENCE	-0.110	-1.29	-0.272	-3.22	-0.075	-0.97	-0.154	-2.48
ADMIN	-0.209	-0.87	-0.063	-0.51	-0.012	-0.05	-0.034	-0.37
OTHER	-0.063	-0.77	0.247	2.91	-0.122	-1.67	0.025	0.40
HEAT	0.132	1.87	0.174	1.58	0.166	2.58	0.151	1.87
HAZARD	0.055	0.96	0.096	1.31	0.038	0.73	0.054	1.01
DUST	0.013	0.20	0.028	0.35	0.014	0.24	0.042	0.72
HARDTE	0.019	0.27	0.028	0.43	0.051	0.80	0.094	1.98
HEAVY	0.022	0.35	0.155	2.21	0.012	0.22	0.123	2.41
DIRT	0.016	0.30	0.012	0.20	-0.026	-0.54	0.004	0.08
NOISE	-0.012	-0.21	0.044	0.58	0.009	0.18	0.033	0.61
TEMP	-0.003	-0.05	-0.070	-1.17	-0.013	-0.22	-0.058	-1.32
NERVOUS	-0.144	-3.36	-0.119	-2.75	-0.103	-2.62	-0.031	-0.97
NOSPACE	-0.071	-0.90	0.030	-0.42	-0.028	-0.39	-0.025	-0.46
Adj. R^2	0.18		0.25		0.24		0.39	

Table A5.5   Variable means for Soviet and sample workers and employees for Model C

	Soviet men	Sample men	Soviet women	Sample women
AGE	38.4	41.6	37.4	39.8
MANUAL[a]	0.743	0.704	0.535	0.552
HIGHQUAL[b]	0.046	0.039	0.044	0.028
BADCOND[c]	0.129	0.351	0.055	0.171
HIGHED	0.138	0.296	0.148	0.262
SECSPEC[d]	0.204	0.322	0.291	0.332
GENSEC	0.249	0.156	0.248	0.303
PTU1	0.149	0.066	0.094	0.044
PTU2	0.054	0.066	0.020	0.009
INCSEC	0.128	0.082	0.128	0.087
LOWED	0.078	0.010	0.071	0.025
LIGHT	0.023	0.026	0.070	0.033
FOOD	0.030	0.016	0.027	0.033
HEAVY	0.374	0.543	0.201	0.430
TRANSP	0.150	0.080	0.056	0.039
CONSTR	0.207	0.064	0.060	0.042
SERV	0.048	0.048	0.084	0.061
TRADE	0.011	0.021	0.141	0.072
TEACH	0.058	0.053	0.154	0.123
HEALTH	0.030	0.021	0.113	0.059
ART	0.014	0.013	0.026	0.015
SCIENCE	0.021	0.056	0.039	0.044
ADMIN	0.014	0.005	0.030	0.017

[a] Corresponds to qual1, qual2 or qual3.
[b] Corresponds roughly to qual5 or qual6.
[c] Manual worker with unsuitable conditions of work.
[d] Secondary specialist or incomplete higher educ.
Since the residual category in the national statistics is not the same as those coded as 'other' in the sample this parameter was not used to calculate the 'predicted values'. For details of definition, sources and methods of imputation, see Katz (1994, chapter 5, appendix II).

6
Pay and Education

6.1 Introduction: the debate over 'wage-levelling'

It is a common view that wage differentials during the Soviet period were too narrow and that this contributed to the inefficiency of the Soviet economy. In particular, the economic incentives for acquiring education were considered very small (Gordon, 1987, Rimashevskaia and Onikov, 1991). The views of Western researchers were mixed, but many agreed. (Ofer and Vinokur, 1992, can be cited as an exception.) Granick (1987) claims that returns to education in the USSR were negative, while Chapman (1988) describes 'wage-levelling' as a problem for the Soviet economy.

Low returns to schooling in the USSR are often explained as the result of an ideologically inspired policy of wage compression or 'levelling' (*uravnilovka*).[1] The criticisms of 'levelling' easily give the impression that official wage policy was egalitarian. But this was not the case. On the contrary, the USSR was a deeply inegalitarian society. The argument of the present study is that, if the pressure of demand and supply had been given freer play, given the institutions and conditions of the USSR, differentiation is more likely to have decreased than increased. The claim that larger wage premia to the highly educated would have reduced the inefficiencies of the Soviet economy has not been properly substantiated, either empirically or theoretically. Here, the question of whether there really was a conflict between equality and efficiency is discussed only in the Soviet context, but it does have a wider relevance.

In section 6.2 earlier empirical studies of wage differentiation according to education and skill in the USSR are presented. In section 6.3 problems of definition and measurement are raised. Section 6.4 reports empirical results from the 1989 Taganrog study. Section 6.5 returns to the 'levelling' debate. Sections 6.6–6.8 survey the available evidence on demand and supply of labour with different levels of education and discuss the relevance of wage incentives for problems of labour shortage and job rationing.

6.2   Pay and education in the USSR. What is known?[2]

In its early years, the USSR urgently needed to train millions of poorly educated peasants to become urban skilled workers and professionals. The large wage differentials of the Stalin period provided substantial incentives both for unskilled workers to learn industrial skills and for young people to achieve much higher schooling levels than their parents or grandparents.

Although social inequality was less blatant after Stalin, the emphasis on substantial wage differentials as incentives for vocational training continued, sustained by the continuing shortage of qualified workers, technicians and engineers

Conditions, however, changed. By the 1950s there were more applicants for higher education than there were places (Marnie, 1986, p. 211). Kirsch (1972, p. 102) quotes a Soviet study from 1968[3] which found that workers with secondary schooling were better able to acquire new industrial skills, and recommended that general schooling should be encouraged by a higher starting wage for those who had completed secondary education. By the 1980s, there was no point in a wage premium as an incentive for secondary schooling, since it was practically universal.[4]

But, since the mid- or late 1960s, more and more had been written on the low relative wages of 'specialists' – that is, people with specialised secondary or university education. What is best known in the West is the comparatively low pay of Soviet doctors and teachers. The salaries of engineers also declined relative to those of skilled workers.

While relative pay decreased, the proportion of women increased among engineers, accountants, physicians and schoolteachers. The percentage of women among ITR doubled from 22 per cent in 1939 to 44 per cent in 1970 and increased further to 50 per cent in 1989. Among engineers the proportion of women was 42 per cent in 1970 and 52 per cent in 1989. At the same time, the wages of ITR fell from more than double those of workers (214 per cent) to only 15 per cent above them.[5]

The three Taganrog studies offer comparable data on wage differentiation over time. Rimashevskaia and Onikov (1991, p. 19) conclude that between the first (1967–68) and the second Taganrog (1978–79) surveys there was an 'inversion' in relative wages as 'the result of which ... staff with low qualifications became predominantly middle- and highly paid, while among highly qualified workers and particularly specialists with higher education the proportion with low pay increased significantly . . .'. Technicians with secondary specialised education earned 91 per cent of the average for low-skilled workers, technicians with higher education 108 per cent. The authors conclude that 'the process of levelling of wages . . . had a negative impact on the material incentives [*zainteresovannost'*] of in the first place qualified and highly achieving [*rezul'tativnye*] staff.'

Figure 6.1 shows relative wages according to Taganrog I–III. It indicates that, in 1968, the average wage of specialists was below that of highly skilled workers, but well above that of the unskilled. In 1978, it had fallen below that of the unskilled too. From 1978 to 1989 we see an increase in the wages of specialists relative to all workers, but not back to the 1968 levels.

The source for Figure 6.1 does not report wages separately for men and women. Tables 4.10 and 4.11 showed that in Taganrog, in 1989, the wage advantage of education, or of a qualified job, was larger within each sex than for the mixed sample, although still not very large. They also showed that average wages for women in all educational groups were lower than

Figure 6.1 Relative wages in Taganrog, 1968–89

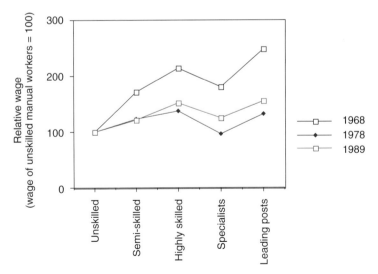

Sources: Rimashevskaia and Patsiorkovskii (1992, p. 69), Rimashevskaia and Onikov (1991, p. 33).

the lowest such average for men. (See also the March Census, 1989, reported in *Nar. Khoz.*, 1989, p. 81, and Katz, 1994, p. 306.)

Account should also be taken of cohort effects. Lower formal education is correlated with more experience and seniority. This is to some extent controlled for in multivariate models, as in this study. It is harder to model that when the older generations first started to work, the shortage of educated staff created openings for workers with low formal qualifications relative to the job. If a self-taught skilled worker had been doing an engineer's job for 20 or 30 years, he wouldn't be sacked because a young engineering graduate had become available. All this may bias education coefficients downwards and experience coefficients upwards. An ideal model of experience – cohort – education – job-type interactions would require a much larger data set than this.

Ofer and Vinokur estimate multivariate models, using retrospective data for the early 1970s, from an émigré sample, restricted to two-earner married couples. They conclude that returns to education were considerably lower in the USSR than in the United States, but that there nevertheless was a 'relatively high yield [to human capital] in the form of higher status and life-time income' (1992, p. 115).

With a model of monthly wages – including years in various forms of education, experience, experience squared, age and regular hours of work – their results indicate a parameter of 2.5 per cent per year of regular schooling for both sexes (ibid., table 7.2). This implies a 5 per cent difference between having incomplete secondary school (8 years) and full secondary education (10 years). For men the return per year of study is slightly bigger in specialised secondary than in general secondary school, for women it is somewhat smaller. Five years of university education add a quarter to men's wages and a third to women's. The authors note that the returns are larger, the higher the level of the education, and also that the relative return to education is higher for women than it is for men. In a model, which also includes sector of occupation and occupational roles, education parameters are larger, except that for an ordinary university degree. Another model, estimated for married women, showed that those with a completed university degree earned one and a half times as much as those with only secondary education and those with an advanced degree nearly two times as much (89 per cent more).

The period between their survey and 1989 had seen an increase in the supply of highly educated workers. This would tend to decrease education premia. On the other hand, there had been a strong effort to increase the relative wages for professionals and semi-professionals during the Gorbachev wage reform (see section 3.2.2).

6.3   Methodological issues

6.3.1   Western theory and the Soviet context

In Western economics, the relation between earnings, or wage rates, on the one hand, and level, or years, of education on the other, is usually treated within the frame work of 'human capital' theory. (See chapter 2.) Even those who accept human capital theory, as applied to market economies, may question its relevance for labour demand in the USSR. There was no well-defined, or even approximate, measure of marginal productivity in the Soviet context, both because prices were set administratively and because the 'production function' of the Soviet enterprise was anything but smooth.

An essential tenet of Soviet wage doctrine was that wages should correspond to the 'final results of labour'. (See for example, the guidelines for the 1986 wage reform.) This term was used in much the same ways as a neoclassical economist would use 'productivity' or 'marginal productivity' of labour. As in human capital theory, productivity was assumed to depend on age and to increase with work experience – including on-the-job training – and formal schooling. In addition, both theories allow for compensating differentials, and in both systems the construction of 'skill' is gender-biased.

Interestingly, the Soviet economist and statistician Strumilin, in effect, estimated a multivariate model of productivity, as a function of age, experience and schooling in 1921 (Strumilin, 1966, originally published 1925). Without computers, multivariate regressions on a large data set were impossible, yet Strumilin can be said to have anticipated the human capital theory of Mincer (1974) and Becker (1964) by decades. Like many intellectual and cultural achievements of the early 1920s, such cost-benefit studies of public investment in education were discontinued under and after Stalin. However, the main criteria of 'quality of work' (productivity) remained.

This is not to say that the theories were identical, nor that Soviet practice was identical to Soviet theory. The theory applied mainly to the centrally determined wage scales, and bonus regulations, less to what the enterprise did with them. The incentives and objectives of the Soviet enterprise were *not* those of the archetypical capitalist profit-maximiser. The number one criterion for an enterprise wanting to hire more workers was not whether their marginal product was equal to the marginal wage, but whether planners could be persuaded to add to its Wage Fund.[6] (See p. 59.)

Theories oversimplify both market and Soviet-type economies. The market-clearing prices of general equilibrium theory are abstractions, and so is the enterprise, which produces with perfect substitutability of inputs. Conversely, labour power was the least planned of 'goods' in the Soviet state sector, and hence, the good for whose price demand and supply mattered most. Yet, the difference between these economic systems is not merely quantitative but qualitative. The inherent logic of the Soviet system made waste, bottlenecks, erratic supplies and erratic labour productivity pervasive. (It would take another book to analyse 'the nature of the USSR'. See, however, Ticktin, 1973, 1992.)

6.3.2 Problems of definition

From the point of view of labour supply and occupational choice, the size of wage-differentials according to education reflects the availability and cost of schooling (including earnings forgone while studying), the job options available for those with or without a given education and the non-monetary advantages associated with these options. Economic theory cannot claim a *priori* that those with more years of schooling will earn more than those with less schooling. Neoclassical economists expect better educated workers to have higher marginal productivity and that this will tend to increase wages. On the other hand, both the period of study, and the jobs that become available, may be intrinsically pleasant and imply negative equalising differentials. The low private cost of schooling, as well as broad access to education, will also tend to decrease relative wages for the educated.

'Returns to education' are wage differentials due to differences in schooling, other things being equal. Yet, when some of the 'other things' are intrinsically connected with choice of education, it is not conceptually clear whether it should be held 'equal'. There is no one 'correct' way of perceiving this choice and from each perception follows a different specification of the wage model used to estimate the returns.

The choice of an education is not only a choice of number of years of schooling, but also of field of employment and type of work. Hence, if the objective is to study the consequences of choices, there is no clear-cut distinction between what should be attributed to education and what to job characteristics. To measure the rewards for having been to university, net of the addition to wages attributed to having jobs that require higher education, is to underestimate even the monetary benefits of getting a degree. Yet, getting and holding a highly qualified job may require other qualities, beyond those that are necessary for, or 'signalled by', a particular education. Like the wage differentials according to education, the 'returns' to the characteristics of qualified jobs could have any sign and size. In those humanist traditions – that of the young Marx, among others – which see a potential for human self-realisation or self-expression in work, it is natural to consider autonomy, creativity and intellectual challenge as advantages of the job, and monotonous, uncreative work as something that – if it cannot be avoided – should be compensated by higher wages. Most Soviet and Western economists alike seem to assume the opposite to be the 'normal' case.

If personal characteristics, which affect careers, but are not included in the model, are correlated with education or job type, wage coefficients for these may be biased.

Similarly, if the physical conditions of work are excluded from the model, theoretical schooling is seen as having lower returns than if they are included. Certainly, the wish to avoid dangerous, dirty or heavy work is likely to be a motive for choosing an academic education in order to get a white-collar job. To capture this advantage of schooling, education premia should be estimated net of compensation for poor working conditions.

Further, as discussed in sections 4.5.4 and 5.2.2, training for certain professions gave the option of having a shorter working week. If many women entered medical school or teacher training colleges because they wanted a 30-hour week, what was, then, the 'real', 'pure' rate of return to this education? Shouldn't it include at least some of the increase in hourly wage we find for those with short working weeks? How do we describe the 'returns' of a choice of education and sector, which has no effect on monthly earnings, when – precisely because of this choice – the wage is earned in considerably fewer hours?

To make simultaneous estimates of wages, years of education, job qualities and hours of work would require a very large data set. The compromise chosen here is to estimate a range of models. The shifts in the coefficients for education as new variables are included offer a picture of the complex relation between education and earnings.

6.3.3 Problems in modelling returns to education[7]

In econometrics, two measures of the pay-off to education are standard. The one used in this study is coefficients estimated from wage regressions; the other is internal rates of return, that is, the rate of discount which would equate expected lifetime earnings, given different choices of years of schooling. Under certain restrictions on the wage functions, the two rates will be approximately equal (Psacharopoulos, 1981, Willis, 1986). In what follows, for convenience, 'rates of return to education' and 'education premia' both refer to parameters estimated from wage functions.

Whichever the measure chosen, some econometric problems are generally acknowledged. The scope of this study allows only a brief note on some of them and their relevance to the USSR.

1. There may be errors in the measurement of education. Even random error, uncorrelated with education, biases the estimated coefficients for education in the wage equation downwards, by increasing variation. (See Lam and Schoeni, 1993 and references therein.) In Soviet surveys such problems are likely to occur because the quality of a given level of education is likely to vary a lot between institutes. Worse still, people whose level of schooling was low may have said that it was higher because they were embarrassed to admit it. In this case, our measure of education is upward biased and the returns underestimated.

2. Sample selection bias, if labour force participation is correlated with earnings, is a potential problem, but not likely to be grave in this case because of the high participation rates in the Taganrog sample.

3. If any factor not included in the wage equation is correlated with both earnings and education, this produces an omitted variable bias. If, for instance, unobserved ability is positively correlated with education, and at the same time increases wages, given the level of schooling, then estimates of returns to education will be exaggerated. (See Blackburn and Neumark, 1992, and references therein.)

4. Earnings may depend on 'social capital', which affects the ability to be perceived as able, or to get the chance to show or develop potential ability. Obvious candidates are the position of the respondent's family of origin and membership of formal or informal organisations and networks. In the USSR, it is very likely that family affluence and influence, party and other contacts affected careers. Nevertheless, attempts to model their effects did not produce any substantive results. Parents' education could not be shown to have a significant impact on either wages or returns to education in Taganrog.[8] This could be due to measurement error. The levels of education that Taganrog respondents attribute to their parents are very much higher than the schooling of the Soviet workforce a generation back and could be exaggerated.

5. As discussed above, the incentives for acquiring an education include non-wage benefits, which we cannot measure.

6.4 Results from the survey

6.4.1 Issues

The estimates reported in this section will indicate the actual size of wage incentives for education in Taganrog. Beyond that, six issues, each with important gender dimensions, will be raised.

1. Did the rate of wage increase with experience depend on education?

2. To what extent do the estimated returns to education depend on whether working conditions are controlled for?
3. What were the combined effects of related education and job choices? The emphasis will be on a set of 'stylised', 'typical' combinations, to which a person choosing a level of education may have expected it to lead.
4. How did the career options of Soviet men and women differ, when we take into account both occupational segregation and differential returns to education?
5. For which kinds of schooling were 'reduced working hours' part of the 'returns' and how did this show in hourly wages?

An additional essential question that the Taganrog data are not really suited to answering is whether the coincidence of low priority and high average level of schooling in certain sectors reduced average returns to education.

6.4.2   Data and models

The analysis will start with Model C, which includes education only. Gradually, more and more factors will be controlled for and the estimates discussed in terms of the question implicit in each model. (For definitions and means of all variables, see Table A5.1.)

As in chapter 5, wage functions will be estimated for women and men separately and for both hourly and monthly wages of one respondent per household. The selectivity problems related to this sub-sample, discussed in chapter 5, are likely to be less serious the more variables are controlled for and most serious for simple variable means.[9] In Table A5.5, a wage equation estimated on both sub-samples, respondents and other household members, are reported. The result does not indicate that the selection of respondents introduces bias in wage equations. (In similar estimates on both the sample of all household members and on the sub-sample of respondents, no parameters differed significantly at the 10 per cent level.[10]) Keep in mind, however, that in the larger and random sample, the coefficients for part-time and incomplete higher education relative to incomplete secondary school are approximately 10 per cent for both men and women, while they are negligible for the main respondents.

Education is often measured as years of schooling, instead of as highest achieved level. With these data, length of schooling would have to be inferred from the kind of education. (See Table A5.2.) The error involved should be small, except for advanced degrees.[11] Nevertheless, dummy variables were preferred, since premia for different kinds of schooling differed.

For completeness, however, three models with a continuous length-of-education variable were estimated, for hourly and monthly wages. These models were constructed by replacing the education dummies in models E, J and K (below) by imputed years of schooling (edyrs). For women, the parameter for edyrs has high precision. Its size varies between 1.5 and 4 per cent depending on the model. For men, the parameter is in the order of 2 per cent and significant at the 5 per cent level, in the models corresponding to E and J. The addition of a dummy for PTU in the model does not change either size or precision of edyrs much for women, but for men it increases them.

6.4.3 Interaction of education with age, experience and working conditions

Estimates of Models C–E are reported in Tables 6.1 and 6.2. The reference group is those with incomplete secondary education (incsec). In Model D age and experience (general and firm-specific) and their squares are added to Model C.

Age and general work experience (*stazh*) have low precision and adding them to the model induces only small changes in the education coefficients. The largest is that, for men, the parameters for PTU without secondary education increase when age and experience are controlled for. The average age of these respondents is 51 years. Most started working in the 1950s or earlier when the skills they have may have been quite scarce, giving them an advantage in terms of wage or jobs, which they have been able to maintain. For women, the coefficients for all three forms of secondary school decline when age and experience are controlled for, for both monthly and hourly wages.

In this model, for both women and men, full-time higher education increases hourly earnings by 35–40 per cent and monthly wages by 25–30 per cent. General and specialised secondary school brings approximately 20 per cent for men, and PTU on average a little more. For women the pay-off to secondary education is small. PTU with secondary has a higher coefficient than specialised secondary schooling. (The difference in years of schooling between PTU with secondary and specialised secondary is usually only 1–2 years.) PTU without secondary for women in the sample is connected with low monthly and very high hourly wages. This sub-sample is very small and quite peculiar.[12] It would be unwise to draw any general conclusions about women with PTU or the frequency of 'unofficial part-time' work from these very few individuals.

Table 6.1   Models C–E for hourly wages

	Men			**Women**		
	Model C	Model D	Model E	Model C	Model D	Model E
Intercept	0.028	–0.237	–0.371	–0.257	–0.430	–0.570
Age		3E-5	0.008		2E-4	0.005
Agesq		–6E-5	–2E-4		–4E-5	–8E-5
Stazh		0.024¤	0.020		0.010	0.010
Stsq		–4E-4	–3E-4		–2E-4	–2E-4
Senior		0.014*	0.015*		0.022**	0.018**
Sensq		–3E-4	–3E-4		–0.001**	–5E-4*
HIGHED1	0.319**	0.323**	0.347**	0.346**	0.337**	0.423**
HIGHED2	3E-4	–0.012	0.032	0.163¤	0.169¤	0.238*
INCHIGH	0.050	0.080	0.074	0.115	0.132	0.194¤
SPECSEC	0.183*	0.174*	0.171*	0.109¤	0.073	0.136*
GENSEC	0.190*	0.157*	0.151*	0.088	0.056	0.099
PTU1	0.239*	0.230*	0.234*	0.170¤	0.131	0.166¤
PTU2	0.153	0.212*	0.190*	0.532**	0.578**	0.545**
INCSEC	0	0	0	0	0	0
LOWED	0.199	0.229	0.154	0.003	0.050	0.031
Heat			0.139*			0.195¤
Heavy			–0.008			0.107
Nervous			–0.112**			–0.098*
OTHCOND			0.092*			0.121*
Adj. R^2	0.05	0.14	0.17	0.07	0.10	0.13
Prob < W	0.99	0.97	0.97	0.0001	0.0001	0.0001

Note: W is the Wilk-Shapiro test statistic for normal distribution of residuals. The indicated significance levels are calculated on the assumption of normality.
¤ Significant at 10 per cent.   * Significant at 5 per cent   ** Significant at 1 per cent.
Full estimates including standard deviations are available from the author on request.

Adding working conditions to the age–experience–education model (Model D) produces Model E. A comparison shows that, for men, this changes the coefficients for education only marginally in equations for hourly as well as monthly wages.

For women the inclusion of compensating differentials makes a larger difference. For full-time higher education, the premium to hourly wages increases from 39 per cent in Model D to 52 per cent in Model E. For specialised secondary education it rises from 7 per cent to 14 per cent, for general secondary from 6 per cent to 10 per cent. The results for monthly wages are analogous. Omitting the working condition variables from models with more factors included produces similar conclusions, at least for monthly wages.

Starting from Model E, some attempts, constrained by the size of the data set, were made to investigate whether the level of education affected

172 Gender, Work and Wages in the Soviet Union

Table 6.2 Models C–E of monthly wages

Variable	Men			Women		
	Model C	Model D	Model E	Model C	Model D	Model E
Intercept	5.252	5.105	4.921	4.909	4.306	4.126
Age		–0.005	0.004		0.020	0.026¤
Agesq		–5E-5	–2E-4		–3E-4*	–4E-4*
Stazh		0.027*	0.022¤		0.023**	0.019*
Stsq		–4E-4	–3E-4		–4E-4*	–4E-4*
Senior		0.014*	0.015*		0.020**	0.017**
Sensq		–2E-4	–2E-4		–4E-4	–3E-4*
HIGHED1	0.273**	0.292**	0.317**	0.240**	0.214**	0.302**
HIGHED2	0.040	0.029	0.067	0.082	0.062	0.141¤
INCHIGH	0.018	0.065	0.051	0.161¤	0.168*	0.225**
SPECSEC	0.185**	0.180**	0.180**	0.104*	0.034	0.106*
GENSEC	0.183*	0.152*	0.148*	0.048	–0.011	0.044
PTU1	0.226*	0.223*	0.230**	0.171*	0.100	0.134¤
PTU2	0.135	0.209*	0.194*	–0.242	–0.080	–0.099
INCSEC	0	0	0	0	0	0
LOWED	0.141	0.189	0.129	–0.328**	–0.141	–0.150¤
Heat			0.158**			0.219**
Heavy			–0.013			0.110*
Nervous			–0.058			–0.020
OTHCOND			0.091*			0.160**
						0.037
Adj. R^2	0.04	0.16	0.19	0.10	0.26	0.31
Prob < W	0.87	0.96	0.95	0.05	0.12	0.19

Note: ¤, *, ** See notes to Table 6.1.

the rate at which wages grew with experience and seniority. 'Stazh' and 'senior' were each replaced by three variables. 'Stazh1' was equal to '*stazh*' for respondents with full-time higher education, and zero for the others. 'Stazh2' was defined analogously for those with part-time higher or incomplete higher education or with specialised or general secondary education and Stazh3 for those with PTU or less than secondary education. Senior1–senior3 were defined analogously for seniority.

For male monthly wages, all seniority variables are significant, but none for *stazh*. This does lend some support to the assumption that enterprises set wages so as to encourage 'stayers'. Both *stazh* and seniority coefficients are nearly twice as large for the university educated as for others. For male hourly wages, it is hard to draw any conclusions about the relative importance of general and firm-specific experience. All the seniority parameters are in the order of 0.5 per cent per year, but only senior2 has a probability value below 10 per cent. All *stazh* parameters have low precision, but stazh1 is larger than the others, at 1.2 per cent. (If second-order terms are included, stazh1 and senior2 are significant.)[13]

For women's hourly wages, stazh1 is large (1.6 per cent) and significant at 1 per cent, while stazh2 and stazh3 are even slightly negative. The only significant seniority coefficient is that for senior2, which is equal to 1.1 per cent. The results when only one of *stazh* and senior is divided, or when Model J is used instead, are very similar. So are estimates for monthly wages. For highly educated women, experience pays, but not staying with one employer; the opposite is the case for those with middle-level education. Women manual workers, unlike both other women and male workers, appear to enter employment in low-paid jobs and stay there.

6.4.4   Interaction of education with occupation

Before job-type variables are introduced, the model will be modified in two respects. First, according to the estimates of chapter 5, the variable 'pens' for pensioner was important in the USSR. It is included from Model F onwards. Second, since both Highed2 and Inchighed correspond to sub-samples too small to be really interesting and since their parameters have been of similar size, they are combined into 'parthigh' in Model G.[14]

In Model H (Tables 6.3–6.4), four broad job types are introduced: managerial or highly qualified and creative white-collar work (highqual), other non-manual work (qual4), skilled physical or partly physical work (physqual) and unskilled manual work (the reference).

Male 'highqual' staff earn a premium of 23 per cent on hourly wages, female 37 per cent, both add 31 per cent to monthly wages. 'Other white-collar work' had very small coefficients. Skilled manual work has pay-offs in the order of 6–11 per cent. This is not very much either, and considerably less than the skilled/unskilled differential found by Ofer and Vinokur (1992, p. 246f).

As expected, education parameters decrease when job types are included in the equation, since more education goes with better-paid jobs. The shift is, however, negligible: just 1–3 percentage points. It makes a larger difference to do the reverse, omit education variables while keeping the job types. In such a model (not reported), the parameter for qual4 is about 20 per cent, for male and female, hourly and monthly wages.

Skilled workers often had PTU training or specialised secondary school and the education premia for this added to earnings. Most people with university degrees worked as managers or professionals and had a premium for highqual or qual4 in addition to that for higher education.

Table 6.3A   Hourly wages for men, Models E–I

	Model E	Model F	Model G	Model H	Model I
Age & exp.[a]	x	x	x	x	x
Pens		x	x	x	x
HIGHQUAL				0.21¤	0.17
QUAL4				0.01	−0.46¤
PHYSQUAL				0.06	0.07
HIGH4					0.40*
MID4					0.52*
SEC4					0.57
HIGHED1	0.35**	0.34**	0.34**	0.33**	0.39**
HIGHED2	0.03	0.01			
INCHIGH	0.07	0.07			
PARTHIGH			0.03	0.03	0.01
SPECSEC	0.17*	0.15*	0.15*	0.14¤	0.12¤
GENSEC	0.15*	0.12	0.12	0.12	0.13¤
PTU1	0.23*	0.21*	0.21*	0.19*	0.21*
PTU2	0.19*	0.18*	0.18	0.16¤	0.18*
LOWED	0.15	0.12	0.12	0.10	0.09
Working conditions[a]	x	x	x	x	x
Adj. R^2	0.17	0.19	0.19	0.20	0.20
Prob > W	0.97	0.96	0.97	0.16	0.18

Notes: [a] Age, experience and working condition variables as in Model D. Reduced working time variables: Reduc, reduced, unoff, offpart and sector variables as in Model A.
x Included
¤ Significant at 10 per cent.   * Significant at 5 per cent.   ** Significant at 1 per cent.
Full estimates, including t-statistics available from the author on request.

Even for the white-collar jobs requiring only secondary education, an education premium should be considered. It would be desirable to analyse the effect of a joint education – job-type choice for 'typical' combinations.

Simply to add the parameter of an education to that of a job type is not a reliable method of measuring their combined effects. The coefficients for job types are average effects across education groups, and vice versa. As long as the effect of, say, a skilled manual job depends on whether one has been to PTU, or that of a white-collar job on whether one has higher education, these sums will be incorrect. Nevertheless, the technically correct approach of introducing a variable for each non-empty job type/education combination is not very good either for a sample as small as this. The small number of observations in many categories will not allow sufficient precision.

On the other hand, the more a certain educational group is dominated by a single job type, or conversely, the more homogeneous an

Table 6.3B Hourly wages for women, Models E–I

	Model E	Model F	Model G	Model H	Model I
Age & exp.[a]	x	x	x	x	x
Pens		x	x	x	x
HIGHQUAL				0.31**	0.44**
QUAL4				0.06	0.12
PHYSQUAL				0.07	0.06
HIGH4					0.15
MID4					0.03
SEC4					−0.12
HIGHED1	0.42**	0.39**	0.39**	0.36**	0.17
HIGHED2	0.24*	0.21*			
INCHIGH	0.19¤	0.15			
PARTHIGH			0.19*	0.17*	0.12
SPECSEC	0.14*	0.11	0.11	0.09	0.12¤
GENSEC	0.10	0.07	0.07	0.07	0.09
PTU1	0.17¤	0.14	0.14	0.13	0.13
PTU2	0.55**	0.53**	0.53**	0.58**	0.57**
LOWED	0.03	0.13	0.13	0.17	0.17
Working conditions[b]	x	x	x	x	x
Adj. R^2	0.13	0.15	0.15	0.16	0.16
Prob > W	0.0001	0.0001	0.0001	0.0001	0.0001

Note: See notes to Table 6.3A.

occupational category is with respect to education, or the more similar the parameters for the education levels represented in the same occupational group, the smaller the approximation error when adding education and job-type coefficients.

These considerations led to the approach used in Models I–L. These models include interaction effects between the most heterogeneous group, qual4 and three broad levels of schooling: full-time university education (highed1), other higher education (highed2 and inchighed) and secondary (specsec or gensec). With these models, parameters were added to produce the combined job type and education effects of Tables 6.8–6.9. For the approximations involved and justification for accepting them, see the appendix to this chapter.

In the models with interaction terms, estimates are quite volatile, in the sense that small changes in variable definitions make effects shift between related occupational, education and interaction variables. The inclusion of new variables can cause counteracting changes in group parameters and interaction terms, as happens in the transition from Model I to Model J. Therefore, we will use the approximations in Tables 6.8–6.9.

Table 6.4A   Monthly wages for men, Models E–I

	Model E	Model F	Model G	Model H	Model I
Age & exp.[a]	x	x	x	x	x
Pens		x	x	x	x
HIGHQUA				0.27**	0.26*
QUAL4				0.02	–0.53*
PHYSQUA				0.10□	0.10□
HIGH4					0.52*
MID4					0.63**
SEC4					0.61**
HIGHED1	0.32**	0.31**	0.31**	0.29**	0.32**
HIGHED2	0.07	0.04			
INCHIGH	0.05	0.05			
PARTHIGH			0.04	0.04	0.01
SPECSEC	0.18**	0.16*	0.16*	0.14*	0.13*
GENSEC	0.15*	0.11	0.11	0.09	0.10
PTU1	0.23**	0.20*	0.20*	0.17	0.20*
PTU2	0.19*	0.19*	0.19*	0.15□	0.17*
LOWED	0.13	0.09	0.09	0.05	0.04
Working conditions	x	x	x	x	x
adj. R^2	0.19	0.24	0.24	0.25	0.26
Prob < W	0.95	0.93	0.93	0.98	0.97

Note: See notes to Table 6.3A.

Tables 6.8–6.9 show the sum of education, job type and (for white-collar staff) interaction terms for a number of 'typical' combinations, which are defined in the tables. The numbers indicate, approximately, the difference between the wage of a worker in the given category compared to an unskilled manual worker with incomplete secondary school, in per cent. They are based on Models I, J, K and L. For convenience, the structures of the models are summarised in Table 6.7.

The wage premium for higher education is higher for women than for men in terms of hourly, but not of monthly, wages. Men have higher returns both to secondary school plus white-collar work, and to vocational training plus skilled manual work. For them, the latter was an alternative that competed well with higher education, particularly since male skilled workers tend to work in heavy industry where non-monetary benefits were high. For women, this combination was much less of an option.

In terms of monthly wages, the sum of parameters for higher education and the highest qualification category pay-off is in the order of 70 per cent

Table 6.4B   Monthly wages for women, Models E–I

	Model E	Model F	Model G	Model H	Model I
Age & exp.[a]	x	x	x	x	x
Pens		x	x	x	x
HIGHQUAL				0.27**	0.32**
QUAL4				0.02	0.07
PHYSQUAL				0.09*	0.09*
HIGH4					0.04
MID4					−0.09
SEC4					−0.07
HIGHED1	0.30**	0.28**	0.28**	0.29**	0.21*
HIGHED2	0.14¤	0.13¤			
INCHIGH	0.22**	0.20*			
PARTHIGH			0.15*	0.17*	0.19*
SPECSEC	0.11*	0.09¤	0.09¤	0.08¤	0.09¤
GENSEC	0.04	0.03	0.03	0.03	0.04
PTU1	0.13¤	0.12	0.12	0.10	0.10
PTU2	−0.10	−0.10	−0.10	−0.05	−0.05
LOWED	−0.15¤	−0.09	−0.08	−0.03	−0.03
Working conditions[a]	x	x	x	x	x
Adj. R^2	0.31	0.33	0.33	0.36	0.35
Prob < W	0.19	0.35	0.36	0.39	0.40

Note: See notes to Table 6.3.

for women and 90 per cent for men, when we do not control for sectors. The premium in terms of hourly wages, however, is larger for women.

For both women and men, university training and white-collar work add a little less than 40 per cent to monthly earnings. Yet, while for men the effect on monthly and hourly wages is about the same, for women the increment is larger for hourly wages. Secondary education and white-collar work adds about a quarter to male hourly wages, a little less to monthly wages. For women, the pay-off to jobs that go with any secondary schooling is low.

In model J, sector of occupation is controlled for. Using such a model means seeing choice of sector as independent of choice of education level or job-type. For men, the changes are small. The wage impacts of being a professional and a skilled worker decrease, which indicates that men in these categories have a higher than average probability of working in high-priority sectors. For women professionals, the direction of the shift in wage effect when sector is controlled for depends on whether the models include the short working week variables. There are many women

178

Table 6.5A Hourly wages for men, Models I–L

	Model I	Model J	Model K	Model L
Age, exp., pens	x	x	x	x
Reduced working time[a]			x	x
HIGHED1	0.39**	0.41**	0.31**	0.30**
PARTHIGH	0.01	0.01	–0.02	–0.02
SPECSEC	0.12¤	0.13¤	0.09	0.09
GENSEC	0.13¤	0.13¤	0.08	0.09
PTU1	0.21*	0.20*	0.16¤	0.18
PTU2	0.18*	0.20*	0.16¤	0.15¤
LOWED	0.09	0.08	0.05	0.07
HIGHQUAL	0.17	0.14	0.26*	0.25*
QUAL4	–0.46¤	–0.34	–0.26	–0.41¤
PHYSQUAL	0.07	0.05	0.11¤	0.13*
HIGH4	0.40	0.23	0.22	0.40¤
MID4	0.52*	0.39	0.40	0.55*
SEC4	0.57*	0.43¤	0.33	0.48*
Sectors		x	x	
Working conditions				
Adj. R^2	0.20	0.21	0.34	0.33
Prob > W	0.18	0.22	0.14	0.09

Note: See notes to Table 6.3.

Table 6.5B Hourly wages for women, Models I–L

	Model I	Model J	Model K	Model L
Age, exp., pens	x	x	x	x
Reduced working time			x	x
HIGHED1	0.17	0.16	0.21*	0.20¤
PARTHIGH	0.12	0.17	0.18¤	0.14
SPECSEC	0.12¤	0.14*	0.11¤	0.09
GENSEC	0.09	0.11¤	0.07	0.05
PTU1	0.13	0.17¤	0.16*	0.13
PTU2	0.57**	0.48**	–0.09	–0.08
LOWED	0.17	0.22¤	–0.07	–0.13
HIGHQUAL	0.44**	0.52**	0.42**	0.34**
QUAL4	0.12	0.12	0.07	0.09
PHYSQUAL	0.06	0.07	0.10*	0.10*
HIGH4	0.15	0.13	0.06	0.02
MID4	0.03	0.02	0.07	0.03
SEC4	–0.12	–0.13	–0.05	–0.07
Sectors		x	x	
Working conditions	x	x	x	x
Adj. R^2	0.16	0.24	0.49	0.44
Prob > W	0.0001	0.0001	0.66	0.43

Note: See notes to Table 6.3.

Table 6.6A Monthly wages for men, Models I–L

	Model I	Model J	Model K	Model L
Age, experience,[a] pens	x	x	x	x
Reduced working time[a]			x	x
HIGHED1	0.32**	0.34**	0.29**	0.29**
PARTHIGH	0.01	0.02	–0.01	–0.01
SPECSEC	0.13*	0.13*	0.10	0.11¤
GENSEC	0.10	0.10	0.07	0.08
PTU1	0.20*	0.18*	0.15¤	0.17*
PTU2	0.17*	0.19*	0.17*	0.16¤
LOWED	0.04	0.02	0.00	0.03
HIGHQUAL	0.26*	0.29*	0.35**	0.35**
QUAL4	–0.53*	–0.37	–0.31	–0.48*
PHYSQUAL	0.10¤	0.08	0.11¤	0.14*
HIGH4	0.52*	0.33	0.32	0.51*
MID4	0.63**	0.47¤	0.45¤	0.62**
SEC4	0.61**	0.44¤	0.39¤	0.56*
Sectors		x	x	
Working conditions	x	x	x	x
Adj. R^2	0.26	0.28	0.32	0.30
Prob > W	0.97	0.98	0.61	0.53

Note: See notes to Table 6.3.

Table 6.6B Monthly wages for women, Models I–L

	Model I	Model J	Model K	Model L
Age, experience,[a] pens	x	x	x	x
Reduced working time[a]			x	x
HIGHED1	0.21*	0.24**	0.22*	0.18*
PARTHIGH	0.19*	0.22**	0.22**	0.19*
SPECSEC	0.09¤	0.12*	0.12*	0.10¤
GENSEC	0.04	0.05	0.05	0.04
PTU1	0.10	0.12¤	0.12¤	0.10
PTU2	–0.05	–0.08	–0.16	–0.15
LOWED	–0.03	–0.02	0.04	0.01
HIGHQUAL	0.32**	0.38**	0.39**	0.35**
QUAL4	0.07	0.06	0.06	0.08
PHYSQUAL	0.09*	0.09*	0.10**	0.09*
HIGH4	0.04	0.02	0.04	0.04
MID4	–0.09	–0.06	–0.05	–0.10
SEC4	–0.07	–0.07	–0.06	–0.08
Sectors		x	x	
Working conditions	x	x	x	x
Adj. R^2	0.35	0.41	0.41	0.36
Prob > W	0.40	0.42	0.35	0.68

Note: See notes to Table 6.3.

Table 6.7   Models I, J, K and L

Includes/Model	I	J	K	L
Short working week			X	X
Sectors		X	X	

Table 6.8A   Percentage wage differential over unskilled workers with incomplete secondary school, for selected groups: hourly wages of men

Category	Definition	Model I	Model J	Model K	Model L
Managerial, etc. with full-time VUZ	Highqual + highed1	75	75	76	73
White-collar with full-time VUZ	Qual4 + highed1 + high4	39	36	32	33
White-collar with spec. secondary	Qual4 + specsec + sec4	26	25	17	17
White-collar with gen. secondary	Qual4 + gensec + sec4	26	25	17	16
Skilled worker with PTU	Physqual + PTU1	31	28	30	35

Table 6.8B   Percentage wage differential over unskilled workers with incomplete secondary school, for selected groups: hourly wages of women

Category	Definition	Model I	Model J	Model K	Model L
Managerial, etc. with full-time VUZ	Highqual + highed1	84	96	87	72
White-collar with full-time VUZ	Qual4 + highed1 + high4	56	50	39	37
White-collar with spec. secondary	Qual4 + specsec + sec4	14	15	14	12
White-collar with gen. secondary	Qual4 + gensec + sec4	11	11	9	7
Skilled worker with PTU	Physqual + PTU1	22	28	30	25

with university education in the socio-cultural sectors. In terms of hourly rates, they were relatively well paid – because of short weeks, not fat pay packets. The return to being a skilled worker with PTU increases when sector is controlled for. More female than male skilled manual workers work in the very low-paying consumer, municipal and housing services or in trade and catering. Male skilled workers were more concentrated into the high-priority sectors.

Table 6.9A Percentage wage differential relative to unskilled workers with
incomplete secondary school, for selected groups: monthly wages of men

Category	Definition	Model I	Model J	Model K	Model L
Managerial, etc. with full-time VUZ	Highqual + highed1	89	88	89	89
White-collar with full-time VUZ	Qual4 + highed1 + high4	38	35	34	38
White-collar with spec. secondary	Qual4 + specsec + sec4	24	23	20	21
White-collar with gen. secondary	Qual4 + gensec + sec4	20	19	16	17
Skilled worker with PTU	Physqual + PTU1	35	29	30	37

Table 6.9B Percentage wage differential relative to unskilled workers with
incomplete secondary school, for selected groups: monthly wages of women

Category	Definition	Model I	Model J	Model K	Model L
Managerial, etc. with full-time VUZ	Highqual + highed1	70	86	83	69
White-collar with full-time VUZ	Qual4 + highed1 + high4	38	38	37	34
White-collar with spec. secondary	Qual4 + specsec + sec4	10	12	13	11
White-collar with gen. secondary	Qual4 + gensec + sec4	4	5	5	4
Skilled worker with PTU	Physqual + PTU1	21	24	25	22

6.4.5 Interaction of education with reduced working hours

In chapter 5, the system of reduced working weeks in certain jobs was
found to be very important for relative hourly wages. Another way of
seeing this is to compare Model I with Model L, and Model J with Model K.
For the most highly qualified male white-collar staff, there is hardly any
difference. In other words, they have reduced working weeks to about the
same extent as the reference group of unskilled workers with low
education. The perceived reward for male white-collar staff with higher
education decreases when reduced workingweeks are controlled for. In
other words, some of the education/occupation premium for this group
can be said to take the form of reduced workingweeks without loss of pay.
This is even more true for employees with secondary education. Skilled
manual workers, on the contrary, seem to be the least likely group to
enjoy reductions in the working week.

For hourly wages we see that all categories of white-collar staff have some of their wage reward in the form of short workingweeks.[15] The wage premium for female professionals seems to be as much as 20 percentage points lower, when reduced weeks are included in the model. These effects are slightly smaller if sector is controlled for. The reduced week effect on wage rates was to a considerable extent an education-effect, but concentrated to the 'feminine' socio-cultural sphere. (See also section 5.3.2.)

6.4.6   Returns per year of education

The standard format for rewards to education is per year of schooling (or year of education of a particular type). Such yearly rates are reported in table 6.10, for both monthly and hourly wages. The rates are relatively similar to Ofer and Vinokur's (1992, Table 7.2). They find returns per year of (undergraduate) university studies in the order of 5 per cent, and per year of secondary specialist schooling of 3 per cent for men and 2 per cent for women.

Table 6.10   Average education premia, per year of study, as a percentage of wages (80 per cent confidence interval in parenthesis.)

Type of education	Hourly wages, men	Hourly wages, women	Monthly wages, men	Monthly wages, women
Full time higher/ incomplete secondary	5.9 (3.8–7.9)	7.5 (5.5–9.5)	5.3 (3.5–7.0)	5.0 (3.7–6.3)
Fulltime higher/ specialised secondary	6.1 (3.5–8.7)	11.0 (8.3–13.7)	4.7 (2.4–6.9)	7.1 (5.3–9.0)
Fulltime higher/general secondary	4.3 (2.4–6.2)	7.4 (5.7–9.1)	3.6 (2.2–5.0)	5.7 (4.5–6.9)
Secondary spec./ incomp. sec.	4.8 (2.0–7.7)	3.6 (1.2–6.1)	5.0 (2.4–7.6)	2.7 (1.0–4.5))
Secondary spec./gen. secondary	1.4 (−2.3–5.0)	1.5 (−1.5–4.4)	1.8 (−1.6–5.2)	2.8 (0.6–5.1)
General sec./incomp. secondary	8.1 (2.4–13.9)	5.5 (0.7–10.4)	8.0 (2.7–13.2)	2.5 (−1.1–5.6)
PTU with secondary/ incomp. sec.	9.0 (3.9–14.2)	6.4 (1.3–11.5)	8.7 (4.0–13.3)	5.0 (1.3–5.0)
PTU without secondary/ incomp. secondary	21.9 (7.2–36.6)	72.9 (32.2–113.4)	21.5 (8.2–34.9)	−11.2 (−26.6–4.2)

Note: The percentages are calculated as $f(\beta) = (100 \cdot (\exp(\beta) - 1)/\Delta)$ where β is the estimated coefficient for the first type of education when the second is the omitted category and Δ is the difference in usual years of study for the two levels. The β are assumed to be normally distributed with standard deviation s. Thus, the standard deviation of $f(\beta)$ is $f'(\beta) \cdot S$ and the confidence interval is $f(\beta) \pm t \cdot f'(\beta) \cdot S$ where t is chosen from the t-distribution. (To obtain a symmetrical 80 per cent interval, t = 1.282). Apart from the choice of omitted education category, the models were identical. They included age, experience, seniority and their squares, eight education dummies and ten work-condition variables.

The differences in returns between different types of education are striking, and they do not uniformly increase or decrease with level. For men, each year between year 8 and '*attestat*' (secondary school diploma) produces a return of 8–9 per cent, whether they are in PTU with secondary or in general secondary – but to continue in secondary specialist training after that has a payoff of 1–2 per cent, per year. The three additional years necessary to acquire a university degree instead pay off at the rate of 5–6 per cent. For women, the ranking is similar, although the pay-off to higher education tends to be larger than for men, while those for secondary schools are lower. The high premia for PTU without secondary education for men is likely to reflect a cohort effect. (The estimates for women with this education should, as explained above, be disregarded.)

The confidence intervals in Table 6.10 illustrate the variation in wages, at any given level education, even when age, experience and working conditions are controlled for. Since Soviet books and journals rarely reported either variation or sampling frame, the intervals in Table 6.10 are a rough, but salutary, indication of the margin of error in sample estimates.

The sample is small and local. Yet, the lack of reliable previous knowledge in this field makes it important to know that in this Soviet locality, wage premia for education were not zero.

6.4.7 Summary of results

We can now return to the questions in section 6.4.1. We have found that earnings increase most with experience among those with highest education, for both men and women. Yet, there are also gender differences. For all groups of men, and for female employees, earnings increase with experience, while women workers experience hardly any wage increase. We find some evidence that for women with university education, wage increases were linked to overall work experience, while for clerical workers and semi-professionals they came with staying in the enterprise.[16]

The choice of an education is to a considerable extent a choice of a future job. When education and broad occupation roles are combined, we find that higher education, and to a lesser extent secondary school or PTU have a larger impact on earnings prospects than the education parameters alone would imply.

There are few observations of women with PTU training and skilled manual work, but the crumbs of evidence we have tend to confirm that for Soviet men there were two routes to relatively well-paid work, while women had only one. Men could choose to go to university or to train for highly skilled manual work in material production. Women were discriminated against in access to such vocational training and had less access to jobs even if they had the skills.

Because of reduced working hours, the wage difference between men and women in terms of hourly wages is smaller than for monthly wages. The combination of higher education and white collar work in non-leading positions has a larger effect on the monthly than on the hourly earnings of men, while the opposite is true for women – further evidence of the reduced hours in feminised jobs of this type.

It seems that women with higher, and some women with very low, education gained more in terms of hourly wages from reduced working time than either lower- grade white-collar workers or more skilled manual workers. Hence the benefits to women of higher education are underestimated if we look only at monthly tariffs.

For women, the returns to higher and secondary education appear considerably smaller if working conditions are not controlled for. For men, only the estimates for the most qualified jobs are substantially affected.

6.5   Was there an official policy of 'wage-levelling'?

The Soviet discussion of 'levelling' followed two main tracks. One was that wages were not sufficiently differentiated to correspond to the 'final results' of the individual's labour. It was taken for granted that the incentives created by increased differentiation would improve productivity.[17] This is not a forgone conclusion.

According to most observers, the Soviet public usually preferred small pay differentials, particularly within the workplace.[18] Although Chapman (1988, p. 358) considers 'levelling' to be a serious problem, she notes that managers sometimes find that too much differentiation of pay rates or bonuses 'causes resentments that create more trouble on the shop floor than treating workers equally'. Since resentment and discontent are bad for productivity, widened differentials may actually be counter-productive as work incentives, particularly if they are perceived as arbitrary or unfair. (Cf. the efficiency wage theory, p. 18.)

When Soviet economists called for larger pay differentials according to education they took for granted that highly educated labour power is 'more productive' and that it is, therefore, economically efficient to award it higher wages. For example, Gordon (1987) argues that wages should be increased in the public education sector, because there 'people with higher or secondary specialist education form the majority of the employed, but in industry – only 1/4'. (There were, certainly, other and better reasons for increasing teachers' pay, but these are not mentioned.)

If returns to education are 'too big' or 'too small', it must be relative to a specified standard. The standard must be defined by some ethical norm or some concept of efficiency. (Efficiency in relation to an objective that is determined by a normative choice.) It is, of course, quite legitimate to discuss the issue as an ethical one. Depending on one's values, one could argue for equal wages, for distribution according to need, for rewards according to effort or to achievement. The choice is conditioned by interest, class and experience, but is ultimately ethical.

Wage policy can also be discussed in terms of its economic effects. It is possible to argue about what relative wages would best make people want first, to have the right jobs (according to some criterion), and second, to work hard enough in them. The next question is how large an effect wage policy *could* have on this, in a given society. For instance, surveys of Soviet job-changers indicate that higher wages were only one of many important reason for the change (Baranenkova, 1983). (That the structure of jobs in the USSR – technology as well as priorities – should have been changed is true, but beyond the present study.)

The distinction between 'normative' and 'descriptive' itself is of course neither clear-cut nor objective. The conservative ideological bias inherent in the neoclassical predilection for Pareto-optimality as a welfare criterion is a case in point. The problems inherent in the distinction do not, however, make it meaningless. Thus, depending on values, there are any number of possible views of what wage structure was desirable, and why. What is questioned here is the unspoken assumption that there is one, and only one, value-free 'optimal' choice of system of distribution.

As Strumilin pointed out in his 1925 study of schooling and productivity, productivity could not be measured by the non-market prices of the USSR.[19] How, then, could one measure either the total results or the individual contribution to them? This is also recognised by Gordon (1987), but he writes about 'the social necessity, usefulness of goods and services' as if this could be identified with market value in a *capitalist* economy. Externalities, public goods and the fact that demand – and, hence, market values – are a function of the distribution of wealth and income and do not express '*the* social utility function' are forgotten.

When the authority of Marx was ceremoniously invoked in the USSR, the principle of pay 'according to labour' was simply assumed to mean 'according to the results of labour'. Marx himself, in a brief section of the *Critique of the Gotha Programme*, may have meant that, or according to effort or labour time, or 'in proportion to the labour required to reproduce the necessary labour power' – or something else. As Redor (1992) notes, Marx never identified wages with productivity. As with other issues where no unambiguous opinion can be ascribed to Marx, in the USSR only one interpretation was sanctioned and disagreement was suppressed. At any rate, to transpose Marx's analysis of wages under the social relations of capitalism into a prescription for a non-capitalist society contradicts everything Marx said about his method. What was definitely not adopted by the *nomenklatura* was the most concrete 'recipe for the kitchens of the future' that Marx ever offered – the principle of the Paris Commune that no one representing the working class should earn more than a skilled worker.

Rimashevskaia (1992, p. 18f) explains the swifter growth of wages than of salaries as the result, partly, of 'the attempt to implant "levelling" into the national economy', but partly also of 'the necessity to attract unskilled workers to work and to stimulate it'. In another article Rimashevskaia (1989, p. 38) rightly notes that the 'disproportion between the high level of education, especially among youth, and the structure of employment influenced the formation of wages. The shortage of unskilled manpower . . . is compensated by its higher pay.' Yet her conclusion is that '[t]he relationship between level of education and pay was . . . violated'. Shortage of unskilled labour is, somehow, not sufficient justification for a high relative wage.

Western authors also believe in an official Soviet desire for '*uravnilovka*'. Redor (1992, p. 165) considers that the difference in pay between manual and non-manual staff is smaller in Soviet-type economies than in others, as a 'result, first of all, of the political options chosen by the leaders in these countries'. He asks whether this is connected to 'the leading role of the working class', so often proclaimed in the USSR and Eastern Europe. Yet, as he also notes, the socio-cultural status of workers in these states was by no means that of a privileged class. Newell and Reilly (1996, p. 346) note that the 'relatively low returns to education' in the USSR could reflect 'an over-supply of human capital', but without any argument favour the alternative interpretation that they 'reflect the consequences of egalitarian policies'.

Alternative explanations are there, for he that runs to see. The ruling stratum played off the working class and the intelligentsia against each other. Workers in 'material production' knew that the rulers needed their work and had limited means of disciplining them in the absence of unemployment. Oppositional workers risked repression (see, for instance, Haynes and Semyonova, 1979), but mass terror like that of the 1930s was not politically feasible and, therefore, an implicit 'social contract' was necessary. One element of this 'contract' may have been the level of the minimum wage. This was not intended to reduce differentiation, but since the aggregate Wage Fund did not allow other wages and salaries to be increased in proportion, it did, in fact, compress the wage structure (Malle, 1990, p. 252).

Thus, regardless of what the *nomenklatura* wanted, manual workers had a certain bargaining advantage. The underlying reasons were the importance to the system of the 'priority sectors' (heavy industry, infrastructure, minerals, energy and, above all, military production), the subordination of women, the inflexibility which made it impossible to change the priorities, inherited from the Stalin period, the weakness and instability of the system and, finally, the relativities of supply and demand for labour power. The last point will be discussed below. Here we will note only that enterprises had means of adjusting wages so as to prioritise the staff that management was most anxious not to loose (Granick, 1987, Redor, 1992).

One way in which the authorities tried to deal with the shortage of unskilled labour, without increasing pay, was mandatory secondments of staff from enterprises, to work which was 'low-skilled, physically hard and unattractive at prevailing earning levels' (Granick, 1987, p. 39).[20] The more market-like solution of raising regular earnings in these jobs, and avoiding the disruption and inefficiency of secondments, was rejected because rates for unskilled work *ought* not be higher – a telling example of official anti-levelling ideology.

6.6 Demand and supply of educated labour in the USSR

6.6.1 Increase in the level of non-vocational education

According to a survey cited by Rutkevich (1984), in 1965, about two-fifths of children started to work after incomplete secondary school, while an equal number continued into year 9 of general secondary school. The remainder went to PTU or to specialised secondary school. Ten years later, a very small number started work, after incomplete secondary school, while nearly a third went to PTU and three-fifths continued into year 9. The figures for 1980 are almost the same, except that, by then, most PTU students acquired secondary education.[21]

Of those who completed general secondary school in 1965, 16 per cent started work and about 40 per cent went to SSUZ and 40 per cent to VUZ. In 1980, two-fifths of a much larger number started work after general secondary school, a quarter went to PTU and the remaining third were divided equally between specialised secondary and higher education.

Initially, the vocational-technical schools had difficulty attracting students. Most pupils did not want to become workers, and those who did, preferred on-the-job training. (In the first Taganrog wave of surveys, 1967–68, 70 per cent of blue- collar workers wanted their children to have higher education.) It became easier after PTU with secondary education (SPTU) had been introduced in 1969. In 1989, seven out of eight PTU graduates had full secondary education, or obtained it through part- time studies. The numbers graduating from PTU increased from 1.6 million in 1970 to 2.6 million in 1986. Two-thirds had studied full-time (in day schools) and one third had taken part-time courses (*Nar. Khoz.*, 1988, p. 55, *Nar. Khoz.*, 1989, p. 64).

Nevertheless, as we have seen, the numbers going to general secondary increased too. In former times, those who went to general secondary school expected to continue in higher education and become '*intelligentsia*'. When almost everyone acquired full secondary schooling, the *proportion* of secondary school graduates entering university fell, even though the *numbers* increased by 70 per cent from 1965 to 1980 (Rutkevich, 1980, 1984).

Thus, the supply of educated labour power was drastically increased. This must have exerted a downward pressure on estimated returns to education. If there were fewer qualified jobs than qualified workers, some would have to take jobs requiring less education and with lower pay. Thus our estimates of the wages of the educated would be lower than if we had measured wages in jobs requiring the education. With many highly educated workers employed, their marginal productivity would be lower than if there were few of them.

Unfortunately, the studies cited make little or no distinction by gender. As seen in section 4.3.3, there was a large gender difference in fields and forms or schooling.

It is also interesting to look at studies made after the collapse of the Soviet system, since while the centralised wage-setting was abolished over a short time, it would take longer for the supply of educated labour to change. Brainerd (1998) finds increases in returns to years of schooling for both men and women from 1991 to 1994 but is cautious in interpreting why the 'winners' over this period are 'young, well-educated men whose skills have enabled them to exploit new profit-making opportunities' (Brainerd, 1998, p. 1112). A later study, based on better data and focusing particularly on returns to education, finds very small increases in returns to education in the 1992–99 period (Sheidvasser and Benítez-Silva, 1999). Their analysis leads them to polemicise against the argument of Newell and Reilly (1996, see p. 186) that low returns to education are the consequence of wage equalisation policies originating in the Soviet period and continued by state enterprises. Instead, they conclude that the persisting low education premia were not primarily caused by 'government egalitarian policy, whose influence faded completely over the last seven years' but 'were (and still are) more likely the consequence of over-supply of highly educated workers, combined with high demand for blue-collar jobs' (ibid., p. 29).

Clarke and Kabalina (2000), in a study of the post-Soviet 'new private sector', find that employers 'prefer to hire people with higher education even for low- skilled positions. ... In our case study enterprises, in retail trade it was rare to find an employee without at least middle special education and sometimes even the ordinary sales staff had higher education.' One reason for this preference, stated by employers, was 'the over-supply of people with higher education on the labour market' (ibid., p. 12).

6.6.2 Labour shortages

Soviet educational policies from the 1950s onwards aimed to make more youngsters choose vocational training for skilled manual jobs, instead of aspiring to higher general education. Complete secondary education came to be regarded as the proper basic schooling also for workers (Kirsch, 1972, p. 102), but it needed to be combined with some form of professional training. The Soviet job structure had few clerical jobs that could have suited those with general secondary school.

It was expensive to train people who would not find jobs where they could use what they had learnt. An additional concern was that secondary school graduates, who were frustrated in their hopes for further education, as well as those who got the education but couldn't get a job corresponding to it, would become demoralised. They were said to be indifferent and undisciplined, and to change jobs frequently, something the authorities disapproved of.

Workers, particularly young workers with eleven years or more schooling, would not accept dirty, heavy, boring unqualified jobs unless they were quite well paid for it. Cherednichenko and Shubkin (1985, p. 68) in a study of how Soviet teenagers evaluated different jobs write that 'today society is obliged to give additional pay (*doplachivat'*) not only according to how complicated or heavy the work is, but also because it is unprestigious'.

Soviet industry, however, demanded unskilled manual labour. It was notorious for its large numbers of auxiliary workers, relative to the numbers directly working in production (Granick, 1987, p. 186, Ticktin, 1973). These workers might be skilled, but in very many cases were engaged in very simple, unmechanised tasks.

With the exception of the far north and remote rural areas, it was not hard to recruit doctors, engineers or teachers – while anyone in the USSR would tell you how difficult it was to find someone who would work as a cleaner.

Malle's (1986) conclusion from the Soviet literature is that there were more ITR staff available than necessary and that education of specialists for industry grew much faster than employment. Of course, a general excess supply is compatible with partial shortages in particular localities or particular occupations. The difficulty of enticing specialists to work in remote regions was a problem for new enterprises as well as for health-care and schools. This reflected the deterrent effect of the lack of social and cultural amenities as well as shortages of consumer goods in rural areas and in the far north, in addition to the latter's forbidding climate.

A study of demand and supply for labour with different qualifications in the USSR must differentiate according to the sex, age and nationality of the worker. And, as Malle points out, it must also differentiate according to the 'quality' of the employer. Depending on size, sector and success, there were large differences in the bonuses, promotion prospects and non-monetary benefits different enterprises could offer.

Both this study and Ofer and Vinokur's (1992) find that returns per year of secondary specialist training were lower than for a year of university. Soviet statistics and research tended to aggregate the whole group of 'specialists'. This probably reflected the dated notion that all general education beyond ten years was 'high'. (By 1989, 39 per cent of the employed population were 'specialists'.)

'Secondary specialists' in industry faced competition, both from more and more university graduates, and from more and more PTU graduates with secondary education, as well as from older workers with less schooling but more experience. SPTU provided only one year less of schooling than SSUZ and skills which were in great demand.

The pay of 'secondary specialists' in service jobs was depressed by the low value accorded, not to educated labour, but to female and to service labour. By 1970, 63 per cent of 'secondary specialists' were women, and this reduced their average wage. Ofer and Vinokur (1992, p. 261) found, in a survey of émigrés, that the male/female wage differential was larger among those with specialised secondary school than in other educational groups.

6.7   What determines the choice of education?

In 1980, for each 100 full-time places in institutions of higher education (VUZ), there were 212 applicants for the entrance examinations. For full-time secondary specialised schools, the figure was 175 per 100 places (*Nar. obr.*, 1989, pp. 179 and 229). In 1988 the number of applicants per place was 2.0 for both. In 1988 there were 2.4 applicants for each full-time university place in medical and physical education schools (despite the low pay of doctors) and 1.5 in those linked with industry and construction. In secondary specialist education, the figures were nearly identical.

There are Soviet surveys comparing the preferences of 8th graders with the education they actually got, but it is hard to judge the representativeness of the samples. Granick (1987, p. 209) quotes a survey from the Urals in 1972, according to which 30 per cent of 8th form school-leavers wanted to go to specialised secondary education, but only 10 per cent were admitted. (For further references, see Marnie, 1986.)

There are a number of economic reasons why people in the USSR would aspire to a higher level of education even with a relatively small wage premium. First, as in many West European countries, but unlike the United States, tuition at all levels was free. Most full-time students received non-refundable grants, and for those who did not live with their parents, there were inexpensive hostels. The grants were not very generous, and most hostels were not very attractive – but it was possible to manage even without parental support. The widespread availability of evening and correspondence courses made it possible to study with little loss of earnings. On the other hand, the burden of combining work and study was heavy and for single mothers or married women, with a third shift in the home, it was gruelling. Also, the quality of this education was considered inferior to full-time studies. (This may explain the low wage premiums we have noted for part-time university graduates in Taganrog.)

Since women could rarely get the best paid blue-collar jobs, their opportunity wage was lower than that of men, as were their reservation wages in jobs requiring more education. Hence, and since this education was available to many of them, women crowded into white-collar professions and contributed to depressing wages there.

Jobs for the well-educated were more likely to provide fringe benefits, opportunities for second incomes, shorter working weeks, laxer supervision at work and, not least, escape from the physical strain and health hazards of manual work. It is also essential to keep in mind the prestige and self-esteem connected with a diploma and with a qualified white-collar occupation, as well as the ambiguous demands that Soviet sex-role socialisation made on women. Being a doctor, teacher or secretary could satisfy the expectation that women should be employed, as well as a patriarchal concept of 'femininity'. (See pp. 79ff.) For rural youth, education meant escape from the village and for those in small towns a road to a larger city. Aage (1984) concludes from Soviet evidence that higher prestige, rather than higher wages, was the principal attraction of education.

6.8   Over- and underqualification of staff

A related concern was that people choose jobs that do not match their schooling because of perverse wage incentives. In engineering, about one blue-collar job in eight was held by a university graduate and 22 per cent of engineers worked in jobs that did not require higher education (Malle, 1987, p. 378). The majority (62 per cent) of graduates with higher education, working in blue-collar jobs, were engineers. Of secondary specialists in such jobs, 73 per cent were technicians (*Trud v SSSR*, 1988, p. 121). Granick (1987) doubts whether engineers stayed in blue-collar jobs, but like Gloeckner (1986), he emphasises that many engineers felt that not enough use was made of their knowledge.

Altogether, of the 15.5 million with higher education, in 1987, 3.7 per cent worked in blue-collar jobs (*Trud* ..., 1988). Engineers, which is a mixed profession with access to skilled workers' jobs in industry, were more likely to have a manual job, than low-paid, predominantly female, groups like doctors, teachers or librarians. (See Table 6.11.)

Among 'secondary specialists', 21 per cent had blue-collar jobs. Almost a third of technicians worked in blue-collar jobs, but they were not all

Table 6.11   Proportion of employed specialists* with different professional training working as blue-collar workers (in per cent)

	With higher education	With specialist secondary school
Engineers/technicians	5.5	32.6
Agronomists, veterinaries	4.8	21.2
Economists**	2.5	9.9
Physicians/medical staff	0.3	2.7
Teachers, librarians, cultural workers	2.1	5.6

Sources: Calculated from *Trud v SSSR* (1988, p. 121) and *Nar. obr.* (1989, p. 13f.).
* 'Specialist' refers to the education of the person, not to her/his present occupation.
** The category '*ekonomist*' was wide and included unqualified book-keeping.

overqualified – nearly 400 blue-collar occupations required secondary specialist education (Gloeckner, 1986). In the lowest paid, female-dominated groups in the socio-cultural sphere, few specialists entered manual occupations.

Was it a lack of wage incentives that kept specialists from putting their education to use? Were there other reasons for this choice, or is it not so much a choice as the effect of job rationing? Conclusions differ. Prokofeva (1991, p. 122) writes that in the Taganrog survey of the late 1970s, 40 per cent of 'specialists with secondary education' worked in blue-collar jobs. She considers wage differences to be the main factor, but does not report any figures in evidence.

A factory survey cited by Oxenstierna (1990, pp. 218ff)[22] found that the proportion of staff with higher education working in manual jobs increased from 6 per cent in 1975 to 10 per cent in 1985. According to the study, 'a major part of the ITRs working in blue-collar positions had been offered ITR positions and had refused these offers'. Of those with higher education, 61 per cent cited the low wages of ITRs as the reason for their refusal. According to this study there was a shortage of some categories of ITR staff, especially foremen.

According to another survey of 10,700 specialists in industry, nearly half did not work in the profession they were trained for. Yet, of those who did not, only one in eight said it was because their earnings would have been lower. A quarter had not found any vacancies, nearly two-fifths quoted 'inadequate training, family obligations and other reasons' and one in five found the job they were doing more interesting (*Trud v SSSR*, 1988, p. 123. No information on the sampling provided.) Hence, relative wages do not appear to be the main reason.

School-leavers or university graduates, who were assigned a job in a region where they did not want to live, might take a less qualified job in their home town instead. Those who failed the entrance examination to VUZ might take any job while preparing for the next round of examinations, or work for the two years which gave preferential access to the university. For a young specialist, it could be better to take a manual job with the opportunity for future promotion in a 'strong' enterprise than to get a more qualified position with a 'weak' employer. The carrot of a residence permit (*propiska*) for a large city made it possible to recruit workers into less skilled jobs than they might otherwise have demanded.

Malle (1987, pp. 374–6) emphasises that most vacancies were in 'the least attractive' jobs. Vacancies in blue-collar jobs were 70 per cent of all vacancies and increased faster than the number of such jobs during the

1970s. Both Malle (1987) and Aage (1984) observe that it was more difficult to recruit staff for blue-collar than for white-collar positions.

Of my sources, only Prokofeva discusses different reasons for male or female specialists to be 'downwardly mobile'. A reasonable guess is that men were more likely to enter highly skilled worker occupations, that they would attach more importance to pay and to housing, and women more to access to consumer goods and services (including subsidised child-care). (See pp. 73ff.)

The argument that it was inefficient to have highly educated staff in blue-collar jobs would be strengthened if positions that ought to require secondary specialist or higher education were held by workers who lacked these qualifications.

According to Prokofeva (1991, p. 130) highly qualified staff in teaching, child-care and health-care were discouraged by the low wages in these sectors and therefore the qualified jobs had to be given to people without the necessary qualifications. Her only concrete example, however, is that mothers of young children worked in nurseries even though they lacked professional training as nursery teachers. It is unclear whether these were women with low education, or whether they had high education in some other field, since she also says that a strong incentive for doing so was to provide good quality care for their own children. (In 1988, one fifth of nursery teachers had less than specialised secondary education. *Nar. obr.*, 1989, p. 43.)

Table 6.12, based on the last three Soviet censuses, shows that the number of non-specialists working as managers or professionals decreased substantially over this 20-year period, as did the numbers of secondary specialists in jobs like dentistry or school teaching, despite the low pay. This suggests that such underqualification mainly reflected past, not contemporary, under-supply.[23]

Did skilled workers choose unskilled jobs or did they have to take them? The evidence is ambiguous. According to Komozin (1991), both young specialists and young workers had difficulty finding sufficiently skilled work. Pravda (1982, p. 3f), however, writes that 'young workers have rapidly climbed the skill ladder ... leaving the lower echelons largely to older blue-collar workers'. Yet, Pravda also notes that many skilled young workers, particularly young women, had to do unskilled work. Granick (1987, pp. 112, 187 and 189) quotes Soviet case studies according to which skilled workers had to do work for which they were overqualified because of the shortage of unskilled workers.

Kirsch (1972, p 105) quotes a study of 3,000 workers according to which work in the highest skill grades (V and VI) was scarce, many workers

Table 6.12   Education of staff in selected occupations, 1970–89

	Higher education 1970 1979 1989			Secondary specialists 1970 1979 1989			Not specialists 1970 1979 1989		
Enterprise managers[a]	39	46	58	34	34	30	27	20	12
Heads of departments, sections, etc.	52	60	68	34	30	26	14	10	6
Engineers[b]	53	59	66	37	34	30	10	7	4
Technicians	2	4	7	59	63	65	39	33	28
Foremen (salaried)	7	14	23	49	56	57	44	30	20
University lecturers	96	96	95	3	3	3	1	1	2
School teachers	49	64	69	40	29	26	11	7	5
Nursery teachers[c]	10	16	17	49	54	56	41	30	27
Physicians	89	89	90[d]	9	9	9	2	2	1
Dentists	29	47	57	66	50	39	5	3	4
Medical nurses	1	1	1	78	81	87	21	18	12
Economists, statisticians	31	40	47	43	44	44	26	16	9
Book-keepers	3	7	10	32	46	61	65	47	29
Secretaries, clerical staff[e]	2	5	9	12	21	34	86	74	57

a. For 1989 this also includes 'organisations', i.e. not only 'material production'.
b. Excluding chief-engineers.
c. For 1970 and 1979 heads of nurseries were included, but not in 1989.
d. According to *Trud v SSSR* (1988, p. 126), in 1985, 99 per cent of physicians had higher education.
e. Does not include typists and stenographers.
Sources: *Itogi* ... (1979 Census), vol. IX, table 51, 1989 Census, vol. XI, table 5.

qualified for them remained in grades III and IV, and seniority determined promotion. Other studies in the same period pointed in the same direction.

On the other hand, Swafford (1979, p. 19) writes that in 1975 a shortage of skilled workers 'prevented more than half of all new enterprises scheduled to operate at full capacity from doing so'. Oxenstierna (1990, pp. 221f.) cites complaints that too many skilled workers were trained for industry, construction and agriculture and too few for the service sector.

Demand for skilled workers relative to that for unskilled workers did increase over time. From 1965 to 1985 the average skill grade in industry rose from 3.1 to 3.6. Over these 20 years, twice as many jobs in the two highest skill grades had become available. On the other hand, the supply of workers with technical-vocational training increased considerably from the 1960s, and it is doubtful whether the increase in skilled jobs had kept pace with that of qualifications. The promotion prospects of blue-collar workers were reduced further through competition with technicians and engineers working in blue-collar jobs (usually in the highest skill grades).

Conditions no doubt varied between occupations, sectors and regions. The studies may over-generalise from small and non-random samples of enterprises. Yet, I take the balance of the evidence to be that there was often a surplus, and almost always less shortage, of skilled than of unskilled manual labour.

In the Taganrog sample, of working respondents with higher education, over 20 per cent of the men and 10 per cent of the women are employed as blue-collar workers. Just under half of them (17 individuals) consider that their knowledge and professional skills are higher than required for their job. A larger-than-average proportion received their degree from evening or correspondence courses. Neither men nor women seem to have taken these jobs in connection with having young children.[24]

Of specialists with secondary education (including incomplete higher), the majority are in the 'worker' occupations. A quarter of the male 'secondary specialists', and a tenth of the female, are coded as workers and consider their skills to be higher than necessary for the job. Many are skilled workers in heavy industry. The women report a high degree of satisfaction with their jobs.

The 'overqualified' workers actually earn a little less than others with a similar education. Hence, although not much positive information can be collected from such a small sample, there is no vindication of the hypothesis that relative wages induced people to take jobs in which they earned more but were less productive.

6.9   Conclusions

A quantitative assessment of returns to education in the USSR must take into account, first, that women were paid less than men, controlling for sector, experience and education. As the share of women among the highly educated increased over time, average relative wages for this category decreased. Second, in Soviet literature higher and specialised secondary education were often aggregated, even though the former was much better rewarded. With time, the output of the specialised secondary schools became greater than the economy could usefully absorb, and relative wages fell with marginal productivity.

Two more general points have been emphasised. First, demand for education is not a function of wages only but also of other advantages of schooling and of the jobs that it gives access to. Second, Soviet planners could not totally disregard demand and supply when setting the price of labour power.

Despite the low wages of highly educated staff in the socio-cultural sphere, there does not seem to have been a lack of applicants for such jobs. Staff shortages in lower-level occupations in child-care and health-care reflected that these occupations combined the features of low priority sectors *and* of low-skilled manual work with worse pay and conditions than professionals and semi-professionals in the same sector.

If the Soviet workforce included larger numbers with high education than there were jobs for, higher wage premiums for academic or general schooling are likely to have exacerbated the existing imbalances, rather than to have stimulated people to make better use of their education. Therefore, it is difficult to argue that pay differentials according to skill or education were suppressed, because the central authorities had an ideological preference for equalisation. Compression of the wage structure seems more in accordance with, than contrary to, the pressure of demand and supply conditions. Further, there is evidence of a 'wage-drift' at the enterprise level, not initialised or sanctioned by the authorities, which increased the relative pay of manual workers, particularly the unskilled.

The more qualified jobs were not unfilled. Hence, those who criticise 'levelling' ought to demonstrate, first, that there were people who would have been more competent to do these jobs than those who actually held them, and second, that they would have taken them if pay had been higher. Many writers claim that feminisation meant lower quality or intensity of work[25] (hence, the Soviet authorities' efforts to reduce the share of women in medicine[26]), yet, no one takes this idea to its logical conclusion by saying which men would replace these women and who would replace them, in their turn, in their (skilled blue-collar?) jobs. Nor is it self-evident that those for whom earnings are relatively most important in choice of job necessarily make the best doctors, scientists or teachers!

A more forceful argument is that the low relative pay of engineers, doctors and teachers made them demoralised, less committed to their work and, hence, less productive. The same argument applied, however, to manual workers in industry, who might be handling expensive capital equipment, and this was a reason to pay them relatively well. The issue remains one of priorities.

It is true that the high proportion of blue-collar relative to white-collar jobs in the USSR was evidence of backwardness and inefficiency, as well of the undemocratic character of priority-making. (If the majority of Soviet citizens could have decided, as consumers or as voters, it is unlikely that the service sector would have been so underdeveloped.) The large numbers of manual workers, relative to non-manual, in manufacturing was an indication of poor technology and organisation. My point is that neither of these problems is likely to have been lessened by a rise in the relative wages of white-collar staff with high education.

In developed Western countries too, the level of schooling of the workforce increased in the 1960s and 1970s, and this was followed by a substantial decrease in returns to education (Edin et al., 1994). Note also that in both Western and Soviet-type economies, an expansion of jobs requiring long schooling, performed mainly by women and perceived as 'female' coincided with a decrease in average returns to schooling.

Many Soviet intellectuals believed that a market economy would automatically raise the salaries of the *intelligentsia* relative to those of workers. What existed in the richer Western countries was taken to be 'normal'. But if the availability and private cost of education are different, production priorities, preferences and gender relations are different, nothing implies that it is most efficient for relative wages *not* to be different. What the debate should have focused on are these underlying factors themselves – and perhaps on why the idea of a 'levelling ideology' was so widespread and so emotionally charged. There is also good reason to debate how the outcome of Russian market reforms has been contingent on the reformers' 'aversion to equality ... deeply rooted in their belief that communist egalitarianism played a major part in perpetuating the inefficiencies of the Soviet economy' (Silverman and Yanowitch, 1997, p. 10).

Appendix

Interaction between job type and education

A full job type/education interaction model would have had to take into account 32 possible combinations. With a sample of this size, this was not meaningful. To reduce the problem, education was aggregated into four broad levels: (any) higher education, complete secondary, PTU and incomplete secondary or less. Even so there were 14 parameters to estimate. Only six were signficant, even at the 10 per cent level, for women, three for men. Since most education groups are dominated by one job type, the average represented by an 'education parameter' should be close to the effect for the job-type group in which most observations with this education are found. The 'interaction model' reported in Table A6.1 was used to test whether the illustrative procedure of adding parameters was a reasonable approximation. For men, its coefficients diverged a lot from the simple parameter sums, even for the more

Table A6.1   Estimates of hourly wages with education/job-type combinations

	Men parameter estimate	T for H0: Parameter = 0	Women parameter estimate	T for H0: Parameter = 0
INTERCEP	-0.280170	-0.983	-0.457236	-1.653
AGE	0.015772	1.141	-0.002349	-0.176
AGESQ	-0.000209	-1.371	0.000064995	0.413
STAZH	0.005297	0.969	0.003237	0.858
SENIOR	0.002157	0.947	0.002171	0.851
PENS	-0.297362	-3.402	-0.308576	-3.353
MTS	0.059872	1.121	0.060117	1.646
PARTY	0.065889	1.572	0.035277	0.808
LOW1	0	–	0	–
LOW2	-0.105440	-1.049	0.148700	1.474
LOW4	–	–	-0.099798	-0.276
PTU1	0.103455	0.619	0.254635	1.973
PTU2	0.113001	1.740	0.061836	0.657
PTU4	-0.290451	-1.167	0.238052	1.146
MID1	-0.095079	-0.849	0.151825	1.800
MID2	0.041598	0.545	0.210829	2.681
MID4	0.080170	0.778	0.140856	1.720
MID5	–	–	0.576911	2.939
HIGH1	0.058215	0.234	-0.172784	-0.633
HIGH2	0.173774	1.661	0.214873	1.622
HIGH4	0.078279	0.842	0.404931	4.822
HIGH5	0.326216	2.551	0.657525	4.666
HEAVY	0	–	0	–
TRANSP	-0.028086	-0.425	-0.003897	-0.046
CONSTR	-0.059178	-0.826	-0.065742	-0.816
LIGHT	-0.068866	-0.797	-0.026678	-0.396
SERV	-0.231791	-2.766	0.003824	0.056
TRADE	-0.330138	-2.306	-0.312702	-4.803
TEACH	0.010975	0.125	0.170024	3.055
HEALTH	0.056908	0.442	-0.090817	-1.297
ART	0.017373	0.112	-0.138885	-1.033
SCIENCE	-0.023668	-0.279	-0.198071	-2.422
GOVT	-0.170032	-0.708	-0.089967	-0.726
OTHER	-0.043970	-0.547	0.229891	2.742
HEAT	0.130477	1.941	0.176424	1.689
HEAVY	0.034559	0.633	0.153908	2.353
NERVOUS	-0.157554	-3.796	-0.113479	-2.754

Table A6.1   (continued)

	Men parameter estimate	T for H0: Parameter = 0	Women parameter estimate	T for H0: Parameter = 0
OTHCOND	0.079910	1.889	0.115991	2.262
Adj R^2		0.17		0.22

The qualification/education dummies are defined as follows:
LOW = respondent has incomplete secondary school or less
PTU = respondent has PTU-schooling
MID = respondent has complete secondary but not complete higher education
HIGH = respondent has higher education
The figures refer to qualification categories:
1 = unskilled worker
2 = skilled worker with manual or partly manual work (qual2 and qual3)
4 = non-managerial white collar work (qual4)
5 = managerial or highly qualified creative work (qual5 and qual6)
Thus, LOW2 means 'skilled manual worker with eight or less years of school', HIGH4 means 'white collar worker with higher education' etc. (PN that, PTU1 and PTU2, in this table, both refer to either kind of PTU, but to different job-types.)

common combinations. On the other hand, precision was very low indeed. For women, precision was better, and the effects were close to those obtained by adding parameters.

A Chow-test showed that equality between this model and one without interaction was not rejected for men at the 5 per cent level. It was rejected at the 5 per cent, but not at the 1 per cent, level for women. After a check of how average wages varied with education within job types, a new model was constructed with interaction effects only for qual4. It was enough to divide this group into one with and one without higher education, to produce reassuringly low F-statistics when testing for equality between this model and a model with all 14 combinations. When the new model was tested against no interactions, equality was resoundingly rejected.[27] The acceptance of equality between this intermediate model and that with all combinations included implies that for other job types it is acceptable to assume that wage effects of the job-type do not vary with education.

Using the approximations of Tables 6.8–6.9 involves the following simplifications:

a. All highqual staff are assumed to have full-time university education. In fact, 10 per cent have part-time higher education and 13 per cent secondary education. However, the detailed interaction model shows a rather small difference between highqual with higher and highqual with secondary education.

b. The interaction effect Sec4 does not distinguish between specialised and general secondary education. The reader must judge from the size of the parameters for these groups in other models whether separate interaction effects would have been likely to be very different.

c. Not all skilled workers have PTU with secondary school education. In fact, more have specialised or general secondary education. Yet, the parameters for the two kinds of secondary school and the two kinds of PTU have been of similar magnitudes. The exception is hourly wages for women with PTU2, but this outlier group are not skilled workers and therefore do not affect the coefficient for 'physqual'. To use this coefficient, that is the average premium for skilled workers over educational groups, therefore, involves a relatively small error. (Average monthly and hourly wages for skilled workers with gensec and specsec are a few percentage points lower than for those with PTU.)

7
Taganrog Post-USSR: Patriarchy, Poverty, Perspectives

7.1 Introduction

Earlier chapters have shown some of the many reasons why one should not idealise life in the USSR or regret the demise of the Soviet order. The old days were bad, but, nevertheless, conditions of life have deteriorated drastically for many Russians. In the wake of 'market reform', poverty, social tension, stress and insecurity have taken a tragic toll in terms of well being, health and life expectancy. The labour market is only a part of this scenario, but an essential one on which the majority depend for their livelihood and for important elements of their identity, their status and self-esteem and for social relations well beyond those in the workplace itself.

Russian workers have experienced drastic changes. Instead of job security, they face fear of unemployment. Instead of not being able to find goods, people are unable to afford them. Instead of an all-dominant state sector, in 1998, 43 per cent of the employed population worked in the private sector and an additional 18 per cent in enterprises with mixed ownership (*Rossiiskii* ... 1999, p. 109). Yet, the privatised enterprises most often retain both their old management and much of their old working practices. Firms are supposedly subject to 'the discipline of the market', yet they evade paying what they owe each other, their workers and the tax authorities for years on end. GNP has slumped, yet open unemployment is not higher than in Western Europe. Employers default on wage payments, yet hire new staff. Millions of employees do not get paid, yet do not quit their jobs. Wages do not cover the cost of bare essentials, yet people survive.[1] Although the old system collapsed in disgrace, those who ruled under it (and their offspring) are still likely to be powerful and affluent, while those most nostalgic for the old order tend to be such as it disadvantaged.

The present chapter will limit itself to certain aspects of the gender dimension of employment in Russia. There is, by now, quite an extensive literature in the field, but a shortage of solid empirical analysis, particularly quantitative. Since empirical knowledge beyond impressions, individual cases and anecdotes is a precondition for taking theoretical analysis further, what follows will focus on the empirical and quantitative.

Women in the former Soviet Union encountered the turmoil of post-Soviet economic reform from a relative position of disadvantage, of segregation and discrimination. This chapter will outline the differential impact of post-reform changes on women and men in Taganrog, and in Russia, as concerns labour force participation, unemployment and earnings. A statistical analysis, similar to that of the preceding chapters will be performed on household survey data collected in Taganrog in 1993/94 and comparison made with those of 1989. In addition, official statistics will be used to measure the local situation against the national, and to follow trends up to 1997–98. Analysis of wages will be mainly based on the Taganrog data. The study of changes in employment and unemployment will have heavier emphasis on the national statistics, since the number of observations of unemployed and of employed in smaller sectors are not large enough in the sample.

The study is limited to paid work even though this is unsatisfactory, particularly for a gender analysis. Contrary to what was expected before the transition, it is not likely that housework has been reduced. The need to search for the cheapest goods and to forgo services that have become unaffordable (such as laundries) and the increased need for subsistence gardening, take up time that earlier was spent in queues. (Eremitcheva, 1995, is one of the few sources to discuss this issue, but does not have representative or quantitative data.) According to official statistics the volume of consumer services in 1996 was less than a quarter of the 1990 level (*Rossiiskii ... 1999*, p. 457). The statistics no doubt exaggerate the size of the drop since some service production has transferred to the 'shadow', grey or black economy, but it would be surprising if *none* of the decline was real. Since no fully-fledged time-use studies are made in Russia today, we will not go deeper into the issue of housework here.

A summary of the findings and a discussion of the conclusions that can be drawn from them is deferred to chapter 8.

7.2 Women in post-reform Russia

7.2.1 'Backlash'

One very visible phenomenon starting in the *glasnost'* years and continuing in post-Soviet Russia was – to use a perhaps inappropriately

Western term – a 'backlash' in the media, in politics, culture and entertainment. One important aspect concerned women and sexuality. All forms of commercial exploitation of the female body – from naked women in advertisements for carpenters' tools to prostitution – became rampant. During the Soviet period, sexual harassment at work had been one of the issues, that could not be discussed and was therefore assumed not to exist. There was now nothing to protect women from the employers whose job advertisements asked for good-looking women, not older than 25, or for secretaries with language skills and long legs.

With the typical dichotomy known from feminist research elsewhere, reducing women to sexual objects went in tandem with glorification of the 'virtuous' woman as wife and mother, patient, tender and – above all – self-sacrificing (Buckley, 1992, Lissyutkina, 1993, Klimenkova, 1994, Kay, 1997).

Another manifestation of 'patriarchal renaissance' was that with a real choice in elections, Soviet and East European voters elected very few women. With the 1989 election to the USSR Supreme Soviet, the percentage of women deputies fell from 33 per cent to 19 per cent (*Zhenshchiny v SSSR*, 1989, 1990).[2] Following the 1999 elections, only 8 per cent of the members of the State Duma (Russian Parliament) are women. (Analogous figures for Eastern Europe are cited in Grapard, 1997.)

A third concerned employment. During Gorbachev's *perestroika*, influential and widespread voices argued that it was time to free the 'over-emancipated' Soviet woman from her double burden and return her to her 'natural' place in life, as the guardian of home and hearth (Buckley, 1992). During the Soviet period, the view that women are less suited for careers than men and have a 'natural propensity' for devoting themselves above all to their homes, husbands and children was only barely covered beneath a thin veneer. Now politicians, employers and academic 'experts' could claim openly that female unemployment did not merit concern so long as men were unemployed and women were better off not working, anyway. Many women also welcomed a reduction in employment. A typical opinion was that 'quite a few more that women wish to return to the kitchen in order to be relieved of doing road work, construction jobs or factory work' (Lissyutkina, 1993, p. 276). According to this view, patriarchal gender roles became a protest against a 'totalitarian system built on force and the demise of individual differences including the differences between men and women' (ibid., p. 277).

As previous chapters have shown, 'the differences between men and women' were far from 'demised' in the USSR. Thus, Bloomsma (1993) points to the continuity between post-Soviet ideology and longstanding

Soviet views on the 'demographic problem' (see p. 101f). Yet, it was perceived by most as a break with the Soviet past. As Waters (1993, p. 288) puts it: 'When the propaganda claims concerning women's emancipation were eventually challenged, it was less to expose their lack of substance than to deny the validity of the professed objectives.' As she says, Soviet ideology, the adherents of market reform and the conservative slavophiles had in common an essentialist perception of femininity and masculinity.

In this atmosphere, the emerging women's movement had an uphill struggle. Yet, the newly obtained freedoms of speech and organisation were a very real gain for Russian women. By the early 1990s, the number of independent women's organisations numbered in their hundreds. Women have organised themselves in groups and networks-producer co-ops, organisations for women in business or in professions, help-lines for battered women, feminist centres for researchers and artists. So far, however, they have had a rather small impact on society (with the possible exception of the organisations of Soldiers' Mothers) and feminism or equal opportunity policies have very limited support.

7.2.2 Marginalisation of women in the labour market?

When market reforms began, scholars of different disciplines, in Russia itself and in the West, noted indications that women were losing out in terms of employment and earnings too (Khotkina, 1994, Buckley, 1992, 1997, Fong, 1994, Lissyutkina, 1993, Posadskaya, 1994, Malysheva, 1996). A number of authors asserted that marginalisation had already occurred (Fong, 1995, Posadskaia, 1996, Rimashevskaia, 1996). General arguments that there was bias against women in market reforms, in the whole former Soviet bloc, were given (Einhorn, 1993, Funk and Mueller, 1993, Hopkins, 1995, Grapard, 1997), but not substantiated by first-hand empirical studies.

There were a number of reasons why market reforms could squeeze women out of employment:

- The notoriously overstaffed Soviet enterprises were expected to lay off millions of workers. First, it was no longer necessary for managers to protect themselves against inefficiencies in production and planning by 'hoarding labour'. Second, funding for labour costs was no longer allocated by the centre but had to be borne by the enterprise. Third, managers no longer had to find new jobs for those made redundant. Cuts in employment began, and the first to go were administrative staff, almost always female.

- With a market economy, employers were expected to be more sensitive to costs connected with maternity leave, absence for family reasons, protective legislation for women and special rights for mothers. These were maintained or increased in the reform period (Mezentseva, 1994b, Khotkina, 1994, Fong, 1994, Grachev, 1996). Maternity leave, with the right to return to the same job, after the birth of the child was extended from 18 months to 36 in April 1991. Even though government pays the monetary benefits[3] employers might still find the leave a disincentive to hiring women of childbearing age. Women could be considered to be unreliable workers because they have to stay home when children, grandchildren or elderly relatives are ill.

- The demand for fiscal cuts threatened the health-care, child-care, schools and culture sectors which employed about a quarter of the female labour force. Substitution of imported for domestic consumer goods would hit female dominated light and food industries.

- Substitution of home production for previously purchased or free services and goods would increase the burden of housework and subsistence gardening and their negative effects on women's paid work.

- It was hard to believe that the discriminatory attitudes so frequently expressed by politicians, media and business would not end up having practical repercussions on employment practices and labour market policies.

- For the '*noveaux riches*' and those who wanted to emulate them it became a prestigious Veblenian symbol of 'conspicuous consumption' to have a non-working wife.[4]

On the other hand, there were factors working in other directions:

- A crisis in heavy industry and mining would lead to losses of more male than female jobs. Even though many women, particularly engineers and technicians, lost their jobs as the military-industry complex declined (Rzhanitsyna, 1993, Leontieva, 1994) there is no real evidence that – at least in the longer run – it would not affect as many or more men. Budget cuts for the armed forces affected mainly men.

- Since consumer services were so underdeveloped in the USSR, expansion was expected. More retail shops, restaurants, launderettes as well as private child-care and health-care, beauty parlours, dress-makers, and so on would provide employment opportunities for women.

- It was not necessarily less profitable to employ women. Juggling jobs and housework had taught Russian women efficiency and organising skills. They were more likely than men to stay home with a sick child, but less likely to be absent or inefficient because of drinking.[5]
- Women accepted lower wages than men. This implied that rather than being unemployed they might still have jobs, but lose in terms of pay.

The impact of market reforms on the *relative* position of women is, thus, not something that can be determined on first principles. It requires empirical research.

The question in this chapter is not whether gender inequality *exists* in Russia, in terms of work and earnings. It does. Yet, since we have seen that there was gender inequality in the Soviet period too, we may ask whether inequality has increased or decreased. This is a different question, just as to ask if women *and* men have lost or gained equally much during the years of reform is not the same as asking whether Russian women have lost or gained. The living standards of a great many Russian women *and* men have dropped since 1989. Our question is whether the decrease has been the same, or different in size or form. Since male earnings have fallen, lower earnings for women are compatible with an unchanged or even increased gender ratio.

Quantitative studies in social sciences always suffer from imprecision of measurement and crudity of indicators. Their truths are at best partial, but are nevertheless a necessary complement and corrective to qualitative studies which may be based on few and selective observation. In studies of the Russian economy, the difficulties of measurement and of definition are compounded by the existence of a large informal and 'shadowy' sector, and those of interpretation of data and survey responses by traditions and cultural norms different from those of Western market economies. Yet, in this complex social formation, a quantitative 'check' on the validity and generalisability of small-scale qualitative studies or journalistic accounts is particularly urgent.

7.3 Russian survey data

7.3.1 The new Taganrog data

The research projects Taganrog I–III had been carried out at ten-year intervals (p. 82). In 1993/4, the Institute for Socio-Economic Population Studies undertook a smaller-scale intermediate study, Taganrog '3½', while a more ambitious Taganrog IV was planned for the end of the decade. A sample of households was selected, in the same way as in the previous

Taganrog surveys and 2,095 households were interviewed, mostly between November 1993 and April 1994.

These data have the advantage over those of 1989 in that information was obtained about employment and income of all household members – 4,349 individuals, aged 15–72. The 1993/4 sample is a probability sample of the non-institutionalised population of Taganrog, excluding hostel residents.[6] The set of variables, however, is narrower. Non-response was low, as in 1989, but partial non-response to questions about incomes has increased. The measurement error when imputing hourly wage rates from earnings the preceding month and 'usual hours of work per week' is probably aggravated since fluctuations in working hours from month to month are larger. (See p. 153.) Therefore section 7.7 will focus on models of monthly earnings

Generalisation from a local sample to urban Russia could be justified in 1989, under a system of central planning. *Wage levels* varied between regions, but the *determinants of wages*, which are described by wage equations, could be expected to be similar. In 1993/4, much greater qualifications must be made. Rimashevskaya considers that when Taganrog I–III, were done, the samples were 'representative of urban Russia'. In 1993/4 she notes an above-average incidence of poverty in Taganrog which is 'related to the particular situation of its working population and the nature of the city's industrial development, Significant output declines have led to high unemployment, particularly hidden unemployment, and wage arrears' (Rimashevskaya 1997, p. 127).

There are some data sets which cover a probability sample of Russian regions or localities, and in that respect are superior to these, but none of them goes back further than 1991. The unique contribution of the Taganrog data is that we can compare a pre- and post-reform situation in at least this town. It can indicate some directions of change that apply in other places too, and raise issues for further research. Figures A7.1 and A7.2 and Tables A7.1 and A7.2 compare the sample with national data on employment and relative wages.

Our information on earnings is given to us by respondents. All studies using interview data on incomes suffer from intentional or unintentional misreporting. In Russia at this time, earnings varied greatly from month to month, even from week to week. A number of people had regular or irregular side-earnings; wages due may not have been paid or paid only in part or paid for more than one month at the same time. Furthermore, inflation was high. All this may have made it difficult for respondents to recall incomes accurately. It is likely that some incomes kept secret from the tax authorities were not disclosed to interviewers either.[7] These problems should affect all Russian survey earnings data. (See also section 7.7.)

7.3.2 Other data

The official statistical agency, Goskomstat, publishes wage data collected from enterprises, but until recently has never done it separately by gender.[8] Further, enterprise-based statistics cannot take into account second jobs at other workplaces nor incomes from self-employment (nor, of course, informal, illegal or unregistered earnings). They provide information of how *a job* is paid, depending on sector and type of enterprise.

Goskomstat also conducts Labour Force Surveys of 0.55 per cent of the adult population, providing data on labour market status according to gender, education, socio-economic category and age. Some research teams have been allowed to add questions to a subsample of the survey (Lehmann, et al., 1998, 1999, Clarke, 1999, p. 6). The Federal Employment Service publishes similar data, but these only cover those who turn to it for help and registration.

Four sources of household survey data will be referred to in the following: the All-Russian Centre for Study of Public Opinion (VTsIOM) has carried out regular all-Russian repeated cross-section surveys since 1991. The widely used Russian Longitudinal Monitoring Survey (RLMS) was started in 1992. Unlike the VTsIOM, the RLMS has been conducted as a panel study. At the time of writing, there have been eight waves of interviews, starting 1992 (with one change of panel) on a stratified all-Russian sample. The first panel included 6,500 households, the second 4,700. (Klugman and Braithwaite, 1997, describe these sources, as well as the Taganrog data and Goskomstat's Family Budget Surveys.) The Centre for Comparative Labour Studies, University of Warwick the and Institute for Comparative Labour Relations Research (ISITO), Moscow have carried out household surveys in four Russian cities (see e.g. Clarke, 1996a, 1996b, 1999. For brevity, I will refer to these as 'the CCLS data'.)[9]

7.4 Gender and employment in Russia

This section will discuss the extent of labour force participation, employment and unemployment of men and women in Russia. The standard concepts of labour economics and statistics are helpful in structuring this information, but are not necessarily sufficient. Figure 7.1 provides a chart to guide the reader through the terminology. Henceforth, numbers in square brackets, [n], refer to Figure 7.1.

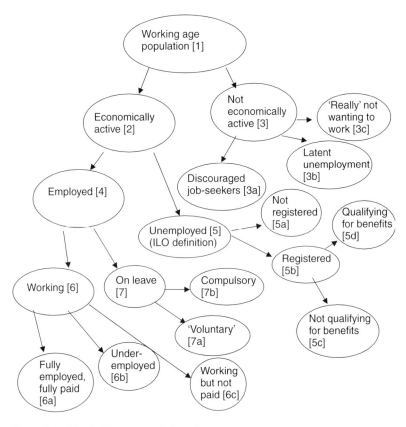

Figure 7.1   Chart of labour market positions

7.4.1   Labour force participation

We divide the working-age[10] population [1] into the 'economically active' ('labour force participants') [2] and the 'not economically active' ('outside the labour force') [3]. Participation (or employment) rates can be low because many people are excluded from the labour market, but also because people leave school late or retire early. The economically active – those able and willing to work – are divided into employed [4] and unemployed [5]. An employed person has either worked for pay or profit during a reference period before the interview (usually a week) [6] or is on leave from a job she or he expects to return to [7]. An unemployed person, according to the International Labour Organisation (ILO), is one willing and able to take up work, who has not worked, but actively looked for work, during the reference period.

Table 7.1 Self-defined main occupation of men aged 16–59 and women aged 16–54 in the samples of 1989* and 1993/4 (%)

Occupation	Men 1989	Men 1993/94	Women 1989	Women 1993/94
Working	87.5	79.8	79.4	72.4
Non-working pensioner	0.6	3.7	0.7	1.7
Disabled	0.4	1.9	0.7	1.4
Housewife	0	0.2	1.9	5.8
Temporarily not employed	0.5		0.7	
Unemployed		4.5		1.8
Leave for pregnancy/childbirth/paid or unpaid maternity leave	0.1	0	5.2	7.2
Student	8.8	7.4	11.1	8.7
Other	2.2	2.6	0.4	1.1
N	1120	1591	1185	1647
Non-response	3	2	7	3

* All household members.

Table 7.1 shows that in 1989 the difference in participation rates between men and women in Taganrog from 16 years to pension age was about 3 percentage points. (Women on maternity leave count as employed.) If the age-bracket is cut at 20 years the difference is less than 2 percentage points,[11] but in the 15–72 age group, 81 per cent of men and only 72 per cent of women were employed, due to the lower pension age for women. In the 1993/94 sample, in the 15–72 age range, male LFPR is 77 per cent and the female 65 per cent. Between 20 and pension age, the difference between male and female rates has increased to over 3 percentage points. Comparing over time, we see that in Taganrog, the proportion of respondents aged 16 to pension age who are 'economically active', is down by 3–4 percentage points for both men and women. The proportion who defines itself as 'working' has fallen by 7–8 percentage points.

Figure 7.2 indicates changes in participation and employment from 1989 to 1998 in Russia as a whole.[12] It shows that the number of labour force participants has decreased for both sexes. In 1989 the census registered 37.2 million employed women. In 1998, 31.5 million women were in the labour force, a drop of 5.7 million. The number of employed women had fallen by nearly 10 million since four million were unemployed. While 39.7 million men were employed in 1989, 35.3 million were in the labour force in 1998, a decrease of 4.4 million. With nearly 5 million men unemployed, male employment had fallen by over 9 million. Thus, more women have left the labour force, the fall in female

Figure 7.2 Numbers of men and women employed in 1989 and change in economically active population, 1989–98

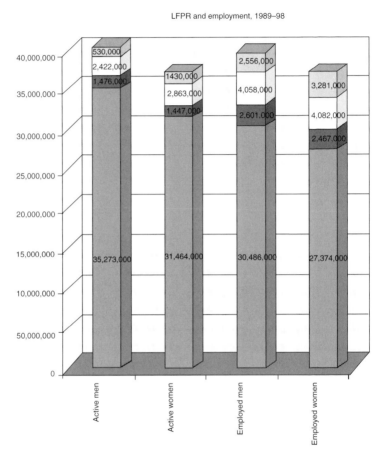

LFPR and employment, 1989–98

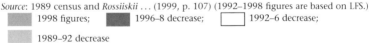

Source: 1989 census and *Rossiiskii* ... (1999, p. 107) (1992–1998 figures are based on LFS.)
    1998 figures;   1996–8 decrease;   1992–6 decrease;
    1989–92 decrease

employment was larger and more men were unemployed, but none of these gender differences are dramatic in size.

Admittedly, census data and (Labour Force) Survey data are not strictly comparable and ought not to be joined in one time-series. On the other hand, there few alternatives if one wants to analyse the different changes in male and female labour market status since the LFS began only in 1992. Redundancies began earlier than that, and there is reason to believe that the earliest cuts in staff were most strongly biased against women. Goskomstat publishes data on aggregate employment for earlier years too, but they are from register data, that is to say, reports from firms above a certain size, complemented by guesstimates for small firms, unregistered employment and self-employment which would otherwise not be included. According to these data, male employment decreased from 37.2 to 33.4 million from 1990 to 1998, and female from 38.1 to 30.3 million, that is to say, considerably more. Doubts about the quality of data make me prefer the combination of census and LFS figures, although the latter are also open to criticism. The numbers in this paragraph exceed estimates based on the LFS by several million – according to these male employment in 1998 was 30.5 million and female 27.4 million.[13]

Figure 7.3 shows *rates* of participation in Russia, in 1989–98. There is a persistent decline over time. According to the Goskomstat Labour Force

Figure 7.3 Male and female participation rates, Russia, 1989–98

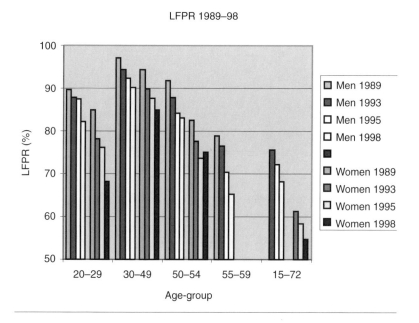

Sources: For 1989 participation is assumed equal to employment. Numbers for RSFSR calculated from census, vol. 10, tables 1 and 2. Rates for 15–72 years are not available in 1989 census. 1993, 1995 and 1998 figures are based on LFS (*Trud i . . .* 1999, p. 35). For women aged 55–59, the numbers are 34 per cent in 1989, 37 per cent in 1993, 30 per cent in 1995 and 28 per cent in 1998.

Survey on which Figure 7.3 is based, overall male and female participation rates have fallen almost as much in 1992–98 and the male employment rate slightly more than the female. (In 1992, large numbers of female office staff had already been made redundant.) The male employment rate remains 11 percentage points higher than the female, but only four points higher in 'working age' because this ends at 54 years for women and 59 for men.[14]

The decrease in female participation rates (measured in percentage points) is 1.5–2 times as large as that in male rates for age-groups 20–39, that is to say at child-bearing and child-rearing age. Judging from international experience, if young mothers stay out of work for several years – even if intending to return – this could leave whole cohorts of women in a disadvantaged position throughout their entire working life. If instead of participation we were to look at 'at work rates' about 2 million[15] women on maternity leave would also be subtracted from the approximately 14 million employed women aged 20–39. Thus, 'at work rates' for women of reproductive age should be some 10 percentage points lower than those of men, with the consequent erosion of skills, loss in work experience and missed chances of promotion.

In multivariate analysis of labour market transitions both Foley (1997b) and Grogan (1999) find that being a woman significantly increases the likelihood of leaving the labour force.

Figures A7.1 and A7.2 compare sample and national data on employment rates in 1989 and participation rates in 1993 in different age cohorts. Despite measurement problems, the deviation of the sample from national data is small in 1989.[16] In 1993 the rate is higher than the national average[17] in the core 30–49 age group and among older women, but if we exclude those who did not report earnings, average participation rates in Taganrog for men and women drop by 3 percentage point to quite close to the national figures.[18] The decrease in participation is smaller in Taganrog than in Russia as a whole, particularly for women.

7.4.2 Mothers and work

As Table 7.2 indicates, mothers of children aged 1–3 are much more likely, and mothers of children aged 3–7 somewhat more likely, to be full-time home-makers in 1993/94 than they were in 1989. (The proportion of women who have young children is lower, however. The total fertility rate in Russia fell from 1.9 in 1990 to 1.4 in 1993[19].)

The extent to which Russian mothers actually want to be at home is hotly debated. Many resented what was perceived as Soviet 'over-employment' of women and in the early 1990s there was an idealisation

Table 7.2 Occupation of mothers according to age of youngest child (%)

	Age < 1 yr 1989	Age < 1 yr 1993	1 < age < 3 1989	1 < age < 3 1993	3 < age < 7 1989	3 < age < 7 1993
Working	0	7	65	20	93	80
Student	0	10	4	1	1	0
Unemployed	0	2	0	0	0	4
At home*	100	80	26	77	4	14
Other or missing	0	0	5	2	2	3
N	41	41	76	97	164	250

Note: Only mothers who live in the same household as the child are included.
* Those who describe their occupation either as 'on maternity leave' or as 'housewife'.

of a Western lifestyle where – it was widely believed – 'mothers do not work' (Fong, 1994). Exactly how many women preferred to stay home for as long as 3–7 years is another matter. There were considerable differences between educational and socio-economic groups.[20]

Women who wish to be at home may not be able to afford it. On the other hand, mothers may be under pressure from employers to stay away when there are redundancies or non-payment of wages. It may also be difficult to find child-care. The number of children in nurseries fell by more than a third between 1989 and 1994 (*Rossiiskii*, 1996, p. 151). The greater part of this decrease is likely to be in the 1–3 age group, whose mothers are covered by the extended maternity leave, but no statistics are available. Child-care fees have increased relative to the wages of most mothers. In some regions a benefit is paid if the child does not use public child-care (*O polozhenie semei . . .*, 1994). The number of places in afternoon activities and summer camps for school children has also declined sharply. These problems could create latent or hidden unemployment [3b].

7.4.3 Working where?

As described in sections 3.3 and 5.6, in the Soviet shortage economy 'priority branches' got the most and the best of human and material resources, while others were disadvantaged. Pay was positively correlated with priority, and female share negatively. (See section 5.7.) In the wake of market reforms, the relative position of some sectors has changed, although certain former 'priority branches' retain some of their advantage.

The proportion of the Russian workforce employed in industry declined from 30 per cent in 1990 to 27 per cent in 1994. (By 1998 it was down to

22 per cent.) The change was similar in Taganrog, although the total share of industry in employment was higher: it fell from 59 per cent in 1989 to 54 per cent in 1993/94, for men, and from 49 per cent to 42 per cent for women.[21] Table A7.1, which compares the sector composition of employment in the Taganrog samples and in Russia in 1990–94, shows that most of the decrease in industrial employment was borne by women nationally too. Female-dominated light industry has lost most, in percentage terms. It was halved from 1990 to 1996 by a loss of 1.1 million jobs. The decline of 40 per cent in engineering industry, however, implies a loss of 4 million jobs. This branch is male-dominated (58 per cent men in 1989), but we do not know the gender distribution of lost jobs.

In Russia as a whole the shares working in health-care, education, science and art and culture increased for both women and men, but not by much. In the Taganrog sample they have increased slightly more for women and decreased a little for men. Employment in construction has declined nationally, but not in Taganrog. The proportion of the workforce employed in finance, banking and insurance has doubled, but only from 0.5 to 1 per cent.

The percentage of women among the employed is shown in Table 7.3. The average decline of 3 percentage points from 1990 to 1998 was unevenly distributed over sectors. The greatest fall in female employment in absolute numbers was in industry, over 5.5 million, or a drop in the

Table 7.3   Percentage women among the employed in economic sectors

Sector	1990	1993	1996	1998
Industry	48	44	41	38
Agriculture and forestry	39	35	34	31
Transport	25	26	26	26
Communications	71	70	62	60
Construction	27	25	24	24
Trade, catering	80	66	62	62
Services	52	46	47	46
Health care & sports	83	82	82	81
Education	79	80	82	80
Art & culture	71	68	69	68
Science	53	53	51	50
Public administration	67	68	62[a]	48
Banking finance, insurance	90	78	74	71
Total	51	48	48[b]	48

[a] In *Rossiiskii* ... (1998) this figure is reported as 50 per cent.
[b] In *Rossiiskii* ... (1998) this figure is reported as 47 per cent.
Source: *Rossiiskii* ... (1996, p. 89, 1997 p. 115 and, for 1998 figures, 1999, p. 115).

proportion of women of 10 percentage points. The greatest decline in the share of females was in trade and catering, in banking and finance, in administration and in consumer services. As these traditionally female-dominated sectors have became more attractive, they have been 'masculinised'. (Table A7.2 shows changes in relative wages between sectors for 1989–98.)

Unfortunately, the statistics on employment in public institutions and enterprises, private enterprises, etc. are not divided by gender. Clarke and Kabalina (2000) find in case studies of new private enterprises that 'other things being equal, employers tended to prefer to employ younger men with higher levels of education and some work experience.' As they note, such preferences are not unique to the new private sector, but if these well-paid jobs are attractive and have many applicants, employers have more scope for discrimination. They also find, using the CCLS surveys, that a change to a job in the new private sector is 'significantly more likely to be associated with an increase in pay' than other job changes, while Grogan (1999) finds from the same data that – controlling for age, education and other characteristics – men are more likely to make moves into jobs in such firms.

Foley (1997b) uses RLMS data to study movements in and out of jobs for 1992–93 and 1995–96. He finds that 'men are more likely to make a transition to non-state employment while women are more apt not only to move into the state sector but also to remain in a state sector job. Thus, it appears that men are more willing to move away from traditional employment and take on the more novel, market-oriented jobs' (p. 21. There is no indication how he knows whether it is women who are not 'willing' or prospective employers.)

Men predominate among entrepreneurs and in individual labour activity, another group that have above average earnings. According to the 1998 LFS, of those gainfully employed in non-wage labour (*nenaemnyi trud*), 62 per cent were men (5.4 per cent of male employment and 3.7 per cent of the female was in this category) (*Trud* . . ., 1999, pp. 84 and 215.).[22] Grogan (1999) finds that controlling for age, education and other characteristics, men are more likely to move into self-employment. In Taganrog in 1993/94 2,790 respondents, aged 15 or older, reported labour income for the previous month. Of these, 349 received all or part of their earnings from self-employment. Among these are more male than female respondents, but nearly as many women as men do it as their sole employment. Table 7.4 indicates the proportions. As the table shows, in the survey a distinction was made between 'entrepreneurial activity' and 'individual labour activity' (ITD). People who engage in very small-scale

Table 7.4   Percentage men and women with entrepreneurial or ITD incomes, Taganrog 1993/4 (of all with earnings previous month, aged 15+)

	With any ITD earnings	Earnings only from ITD	With any entrepreneurial earnings	Only entrepreneurial earnings
Men	9.0	3.0	5.6	2.8
Women	6.3	2.6	4.2	2.9

self-employment activities are likely to find the traditional concept of 'ITD' a better description of what they do than entrepreneurship. (See p. 76f.)

7.4.4   Multiple jobs and hours of work

In the 1993/4 Taganrog sample, 13 per cent of women earning a wage[23] said that they had more than one job, and an additional 4 per cent reported at least two sources of labour income for the preceding month. For men, the figures were 12 per cent and 5 per cent respectively. It is worth noting that among women working in the 'socio-cultural sphere', the numbers are higher – 24 per cent answer that they have more than one job and another 3 per cent report earnings in addition to their primary wage.

Roshin (1995) also finds, in two local samples, that many of the women who have second jobs are employed in the public ('budget') sector. Supplementary work may be the means whereby these women can stay in their public sector jobs, despite the very low wages. (Although in 1994 the ratio between the average wages in these sectors and that in the economy as a whole had not changed much, it was the same percentage of a much lower wage.)

The Taganrog figures are relatively high compared to the frequency of regular and irregular secondary employment found in other surveys. According to Khibovskaya (1995b), in 1993/4 the frequency varied between 14 and 20 per cent.[24] Of these about two-thirds worked extra irregularly and may well have replied 'no' to the question as it was formulated in the Taganrog survey. The VTsIOM figures include secondary earnings of students and pensioners with one job, unlike the Taganrog data or the RLMS.[25] According to the RLMS, about 5 per cent of working respondents held multiple jobs in 1992, and twice as many in 1996 (Foley, 1997c). Foley finds that women are less likely than men to hold multiple jobs, particularly if they are married or have children, and the gender difference increases over time. In 1996 among working age respondents, 12 per cent of men and 8 per cent of women held multiple jobs. He also finds that the gender wage gap is substantially larger in second jobs – while according to his estimates the ratio of female to male hourly wages was 82 per cent in primary jobs, it was 31 per cent (!) in second jobs, in 1996. Note that among those who do have second jobs, women do not work fewer hours per week than men do.

Thus, multiple job-holding increases the gender earnings differential in three ways: (1), men more often have such earnings (work more total hours); (2), hours in second jobs pay better; (3), the gender gap in earnings per hour is larger.

All survey studies of second jobs are likely to suffer from under-reporting. Khibovskaya's estimate is that the real figure is about twice as large as the one that the VTsIOM studies report. Both Khibovskaya (1995b, 1996) and Roshin (1995) find a higher frequency of second jobs among men than among women.

According to the VTsIOM data average hours per week in second jobs varied between the different monthly surveys, from 13 to 21 hours. The 1993/4 Taganrog survey included a question about total usual hours of work per week only. Average hours of work per week (thus measured) decreased by about an hour for both men and women, from 1989 to 1993/94. Standard deviation increased, but the numbers with very short working weeks do not indicate that many work part-time, particularly since some of the women with short working weeks are teachers and probably report hours in class. There is more to indicate multiple jobs, or large amounts of overtime among men, but it is still a minority (Table A7.4).

According to official statistics, the hours worked per week of employed women increased from 34.8 to 36.0 for women between 1992 and 1999 and decreased from just over to just under 39 hours for men (*Trud* ... 1999, p. 211). According to RLMS for 1996 (Foley, 1997c), among those who report positive hours of work at their primary job the preceding months, men report an average of 45 hours and women one of only 39. The Taganrog figures for average total hours per week (42 for men and 38 for women) are in between the RLMS and Goskomstat data.

7.5 Unemployment

7.5.1 Open unemployment

From 1991 onwards, media reports as well as case studies indicated that when layoffs began 70–80 per cent of those affected were women. In the middle of 1991, when the recently established Federal Employment Service began to publish data on those registered as unemployed, the share of women was 69 per cent (*Trud* ..., 1995, p. 84). Researchers wrote that 'unemployment is a female problem' and of the 'female face of unemployment' (Khotkina, 1994, p. 98). Rimashevskaia (1996, p. 39) concluded that women were losing in 'competitive force' and, therefore, more women than men were unemployed and the gender differential in wages increased. According to Posadskaia (1996, p. 16), the 'prognosis of great losses which women would have to carry in the sphere of employment in the reform period, have come true'.

In 1992, the Goskomstat labour force surveys began. These showed that, when 'unemployment' was defined according to the ILO standard (p. 210), 51 per cent of the unemployed were women. The number of registered unemployed has remained well below that of 'ILO-unemployed' and with a larger proportion of women. (Table 7.5 shows 1992–98 data.) Reasons for non-registration could be the bureaucratic hassle it involves, the restrictive conditions and low rates of benefits and the low expectations that the Employment Service will be of help in finding a job.

Among both men and women, the higher the education, the lower the unemployment rate. In 1993, overall unemployment rates for both men and women were just under 6 per cent whereas for those with higher education they were 3.1 per cent for men and 3.9 per cent for women. In 1998, the unemployment rate for women with higher education was 6.9 per cent and for men 7.3 per cent – a little more than half the average.[26] Rates for those with specialised secondary education were slightly below the average. The widespread claim that 'the typical unemployed' is a woman with university or specialised secondary education (Vlasova et al., 1994, Khotkina, 1994) was a misconception, due partly to the greater propensity of the highly educated to register.[27] Kalabakhina (1995) complains that highly educated and committed female engineers have to leave their jobs while unskilled women workers run no risk of unemployment – even though they would probably prefer to stay at home since their jobs are so boring and badly paid. The latter belief does not seem to be based on any actual research. There is some

Table 7.5   Unemployment rates, 1992–98 (%)

| | Labour Force Survey | | | Registered | | |
	1992	1994	1998	1992	1994	1998
Men	5.2	8.3	13.6	0.4	1.6	1.9
Women	5.2	7.9	13.0	1.2	3.2	4.0

Source: *Rossiiskii* ... (1999, p. 107), for population aged 15–72.

survey support for her view of the attitudes of female unskilled workers in Bodrova (1995), while Ashwin and Bowers (1997) find the opposite in an anthropological workplace study.

Although there are more unemployed men than women, it takes longer, on average, for unemployed women to find a job. According to the 1998 LFS, unemployed men had been unemployed 0.4 months less than unemployed women.[28] This is consistent with the results of duration analysis based on the RLMS in Foley (1997a) and Grogan and van den Berg (1998), although the RLMS is not ideal for quantifying unemployment spells.

Another approach is to estimate the probability that a person who is unemployed at a given time has found a job a year later. This is done by Foley (1997b) who compares responses to the RLMS survey in 1992 and 1993, and in 1995 and 1996 respectively. Of those employed in 1992, married men ran the smallest risk of being unemployed in 1993, single women the second lowest and married women the highest. In 1995/96, the order of likelihood had shifted between married women and single men so that the latter ran the highest risk. In this case, however, while the parameter for 'female' is negative and significant, those for 'married' and 'married and female' are not significant. At both points in time employed women, particularly married women, run a greater risk of leaving the labour force than employed men.

Among the unemployed, married men are the most likely to find a job and married women the most likely to leave the labour force. Unmarried women (inclucing widowed and divorced are more likely to find employment than single men but also more likely to leave the labour force. This agrees with Grogan and van den Berg, who find that unemployed men are more likely to find a new job if they are married but unemployed women less likely.

A larger percentage of unemployed men than of unemployed women have quit their previous jobs voluntarily, while a larger percentage of women have been made redundant (*Rossiiski* ..., 1997). Since unemployed men find new jobs more easily than unemployed women do, men may be more inclined to leave a job with low pay, arrears or poor working conditions. In a case study of a factory, Monosouva, (1996, p. 172) quotes a manager who does not fear losing the female workers, almost irrespective of conditions. 'They are women. Where are they going to disappear to?' This, too, is an issue requiring more research.

7.5.2 'Hidden' unemployment

The extent of 'unemployment' depends on the choice of definition and the choice of definition should depend on the issues under discussion. People who work but do not pay taxes, or have earnings from the informal sector or from more or less illegal activities, are likely not to disclose this to the LFS interviewer. In this case, the LFS unemployment figures are exaggerated.

According to Khibovskaya (1995a), in VTsIOM surveys of 1994 and 1995, among 1434 individuals, defining themselves as 'temporarily not working, unemployed', 24 per cent were involved in some kind of income-raising activity. In addition, as with second jobs, there are probably individuals who have such income but do not tell the interviewer.

Commander and Yemtsov (1997) differentiate among the unemployed, using VTsIOM data from 1994. Those whom they call 'true unemployed' make up 3.5 per cent of the sample. These are people without any employment at all the preceding month. 59 per cent of them are women. An additional 1.2 per cent are passively waiting for re-employment, half of them because they expect to be re-employed by their previous employer. Of these 70 per cent are women. Another 1.6 per cent, a small majority of them male, define themselves as unemployed [6b], but have some 'secondary employment'.

In the Taganrog 1993/94 sample, 24 per cent of unemployed women had some self-employment or entrepreneurial incomes in the preceding months, as did 16 per cent of the unemployed men and 15 per cent of women who defined themselves as 'housewives'.[29]

On the other hand, these 'false unemployed', who have some labour income, but not a regular full-time job, may have good reason to consider themselves unemployed even though they do not satisfy the ILO definition of unemployment. They may have very low earnings and they may well have wanted to work more hours than they did, and, therefore, be *under*-employed according to standard definitions [6b]. Even those who reported relatively high earnings may have considered themselves unemployed because they did not have a reasonably permanent job with a reasonably stable income. The economic and psychological suffering caused by insecurity is an evil in itself.[30]

Another group to note are the discouraged job-seekers [3a], people who would accept a reasonable job offer, but who have given up actively seeking work, because they are convinced that they will not find any, perhaps after many attempts.

In October 1993 the unemployment rates for men and women were about 5 per cent, both in Russia and in Rostov *oblast' to* which Taganrog belongs. Yet, in the sample, the rate of self-defined unemployment is 4.9 per cent among men, but only 1.9 per cent among women.[31] At the same time, among prime working age women, nearly 6 per cent define themselves as 'housewives', or about three times as many as in 1989. This is even though in 1993/4 women at home with children under three years describe themselves as on maternity leave, not as housewives, while in 1989 the maximum maternity leave was 18 months. Could some of them be 'ILO unemployed' or 'discouraged job-seekers' in the terminology of labour economics but 'housewives' in their own? According to Grogan and van den Berg (1998), in the 1994–96 RLMS surveys, about one in six self-defined housewives had actively searched for a job the last month (as had a fifth of VUZ students and more than a tenth of pensioners). This raises questions for further research about how Russians see being unemployed or being a housewife in terms of status or self-esteem.

Probit estimates of the likelihood of being unemployed were made for men, and of being unemployed or of being a housewife were made for women.[32] Results should be generalised with great caution, because of the smallness and local character of the sample. Both men and women are significantly more likely to be unemployed if they are under than over 35. Women aged 25–34 are more likely, and those aged 45–54 less likely, than the 35–44 age group to be housewives. Dummy variables for children aged 3–7 or of school age are not significant in any estimates. (Coefficients for having children under three years are negative, since their mothers define themselves as 'being on maternity leave' not as housewives.)

The probability of unemployment falls steadily with levels of education. This agrees with the national statistics (see above) and with Foley (1999b). The likelihood of being a housewife is smaller with university or vocational education than with secondary. (The coefficient for university schooling is significant at the 10 per cent level.) The likelihood of being a housewife increases with the income of other household members (probability value below 0.1 per cent!), while this variable has no effect on the probability of unemployment for either men or women.

The negative correlation between household income and female employment agrees with neoclassical economic theory, according to which the marginal utility of the woman's wage decreases and that of leisure or her time in household production increases when other household income is higher. Yet, when conflicts of interest, in the household and workplace are allowed for, interpretations of the 'choice to stay at home' are more complex. A woman in a high-income household may be happy 'not to have to work'. Yet, if she is not happy, she might find it more difficult to convince her husband that she wants to work, than if household income were lower.

7.5.3 Unpaid leave and unpaid work

Even among the 'employed' we find hidden unemployment. Both wage arrears (non-payment of wages by employers) [6c], forced part-time [6b] and involuntary temporary redundancies with loss of part or the whole of the wage [7b] have become widespread. Part of the reason why employment has not decreased in proportion to output is that it is relatively cheap to keep staff, since wages have fallen so dramatically. In addition, employers can refrain from paying even these depreciated wages, while avoiding statutory severance pay. The Taganrog survey has no data on wage arrears. Both Earle and Sabirianova (1998) and Lehmann et al. (1998) study wage arrears using the RLMS data. They find that men are more likely to have experienced non-payment of wages. The gender difference is small, but significant in multivariate (probit) estimates. In the RLMS sample, about 40 per cent were owed wages at their place of work in 1994 and 1995, with the share rising to 60 per cent in 1996 (Earle and Sabirianova, 1998).

Grogan (1998) estimates the probability of compulsory temporary redundancies ('administrative leave'). She controls for both the gender of the individual and for the per cent of women in occupational category. Being female increases the likelihood of experiencing unpaid leave, given occupation, but working in a female-dominated occupation decreases it, given gender. The numbers on unpaid or partly paid compulsory leave at any one moment in time was under 2 per cent according to the 1995 RLMS.

7.6   The gender earnings gap

7.6.1   Previous studies

Brainerd (1996, 1997)[33] uses VTsIOM data to compare male and female wages in 1991 (1,695 observations) and 1994 (4,827 observations). She estimates equations for monthly wages, unadjusted for hours, and not including earnings from ITD, entrepreneurial activity or the informal sector.

Brainerd (1997) finds that the female/male ratio of mean monthly wages has fallen from 80 per cent in 1991 to 68 per cent in 1994 in Russia, while it has actually increased in five Eastern European countries for which she has data. (In the Ukraine, as in Russia, she finds a decrease.) The 80 per cent figure for 1991 raises some concern about the reliability of the data. All Soviet period evidence indicates a gender ratio of 65–70 per cent for monthly wages (see section 4.8). Newell and Reilly (1996) find one of 65 per cent in 1992 and according to the present study – albeit in a local sample – it was 66 per cent in 1989 and approximately 62 per cent[34] in 1993.

Brainerd finds increases in the returns to university education relative to both secondary and vocational schooling, for both men and women and a flattening of the wage-potential experience[35] profile.

Newell and Reilly (1996), Glinskaya and Mroz (1998), Sheidvasser and Benítez-Silva (1999) as well as Ogloblin (1999) use the RLMS data, but with some differences of years, models and focus. Newell and Reilly find a larger female/male wage ratio for hourly (71 per cent) than for monthly (65 per cent) wages in 1992. Their study, as well as that of Glinskaya and Mroz, finds that bulk of the gender gap is attributable to difference in rewards to particular labour market characteristics, rather than to different endowments of these characteristics. (See section 2.6.2.1.) Ogloblin uses a model which accounts for three-quarters of the gross wage gap (more when a selectivity adjustment is made). Among his explanatory factors are a number of dummies for being in female- or male-dominated occupation within broader categories. To include these variables in the regression gives valuable information on the relation between gendering and wages but for the decomposition it means that a discrimination which takes the form of lower wages in occupations constructed as 'female' will be included in the 'endowment term'. (See section 2.6.2.1.) He reports only a decomposition using the pooled OLS parameters, which, as argued in chapter 2, will produce a spuriously large 'explained' part.

Glinskaya and Mroz (1998) compare gender wage ratios for each year from 1992 to 1995, overall and at corresponding points in the male and female wage distributions. For the ratio of mean hourly wages, there is oscillation, rather than a clear trend. (The female to male ratio was 75 per cent in 1992, increased to 80 per cent in 1993, fell again to 71 per cent in 1994 and increased to 75 per cent in 1995.) The most striking result is that the 10 or 20 per cent of men with highest wages have increased their relative advantage noticeably, both relative to lower-paid men and to all women, including those in the corresponding percentiles.

Ogloblin (1999) using 1994–96 RLMS data finds a ratio for monthly earnings in primary place of work of 67 per cent for those who were not owed back wages. Correcting for hours of work reduces the differential to 72 per cent. Sheidvasser and Benítez-Silva use 1996–98 RLMS data and find a female/male ratio for monthly wages of 63 per cent, somewhat lower than in the earlier rounds of the RLMS. Controlling for education, region and potential experience they find an adjusted ratio of 66 per cent.

7.6.2   The gender wage gap in Taganrog

Informative as they are, these studies only partly describe the transition from a Soviet to a post-Soviet economy, since the earliest data in the VTsIOM and RLMS data sets are from 1991 and 1992 respectively. At these times, the centralised wage-setting system of the USSR was already gone. As noted in section 3.1.1, even the 1989 data used here reflect some degree of erosion of the Soviet system of remuneration. The approach chosen here is to compare Soviet and post-Soviet societies by comparing 1989 state sector wages[36] to two different measures of earnings for 1993/94. Wages (from state and non-state employment) and total labour incomes (from wage-labour, self-employment and entrepreneurial activity).[37]

The forms and mores of 'New Russian' business combined with the predominant conceptions of gender, did not encourage women to become entrepreneurs They might, however, have some advantage from their experience of managing the contradictory demands of employment, housekeeping and child-care and of informal networking.[38] It is a common assumption in the literature that women's commercial activities are smaller and less 'ugly *biznis*' than men's and also that this is the general opinion among the public.[39]

Yet, most Russians with non-wage earnings are not *nouveaux riches*. Much 'business' is rather modest, like going abroad to buy a couple of suitcases of cheap clothing to sell, or doing odd jobs in the neighbourhood. Many women combine knitting, sewing, pickling and jam-making for sale with home-making, while men with such very small scale non-wage earnings would be more likely to combine it with a job (Babaeva and Chirikova, 1995).

Irrespective of whether we include non-wage earnings or not, the gender gap increased relative to the wage gap in the Soviet period. Table 7.6 shows female/male wage ratios.[40] In 1989 the female/male wage ratio was 66 per cent, for monthly wages.[41] The earnings ratio in the 1993/4 sample was 61 per cent, and 62 per cent for wages in primary job. Among the sub-sample whose earnings were entirely from ITD or entrepreneurial activity the ratio was 59 per cent.

A major factor behind the Soviet gender differential was the low wages in the 'socio-cultural sphere'. Given the Russian fiscal crisis, one would expect wages in sectors dependent on public funding to have fallen even further behind. Surprisingly, until 1996 the ratios between average wages in health-

Table 7.6   Ratio of female to male earnings (%)

1989	Monthly wage (all household members)	Monthly wage (main respondents*)	Hourly wage (main respondents)
At mean	66.1	65.6	73.3
At median	68.2	71.4	72.7

* See section 5.1.1.

1993/4	Wage at primary job	All labour income	Labour income/hour
At mean	62.1	60.8	69.7
At median	67.1	66.1	72.4

care and schools and the national average remained in the range within they oscillated in the later Soviet period. There seems, however, to have been a drastic turn for the worse in late 1996. (See Table A7.2.) In Taganrog the gender wage ratio dropped by some 5–6 percentage in the less than five years between the surveys, even though relative wages in these female-dominated sectors kept up. If that was the case in Russia generally, the increase in the gender gap from 1989 to the present must be larger, given how dramatically these sectors have fallen behind since 1997.

It is important to remember that the male average we compare women's wages with has slumped, in real terms. To analyse the real standard of living and poverty in Russia is beyond this chapter. (See, for instance, Klugman, 1997, Silverman and Yanowitch, 1997, and Rimashevskaia, 1998.) Yet, there is no doubt that severe hardship has both widened and deepened since the late 1980s. Even though the officially recorded falls in average real wage, GNP and consumption are exaggerated, because of the growth of the informal and illegal sectors and of non-reporting of incomes and economic activity, by no stretch of the imagination could living standards be believed to be maintained. Health has deteriorated and the increase in mortality is staggering, particularly for men. (Male life expectancy dropped from 65 years in 1989 to a low point of 58 in 1994 and was 61 in 1998. The female decreased from 74 years to 71 in 1994 and was 73 in 1998.)

Braithwaite (1997, p. 50) analyses the available statistics and concludes that that there was a sharp increase in poverty in 1992 and 'a real explosion' in 1993. The likelihood of poverty was greater among women than among men and greatest among children. The picture is similar in the Taganrog sample. The share living in poor households is 35 per cent among women, 32 per cent among men, and 44 per cent among children under 18. Among adult women who do not live with a husband or with working parents, 49 per cent are poor.[42] ('Poor' here means that reported household income is below the national official subsistence level.)

What is also beyond doubt is that inequality has increased, from being more or less on a par with Western Europe to a much higher level. According to Brainerd (1996) wage inequality doubled from 1991 to 1994 and Russia 'appears to have won the dubious distinction of achieving the most unequal wage distribution in the shortest period of time of any industrialised country for which reliable data are available' (ibid., p. 34).[43]

7.7 Estimates of wage and earnings models

As in chapters 5 and 6, models were estimated for earnings, to see how the relation between female and male earnings and characteristics like age, experience, education and sector had changed. In this chapter, total monthly earnings in 1993/4 will be analysed. 'Earnings' include wages in primary and secondary jobs, entrepreneurial and self-employment incomes. The estimates are compared with those from an analogous model applied to monthly wages from the state sector in the 1989 data.[44] The estimates reported here are for prime working age individuals, 18 to pension age. (Table A7.3 shows numbers of respondent in this age group not included in regressions.)

Earnings from individual labour activity and entrepreneurial incomes are probably less openly and accurately reported than wages. They are, on the other hand, an important component of earnings, and contribute to the gender gap as well as to overall differentiation. I therefore chose to include them. (I will call them 'non-wage earnings', for short.)

The 1993/4 data did not include work experience (*stazh*) or tenure. Therefore, the estimated equations include only age and age squared.[45] They also included the logarithm of usual hours of work per week and dummies for age groups and for levels of education,[46] sectors and conditions of work. For 1993/94 the model includes dummies for ITD and entrepreneurial activity.[47] (See Table A7.5 for definitions and means of variables.)

In the 1989 sample, labour force participation was too high to call for a Heckman-type correction for selectivity (see p. 121). With the 1993/4 sample, the method was tried but it could not be shown that selectivity in employment affected male or female earnings.[48]

As Table 7.7 shows, the negative coefficients for the age-groups 18–24 and 25–34, relative to 35–44 year olds, have declined in size and precision from 1989 to 1993/94. The reverse is true for those aged 45 and over. The shifts are similar for hourly and monthly wages/earnings. This agrees with Brainerd (1996) and with Glinskaya and Mroz (1998) who find insignificant age parameters. That age is unimportant for earnings could mean that experience acquired under Soviet conditions is not valued by employers. Employers may also believe it to be more profitable to employ staff who does not have Soviet work experience and work habits. Changes in output structure may have outmoded some skills and created demand for new ones. Clarke and Kabalina (2000) find almost twice as high wage premia for higher education in 1998 if it has been acquired after 1991.

The premium for higher and specialised secondary education has increased. This does not increase the gender gap since the level of education of employed women is as high as that of men. In the model for monthly 1989 wages and 1993/94 earnings, the premium for university education has increased from 17 per cent to 23 per cent for men and from 25 per cent to 44 per cent for women. In terms of hourly rates there is a

Table 7.7 Model of 1989 monthly wages and 1993/4 monthly earnings*

	Male wages 1989	*t-value*	Female wages 1989	*t-value*	Male earnings 1993/94	*t-value*	Female earnings 1993/94	*t-value*
INTERCEP	5.10	9.64	4.64	18.5	8.07	26.0	7.85	27.3
AGE 18–24	−0.16*	−2.17	−0.24**	−3.9	−0.12¤	−1.9	−0.14*	−2.2
AGE 25–34	−0.10*	−2.39	−0.12**	−4.1	−0.02	−0.3	−0.03	−0.7
AGE 35–44	0		0		0		0	
AGE 45–59	−0.01	−0.14	0.00	0.1	−0.08¤	−1.8	−0.05	−1.3
HIGHED	0.16**	3.02	0.23**	6.4	0.21**	3.8	0.39**	7.6
SPEC2	0.04	0.94	0.08**	2.8	0.08¤	1.7	0.11*	2.5
GENSEC	0		0		0		0	
INCSEC	−0.15**	−3.49	−0.04	−0.6	−0.18*	−2.2	−0.03	−0.3
PTU	0.08	1.59	0.07	1.0	−0.07	−1.0	0.03	0.4
LOWED	−0.08	−0.94	−0.01	−0.1	−0.15	−1.3	−0.08	−0.5
INDUSTRY	0		0		0		0	
CONSTR	−0.09	−1.28	−0.03	−0.4	0.09	1.6	0.16¤	1.8
TRANS	−0.02	−0.37	−0.10*	−2.2	0.23**	3.6	0.35**	4.2
TRADE	−0.38**	−2.65	−0.25**	−4.8	0.13	1.5	0.12*	2.1
SERV	−0.29**	−3.42	0.05	1.1				
MUNSERV					−0.01	−0.1	−0.12	−1.3
OTHSERV					0.25*	2.2	0.15¤	1.9
HEALTH	0.00	0.00	−0.18	−3.0	0.44**	3.4	0.19**	3.5
SCEDCULT					−0.08	−1.0	0.04	0.8
TEACH	−0.10	−1.60	−0.02	−0.4				
ART	−0.04	−0.44	−0.35**	−3.1				
SCIENCE	−0.11	−1.46	−0.11	−1.9				
FINANCE					0.70**	2.9	0.51**	4.3
ARMYMILI					0.47**	6.6	0.34¤	1.9
ADMIN	−0.04	−0.24	−0.14	−1.5	0.04	0.2	0.12	1.0
OTHER	−0.11	−1.37	−0.01	−0.1	0.40**	3.3	0.24	1.5
AIR	0.04	0.90	0.08	1.6	0.06	1.4	0.00	0.0
HEAT	0.07	1.30	0.02	0.4	0.18*	2.3	0.00	0.0
HARDPHYS	−0.01	−0.28	0.13	2.2	0.01	0.2	−0.06	−0.9
NOICEVIB	−0.01	−0.12	0.09	1.4	0.11**	2.6	0.01	0.2
MTS	0.08	1.45	0.05¤	1.9	0.06	1.3	0.07*	2.0
LNH	0.08	0.57	0.10	1.5	0.69**	8.3	0.64**	8.3
PARTITD					0.50**	7.0	0.55*	7.4
PARTENTR					0.55**	5.4	0.80**	5.3
ONLYITD					0.11	0.6	0.72**	2.6
ONLYENTR					0.68**	5.5	0.36	1.5
adj. R²	0.08		0.19		0.24		0.26	
N	354		488		1183		1098	
Dep. mean	5.45		5.05		10.92		10.46	
Prob > W	0.98		0.26		0.53		0.62	

* t-statistics are (White-) adjusted for heterosedasticity.
W is Wilks-Shapiro's test statistic for normal distribution of residuals.

similar increase for women, but not for men. The increase for specialised secondary schooling is smaller. The coefficients for PTU have dropped by 12–15 percentage points, from positive to (insignificantly) negative for men. This reflects the decrease in relative pay for skilled, male workers in heavy industry. For women the change is smaller.

Sheidvasser and Benítez-Silva (1999), in a 'human capital'-type model, find returns to university education of 38 per cent for women and 23 per cent for men, in terms of monthly wages in 1992–98. They do not report separate estimates for returns to level of education for each year, but estimating wage premia for years of schooling they find no increasing trend over the period. Ogloblin (1999) finds a 'university premium' of 48 per cent for women in a similar model (but he does not control for regions) and 37 per cent in one with detailed controls for sector and occupation. For men the premia are 19 per cent and 11 per cent.

The increase in most sector coefficients is better described as a drop for the reference category industry. The military-industrial sector was in deep crisis in 1993. That this type of industry was so dominant in Taganrog explains why industrial wages have fallen more (relative to other sectors) here than in Russia as a whole. While wages in the education sector have fallen about as much as those in industry, those in health- care have not. Banking and finance stands out as the highest paying sector, particularly for men, both in terms of monthly and hourly earnings.

Note that the coefficients for the logarithm of hours of work (technically, the hours elasticities of earnings) were small and insignificant in 1989. In 1993/94, by contrast, the coefficient is large and has high precision for both men and women. Part of the explanation could be the way monthly wages and statutory working weeks for specific occupations were set in the Soviet system. (See sections 4.5.4 and 5.2.2.)

The premia for having other kinds of earnings than wages are rather high, except for women with all their earnings from entrepreneurial activity. (A coefficient of 0.5 implies an addition of 65 per cent and one of 0.7 implies a doubling.) Note, however, that about a quarter of respondents with non-wage earnings are not included in the estimates because they do not report hours of work. Earnings of these respondents are about half as high as for men and women with non-wage earnings who do report hours. Thus, we are likely to be selective in the direction of those with more regular ITD and business activity.

As in section 5.4, Oaxaca decompositions were made for monthly and hourly wages, for 1989, monthly and hourly labour income for 1993/94. Those of monthly earnings are reported in Table 7.8. In 1993/94 characteristics account for a quarter of the gender gap, as compared to

Table 7.8 Decomposition of the gender gap in monthly wages, 1989, and earnings, 1993 (% of the log differential)

Total	Weighted by 'female' pms 1989	1993/4	Weighted by 'male' pms 1989	1993/4
Unexplained	82.7	76.0	85.7	75.5
Explained of which	17.3	24.0	14.3	24.5
Age	1.1	–1.2	0.9	–1.2
Education	1.3	–2.0	1.2	–3.3
Sector (branch)	4.5	3.5	6.8	1.1
Working conditions	6.9	–1.3	1.5	4.4
Hours of work	1.9	15.3	1.5	16.3
Marital status	1.6	2.4	2.4	1.9
Entrepreneurial activity	–	3.0	–	2.7
Self-employment	–	4.3	–	2.6

Total log differential 1989: 0.40; 1993/94: 0.46.

one sixth or one seventh in 1989; 5–10 per cent are attributable to the dummy variables for non-wage labour and 15–16 per cent to difference in hours of work. In the decompositions of the difference in hourly earnings 14 per cent or 9 per cent are accounted for by characteristics in 1993/4, depending on weighting, – some 4 percentage points more than in 1989.

232

Appendix

Figure A7.1 Employment rates for men and women, 1989. RSFSR census and Taganrog sample

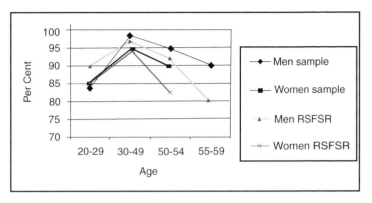

Sources: See note to Figure 7.2.

Figure A7.2 Labour force participation rates for men and women in the Russian Federation, 1993, and Taganrog sample, 1993/4

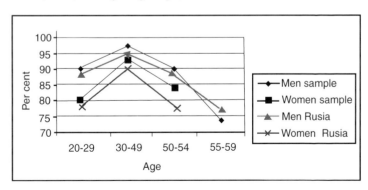

Sources: See Figure 7.2.

Table A7.1 Distribution of male and female workforce by sector in Taganrog and the RSFSR/Russian Federation (%)

Branch	Men Sample 1989	Women Sample 1989	Men Sample 1993/4	Women Sample 1993/4	Men Russia 1990	Women Russia 1990	Men Russia 1994	Women Russia 1994
Industry	58.5	49.0	54.5	41.8	32.0	28.6	30.1	23.9
Agriculture and forestry	–	–	–	–	16.5	10.1	19.5	11.0
Transport & communication	8.0	3.9	9.0	3.4	10.6	4.9	10.1	5.4
Construction	6.4	4.2	8.0	3.3	17.8	6.3	14.5	4.9
Trade, catering	2.1	7.2	5.8	10.5	3.2	12.2	6.4	12.8
Services	4.8	6.1	6.2	8.9	4.2	4.3	4.8	4.0
Health-care, sports	2.1	5.9	1.6	9.5	2.0	9.2	2.3	10.8
Science, education & culture	12.2	18.2	6.2	17.8				
Education and culture					4.4	14.7	4.5	17.5
Science					3.6	3.9	2.5	2.9
Public administration	0.5	1.7	0.5	0.7	1.4	2.8	1.3	3.2
Banking finance, insurance			0.9	1.5	0.1	0.9	0.5	1.7
Other	5.6	4.0	7.4	1.7	4.2	2.1	3.5	1.8
Total	100	100	100	100	100	100	100	100
Number (1000s)					37,211	38,114	35,466	33,018

Source: Samples and *Rossiiskii Statisticheskii Ezhegodnik* (1996, p. 85).

Table A7.2 Average monthly wages for workers and employees in different branches of economy in percentages of the average wage and the female/male wage ratios 1998[a]

Branch	USSR 1989[b]	Sample 1989 Weighted[c]	Russia 1993[d]	Sample 1993/94[e]	Russia 1996	Russia 1998	Gender wage ratio 1998 (%)
Industry	109.7	106.9	108.2	89.2	110	115	69
Construction	131.5	107.2	132.9	103.0	122	127	79
Transport & communication	111.9	107.3		141.2			
Transport			150.6		144	144	77
Communications			107.3		130	140	70
Trade and catering	77.8	63.9	79.7	98.2	77	82	73
Service	75.1	82.7[f]	92.1	87.2	106	105	78
Health-care & sports	67.9	79.2	76.0	92.0	77	69	79
Science, education & culture				89.3			
Education	73.0	90.2	68.4		70	63	83
Science	126.1	100.7	67.6		83	99	74
Culture & art	59.5	71.0	62.0		65	62	81
Administration	97.9	92.3[f]	115.4	102.9	120	129	84
Banking, finance, insurance	97.9		243.0	196.9	192	199	77
All (roubles)	240.4	225.8	58663	65140	790210	1051[g]	70

Notes:

[a] In medium and large enterprises (multiple jobs not included).

[b] Average gross wage over the year, including bonuses for workers and employees in one job.

[c] Imputed gross wages including monthly bonus in all state sector jobs, month preceding interview. Male and female averages weighted by proportion male and female in sector in the USSR (since women are overrepresented in the sample).

[d] Average monthly gross wage in one job for those employed in enterprises and organisations.

[e] Net wage in month preceding interview.

[f] Unweighted (weights not available).

[g] New roubles, equivalent to 1,000 old roubles

Sources: Taganrog samples, Nar. Khoz (1989 g, pp. 76–77), Trud ... (1995 p. 49), Rossiiskii ... (1997 p. 144, 145, 147), Rossiiskii (1999, p. 156), Zhenshchiny i muzhchiny Rossii (1999 p. 71).

Table A7.3   Non-response of men and women aged 18 to pension age, 1993/4

	Men	Women
Total number in age-group	1,516	1,579
Not working at time of interview	211	343
Do no report any earnings	40	35
Date missing or not Nov. 1993–March 1994*	30	25
Do not report hours of work per week	43	61
Other partial non-response (sector, education, marital status)	9	17
Included in earnings-function estimates	1,183	1,098

* The data include month of interview. Since the income of individuals for whom this information is missing or misspunched could not be indexed for inflation, they are not included in the analysis of earnings. To reduce the error in the indexation, the respondents – 14 in this age range – who had been interviewed before November 1993 or after March 1994 were also excluded. There is no reason to suspect a systematic bias in this selection.

Table A7.4   Usual hours of work per week of men and women 1989 and 1993/4 (%)

Hours	Women			Men		
	State sector 1989	Total 1989	Total 1993/94	State sector 1989	Total 1989	Total 1993/94
1–19	3.3	3.5	2.7	–	–	0.9
21–29	4.7	4.6	8.8	2.1	2.1	3.6
30–35	5.1	5.0	12.1	2.4	2.4	6.8
36–39	6.0	5.9	2.2	3.3	2.9	0.4
40–42	65.5	65.3	62.0	61.1	58.9	67.0
43–48	11.1	11.1	4.4	19.2	19.1	4.9
49–56	2.8	2.9	5.1	9.3	10.4	7.2
57–	1.3	1.7		2.7	4.2	9.7
Range	4–84	4–84	8–99	20–76	20–80	10–99
Mean	39.5	39.6	38.1	42.6	43.2	42.3
Std. Dev.	7.68	7.85	8.99	6.22	7.03	10.27
N	540	541	1363	375	377	1370

Note: The 1989 observations exclude 32 individuals who are employed but only in 'cooperatives' or self-employment which had not been possible earlier in the Soviet period. Thus the 1989 'total' includes such work only as a complement to state sector work.

Table A7.5 Definition and means of variables used in wage or earning models (respondents aged 18 to pension age included in earnings estimates)

Variable	Definition	Men 1989	Women 1989	Men 1993	Women 1993
WAGE	Wages previous month*	245	162	60505.58	38663.46
W	Wage/h	1.35	0.98		
EARN	All earnings previous month			69626.69	41771.85
EARNH	Earn/h			1625.54	1116.40
H	Usual hours of work/week	42.7	39.9	42.79	38.59
AGE 24	Age 18–24	0.06	0.04	0.12	0.10
AGE 34	Age 25–34	0.22	0.30	0.26	0.23
AGE 44	Age 35–44	0.33	0.41	0.32	0.39
AGE 59	Age 44–pension age	0.39	0.25	0.30	0.28
HIGHED	University degree	0.30	0.27	0.26	0.27
SPEC2	Spec. sec. or some univ.	0.33	0.34	0.34	0.40
GENSEC	General secondary school	0.16	0.26	0.22	0.23
INCSEC	Incompl. secondary school	0.08	0.07	0.06	0.03
PTU	Vocational school	0.12	0.06	0.11	0.06
LOWED	Less than 8 yrs of school	0.01	0.00	0.01	0.00
INDUSTRY	Industry	0.59	0.50	0.53	0.41
CONSTR	Construction	0.07	0.04	0.08	0.03
TRANSP	Transport & communications	0.08	0.04	0.10	0.04
TRADE	Trade and catering	0.01	0.07	0.06	0.11
SERV	Housing, municipal and consumer services	0.05	0.06		
MUNSERV	Municipal services			0.02	0.04
OTHSERV	Other services			0.04	0.05
HEALTH	Health care	0.02	0.05	0.02	0.09
SCEDCULT	Schools, culture, science			0.06	0.18
TEACH	Schools	0.05	0.12		
ART	Art and culture	0.01	0.01		
SCIENCE	Science	0.06	0.05		
FINANCE	Finance, insurance, banking			0.01	0.02
ARMYMILI	Army, police			0.04	0.01
ADMIN	Public administration	0.01	0.02	0.01	0.01
OTHER	Other sector	0.06	0.04	0.04	0.01
AIR	Dust, fumes, gas	0.16	0.07	0.23	0.10
HEAT	Heat	0.20	0.13	0.05	0.04
HARDPHYS	Physically hard work	0.16	0.07	0.16	0.06
NOICEVIB	Noice or vibrations	0.16	0.07	0.18	0.09
MTS	Married	0.87	0.75	0.83	0.68
PARTITD				0.06	0.04
PARTENTR				0.03	0.02
ONLYITD				0.02	0.01
ONLYENTR				0.01	0.01
N		354	488	1183	1098

For the 1989 data 'wages' are defined as all wages from the state sector, for 1993 as wage in primary job.

8
Summary and Conclusions

8.1 The 'Woman Question' in Soviet ideology

In the USSR, secrecy prevailed about any facts of Soviet life, which contradicted the officially sanctioned picture. Officially 'The Woman Question' had been 'solved' in the 1930s. Why allow research and publication on a problem which ought not to exist and run the risk of revealing that it did? This is one reason why Western research on women, work and wages in the USSR suffered from such poor availability of data. Another problem was that Soviet sociological research rarely included multivariate, quantitative analysis and that there were often problems of non-random sampling.

Secrecy and poor reporting of Soviet research plagued Western Soviet studies generally. Gender studies, however, also encountered specific conceptual problems. Statistics were published about women and some of their problems were discussed – but always on the implicit assumption that women were 'the problem'. Much of the official labour market statistics was not separated by gender. When it was, there were not two corresponding tables for women and men. There was one general table for the USSR plus one on women, the 'exceptions'. Often these were not of the same format, making comparison by gender impossible.

There was no 'Man Question', no critical discussion of male roles or of perceptions of masculinity. Occupational segregation was often taken to reflect 'natural' dispositions of women and men. It could occasionally be asked why so few women were professors, managers, politicians or successful artists (though it was not uncommon to hear even that explained by 'natural', 'innate' differences between the sexes). It was even rarer to question why so few women worked in heavy industry, construction and transport and before *glasnost'* no one asked – publicly –

why Soviet men were to such an extent confined to these three sectors that nearly three-quarters of male workers and employees were found in them. It was not a problem. 'Henpecked', 'feminised' husbands were perceived as needing support, fathers who wanted to be closer to their children were not, and domestic violence was not publicly discussed. The role of mother could contradict the role of worker, that of father could not.

Of course, this is by no means unique to the USSR. If it had been, it would not have required three decades of gender studies, of feminist theory and activism to gain partial recognition in the West of how women have been excluded and marginalised and some acknowledgement that the construction of gender is social, and depends on power relations in the society. To the extent that this has been achieved, it has been through massive criticism of prevailing theories and practice, including the academic. Academic feminism in the West has needed both the changes in the economic and social position of women in society and the existence of an extra-academic women's movement. Soviet women had also entered employment and education, but under bleaker material conditions and a repression which did not allow an independent women's movement.

8.2   Economic theory and statistical methods

This study has used econometric models, which are very similar in form to those in neoclassical labour economics. They are not, however, used and interpreted with neoclassical theory as a canon, but employed as tools for an empirical, statistical description. One reason for this is that neoclassical wage theory assumes an institutional context which is very different from the non-market economy of the USSR. Another is that the author is critical of some fundamental assumptions of neoclassical microeconomics, not least in its applications to gender issues. In chapter 2, an outline is presented of how wages, occupational segregation and discrimination have been perceived and modelled within different economic theories. Institutional, sociological, Marxist and feminist perspectives on gender issues relevant to wage formation can be seen, partly as complements, partly as alternatives to neoclassical theory.

Inequality between men and women outside the labour market has an impact on their behaviour and commitments inside it, but much empirical evidence indicates that this can only explain a minor part of the gender earnings gap. There are no simple 'either one or the other' answers to the questions of whether women are discriminated against or choose different roles, whether the root of inequality rests in the household or in the labour market. It requires a theory of economics which integrates a more complex view of human behaviour and motives; finds a more complex way of posing the questions; and recognises choices as socially structured (not wholly determined) and sees the gendering of jobs and roles as historically and socially created, not as a 'given'.

The standard (Oaxaca/Blinder) method of decomposing the wage gap between men and women (or between other groups) was presented in section 2.6. Neither this method nor any other can assign a unique, well-defined scalar measure to discrimination. The numbers it produces depend crucially on assumptions about what the wage structure would be if no discrimination existed, and this, in turn, assumes knowledge of what a society without discrimination by gender would be like.

A mechanical decomposition of the wage gap into a 'discrimination term' and an 'endowment' term is, on the one hand, always open to the objection that the discrimination term is exaggerated, that women's productivity really is lower than that of men, but that the variables which would measure this are unobserved. (Feminist studies have, however, pointed to a number of hidden 'female' skills that are not recognised. Inclusion of these unobserved variables would instead increase the perceived role of discrimination.)

On the other hand, the decomposition may underestimate the impact of discrimination because it takes the 'explanatory' variables as given, or exogenous. Yet, since choices of occupation, education, etc. are made in the knowledge of existing wages and existing discrimination, the taking 'as given' in itself has a legitimising role relative to the existing structures of gender (and racial and socio-economic) power.

Yet, estimates of wage functions and decomposition of wage gaps are useful as tools for quantifying correlations and of pinpointing different mechanisms of differentiation and discrimination. The numbers produced can indicate trends over time and to some extent differences between societies. With an empirical and pragmatic approach which does not assume an institutional context where wages equal marginal productivity, or that preferences are given and immutable, they serve well as instruments for an empirical analysis.

8.3   Soviet priorities, wages and gender

The account of the regulations and institutions of Soviet wage-setting in chapter 3 describes how they developed through the post-Stalin period and indicates mechanisms through which these rules and institutions may have influenced earnings, and discusses their gender bias.

Under Khrushchev, the very large and often arbitrary wage differentials of the Stalin period began to be reduced. By the 1980s, relative wages had shifted out of line with the intentions of official wage policy and wage differentials decreased more than was intended. The Gorbachev reform of 1986–89 attempted to restore them. It was meant to increase differentiation among manual workers and between white- and blue-collar workers. Like previous reforms, it was said to raise earnings in the female-dominated 'socio-cultural sphere' (schools, health-care, science) relative to other sectors. The words fly up, the wage remains below. In no reform was the fundamental priority accorded to heavy industry, particularly energy, metallurgy, military production and mining, questioned, nor that the wage level should be higher in the priority sector than in the consumer goods industry and in services, including medical, educational and cultural. The limited advance of services in each round of reform was soon outmatched by wage drift in the so-called productive branches, with their powerful branch ministries and predominantly male workforce.

People were, for the most part, not ordered into particular jobs. Therefore planning authorities, branch ministries and enterprises all used wages as an instrument of labour allocation – sometimes at cross-purposes with each other. The enterprise could adjust relative wages to supply and demand of labour power with different characteristics through bonuses, through fiddling with job titles and through job rationing and promotion according to unofficial criteria like seniority or gender.

Formal and informal non-monetary material benefits tended to reinforce the existing wage hierarchies, between the highly educated and manual workers, between men and women, and between priority and non-priority branches. The exception was the substantial opportunities for extra income which staff in certain service jobs had. Beyond this, contradictory and often highly traditional gender-roles directed and constricted the occupational choices of both men and women.

8.4   The male/female wage differential

Women in the USSR were employed almost, but not quite, to the same extent as men. They were as likely as, or likelier than, men to have university or specialised secondary schooling, but less likely to have technical-vocational training. Women did both white-collar and un-skilled blue-collar work more often than men and skilled blue-collar work less often. Women and men were concentrated in different sectors and within each area there were more men the higher the level in the hierarchy. Working women did fewer hours of paid work than men, but the difference was small. The difference in hours of housework was bigger, making women's total workloads much larger than men's.

In these respects, the data from the south Russian city of Taganrog used in this study reflected the national figures. Yet, despite their high levels of education and experience, women in Taganrog earned only two-thirds as much as men.

There are some problems connected with this data set. First, the sample is local and results cannot be automatically generalised to the USSR, or even Russia, as a whole. Second, there are problems with the sample selection and with possible errors in the measurement of wages. These issues are discussed in sections 4.1 and 5.2. Yet, considering the paucity of Soviet data for previous research, and that generalisations from emigrant samples is not unproblematic, as well as the difficulty of retrospective surveys after the fall of the Soviet system, the sample and the data used here do contribute to our knowledge of the then USSR.

The econometric analysis in chapter 5 investigates how female and male wages are correlated with age, experience, education, job level, branch of occupation, hours and conditions of work. Male and female skilled blue-collar workers earn some 8–15 per cent more than unskilled, whereas, on average, non-manual work is paid some 2–4 per cent more than unskilled manual, in terms of hourly and monthly pay.

Women could reduce (but not eliminate) their disadvantage relative to men by acquiring university education or specialised secondary schooling, or by working under hazardous physical conditions. Yet, if we compare the parameters for sectors, for vocational school and for skilled manual work we see that entering male-dominated areas (heavy industry, construction, science, skilled blue-collar work) may give women a better wage compared to other women, but not equal to the wages of men with similar jobs.

In certain professions, often female-dominated, working weeks were shorter than the standard 41 hours. Such a reduced working week must have been an attractive option for young women intending to marry and have children, but aware of the unequally shared burden of housework awaiting them. Compared to other 'women's jobs' many of these – like doctor or teacher – were relatively well paid and relatively well respected.

In a few cases, we find short working weeks and unaccountably high hourly earnings. This is taken to reflect 'unofficial part-time' work, that is opportunities for certain staff (typically cleaners, caretakers, typists and other clerical workers) to work less than the hours they were employed and paid for and perhaps have more than one job. Unofficial part-time work was an illicit adjustment to the fact that the centrally determined wages in these jobs were insufficient to attract workers to them.

Integrating these phenomena into the model for hourly wages increased its explanatory power considerably. The official rationale for the legally reduced working weeks was that these jobs involved a strain, which had to be compensated for, without detriment to monthly earnings. When these variables are included other parameters differ very little between the equations for monthly and hourly wages. Thus, the estimated function appears to model this institutional specificity of Soviet wages quite well.

The average monthly wage for women in the Taganrog sample was 66 per cent of that of men. For hourly wages the female/male ratio was 73 per cent. An Oaxaca/Blinder decomposition showed that even the large set of variables used in this study could 'explain' only a quarter of the difference between the average (of the logarithms of) male and female monthly wages.[1] For hourly wages, the 'endowment term' accounted for about only 15 per cent of the difference. If women and men in the sample had had the same endowments, men would still have earned 35–36 per cent more (depending on which wage equation is used for weighting). The model accounts for a larger share of the variation in wages within gender groups, than of the difference between them. It is difficult to imagine what could have caused such a large unexplained wage gap, unless women were discriminated against – paid less because they were women.

One can compare the gap in monthly wages between men and women in Taganrog with that in earnings for full-time employed in OECD countries (reported in Rosenfeld and Kalleberg, 1991). The Taganrog ratio of 66 per cent is similar to that in Britain, higher than in the United States and Canada and substantially higher than in Japan. In Australia, Denmark, Norway, Sweden and the FRG, however, the ratio ranged from 70 per cent to 80 per cent.[2] The ratio of 73 per cent for hourly wages can be compared to those reported in Blau and Kahn (1992) (see Table 2.3). Here the USSR scores higher in the ranking, but not highest.

In the Taganrog sample education is higher and employment more concentrated to heavy industry than in the Soviet urban workforce as a whole. To estimate the effect this might have on the gender wage gap, the parameters from a wage function estimated for the Taganrog sample was applied to the characteristics of Soviet workers and employees.[3] This model predicts a female/male ratio of 63 per cent for net monthly wages for the USSR – 2.5 percentage points lower than in Taganrog.[4] (For net hourly wages the estimated ratio is 70 per cent, while it is 72 per cent in Taganrog.) According to this model men would still have earned 54 per cent more, if both men and women had possessed the characteristics that the men actually had, in terms of the variables in the model. If both sexes had been endowed like women in fact were, men would still have earned 48 per cent more. There are, certainly, a number of sources of error in these imputations, yet since there are no national probability samples from the Soviet period, it is hard to make a better estimate.

In the absence of micro-data, some information can be obtained from aggregate statistics on wages and workforce characteristics in different sectors. Section 5.7 shows that the percentage of women employed in a sector is very strongly negatively correlated with its wage level. It is a better predictor of the wage than the level of education of the workforce or the average skill grade of workers.

8.5 Rewards to education or 'levelling'?

A number of different models were used to estimate the effect of education on wages. Net of compensation for physically hard or dangerous working conditions, and controlling for age and experience, the return to full-time higher education (relative to incomplete secondary or less)[5] was roughly 40 per cent for men, 50 per cent for women in terms of hourly wages.[6] Specialised secondary education added around 15–20 per cent to wages, while the parameter for general secondary is slightly lower for men and low and insignificant for women. For men, vocational school (PTU) paid somewhat better than general or specialised secondary school. For women this was the case for PTU with secondary education.

When branch, or sector, of employment is controlled for, most education parameters in the female equation increase. Thus, to some extent, the low wages of highly educated women were connected with the sectors they were educated for.

The combination of higher education and managerial work adds nearly 90 per cent to men's monthly earnings. The hourly rates increase by about 75 per cent. For women the pay-off varies from 70 per cent to over 90 per cent depending on what the model controls for. Higher education and 'ordinary' white-collar work makes a difference of 30–40 per cent for monthly wages and for men's hourly rates. For women's hourly wages the differential is 50 per cent. The effect of secondary education and white-collar work differs between hourly and monthly wages and between specialised and general secondary school. For men it ranges roughly between 15 and 25 per cent, but for women only from 5 to 15 per cent.

Wage differentials according to education in the USSR were lower than in many developed market economies. Part of the explanation is the expansion of the educational system, the low private cost of schooling and the unpopularity of working-class jobs, which together made for a large supply of educated labour, even at a relatively low price. But the size of returns to education is easily underestimated, particularly if the analysis is 'gender-blind'.

The priority given to heavy industry, energy and transport, the effort to expand the system of education and gender inequality were all three essential elements of the Stalinist model of development chosen in the 1930s. They were originally combined with high wage differentiation according to education, but eventually, albeit unintentionally, resulted in its decrease.

Paradoxically, to the extent that there was any 'wage-levelling' in the USSR, it was not a result of egalitarianism on the part of the rulers, but of inegalitarianism – of a combination of gender inequality and the low status of workers. Or, more precisely (and more dialectically), it was born of the combination of these inequalities and the relative egalitarianism of giving a large number of girls and a relatively large number of working class children access to education. (Perhaps a taste for education and intellectual jobs in the society should be added.)

There is little reason to think that wage compression was a policy goal in the USSR. Instead, the relatively low wages of the highly educated is one of the clearest instances where supply and demand had an impact in the Soviet economy. It is not at all evident that increased returns to education would have lead to improved efficiency.[7] The result might actually have been the reverse.

The analysis of education, gender and wages in the USSR confirms that gender and social structures interact. Because of the different career options of men and women, and the impact of discrimination, gender-less average education premia do not reflect the realities of individuals' occupational and educational choices. On the other hand, gender differences in jobs and pay must be understood in the context of the Soviet economic and social structure, and the relations between different strata in the society.

8.6   The Soviet legacy of discrimination

We find strong evidence that women and men in the Soviet labour force had very unequal opportunities and were very unequally treated. How could this be after 70 years of formal equal rights? The reasons, I believe, should be sought in three directions. First, the official principle of equal rights was often not observed. Second, the concept of equality applied was too narrow. Third, even if the same activity had been equally rewarded, irrespective of whether it was performed by a woman or a man, the consistently low evaluation of female-dominated areas would have maintained an unequal position for women. These three, of course, reflect deeper causes in the social structure, the material conditions and the history of the USSR, but that falls outside the scope of this study.

Soviet law promised women equality in the sense that if they performed the same work as men, then they should receive equal pay for it. Soviet authors and authorities writing on wage policy emphasise that the role of wages was to 'distribute according to work', not 'according to need'. Social concerns and considerations of equality should be addressed by social policy. Wage policies were explicitly divorced from such considerations.

There were laws giving women workers, especially mothers, particular rights and 'protection', in recognition of their child-bearing and child-rearing roles. Such 'protection' is always double-edged since it makes women less attractive to employers and bars them from certain well-paid jobs. (Women in industry were protected from night-work, but not female nurses.[8]) There were no laws to help men and women take more equal responsibility for children. There was no concept of 'affirmative action' to compensate women for their unequal share of parenting or for the disadvantages left from centuries of traditional subordination and prejudices. Health and safety measures that might have made many jobs more suitable for both women and men were often woefully inadequate.

Soviet women suffered under a 'double burden', the weight of which must have varied with family situation. Yet, attempts to include child-rearing and housework in the wage models produced very weak results. My interpretation of this is that it was so much taken for granted that a woman could not give her full commitment to work, that even if she did, statistical discrimination would still set the odds against her.

That the relative value accorded to different work and different areas of work is biased against female-dominated activities is a feature that the USSR shares with other societies (and much was inherited from patriarchal, pre-Soviet Russia). Both pay and prestige are low in caring and curing work, in market economies as well as in Soviet-type societies. In both systems these activities are considered as 'feminine' rather than 'masculine'.

Yet, some specific and essential traits of the Soviet system produced a specific Soviet version of this bias. The priorities established in the 1930s always set health-care and education in second place, and consumer goods and services in the third. The fundamental weakness and instability of the system resulted in rigidity, in the inability of the ruling stratum to upset precarious balances of power by modifying these priorities, even when it was in their interest to do so. The only instruments for controlling the economy were quantitative criteria. These were enforced at the expense of quality even in the production of material goods. In 'soft' activities, results are often difficult even to measure, let alone to achieve by command. On the political and ideological level, without democracy the majority of the population could not enforce other values or priorities. The repression of open, critical discussion and of any collective activity not controlled from above prevented the emergence of movements that might have questioned hidden biases as well as glaring inequities.

8.7   Women in post-Soviet Russia

To put it mildly, the market economy has not shown any indications so far of decreasing the prejudice, discrimination and inequality that the Soviet order held for women. Instead, the situation of women in the former USSR causes grave concern. The patriarchal norms, the gender stereotypes of who should do what in paid work and in unpaid were reinforced. Soviet ideology had been contradictory. On the one hand, it proclaimed that women could and should work full-time and be economically independent, just as men. On the other, the responsibility of the woman for housework, for bringing up children and for the happiness of the family was quite different from that of the man. Post-Soviet ideology wanted to solve the contradiction, free women from 'the double burden', through a return to the home and hearth. These ideas were reinforced by the fears of mass unemployment.

Have the reforms marginalised women in terms of employment and earnings? The last chapter of this study looked for answers to this question in a set of post-Soviet data, also from Taganrog. This data set from late 1993, early 1994 was analysed and compared with that from 1989.

We find indications of decreased labour force participation in prime working age. There is not a massive exodus of either women or men from the Taganrog labour market, but in only four years that would have been remarkable. Whatever may have been said or thought about the desirability of returning women to the kitchen, the plunge in real earnings of most husbands has not allowed it.

The decrease in participation rates in Taganrog is a little larger for women than for men. This appears to be the case for Russia as a whole as well, even though the 1989 census data and the later labour market statistics are not wholly comparable. In 1992–96, according to the statistical publications, the drop in total participation rate (15–72) was slightly larger for men, and the absolute decrease slightly larger for women. Labour force participation among women aged 20–34, that is at the usual child-bearing age, has declined by about 18 percentage points.

More women in Taganrog describe themselves as 'housewives' than as 'unemployed', but non-participation can be the effect of discrimination or pressure on women to 'leave the jobs for the men'. The latter would apply more to female engineers, technicians and manual workers in mixed or male-dominated sectors than in the 'female ghettos' of health-care, teaching or textiles, where wages are too low to tempt male competition for jobs. Although it does not formally affect participation rates, the longer maternity leave may reflect a larger decline in labour force attachment among women.

Comparison of male and female earnings equations for 1989 and for 1993/94 shows that the difference in wages between young and old has become very small – the skills and experience of older workers have been devalued by the changes. The earnings differential associated with higher education has increased, particularly for women. This is most likely to reflect a shift in demand away from blue-collar and older workers and a greater ability or readiness of the highly educated to enter the more profitable 'new' sectors, professions and business opportunities.

If the data are at all to be trusted, there has been a great increase in earnings differentiation from 1989 to 1993/94, both in total and within gender. Since women are over-represented at the lower end of the scale, an increase in distance between high and low income earners will in itself depress the female to male earnings ratio. The female/male ratio of wages and earnings has fallen although not as dramatically as has been claimed – in the press figures as low as 40 per cent have been current. Yet, what we find is a noticeable setback for gender equality, already within a short period of time. Although women in Taganrog participate in self-employment, second jobs and entrepreneurial activity to a relatively large extent, the gender gap is larger if we include earnings from such employment. The gap has increased despite increased premia for higher education for women and a fall in the wages of workers trained for skilled, male-dominated manual occupations. Decomposition indicates that age, education, working conditions, even sector of occupation, account for only small parts of the wage gap.

The decline in the female/male earnings ratio is serious, for several reasons. First, gender inequality and indications of discrimination were considerable already in the Soviet period. Second, women's wages have declined relative to men's at a moment when real wages for the latter have fallen dramatically. Thus, even an unchanged position relative to men would have meant a worse position in absolute terms, for Russian women. A drop in the gender wage ratio of a few percentage points may not sound dramatic, but that the trend is in this direction is disconcerting in itself. What is more, if we ask instead what has happened to women's wages the answer *is* dramatic. The real earnings of the majority of Russian women have fallen to a very low level. The Taganrog data confirm what other studies show. More people, both women and men, are under the official poverty line than before, but whatever definition of 'poverty' is chosen, more women than men are poor. This was the case also during the Soviet period, but the absolute poverty of the 'relatively' poor has become grimmer.

Nor do data from 1993/4 tell us whether these limited changes in employment and wage ratios were the trough or only the beginning of a decline. The 1995–98 employment statistics and 1996–98 changes in sectoral wages give reason to fear that the situation is becoming worse.

The early predictions of a huge increase in gender equality were exaggerated and based on too little evidence. Nevertheless, labour market, health and mortality statistics lend support to the impression of a previously unequal gender order, which has become even more polarised. The cost of polarisation is borne by women, who suffer a disproportionate share of the burden of poverty and of the increase in total labour (paid and unpaid) as well as suffering from the consequences of discrimination, sexual exploitation and violence. It is also borne by the many men whose material living standards decline and who suffer from the increased violence, social tension and insecurity, to which the gap between the breadwinner ideology, on the one hand, and their real possibilities, on the other, contribute. These in turn contribute to the terrific increase in male mortality.

The problems of the majority of Russian women cannot be seen as an unfortunate blemish of gender bias in an otherwise beneficent process of reform. They are integral to the whole experiment of Russian 'market reforms', the economic and social policies conducted and it is these that must be called into question.

Notes

1 Introduction

1. For instance, *Journal of Comparative Economics* 2/1983, special issue on women.
2. Tables of the percentages of employed men and women, divided by education or in age-groups, found in given wage-brackets, based on a survey of 310,000 households, sampling frame not reported.
3. There is, however, a loss of efficiency. That is, the expected values are the same as they would be with individual data, there is no systematic distortion, but random errors are larger.

2 Gender, Discrimination and Western Economic Theory

1. This survey spans a wide range of topics and cannot aim to be comprehensive. I refer to Blau and Ferber (1986), Humphries (1995a), Humphries and Rubery (1995) and Persson and Jonung (1997, 1998) for more extensive introductions to the economics of gender, and to Ferber and Nelson (1993) for feminist critiques of economic theories. The reader is also recommended the journal *Feminist Economics*, published since 1995. References to specific topics are interspersed in the text.
2. Excluding countries with extremely low female participation rates did not improve precision, nor did regressing the wage ratio on the participation and segregation measures simultaneously.
3. For hourly wage rates the difference was somewhat smaller than for annual earnings, but the trend similar.
4. Katz (1986), Himmelweit (1995).
5. In neoclassical economics what is sold by the employee is described as a quantity of labour, measured in hours of work. I consider more appropriate the Marxist view of the stylised employment contract, as a sale of the employee's labour power (capacity for work) for a certain period of time. This is more consistent with the form of most such contracts, and more fruitful, since it highlights the intrinsic conflict over intensity, forms and content of work.
6. Although it is rarely formally acknowledged, neoclassical microeconomics makes heavy use of metaphors. These are usually images of people as objects, or as treating themselves or each other as objects. Yet there is no *a priori* reason why atomistic market-exchange metaphors should describe outside-the-market behaviour better than metaphors from other social relations, such as gift-exchange or nurturing. (See Strassman, 1993, Klamer, McCloskey and Solow, 1988.)
7. Translated from the 3rd edition, 1928. This work, originally published as *Ocherki po teorii stoimosti Marksa*, probably remains the best exposition of the crucial concept of 'commodity fetishism' in Marxist political economy. Like

much of the best of the Marxist heritage, this was repressed and buried under decades of Stalinism.

8. Both approaches are 'individualist', in the sense of taking the individual as the unit of analysis. The traditional approach is also 'atomistic', that is, treats these individuals as disconnected from social interaction.

9. For a brief exposition, see Layard et al. (1991, chapter 3). For a discussion of how different versions of efficiency wage theory relate to neoclassical and critical economic theories, see Costabile (1995).

10. Akerlof (1982, p. 545) notes that the focus on effort in his article 'could also be expressed in Marxian terminology via the distinction between *labor power* and *labor*' (emphasis in the original). In my view, the emphasis on 'fair wages' and wage-dependent effort, on social conventions and worker/employer relations in Akerlof and Solow is in line with Marx's view of the wage as an historically constructed, socially defined subsistence, and, more generally, with the basic idea that wage labour should be analysed as a social relation. However, unlike Marx, they do not describe this in the context of a fundamental conflict between capital and labour. (See note S above.)

11. For instance, Layard et al. (1991, p. 156f) use one model where revenue is a function of effort, E, raised to a coefficient, α_i, which varies between jobs (indexed with i). Effort is specified as $E_i = (W_i - A)^\lambda$, where w_i is the wage and A is a constant Applying the 'Solow condition' that $\dfrac{d \ln E_i}{d \ln W_i} = \dfrac{1}{\alpha_i}$ the wage is determined by $\dfrac{W_i - A}{W_i} = \alpha_i \lambda$ and hence varies over jobs even when workers have the same attributes. If, instead, we keep α constant over jobs, but let the effort function vary over groups of workers (with different reactions to wage rates, but otherwise equal) as $E_i = (W_i - A)^{\lambda i}$ (where i is now a group index instead of a job index), the wage is determined by $\dfrac{W_i - A}{W_i} = \alpha \lambda_i$. Hence the efficiency wage varies with the sensitivity of effort to wage rates. If A is positive (Layard's specification [ibid., p. 156] implies it must be), the derivative of W with respect to λ is also positive. Hence, it is profitable for the employer to wage-discriminate if, hypothetically, men get more upset than women if their wages – absolute or relative to the other sex – are perceived as too low, and are more likely to reduce their effort, or if men hold more key positions where a slackening of effort affects profits more.

12. This concept was used to explain women's low wages by Millicent Fawcett at the beginning of the twentieth century. It was taken up and developed in the 1970s, most prominently by Barbara Bergmann.

13. Becker's model, which places power in the household in the hands of an 'altruistic household head', leads to similar conclusions and analogous criticisms apply.

14. This need not imply that he earns more, only that if her wage is higher, this difference is smaller than her advantage in non-market work.

15. For the United States, see Beller (1982) and Bergmann (1989).

16. Most prominently those by Catherine Hakim.

17. For white women the effect is significant, for black women it is not.

18. It is, of course, feasible that a more detailed classification of occupations would produce different results. A classification may, however, be too fine as well as

too broad. The same job could be labelled and paid differently according to the gender of the incumbent. Also, with the same qualifications and within the same field of activity, men might have easier access to positions with better promotion prospects.

19. The weak point of the argument is that the measure for 'job requirements' is the respondent's own estimate of how long it would take for a new employee to become fully qualified in the job.

20. Time in education is not included in 'time out of employment'.

21. Controlling for full-time/part-time changes and changes between 42 occupational categories.

22. Or, to be more precise, to increase the probability more for women than for men, in order to control for shifts in the overall occupational structure towards traditionally male-intensive occupations.

23. For a survey of literature and results up to the late 1980s, see Gundersson (1989).

24. They use a sub-sample from the National Longitudinal Studies of college graduates from the High School Class of 1972.

25. For the formal reasoning behind this, see Cain (1986) and Lundahl and Wadensjö (1984). As noted above (section 2.2), with above-productivity efficiency wages, discrimination need not mean competitive failure. It is possible to formulate conditions, also in a neoclassical framework, under which competition will not necessarily do away with discrimination, as in Becker (1993) and Goldberg (1982).

26. The occupational variables should, ideally, eliminate the effect of crowding, but in practice the occupational categories used had to be broad.

27. She defines 'male-dominated' as an occupation in which the proportion of males exceeds that in the overall civilian labour force by more than 5 per cent.

28. This social loss due to discrimination is noted by both feminist economists (e.g. Blau and Ferber, 1987) and Becker (1993).

29. '[S]elf-fulfilling prophecies have been shown to operate so as to confirm various social stereotypes. Expectancy effects have been implicated in the creation of apparent sex differences in behavior ...' (Darley and Fazio, 1980, p. 868).

30. Since this study is about gender differences, the rest of this chapter will focus on women. Obviously a lot of points about the effects of stereotyping and prejudice, about endogenous preferences, about 'cultural capital' and 'old boy networks' and about devaluation of work usually performed by a subordinate group, are relevant not only to gender, but also to race, ethnicity, sexual orientation and social class, but I will not explicitly deal with these, nor with the compounded impact on women in minority groups.

31. Inter-industry wage differentials could reflect unobserved differences in ability. Blackburn and Neumark (1992) find, however, that (net of standard 'human capital' factors) IQ and scores on a number of other psychological tests explain little of these wage differentials. These scores are not a perfect measure of ability, but should be positively correlated with it.

32. For an introduction to the gendering of jobs, see Cockburn (1988).

33. This notion has been dissected by critical economists from Veblen to Sen. For explicitly feminist criticisms, see Nelson, England and Strassman, in Ferber and Nelson (1993), Folbre (1994) and Grapard (1995).

34. Becker notes that 'specialized investments begin while boys and girls are young … prior to full knowledge of the biological orientation of children'. If most girls are, in his phrase, 'biologically oriented' (*sic!*) to household activities and most boys to market work, and if parents have to make choices before individual innate inclinations can show, it is optimal to train all little girls for 'non-market specialisation', but no little boys. But for the 'small fraction of girls [who] are biologically oriented to the market' or of boys 'biologically' inclined to be househusbands, these 'investments' 'conflict with their biology' (Becker, 1991, p. 40). Becker sees a problem of information, but none of defining 'true preferences' (since inclinations are 'biological').

35. For an explanation of these terms and what the choice of such wage functions implies, the non-mathematical reader can consult the Appendix to this chapter.

36. Being married is usually positively correlated with wage for men, while for women the relation tends to be negative or insignificant. Korenman and Neumark (1992) emphasise the importance of the different effects marriage have on the wages of women and of men for the total gender gap.

37. The main idea can be understood informally from a fictitious example. (For simplicity we assume a linear wage function.) Suppose that the only difference between male and female workers we consider is that 15 per cent of men have technical-engineering degrees and 10 per cent of women. Assume also that male engineers receive 120 'monies' more than other men while female engineers get only 80 'monies' extra for being engineers.

    We first divide the average difference in wages according to equation (2) (p. 40). The difference in number of male and female engineers times the wage premium for female engineers is $0.05 \times 80 = 4$. If as many women as men were engineers, the wage gap would be reduced by 4 monies. But there is also a difference due to the fact that the 15 per cent male engineers are paid $120 - 80 = 40$ monies more. On average this makes 6 monies due to preferential treatment of male engineers.

    To follow equation (3) we multiply the difference in number of engineers by the wage premium that male engineers receive and get $120 \times 0.05 = 6$ monies which is how much less men would earn on average if as few men as women were engineers. The remainder of the wage gap is equal to the difference between the premia, $120 - 80$ monies times the number of female engineers, that is to say $40 \times 0.10 = 4$ monies due to discrimination of female engineers.

    Thus, the total differential of 10 monies depends both on differences in characteristics and on discrimination. How much is ascribed to which depends on whether we believe that female engineers are paid too little or male are paid too much.

38. The arithmetic averages of the logarithms which are the logarithms of the geometric averages of the wages.

39. Some authors use this to define various measures of discrimination. Thus, the *unadjusted ratio* $U_r = \dfrac{W_f}{W_m}$ where W_f and W_m are the average wages of women and men and the adjusted ratio $A_r = \dfrac{e^{b_f X_m}}{e^{b_m X_m}} = \dfrac{e^{b_f X_m}}{W_m}$ is equal to what men would get if they were paid like women, as a proportion of their actual wage; or what the female/male wage ratio would be if women were endowed like

men but paid as women are. These are used to define a measure, $G = \dfrac{1 - Ar}{1 - Ur}$ which can be interpreted as the proportion of the wage gap not attributable to endowments. (The notation follows Cain, 1986, p. 746. Cain, however, uses a linear, not a log-linear, wage equation and, thus defines $A_r = \dfrac{b_f X_m}{b_m X_m} = \dfrac{b_f X_m}{W_m}$.)

Another current indicator is the discrimination index $D_f = [e^{(b_m - b_f)Xf} - 1]$, or the percentage increase in pay that women would receive if they retained their present labour market characteristics but were paid according to the male wage function.

40. Of course, an analogous index problem arises with the measure described in note 39. One might equally well have used X_f as weights for the adjusted ratio.

41. When scalars (numbers) are used as weights as in equation (6), the same pair of weights – one for the 'male' and one for the 'female' – is used for every kind of parameter. With a matrix, as in equation (7), there is a special pair of weights corresponding to each variable.

42. $\Omega = (X^T X)^{-1}(X_m^T X_m)$ (I have changed the subscripts from w and b, for white and black, to m and f.)
$X^T X = X_m^T X_m + X_f^T X_f$ and $X^T Y = X_m^T Y_m + X_f^T Y_f$. Hence with this choice of Ω:
$$\beta_* = \Omega \beta_m + (I - \Omega) \beta_f$$
$$= (X^T X)^{-1}(X_m^T X_m)(X_m^T X_m)^{-1} (X_m^T Y_m) + (X^T X)^{-1} (X_f^T X_f)(X_f^T X_f)^{-1} (X_f^T Y_f)$$
$$= (X^T X)^{-1}(X^T Y),$$
where $(X^T X)^{-1}(X^T Y)$ is the ordinary least squares (OLS) estimator for β on the pooled sample.

43. Formally, the utility function is assumed to be homogeneous of degree zero in the number of male and female workers for each category.

44. This effect would operate even with a textbook kind of market. It is all the stronger because the labour market is very far from the ideal type market of the textbooks.

45. I will omit a discussion of this method, since it is not used in the following empirical analysis. The same applies to Butler's (1982) attempt to separate the effects of demand and supply factors in the formation of male and female wages and to the method of 'reverse regression' (Cain, 1986, Slottje et al., 1994). For summaries, see Katz, (1994).

46. The total 'discrimination term' does not change.

47. They estimate a joint semi-logarithmic wage equation for men and women with a dummy variable for sex.

48. If it is correlated with gender, however, we are back to square one. In the standard models a coefficient for gender tells us that something about being female, something which is not controlled for in the model, results in lower wages. In the individual-specific effect models, we find that some individual characteristic correlated with gender results in lower wages for individuals who are female. In neither case does this tell us whether to describe this 'something' as productivity or as being discriminated. If the assumption of no correlation is correct, then the OLS estimator is not biased, only inefficient, and it is surprising that with a relatively large sample, the difference it makes to their estimates is so large.

49. The simultaneous two equation model of Gronau (1988) showed a significant effect of low wages on labour force separations, while the 'negative effect of

separations on wages seems to be an artefact created by the negative effect of wages on separations' (ibid., p. 285). According to Bergmann (1989), with equal earnings, men and women have almost equal quit rates.

3   Soviet Wages and Salaries

1. I have used Rofe et al. (1991) (a manual for trade union officials, published by Profizdat) and the *Short Economic Dictionary* (*Kratkii ekonomicheskii slovar'*, 1989) henceforth *Kratkii* ..., published by Politizdat. The number of articles drawn on multiplied in the course of the work, but nevertheless, this survey does not pretend to be comprehensive.
2. I am indebted to Ludmila Nivorozhkina, Lidia Prokofeva, Natalia Rimashev-skaia, Leonid Kunel'skii, Ludmila Rzhanitsyna, Yuri Kokin and the late Marina Mozhina for patiently answering a great number of questions. They are, of course, not responsible for any remaining errors.
3. Furthermore, students could 'influence' their assignment by bribes or through 'friends' on the assignment commission, by getting a manager to ask for them to be assigned to his or her enterprise or by marrying someone in the place where they wanted to live. In the emigrant survey used by DiFranceisco and Gitelman, respondents were asked what a graduate should do if assigned a job in a remote area – 20 per cent would use bribes, 38 per cent 'connections' and only 21 per cent passively accept the decision! Graduates from technical vocational schools were given two-year assignments, but these appear to have been even less strictly enforced (Granick, 1987).
4. Big 'mobilisations of volunteers' lost importance after the 1950s. Labour allocation agencies as the Orgnabor or the Job Placement Bureaux and 'Komsomol appeals' accounted for a few percent each of hirings (Oxenstierna, 1990), but people were not obliged to accept the jobs they offered.
5. About trade unions as protectors of individual rights, see Godson, (1981) and Ruble, (1979). Victimisation of dissident workers is documented in Haynes and Semionova (1979) and for the wave of illegal industrial action of the early 1960s, see Holubenko (1975).
6. An earlier study, by Mary McAuley, found 52 per cent were reinstated in 1967.
7. Further (older) references in Granick (1987, p. 288).
8. The decile ratio (the ratio of the incomes/earnings of the two individuals who make up the bottom line of the top 10 per cent and the top of the bottom 10 per cent) is a crude indicator of income dispersion, but it was often used in Soviet and East European literature and requires less data than more sophisticated measures. For an East/West comparison it probably matters which measure of differentiation is chosen. The decile ratio does not take into account the extreme tails of the distribution, if these are smaller than 10 per cent. I suspect that the difference between the top 1–2 per cent and the rest of the population is larger in the Western market economies than it was in the USSR. (Certainly, if income from capital is included). In that case, the decile ratio would make the country look more inegalitarian compared with, say, the United States or the United Kingdom, than a Gini coefficient or Lorenz curve would.
9. First, regional differences cannot be taken into account. Second, the ministries, the central planning organs, the most prestigious academic

institutes, the top officials in the party and government, the most celebrated artists, are found in Moscow, Leningrad and the republican capitals, those next in rank live there or in regional (*oblast'*) capitals (which Taganrog is not). Third, being so dominated by heavy industry, Taganrog has an under-representation of the lower paid light industry, service or social sector jobs.

10. Chapman writes, in 1988, that 2 million workers had been made redundant as a result of the reform and a further 300,000 vacant positions had been eliminated. 1.6 million employees found other jobs, half of them in the same enterprise; 400,000 went into retirement.

11. Thus it was still possible in 1989 to use – with some caution – sources such as Kirsch (1972) and McAuley (1979).

12. Each new minimum was introduced sector by sector, and the sources differ as to when they prevailed in the whole economy (see Katz, 1994, p. 97).

13. See, however, Chapman (1983) on the difficulties of inferring from the available data what really happened in the 1968–76 period.

14. If this is not obvious, imagine an economy with three men, all working and with an average wage of 100, and three women, one of whom earns 80, and one the minimum wage of 40 and one is not employed. The female/male wage ratio is 60 per cent. An increase in minimum wage induces the third woman to join the labour force. If the new minimum is more than 50 the female/male average ratio increases, if it is less than 50 it falls. (Assuming the third woman earns the minimum.)

15. Rules regulating use of the Wage Fund were altered a number of times. For more detail, see Kirsch (1972, chapter 7), Oxenstierna (1990, section 3.5), *Kratkii ...*, (1989, p. 75f and 235ff) and Chapman (1988). Further, a number of experiments were carried out with individual enterprises. The best known is that of Shchekino, where management was allowed to use a part of savings from the Wage Fund made through reduction in staff numbers to increase the pay of the remaining workforce. (Among the literature on Shchekino, see Arnot, 1988.)

16. Transport and construction will not be discussed separately here, since their pay systems were very similar to that in industry.

17. English does not have corresponding terminology for these distinctions. 'Rabochii' corresponds to the French 'ouvrier', Spanish 'obrero' or Scandinavian 'arbetare' (or would, if it includes MOP), 'rabotnik' to 'travailleur', 'trabajador' or 'anställd', and 'slushashchii' to 'employé' or 'tjänsteman'.

18. 'Light industry' in Soviet terminology includes textiles, garments and leather, fur and shoe production. According to a table of industrial employment (*Trud v SSSR*, 1988, p. 50) these three sub-sectors make up 99.5 per cent of the 'production staff' of light industry. (Note that the distinction between 'light' and 'heavy' industry is not the same as between production of capital goods (means of production) and consumer goods (means of consumption).)

19. Some of the least skilled (MOP) and most skilled workers had monthly wages.

20. For the proportion of blue-collar wages paid as piece- and time-rates, see Katz (1994, p. 108), in different branches, *Trud v SSSR* (1988, pp. 215–20). For a full list of forms of payment in industry, see Rofe et al. (1991).

21. See *Trud v SSSR* (1988, p. 139) for the percentages receiving these benefits in industry and construction.

22. Quoted by Kirsch (1972, p. 56). For examples, see ibid. and Filtzer (1989).
23. See, for instance, Malle (1987, p. 363), Oxenstierna (1990, pp. 124f), Rofe et al. (1991, p. 107f), *Kratkii* ... (1989, p. 321).
24. Which includes the greater part of military production.
25. There are two kinds of day-care institutions for pre-school children, '*iasly*' for the smaller ones and '*detskie sady*' for the older. I use 'nurseries' and 'kindergartens' to distinguish them.
26. Cf. Chapman (1978).
27. For the education of women and men in each sector, see 1989 Census, vol. X, table 3 (diagram in Katz, 1994, p. 130f).
28. For reasons of space, I will not describe the pension system here. The reader is referred to McAuley (1981) or Katz (1994).
29. 'Tremendous' in comparison to the lives of ordinary Soviet citizens and in relation to what they admitted to having, but compared with the equivalent top few of Western countries, the luxuries of the Brezhnevite *vieillesse dorée* were probably not only less conspicuous but less sumptuous.
30. In the nurseries subsidised by enterprises, staff wages were still paid by the government but the enterprise paid for the premises, toys and other equipment and for better food.
31. *Vedomstvennaia zhilaia ploshchad'*. This includes hostels, but hostels made up less than 3 per cent of the housing stock (Pavlichenko, 1992, p. 90).
32. The survey was carried out by the All-Union Centre for the Study of Public Opinion, with 1,913 respondents in six republics. It is said to be 'representative of the employed population of the USSR with regard to sex, age, and spheres of employment ...' (Kupriianova and Kosmarskii, 1991, p. 61).
33. Quoted in *Vestnik Statistiki* 1/90, p. 45, without source or information about the sampling.
34. The interesting subject of extra benefits for those employed in the military-industrial complex is further obscured by the fact that most military production was hidden under other headings, mainly 'machine-building', which also included civilian industries.
35. Some of those on low incomes were pensioners, but some were 'workers in unprestiguous occupations and low-skilled work, who were thus doubly disadvantaged' (Rimashevskaia and Onikov, 1991, p. 16f).
36. See Arnot (1988, pp. 72–5) for references to Soviet accounts.
37. Jacoby (1975) describes how widespread this 'far from illegal' phenomenon was and comments that it was probably quite well accepted by both party officials and higher level educators since it benefited their children.
38. Income from subsidiary agriculture (gardens, allotments or 'private plots') and from renting housing, although legal and important, are not included here.
39. The female/male ratio for hourly earnings in private work was 0.73 as compared with 0.63 in the state sector, but this is a selection effect, not an indication of greater equality in the private sector. For those men and women who did private work, the wage ratio in the state sector was 0.90. Hence male/female wage differences were reinforced by private sector activities.
40. It is larger than in the Taganrog sample, but the number of respondents doing private work in this data set is too small for a reliable analysis. What little information can be found is reported in Katz (1994).

41. The Tbilisi Medical Institute was an extreme case (as is shown by the fact that its rector and some members of staff were actually convicted in 1975). Of 200 entrants in 1967, 170 were found to have been admitted illegally. 500,000 roubles (286 times the average yearly wage!) were confiscated from the arrested members of staff who had been bribed to admit 29 students (Dobson, 1988, p. 46).

42. No source or information on sampling is given.

43. 1,161 people who had left the USSR in 1977–80, interviewed in Israel, Germany and the United States. For more information on the sampling see DiFranceisco and Gitelman (1984). Their article also contains examples of corrupt practices, described by their respondents.

44. The figures are taken from a table of incomes of the 'shadow economy', which is said to be estimated from 'data from mass statistics, sociological investigations, materials from research on household budgets and estimates by experts of the minimal size of incomes' (*Nar. Khoz. v 1990 g.*, p. 50). The same figures are presented in Gur'ev and Zaitseva (1990, p. 29). According to them, 'illegal additions to income for staff' in trade, catering, housing and municipal services, etc. totalled 15 billion roubles, that is an average of 1,000 roubles per person per year, but there is little information on how this estimate was arrived at. See also Gorianovskii (1990).

45. Cherednichenko and Shubkin (1985), Babushkina and Shubkin (1986). For an English-language source, see Yanowitch and Dodge (1969). See further chapter 6, section 6.3.2.2, below.

46. G. Bel'skaia, quoted and translated in Buckley (1981, p. 92).

47. See Schwartz Rosenhan (1977), Liljeström (1993) and Atwood (1991).

48. '. . . a weak husband loathes his strong wife . . . [but] a strong wife loathes with the same cruelty the weak husband . . . She wants to be weak! And in the end we see that the ideal variant of family relations is a strong husband and a weak wife' (L. Zhukovitskii in *Literaturnaia Gazeta*, 10/1984, quoted in Liljeström, 1993). In the popular 'thaw period' film 'Moscow Does Not Believe in Tears', a professionally successful single mother carefully hides from her lover that she has higher pay and status than he – and he has a fit of hysterical rage when he finds out.

49. Soviet writers made this point early, for instance the sociologist G. M. Kochetov, quoted in Yanowitch and Dodge (1969).

4   Women and Men in Taganrog and in the USSR

1. Topics included incomes, employment, consumption, health, leisure and cultural activities and time-use. A series of studies were undertaken by researchers from the Central Mathematical-Economic Institute headed by Professor Natalia Rimashevskaia. At about the same time, other studies were carried out in Taganrog, such as those by Gordon and Klopov on time-use, and by Grushev on leisure activities.

2. When the later studies were done, Rimashevskaia was Director of the newly founded Institute for Socio-Economic Population Studies, to which most of her Taganrog team had also moved.

3. It had been designed by Professor Ludmila Nivorozhkina and by two feminist scholars, Anastasia Posadskaia and Natalia Zakharova.

4. In 1989, 7 per cent of the adult population of Taganrog lived in hostels. Unpublished census figures from the Rostov *oblast'* statistical office.
5. Of the 58 individuals whose sex we don't know, 40 are children under 18.
6. Since the term 'wage function', explained in section 2.6.1, may feel unfamiliar to the non-economist, I use 'wage structure' instead to denote the relationship between individual wages and various wage determinants.
7. Aged 9–49. Among the urban population of this age, nearly 50 per cent of women and 70 per cent of men were literate in 1897 (Narodnoe Khoziaistvo SSSR 1922–82).
8. Eleven in 1958–66. (see Swafford, 1979, Marnie, 1986).
9. SSUZ have several different names in English. Many translate it as 'specialised secondary schools', some use the current Russian term 'tekhnikum' or anglicise it as 'technical college'. Granick (1987) calls them 'junior colleges', Ofer and Vinokur (1992) 'secondary vocational (professional)' schools and McAuley (1981) 'secondary semi-professional schools' or 'professional training institutions'.
10. I follow Soviet usage, according to which 'higher education' is at university level.
11. The proportions of women students in SSUZ and VUZ were published but not in the male-dominated PTU.
12. As usual no comparison with men is reported in the sources. Even when information on the situation of women is published, there is hardly ever a critical investigation of both male and female roles. For a rare exception, see Posadskaia and Zakharova (1992) and Posadskaia (1992).
13. Tables of education of men and women aged 10+ in Taganrog (sample and census data, are available from the author and in Katz, 1994, p. 173).
14. The parasitism laws applied only after a few months of non-employment. (Four according to Godson, 1981, p. 117, three according to Oxenstierna, 1990, p. 223. There may have been a change in legislation between the times of publication of these sources.)
15. Defined as the percentage of women who have higher, incomplete higher or specialised secondary education (see p. 87).
16. Technically, they use a logit model for participation and an OLS estimate for hours worked.
17. It is not clear from the text how large the sample was, nor, of course, the sub-samples of mothers of pre-school children or of non-employed women. Hence it is impossible to tell if the differences are significant.
18. Since selection of respondents favoured the employed, figures concerning rates of employment are for all household members.
19. Most of this section is based on Terebilova (1981).
20. It is not clear how many hours per week this comes to. Preceding paragraphs in the Labour Code defined working time in dangerous jobs as '6 hours per day or 36 per week', '5 hours per day or 30 per week', etc. In other words, they assume a six-day week, even though the same law stipulates a normal working week of five days! For teaching staff only hours per week are given and for health sector staff 'hours per day'. Probably the hours per day should be multiplied by six.
21. Co-operatives had been legalised by Gorbachev. At this time, they were better described as small businesses than as traditional worker co-operatives.

22. Since it is impossible to know whether teachers report their teaching hours or their total hours of work, respondents working in the education sector have been excluded in the calculations in this section.
23. Unfortunately, the coding of the answers makes it impossible to distinguish a non-answer ('don't know') from a zero answer ('no overtime').
24. In 1990, the annual official publication '*Zhenshchiny v SSSR*' ('Women in the USSR'), suddenly, and without giving any reasons, declared that homeworking and part-time work are 'the most suitable forms' of work for women with children.
25. Hence, without loss of pension rights or benefits.
26. Personal communication from Iraida Manikyna, Goskomstat.
27. For more detail on household composition, see Katz (1994).
28. Personal communication from Neli Pavlova, ISEPS.
29. The data were collected in one or a few cities per country. The Soviet data are from the Russian town Pskov and the Polish data from Torun.
30. Respondents were asked 'how many hours did you spend doing x?', which is to invite errors of recall. To weed out the worst measurement errors, observations for which the answers accounted for less than 20 hours of the previous working day have been excluded (6 per cent of respondents).
31. The problems with using 'working day' and 'day off' values are discussed below.
32. Compare p. 95, above.
33. Not controlling for the number of children, which may be lower in the second group. Swedish full-time employed mothers of young children also spend more time on housework if they are married than if they are single (SCB, 1992).
34. Their source is the so-called March census 1989.
35. These calculations were based on Newcity (1986) and took into account income tax and so-called bachelor's taxes. They are described in Katz (1994).
36. Average hours of work per week and hourly wage rates for female and male respondents in each sector are reported in Katz (1994).

5   The Wages of Soviet Women and Men

1. In the following, if nothing else is indicated, 'significant' is taken to mean at the 5 per cent level.
2. The significant differences are for agecube and pens for women. Since they change in opposite directions their combined effect in the two sub-samples is very similar.
3. Using the term ESS for the sum of squares of unexplained residuals and the subscripts a, r and nr to denote all observations, respondents and non-respondents, k for number of parameters, N for number of observations we have

$$F(k, N_a - 2k) = \frac{\frac{ESS_a - ESS_r - ESS_{nr}}{k}}{\frac{ESS_r + ESS_{nr}}{N_a - 2k}}$$

For men we get $F = 0.56$ and for women $F = 1.06$, both of which are well below the critical point for significance at the 5 per cent level at 1.6.

4. See appendix to Chapter 2.
5. As noted in chapter 4, wage data from the Taganrog survey are taken to be after-tax, unless otherwise stated. For imputed pre-tax wages, the female/male ratio is 64 per cent.
6. The ratio of 66 per cent for monthly wages was calculated for all household members, whereas we have information on working hours and, thus, on hourly wage rates only, for the main respondents. Among respondents monthly wages were slightly higher, but the female/male ratio was the same.
7. According to Table 4.12, average wages in the sample were low compared to national statistics, precisely in the sectors where bonuses are most important. This suggests that few respondents did include yearly and quarterly bonuses.
8. An attempt to approximate 'real' work experience by subtracting one year per child did not increase either the precision of the parameter or R^2 for the regression for women. (It did, very, very slightly for men!)
9. Coding involved finding the original questionnaires to compare data on hours and pay with the uncoded job title for approximately 60 individuals who stated that they worked 'not a full week' or 'not a full day'. Usually, classification was relatively straightforward, but in a few cases the guess was difficult. I am grateful to Ludmila Nivorozhkina who did this with me and supplied the necessary knowledge and '*fingerspitzgefühl*'. For those who stated that they worked 'a full working week' with usual hours of 39 or less 'short' was automatically set to one.
10. To include hours of work in the wage equation could involve an endogeneity problem. In that case, hours and wages ought to be estimated simultaneously. In this study, however, the wage equations estimated are not interpreted as models of individual choice, but as instruments to describe and investigate statistical relations. The relative inflexibility of hours of work in the Soviet context, given occupation, also weakens the influence of earnings on choice of working hours, compared to market economies.
11. For convenience, I will speak of qual4 as 'non-managerial white collar', even though among those not included in it are highly qualified employees who are not 'managers' (qual6).
12. The precision of a parameter is the probability that random variation would have made the estimate at least as large as it is, in the event that there was in fact no underlying relation. (It is, in unstatistical language, 'the level at which the estimate is significant'.)
13. See the appendix to Chapter 2.
14. These partial derivates of hourly wage with respect to age take into account all three age terms.
15. The Pearson coefficients are 0.9 for age/*stazh*, 0.6 for age/seniority and 0.7 for seniority/*stazh*. (Of course, the observations with imputed values for *stazh* were not used in these calculations. See p. 150.)
16. 'Retirement age' here means 60 for men and 55 for women. Respondents who had retired earlier and started a new job between that and the usual retirement age cannot be identified in the data set.
17. This change in the model induced only minuscule changes in other parameters.
18. The parameters for 'administration' and 'health-care' also change, but are based on very few observations.

19. The word 'explained' is not really appropriate, first, since the difference in variable means themselves need to be explained and, second, because we have shown correlation, not causality.
20. These percentages are $[1 - \exp(D_i)] \times 100$, i = f, m, where D_m and D_f are the discrimination terms from equations (1) and (2) in section 2.6.2.1.
21. This is a minor problem for the predicted average male wage, since only one man in seven or eight worked in these sectors. It has a greater impact when we apply these coefficients to women, nearly a third of whom worked in the socio-cultural sphere.
22. Although the industrio-physiocratic Soviet usage of the terms 'productive' and 'non-productive' puzzles a reader of Marx, it does have familiar ring to those who have heard present-day economists proclaim that public sector services are a burden on the 'real' productive economy.
23. If the share of the workforce of the sector with a given level of education is N and the shares among men and women are N_m and N_f, respectively, the proportion of women in the sector is $\dfrac{N - N_m}{N_f - N_m}$ Since the N's are given as (integer) number per 1,000 the numerator and denominator each has a maximal absolute rounding error of 1. The proportion of women is calculated as the ratio of two differences, both of which include a rounding error and both of which are usually small. Hence, the relative error in the quotient can be substantial. To reduce this error, the proportion reported here is calculated, using figures for the type of education in which, for this particular sector, the male/female difference is largest, and for which the expected value of the relative error should therefore be smallest. In most cases this choice is equal to the median of the seven proportions calculated for the sector, or differs from it by less than 1 percentage point. In no case is it more than 3 percentage points different from the median.
24. For branches of industry I did not have employment figures for 1989. Instead I used the numbers for 1987, scaled down by the 5 per cent decrease in overall industrial employment from 1987 to 1989.
25. Ideally, one would have wanted a variable for 'core' priority sectors, but since data were not published for mining or for nuclear or other power production and data for military industry were 'hidden' among those for broader branches, this did not succeed.
26. Half the interviews were done in March, and a further 45 per cent in April. If among those who received bonuses, the proportion who did so in March was p, and in February (1–p), then the chance that the bonus would be in the month that the interview referred to is (0.5–0.05p). In the judgement of Professor Nivorozhkina, who led the survey, because of the crisis of military industry, in 1989 those enterprises postponed the payment of yearly bonuses and were unlikely to have paid any in February.
27. Wage and monthly bonus for the preceding month plus a third of the latest quarterly and a twelfth of the latest yearly bonus.
28. These 45 per cent were intended to simulate the approximately 45 per cent of respondents in '*Obraz*' receiving a yearly bonus who could have included it in the wage they reported. (The selection was done through a random mechanism.) The equations included first- and second-order terms for age, experience and seniority and distinguished nine levels of education, four job

types and eleven branches. They were estimated separately for men and women.

29. For the models where a normal distribution of residuals is not rejected, we can divide parameters into four 'probability value classes'. (Those significant at 1 per cent, those significant at 5 per cent, but not at 1 per cent, those significant at 10 per cent but not at 5 per cent and, finally, those that are not significant even at 10 per cent). For the models for which normality is rejected we can still calculate the probability values that the t-values would have implied if we did have a normal distribution of residuals. It turns out that almost every parameter is in the same probability value class in both types of models and in no case is the difference more than one step.

6 Pay and Education

1. Nevertheless, as noted in chapter 3, several Western studies of earnings and income differentiation in post-war USSR did not find them strikingly small, compared to Western Europe. (For references, see section 3.1.4.)

2. See section 4.3.2 for a description of the Soviet system of education.

3. V. A. Zhamin and G. A. Egiazarian, *Effektivnost' Kvalifitsirovannogo Truda* (Moscow, Ekonomika, 1968). I have not been able to consult this source in the original.

4. In 1982, 98.5 per cent of eighth-graders acquired some form of full secondary education (Marnie, 1986, n. 4).

5. *Nar. Kh.* (1982 p. 370), *Nar. Kh.* (1989, p. 76), McAuley (1981, p. 87).

6. There are many attempts to model maximising behaviour on the part of the Soviet enterprise. I will not go into this, partly because I share Alec Nove's doubts (1977, p. 95f) of its usefulness for empirical analysis. See, however, Oxenstierna's formal deduction of labour demand under various bonus regimes – as she notes, they help clarify the intentions imbedded in the bonus schemes even if they do not explain the actual behaviour of Soviet management. (1990, p. 181).

7. This section is mainly intended for readers interested in the econometric aspects.

8. Active party membership, however, had a significant positive parameter in an estimate of female monthly wages and probability values below 20 per cent for male wages and hourly female wages. Gregory and Kohlhase (1988) emphasise the positive wage coefficients they find for active regime loyalty, but the direction of causality is not clear – people may have got better jobs because they were active in the Party or they may have had to become active in the Party because this was expected of them when they got the job.

9. Average wages by educational group, for all household members, are reported in Table 4.14. For quartiles, geometric means and confidence intervals, see Katz (1994).

10. The procedure was repeated with a model including education and age only. Again, equality was not rejected at conventional levels and most education coefficients differ by only 1–2 percentage points between the sub-samples.

11. Ofer and Vinokur (1992) find that a postgraduate education results in wage increases, per year of study, of about a dozen percentage points more than those for undergraduate university studies. The Taganrog data do not

distinguish between different levels of university training. However, the sample of emigrants is largely metropolitan and highly educated, and must have had much higher frequency of advanced degrees than a provincial town like Taganrog.

12. There are only five female respondents with 'PTU2'. They all have unskilled manual jobs and three work very few hours per week. At least two are cleaners and one is a pensioner. The coefficient for PTU2 is highly influenced by these few individuals whose hourly earnings are likely to be atypical. (Note the coefficients for PTU1 and PTU2 in Table 6.6.)

13. The model was also run with seniority restricted to be uniform, but *stazh* divided, and vice versa. In the first case, both stazh1 and stazh3 have probability values below 6 per cent and are over 1 per cent in size. In the second, senior1 increases to 1 per cent and is significant. (The whole procedure was repeated, starting from Model J. The results were very similar.)

14. These models are reported only in order to allow the reader to check the step-by-step transformation from Model E to Model H. The main result is, as was to be expected, that age variables lose somewhat in precision and the wage impact of levels of education that are common among pensioners is seen as less negative.

15. This is even despite the small group of women with 'unofficial part-time' work who inflate the hourly wage rates connected with unskilled blue-collar work.

16. The low precision of the parameters (probably due to the smallness of the sample) makes these conclusions very tentative.

17. Assuming, of course, that differentiation corresponded to productivity – there were Soviet criticisms of sector differentials not based on skill or schooling. (For example, Rimashevskaia and Onikov, 1991.)

18. Aage (1984) notes that this is generally assumed, though 'difficult to document'.

19. He therefore used pre-war wage rates instead.

20. Those 'seconded' were paid at the rates for their normal jobs, not those for the ones they were seconded to.

21. Survey data from Rutkevich (1984) are reproduced in Katz (1994, pp. 338–9): Swafford (1979) reports destination of year 8 graduates in 1980 from another Soviet survey. His figures are similar, except that only just over 20 per cent enter PTU. Neither source includes information on sampling.

22. S. A. Belanovskii (1988) *Faktory effektivnosti upravlencheskogo truda v promysh-lennosti*. The study is based on a survey of 200 industrial enterprises. I have not been able to consult this source in the original and have no information about the sex composition of the sample or of responses.

23. For non-specialists holding specialist jobs in industry, see Gloeckner (1986).

24. Years in the occupation was checked against the ages of their children.

25. '...the medical profession was opened to women and adapted to their needs; the rate of pay was reduced accordingly,' write Ofer and Vinokur (1992).

26. Earnings were somewhat increased to make the profession at all attractive to men. According to several sources, men also needed to do less well in entrance exams to enter medical schools (Dobson, 1978, p. 286f, Dodge, 1966, pp. 113, 116f). In SOU 1938(!): 47, (p. 239), the economist Karin Kock, mentions a regulation aiming to increase the proportion of male medical students in

'Russia'. In 1960, 76 per cent of Soviet doctors were women, in 1988, 65 per cent, not much above the 1940 figure of 62 per cent.

27. Formally, the test was of the restriction that the wage effect of being a white-collar worker did not vary with education. Rejection of equality means that this simplifying assumption is not justified.

7   Taganrog post-USSR: Patriarchy, Poverty, Perspectives

1. For an introduction to the Russian art of survival, see Alasheev and Kiblitskaya (1996). People survive in the sense that there is no mass famine. Health and life expectancy however, have declined drastically.
2. This is important because of what it reveals about voters' attitudes to women and power. The loss of these Soviet female deputies in itself did not make much difference.
3. As before, full compensation is paid no longer than 10 weeks after the birth. From then, until the child is 18 months there is a low, flat-rate benefit and from 18 months to three years none at all (except the universal, very meagre child benefit).
4. In Roshin's and Roshina's (1994) small survey of Moscow managers and businessmen, the majority of the male respondents wanted their wives to devote themselves to the household full-time.
5. According to the official statistics, there were nearly 650 alcohol-related deaths per million of the male population in 1995, which is four times as much as among women (and more than three times the rate in 1990) (*Rossiiskii . . .*, 1996, p. 58).
6. The 1989 sample of all household members is also a probability sample, while the sub-sample of 'main respondents' was not. (See pp. 84 and 121.)
7. Tax evasion in Russia is generally believed to be quite widespread. Rimashevskaia (ed., 1998, p. 128) quotes unnamed 'experts' working for the tax authorities according to whom about 20 million Russians have declared supplementary work and an equal number work without declaring it.
8. The exceptions are booklets (*Zhenshchiny i muzhchiny Rossii*, 1997, 1999), produced in co-operation with *Statistics Sweden*. The 1997 edition includes examples of female/male wage ratios in professions and sectors and the 1999 one the ratios in all major sectors of the economy and several branches of industry.
9. See also the studies cited in the following and the RLMS web-site http://www.cpc.unc.edu/projects/rlms/rlms_home.html. and that of the University of Warwick: http://www.csv.warwick.ac.uk/fac/soc/complabstuds/russia/rus-sint.htm.
10. In international statistics this usually means 15–72 years.
11. But nearly 5 per cent of the employed women are on leave.
12. The data are census data 1989 are of employment. Since there was no open and little hidden unemployment in urban Russia, I have equated employment and participation. From 1992 Goskomstat applied the international standard.
13. *Rossiiskii, . . .* (1999, pp. 107 and 116–17).
14. These figures are calculated from *Rossiiskii . . .* (1999). In this edition the figures for earlier years had been revised compared to previous yearbooks, some numbers by more than 2 million people. This explains some of the

inconsistencies in earlier publications but does not increase confidence in the statistics.

15. Clarke (1999b), based on LFS data.
16. Taganrog respondents define their 'main occupation' themselves and their definitions are unlikely to be exactly those of the statistical authorities. I have considered as employed those who either define themselves as 'working', 'working pensioner' or 'on maternity leave' or have reported earnings from the preceding month. In 1989 'labour force participant' is the same as 'employed', in 1993/94 it is employed or self-defined unemployed. Except in the 15–19 age group where the non-sampling of conscripts and hostel-dwellers creates a problem (see section 4.2) and near or over pension age where employment rates in Taganrog appear to have been above average the numbers are close. The figures are reported in table form in Katz (2001), with standard deviations and numbers of observations in sample cohorts.
17. Significantly at 5 per cent.
18. In the 30–49 age group the difference from the national rates becomes less than 1 percentage point. On the other hand, those who did 'work for pay or profit' but did not receive the payment due should have been included. Thus, if we had been able to follow the Goskomstat definition exactly, the Taganrog rate would have been lower than the ones in Figure A7.2 but less than 3 percentage points lower.
19. 1.2 in 1998 (*Rossiiskii ...*, 1999).
20. For reasons of space, I refer to Lissyutkina (1993), Bodrova (1994), Ashwin and Bowers, (1997) for different points of view.
21. Because of the oversampling of women in 1989 it is not meaningful to report totals.
22. *Zhenshchiny i muzhchiny* (1997) reported much higher figures for 1996 but a similar gender proportion. Foley (1997b) finds that just under 3 per cent of employed respondents in 1995 and 1996 were self-employed.
23. The percentages of those with any labour income or of self-defined working are the same.
24. This average may conceal large regional differences. Roshin (1995) finds a frequency of secondary employment of 18 per cent in Ivanovo, and 9 per cent in Nizhniy Novgorod.
25. Rimashevskaia (ed., 1998, pp. 121–36) provides a useful discussion of the different estimates of the share of the population with secondary earnings and the different definitions.
26. Calculated from *Trud ...* (1999, pp. 37, 118 and 145).
27. Rzhanitsyna (1993, p. 16) and Bodrova (1994, p. 41), however, emphasised the risks of unemployment of the least qualified manual workers.
28. Technically, these are uncompleted (right-censored) unemployment spells.
29. These are very small sub-samples so the figures should be taken with caution. For some individuals there could be a difference between employment status at the time of the interview and the previous month.
30. Khibovskaya (1995a, p. 39) finds that among the unemployed in VTsIOM samples more women (65 per cent) than men (48 per cent) would prefer lower income with more security to higher income and less security.
31. The rate is calculated as number unemployed divided by the sum of those working, unemployed and on maternity leave.

32. Estimates included respondents aged 18–pension age. They are reported in Katz (2001).
33. Both papers are based on Brainerd's dissertation, 'Distributional Consequences of Economic Reform in Russia and Eastern Europe', (Harvard University, 1996).
34. Monthly wage in primary job. For other wage measures, see below.
35. Age minus years of schooling minus school-starting age.
36. That is, excluding earnings from ITD, private plots or co-operatives.
37. It is respondents themselves who categorise their income as wages, ITD or entrepreneurial income.
38. Bruno (1996), while agreeing that gender stereotypes work against women in business, also suggests that this capacity for management has led some joint ventures to prefer hiring middle-aged women.
39. 'Male street vendors are seen as greedy speculators while female are poor mothers struggling to support their families', according to Bruno (1996). A number of authors discuss to what extent female entrepreneurs in Russia differ from the male, in terms of the sphere and size of activity and of manner, motives and ethos. (See *inter alia*, Bruno, 1997, Roshin and Roshina, 1994, Babaeva and Chirikova, 1995, Marchenko and Tetrenko, 1994).
40. Since I was primarily interested in the relative wage effects of characteristics, I used changes in the Russian average wage for indexation, rather than CPI. I was not able to take into account local or regional rates of price or wage change. See Table A7.2 on loss of observations due to problems with interview dates and indexation.
41. The coding of the data does not allow us to distinguish between people who did not receive a wage that was due to them; people who have a job at the date of interview but had not earned a wage the previous month; and refusals to answer the question. The ratios in Table 7.6 include only those who report earnings, assuming that all others either did not work the preceding month or refused to respond. The opposite assumption – that all who identify themselves as working but did not report earnings for the previous month were victims of non-payment – produces ratios that differ from these by a few tenths of a percentage point.
42. See Rimashevskaya (1997) for more information on poverty in Taganrog.
43. The Taganrog as well as the RLMS and VTsIOM data sets include data for one month. Due to the frequency of irregular earnings and of wage arrears, the difference between dispersion in monthly and yearly earnings is likely to be greater in Russia than in most countries and larger during transition than in the Soviet period. Having made this caution, we note that according a number of measures, earnings and income differentiation are far greater in Taganrog 1993/94 than in 1989. (See Katz, 2001.)
44. Estimates of the same model for monthly wages in primary job and of hourly total earnings in 1993/4 and for hourly wages in 1989 have been made. (They are reported in Katz, 2001. Estimates of a smaller, 'Mincer-type' model are available from the author.).
45. Estimates were made with potential experience, but it had lower precision than age.
46. Models including years of education and job-types were also tried.
47. Estimates without these variables are available from the author.

48. A probit equation was estimated for the likelihood of having reported earnings for the preceding months it included age-groups, levels of education, number of children (under one year, 1–3 years and of school-age) in the household, marital status, frequency of alcohol consumption, subsidiary agriculture and income of other household members. The inverted Mill's ratios were not significant in any of the earnings/wage equations, even at the 20 per cent level. Given the difficulty of specifying a good model of labour force participation and the sensitivity of this method to model specification, uncorrected OLS estimates were used instead. Estimates are reported in Katz (2001).

8 Summary and Conclusions

1. The male and female equations were used as weights.
2. The figures for the OECD countries refer to different years for different countries, ranging from 1980 to 1986, and are calculated from sample surveys.
3. The model includes those variables for which gender-specific means are reported by (or can be imputed from) Soviet official statistics. The mean gross wage outside forestry and agriculture predicted by this model is 6 per cent lower than the actual national average for all workers and employees in 1988, and 11 per cent lower than that for 1989, which gives an indication of the size of the error. (The sample data are from spring 1989.)
4. Since the estimated wage function is semi-logarithmic, these averages are geometric while those given above are arithmetic.
5. The difference in years of schooling would usually be 6–7 years.
6. For women the effect of higher education is smaller (40 per cent) if working conditions are not controlled for. For other education parameters and for all types of schooling for men, it makes much less difference. Note that the pay-off to higher education in terms of monthly wages is lower for women, less than 40 per cent when work conditions are controlled for.
7. Ofer and Vinokur note that 'so far the explanations of lower rates of return for investment in schooling [in the USSR, compared to the US] should not affect efficiency considerations as they are all consistent with free market forces under the system's constraints' (1992, p. 34).
8. For more detail on the rights of women workers – and of infractions of them – see McAuley (1981), Abramova (1989), Shineleva (1989). Shapiro (1992) describes the working conditions of women industrial workers and discusses the advantages and disadvantages of 'protection'.

References

Aage, H. (1984) 'Uddannelse, prestige og inkomst for forskelige ehrvervsgrupper i Sovjetunionen og i Danmark – nogle forelobige data', *Nordic Journal of Soviet and East European Studies*, 1:1

Abramova, A. (1989) 'Zakonodatel'stvo o trude zhenshchin', *Sotsialisticheskii trud*, 4/89

Acker, J. (1989) *Doing Comparable Worth. Gender, Class and Pay Equity*, Philadelphia

Akerlof, G. (1982) 'Labor Contracts as Partial Gift Exchange', *Quarterly Journal of Economics*, 97:4, pp. 543–69

Akerlof, G. & J. Yellen (1990) 'The Fair Wage – Effort Hypothesis and Unemployment', *Quarterly Journal of Economics*, 105:2, pp. 255–83

Alasheev, S. & M. Kiblitskaya (1996) 'How to Survive on a Russian's Wage' in Clarke (1996a), pp. 99–118

Arnot, B. (1988) *Controlling Soviet Labour. Experimental Change from Brezhnev to Gorbachev*, London

Ashenfelter, O. & R. Layard (1986) *Handbook of Labor Economics*, North Holland

Ashwin, S. & E. Bowers (1997) 'Do Russian Women Want to Work?' in Buckley, (1997), pp. 21–37

Atkinson, A. B. & J. Micklewright (1992) *Economic Transformation in Eastern Europe and the Distribution of Income*, Cambridge

Atkinson, D., Dallin, A. & Lapidus, G. W. (1978) *Women in Russia*, Hassocks

Atwood, L. (1991) *The New Soviet Man and Woman: Sex-role Socialization in the USSR*, Indiana

Babaeva, L. & A. E. Chirikova (1995) 'Zhenshchiny v biznese', *Chelovek i trud* 12, pp. 89–93

Babushkina, T. A. & V. N. Shubkin (1985) 'The Statics and Dynamics of Occupational Prestige', in Yanowitch (1985)

Baranenkova, T. (1983) 'Sokrashchenie tekuchesti kadrov v usloviiakh intensifikatsii proizvodstva', *Voprosy Ekonomiki*, 8, pp. 74–84

Becker, G. (1964) *Human Capital: A Theoretical Analysis with Special Reference to Education*, New York

Becker, G. (1991) *A Treatise on the Family*, Harvard, Mass.

Becker, G. (1993) 'Nobel Lecture: The Economic Way of Looking at Behavior,' *Journal of Political Economy*, 101:3, pp. 385–409

Beechey, V. (1978) 'Women and Production', in A. Kuhn & A. Wolpe (eds), *Feminism and Materialism*, London

Beller, A. H. (1982) 'Occupational Segregation by Sex: Determinants and Changes', *Journal of Human Resources*, 17:3, pp. 371–92

Bergmann, B. (1989) 'Does the Market for Women's Labor Need Fixing?', *Journal of Economic Perspectives*, 3:1, pp. 43–60

Bergson, A. (1984) 'Income Inequality under Soviet Socialism', *Journal of Economic Literature*, 22, pp. 1052–99

Berliner, J. (1983) 'Education, Labor Force-Participation and Fertiliy in the USSR', *Journal of Comparative Economics*, 7:2 (June) pp. 131–57

Berliner, J. (1989) 'Soviet Female Labor Force Participation: A Regional Cross-sectional Analysis', *Journal of Comparative Economics*, 13:4, pp. 446–72

Bielby, D. & Bielby, W. (1988) 'She Works Hard for the Money: Household Responsibilities and the Allocation of Work Effort', *American Journal of Sociology*, 93:5, pp. 1031–59

Blackburn, M. & D. Neumark (1992) 'Unobserved Ability, Efficiency Wages and Interindustry Wage Differentials', *Quarterly Journal of Economics*, 107:4, pp. 1421–36

Blau, F. D. (1995) 'Where Are We in the Economics of Gender? The Gender Pay Gap? Paper presented at the 15th Arne Ryde Symposium, Lund.

Blau, F. D. & M. A. Ferber (1986) *The Economics of Women, Men and Work*, Prentice Hall

Blau, F. D. & M. A. Ferber (1987) 'Discrimination: Empirical Evidence from the United States', *American Economic Review*, 77:2, pp. 316–20

Blau, F. D. & M. A. Ferber (1991) 'Career Plans and Expectations of Young Women and Men. The Earnings Gap and Labor Force Participation', *Journal of Human Resources*, 26:4, pp. 581–607

Blau, F. D. & L. M. Kahn (1992) *The Gender Earnings Gap: Some International Evidence*, National Bureau of Economic Research, Working Paper No. 4224

Blau, F. D. & L. M. Kahn (1997) 'Swimming Upstream: Trends in the Gender Wage Differential in the 1980s', *Journal of Labor Economics*, 15:1, pp. 1–42

Blinder, A. S. (1973) 'Wage Discriminaiton: Reduced Form and Structural Variables', *Journal of Human Resources*, 8, pp. 436–55

Bloomsma, J. (1993) 'Budushchee russkikh zhenshchin: tol'ko dom i sem'ia?', *Sotsial'no-ekonomicheskii zhurnal*, 4, pp. 119–26

Bodrova, V. V. (1994) 'Economic Restructuring, New Social Policies and Working Women in Russia: Tendency and Behaviour', Mimeo, VTsIOM, Moscow

Bodrova, V. V. (1995) 'Rabota ili sem'ia: chto vazhnee dlia sovremmennoi zhenshchiny?', *Ekonomicheskie i sotsial'nye peremeny. Monitoring obshchestvennogo mneniia*, 1, pp. 37–40 (VTsIOM)

Boldyreva, T. (1989) 'Columns of Figures or an Instrument of Social Policy', *Problems of Economics*, 32:3, pp. 89–102

Brainerd, E. (1996) 'Winners and Losers in Russia's Economic Transition', mimeo, Dept. of Economics, William's College, Williamstown, Massachusetts

Brainerd, E. (1997) 'Women in Transition: Changes in Gender Wage Differentials in Eastern Europe and the Former Soviet Union', mimeo, Dept. of Economics, William's College, Williamstown, Massachusetts

Brainerd, E. (1998) 'Winners and Losers in Russia's Economic Transition', *American Economic Review*, 88: 5, pp. 1094–116

Braithwaite, J. (1997) 'The Old and New Poor in Russia', in Klugman (ed.), (1997)

Bruno, M. (1996) 'Employment Strategies and the Formation of New Identities in the Service Sector in Moscow', in Pilkington (ed.) (1996), pp. 39–56

Bruno, M. (1997) 'Women and the Culture of Entrepreneurship', in Buckley (ed.) (1997), pp. 56–74

Buckley, M. (1981) 'Women in the Soviet Union', *Feminist Review*, no. 8.

Buckley, M. (ed.) (1992) *Perestroika and Soviet Women*, Cambridge

Buckley, M. (ed.) (1997) *Post-Soviet Women: from the Baltic to Central Asia*, Cambridge

Butler, R. J. (1982) 'Estimating Wage Discrimination in the Labor Market', *Journal of Human Resources*, 17:4, pp. 606–21

Cain, G. C. (1986) 'The Economic Analysis of Labor Market Discrimination', in O. C. Ashenfelter & R. Layard (eds) (1986)

Carlin, P. S. & L. Flood (1997) 'Do Children Affect the Labour Supply of Swedish Men? Time Diary vs Survey Data', *Labour Economics*, 4:2, pp. 167–84

Chapman J. G. (1978) 'Equal Pay for Equal Work', in Atkinson et al. (1978)

Chapman, J. G. (1979) 'Are Earnings More Equal under Socialism? The Soviet Case, with Some United States Comparisons', in Moroney (1979)

Chapman, J. G. (1983) 'Earnings Distribution in the USSR, 1968–1976, *Soviet Studies*, 35, 410–13

Chapman, J. G. (1988) 'Gorbachev's Wage Reform', *Soviet Economy*, 4, pp. 338–65

Chapman, J. G. (1991) 'Recent and Prospective Trends in Soviet Wage Determination', CA Standing (1991)

Cherednichenko, G. A. & V. N. Shubkin (1985) *Molodezh' vstupaet v zhizn': Sotsiologicheskie issledovania problem vybora professii i trudoustroistva*, Moscow

Clarke, S. (ed.) (1996a) *Labour Relations in Transition*, Cheltenham

Clarke, S. (ed.) (1996b) *Conflict and Change in the Russian Industrial Enterprise*, Cheltenham

Clarke, S (1998) 'New Forms of Employment, Job Creation and Survival Strategies in Russia', mimeo, Centre for Comparative Labour Studies, University of Warwick

Clarke, S. (1999a) 'Making Ends Meet in a Non-monetary Market Economy', mimeo, Centre for Comparative Labour Studies, University of Warwick

Clarke, S. (1999b) *New Forms of Employment and Household Survival Strategies in Russia*, Coventry, Centre for Comparative Labour Market Studies

Clarke, S. & V. Kabalina (2000) 'The New Private Sector in the Russian Labour Market', *Europe-Asia Studies*, 52:1, pp. 7–32

Clayton, E. & J. R. Millar (1991) 'Education, Job Experience and the Gap Between Male and Female Wages in the Soviet Union', *Comparative Economic Studies*, 33:1, pp. 5–22

Cockburn, C. (1988) 'The Gendering of Jobs: Workplace Relations and the Reproduction of Sex Segregation', in Walby (1988)

Commander, S. & Yemtsov, R. (1997) 'Characteristics of the Unemployed', in Klugman (ed.) (1997)

Costabile, L. (1995) 'Institutions, Social Custom and Efficiency Wage Models: Alternative Approaches', *Cambridge Journal of Economics*, 19:5

Cotton, J. (1988) 'On the Decomposition of Wage Differentials', *Review of Economics and Statistics*, 20:2, pp. 236–43

D'Amico, T. F. (1987) 'The Conceit of Labor Market Discrimination', *American Economic Review*, 77:2, pp. 310–15

Danilov, E. (1982) 'Sovershenstvovanie oplaty truda v torgovle', *Voprosy Ekonomiki*, 6

Darley, J. & R. Fazio (1980) 'Expectancy Confirmation Processes Arising in the Social Interaction Sequence', *American Psychologist*, 35 (10) pp. 867–88

Davies, C. & J. Rosser (1986) 'Gendered Jobs in the Health Service: A Problem for Labour Process Analysis, in Knights & Willmott (1986)

Davis, C. M. (1988) 'Organisation and Performance of the Soviet Health Service' in Lapidus & Swanson (1988)

Daymont, T. N. & P. J. Andrisani (1984) 'Job Preferences, College Major and the Gender Gap in Earnings', *Journal of Human Resources*, 19:3, pp. 408–28

Demograficheskii ezhegodnik SSSR (1990) Goskomstat, Moscow

Dex, S. & R. Sewell (1995) 'Equal Opportunities Policies and Women's Labour Market Status in Industrialised Countries' in Humphries & Rubery (1995)

DiFranceisco, W. & Z. Gitelman (1984) 'Soviet Political Culture and "Covert Participation"', in Policy Implementation', *The American Political Science Review*, 78:3, pp. 603–21

Dobson, R. B. (1978) 'Educational Policies and Attainment', in Atkinson et al. (1978)

Dobson, R. B. (1988) 'Higher Education in the Soviet Union: Problems of Access, Equity and Public Policy', in Lapidus & Swanson (1988)

Dodge, N. T. (1966) *Women in the Soviet Economy. Their Role in Economic, Scientific and Technical Development*, Baltimore

Duncan, S. & S. Edwards (1997) 'Lone Mothers and Paid Work: Rational Economic Man or Gendered Moral Rationalities', *Feminist Economics*, 3:2, pp. 29–62

du Plessix Gray, F. (1990) *Soviet Women. Walking the Tightrope*, New York

Earle, J. S. & K. Z. Sabirianova (1998) 'Understanding Wage Arrears in Russia', mimeo, SITE, Stockholm

Edin, P.-A., Fredriksson, P. & B. Holmlund (1994) 'Utbildningsnivå och utbildningsavkastning i Sverige', in *Studier av svensk utbildning*, Ekonomiska Rådets Årsbok 1993, Stockholm

Einhorn, B. (1993) *Cinderella Goes to Market: Citizenship, Gender and Women's Movements in East Central Europe*, London

Ellman, M. (1980) 'A Note on the Distribution of Earnings in the USSR under Brezhnev', *Slavic Review* 39, pp. 669–71

England, P. (1982) 'The Failure of Human Capital Theory to Explain Occupational Segregation by Sex', *Journal of Human Resources*, 17:3, pp. 358–70

England, P., Farkas, G., Kilbourne, B. & T. Dou (1988) 'Explaining Occupational Sex Segregation and Wages: Findings from a Model with Fixed Effects', *American Sociological Review*, 53:2, pp. 544–58

Eremitcheva, G. (1995) 'The Women's Leisure before and after the Beginning of Economic Transformation in Russia', paper presented at the V World Congress for Central and East European Studies, Warsaw

Ericsson, T. (1991) *Systematisk arbetsvärdering. Ett lönesättnings instrument i närbild.* Umeå Studies in Sociology, Umeå

Ferber, M. (1991) 'Women in the Labor Market: The Incomplete Revolution', in Willborn (1991)

Ferber, M. & J. Nelson (1993) *Beyond Economic Man*, Chicago

Filer, R. K. (1985) 'Male–Female Wage Differences : The Importance of Compensating Differentials', *Industrial and Labor Relations Review*, 38:3, pp. 426–37

Filer, R. K. (1986) 'The Role of Personality and Tastes in Determining Occupational Structure', *Industrial and Labor Relations Review*, 39:3, pp. 412–24

Filtzer, D. (1989) 'The Soviet Wage Reform of 1956–62', *Soviet Studies*, 41:1, pp. 88–110

Filtzer D. (1994) *Soviet Workers and the Collapse of Perestroika: The Soviet Labour Process and Gorbachev's Reforms 1985–1991*, Cambridge

Florin, C. & U. Johansson (1990) 'Kunskap och kompetens som vapen', *Häften för Kritiska Studier*, 3, pp. 17–29

Folbre, N. (1994) *Who Pays for the Kids? Gender and the Structures of Constraint*, London

Foley, M. (1997a) 'Determinants of Unemployment Duration in Russia', Economic Growth Center, Yale University, Center Discussion Paper No. 779

Foley, M. (1997b) 'Labour Market Dynamics in Russia', Economic Growth Center, Yale University, Center Discussion Paper No. 780

Foley, M. (1997c) 'Multiple Job Holding in Russia During Transition', Economic Growth Center, Yale University, Center Discussion Paper No. 781

Fong, M. (1994) 'The Role of Women in Rebuilding the Russian Economy' *Studies of Economies in Transformation*, Paper No. 10, World Bank

Fong, M. (1995) 'Zhenshchiny na fone transformatsii rossiiskoi ekonomiki', *Chelovek i trud*, 9

Funk, N. & M. Mueller (eds.) (1993) *Gender Politics and Post-communism: Reflections from Eastern Europe and the Former Soviet Union*, New York and London

Gendler, G. (1988) 'Premirovanie rabotnikov sotsial'no-kul'turnykh otraslei', *Sotsialisticheskii Trud*, 8, pp. 82–6

Glinskaya, E. and T. Mroz (1998) 'The Gender Gap in Wages in Russia from 1992 to 1995', Working paper, Carolina Population Centre, University of North Carolina

Gloeckner, E. (1986) 'Underemployment and Potential Unemployment of the Technical Intelligentsia: Distortions Between Education and Occupation', in Lane (1986)

Godson, J. (1981) 'The Role of the Trade Unions', in L. Schapiro & J. Godson (eds.) *The Soviet Worker*, London

Goldberg, M. (1982) 'Discrimination, Nepotism and Long-run Wage Differentials', *Quarterly Journal of Economics*, 97, pp. 307–19

Gordon, L. A. & Klopov, E. (1975) *Man after Work*, Moscow. (Russian original *Chelovek posle raboty*, 1972)

Gordon, L. A. (1987) 'Sotsial'naia politika v sfere oplaty truda (vchera i segodnia)', *Sotsiologicheskie issledovaniia* 4, pp. 3–19

Gorianovskii, A. (1990) 'Ukrast' mozhno vse (rezultaty vkliuchennogo nabliudeniia)', *Sotsiologicheskie issledovania*, 2, pp. 56–64

Grachev, L. (1996) 'Pravovye garantii i sotsial'nye l'goty zhenshchinam imeiushchim detei', *Sotsial'noe obespechenie*, 2, pp. 42–6

Granick, D. (1987) *Job Rights in the Soviet Union. Their Consequences*, Cambridge

Grapard, U. (1995) 'Robinson Crusoe: The Quintessential Economic Man'?, *Feminist Economics*, 1:1, pp. 33–52

Grapard, U. (1997) 'Theoretical Issues of Gender in the Transition from Socialist Regimes', *Journal of Economic Issues*, 31:3, pp. 665–85

Gregory, P. R. (1982) 'Fertility and Labor Force Participation in the Soviet Union and Eastern Europe', *Review of Economics and Statistics*, 64: 1, pp. 18–31

Gregory, P. R. (1987) 'Productivity, Slack and Time Theft' in Millar (1987)

Gregory, P. R. & J. E. Kohlhase (1988) 'The Earnings of Soviet Workers: Evidence from the SIP', *Review of Economics and Statistics*, 70(1) (February), pp. 23–35

Grogan, L. (1998) 'Worker Characteristics and Administrative Leave in the Russian Federation', mimeo, Tinbergen Institute and Dept. of Economics; University of Amsterdam

Grogan L. & G. van den Berg (1998) 'The Duration of Unemployment in Russia', mimeo, Tinbergen Institute, Amsterdam

Grogan, L. (1999) 'Worker Flows in Russia', mimeo, Tinbergen Institute, Amsterdam

Gronau (1988) 'Sex-Related Wage Differentials and Women's Interrupted Labor Careers – the Chicken or the Egg', *Journal of Labor Economics*, 6:3, pp. 277–301

Groshen, E. (1991) 'The Structure of the Female/Male Wage Differential. Is it Who You Are, What You Do, or Where You Work?', *Journal of Human Resources*, XXVI:3

Gunderson, M. (1989) 'Male–Female Wage Differentials and Policy Responses', *Journal of Economic Literature*, 27:1 (March), pp. 46–72

Gur'ev, V. & Zaitseva, A. (1990) 'Stoimost' zhizni, prozhitochnyi minimum, infliatsiia (metodologiia i analiz)', *Vestnik Statistiki*, 6, pp. 20–9

Gustafsson, B. & L. I. Nivorozhkina (1996) 'Relative Poverty in Two Egalitarian Societies. A Comparison between Taganrog, Russia during the Soviet Era and Sweden', *The Review of Income and Wealth*, 42:3 (September), pp. 321–34

Gustafsson, B. & L. I. Nivorozhkina (1998) 'The Distribution of Economic Well-being in Urban Russia at the End of the Soviet Era', *International Review of Applied Economics*, 12:3, pp. 361–80

Hakim, C. (1991) 'Grateful Slaves and Self-made Women: Fact and Fantasy in Women's Work Orientation', *European Sociological Review*, 7:2 (September), pp. 101–21

Hanson, P. (1986) 'The Serendipitous Soviet Acheivement of Full Employment: Labour Shortage and Labour Hoarding in the Soviet Economy', in Lane (1986)

Haynes, V. & Semyonova, O. (1979) *Workers against the Gulag*, London

Heckman, J. J. (1979) 'Sample Bias as a Specification Error', *Econometrica*, 47:1, pp. 153–61

Herleman, H. (ed.) (1987) *Quality of Life in the Soviet Union*, Boulder, Colorado

Hersch, Joni & Leslie S. Stratton (1997) 'Housework, Fixed Effects and Wages of Married Workers', *Journal of Human Resources*, 32:2, pp. 285–307

Himmelweit, S. (1995) 'The Discovery of "Unpaid Work"', *Feminist Economics*, 1:2, pp. 1–20

Holubenko, M. (1975) 'The Soviet Working Class', *Critique*, 4

Hopkins, B. E. (1995) 'Women and Children Last: A Feminist Redefinition of Privatization and Economic Reform', in Kuiper & Sap (1995), pp. 249–63

Horrell, S., J. Rubery & B. Burchell (1989) 'Unequal Jobs or Unequal Pay?, *Industrial Relations Journal*, 20, 3, pp. 176–91

Humphries, J. (ed.) (1995a) *Gender and Economics*, Aldershot

Humphries, J. (1995b) 'Economics, Gender and Equal Opportunities', in Humphries & Rubery (1995)

Humphries, J. & J. Rubery (eds.) (1995) *The Economics of Equal Opportunities*, EOC, Manchester

Itogi vsesoiuznoi perepisi naseleniia 1979ogo g., (1989) Goskomstat, Moscow

Jackson, L. A., Gardner, P. D. & L. A. Sullivan (1992) 'Explaining Gender Differences in Self-Pay Expectations: Social Comparison Standards and Perceptions of Fair Pay', *Journal of Applied Psychology*, 77:5, pp. 651–63

Jacoby, S. (1975) *Skolan i Sovjet*, Stockholm (English original: *Inside Soviet Schools*, 1974)

Jenkins, S. P. (1994) 'Earnings Discrimination Measurement. A Distributional Approach', *Journal of Econometrics* 61:1, pp. 81–102

Jones, F. L. & J. Kelley (1984) 'Decomposing Differences between Groups. A Cautionary Note in Measuring Discrimination', *Sociological Methods and Research*, 12:3, pp. 323–43

Jonung, C. & I. Persson (1993) 'Women and Market Work: The Misleading Tale of Participation Rates in International Comparisons', *Work, Employment & Society*, 7:2, pp. 259–74

Jonung, C. (1997) 'Economic Theories of Occupational Segregation by Sex – Implications for Change over Time', Dept. of Economics, University of Lund, Reprint Series No. 227

Kagarlitskij, B. (1991) *Sovjetunionen: Monolit i upplösning*, Göteborg

Kahan, A. & Ruble, B. (eds.) (1979) *Industrial Labor in the USSR*, London

Kalabakhina, I. (1995) *Sotsial'nyi pol i problemy naseleniia*, Moscow,

Katz, K. (1986) 'Och hon skall sopa trappan och hon skall skura golv ... Klass, kön och politisk ekonomi', in H. Ganetz, E. Gunnarsson & A. Göransson (eds.) *Marxism och feminism*, Stockholm

Katz, K. 1994. '*Gender Differentiation and Discrimination. A Study of Soviet Wages*', PhD thesis, Dept. of Economics, University of Göteborg

Katz, K. (1997) 'Gender Wages and Discrimination in the USSR', *Cambridge Journal of Economics*, 21:4, pp. 431–52

Katz, K. (2001) 'Labour in Transition. Women and Men in Taganrog, Russia', Working Paper, Department of Economics, University of Stockholm

Kay, R. (1997) 'Images of an Ideal Woman: Perceptions of Russian Womanhood through the Media, Education and Women's Own Eyes', in Buckley (1997), pp. 77–98

Khibovskaia, E. A. (1995a) 'Zaniatost' bezrabotnykh. Otnoshenie k sposobam trudoustroistva', *Ekonomicheskie i sotsial'nye peremeny: monitoring obshchestvennogo mneniia*, VTsIOM, 4, pp. 37–41

Khibovskaia, E. (1995b) 'Vtorichnaia zaniatost' kak sposob adaptatsii k ekonomicheskim reformam', *Voprosy Ekonomiki*, 5, pp. 71–97

Khibovskaia, E. (1996) 'Vtorichnaia zaniatost' v raznykh sektorakh ekonomiki', *Ekonomicheskie i sotsial'nye peremeny:monitoring obshchestvennogo mneniia*, VTsIOM, 3, pp. 24–7

Khotkina, Z. (1994) 'Women in the Labour Market: Yesterday, Today and Tomorrow', in Posadskaya (1994), pp. 85–108

Kim, M. K. & S. W. Polachek (1994) 'Panel Estimates of the Gender Earnings Gap. Individual-specific Intercept and Individual-specific Slope Models', *Journal of Econometrics*, 61:1, pp. 23–42

Kirsch, L. J. (1972) *Soviet Wages. Changes in Structure and Administration since 1956*, Cambridge, Mass.

Klamer, A., McCloskey, D. & R. Solow (eds.) (1988) *The Consequences of Economic Rhetoric*, Cambridge

Klimenkova, T. (1994) 'What Does Our New Democracy Offer Society?', in Posadskaya

Klugman, J. (ed.) (1997) *Poverty in Russia*, EDI Development Studies, World Bank

Klugman, J. & J. Braithwaite (1997) 'Introduction and Overview', in Klugman (ed.)

Knights, D. & H. Willmott (1986) *Gender and the Labour Process*, Aldershot

Komozin, A. N. (1991) 'A Work Career from the Standpoint of the Life Cycle', *Soviet Sociology* 30:5, pp. 49–61

Korenman, S. & D. Neumark (1992) 'Marriage, Motherhood, and Wages', *Journal of Human Resources*, 27:2, pp. 233–55

Kratkii ekonomicheskii slovar' (1989) Moscow

Kuiper, E. & Sap, J. (eds.) (1995) *Out of the Margin. Feminist Perspectives on Economics*, London

Kuniansky, A. (1983) 'Soviet Fertility, Labor-Force Participation and Marital Instability', *Journal of Comparative Economics*, 7:2, pp. 114–30

Kupriianova, Z. & V. Kosmarskii (1991) 'Two Population Surveys on the Motives of Work Activity', *Soviet Sociology*, 30:6, pp. 55–70

Lam, D. & R. F. Schoeni (1993) 'Effects of Family Background on Earnings and Returns to Schooling: Evidence from Brazil', *Journal of Political Economy*, 101:710–40

Lampert, N. (1986) 'Job Security and the Law in the USSR', in Lane (1986)

Lane, D. (ed.) (1986) *Labour and Employment in the USSR*, Brighton

Lapidus, G. W. (1978) *Women in Soviet Society. Equality, Development and Social Change*, Berkeley

Lapidus, G. W. & G. E. Swanson (eds.) (1988) *State and Welfare USA/USSR: Contemporary Policy and Practice*, Berkeley

Layard, R., S. Nickell & R. Jackman (1991) *Unemployment. Macroeconomic Performance and the Labour Market*, Oxford

le Grand, C. (1991) 'Explaining the Male-Female Wage Gap: Job Segregation and Solidartiy Wage Bargaining in Sweden', *Acta Sociologica*, 34, pp. 261–78

Lehmann, H., J. Wadsworth & A. Acquisti (1999) 'Grime and Punishment: Job Insecurity and Wage Arrears in the Russian Federation', *Journal of Comparative Economics* 27, pp. 595–617; and (1998) mimeo

Leontieva, T. (1994) 'The Lost Generation', *Women's Studies International Forum*, 17:5

Liff, S. (1986) 'Technical Change and Occupational Sex-typing', in Knights & Willmot (1986)

Liljeström, M. (1993) 'The Soviet Gender System: The Ideological Construction of Femininity and Masculinity in the 1970s', in Liljeström et al. (eds.) *Gender Restructuring – 'Perestroika' in Russian Studies*, Slavica Tamperiana, Tampere

Liljeström, M. (1995) *Emanciperade till underordning: det sovjetiska könssystemets uppkomst och diskursiva reproduktion*, Åbo

Lindberg, A. (1993) 'Mejerskan som försvann', *Arbetets historia: föreläsningar i Lund*, vol. 6, pp. 61–78

Lingsom, S. (1978) 'Arbeidstid hjemme og ute', in Grenness, R. (ed.) *Hvis husmoren ikke fantes*, Pax Forlag, Oslo

Lissiutkina, L. (1993) 'Soviet Women at the Crossroads of Perestroika', in Funk & Mueller (1993)

Loprest, P. (1992) 'Gender Differences in Wage Growth and Job Mobility', *American Economic Review*, 82:2, pp. 526–32

Lundahl, M. & E. Wadensjö, (1984) *Unequal Treatment. A Study in the Neo-classical Theory of Discrimination*, London

Löfström, Å. (1989) *Diskriminering på svensk arbetsmarknad. En analys av löneskillnader mellan kvinnor och män.*, University of Umeå.

Löfström, Å. (1993) 'Kvinnor föder barn och tror på rättvisa löner', in Nord (1993:16), *Kvinnelønnas mysterier – myter og fakta on lønsdannelsen*, Nordisk Ministerråd

Major, B. & Forcey, B. (1985) 'Social Comparisons and Pay Evaluations: Preferences for Same-Sex and Same-Job Wage Comparisons', *Journal of Experimental Social Psychology*, 21, pp. 393–405

Malle, S. (1986) 'Heterogeneity of the Soviet Labour Market as a Limit to a more Efficient Utilisation of Manpower', in Lane (ed.) (1986)

Malle, S. (1987) 'Planned and Unplanned Mobility in the Soviet Union under the Threat of Labour Shortage', *Soviet Studies*, 39:3, pp. 357–87

Malle, S. (1990) *Employment Planning in the Soviet Union*, Basingstoke

Malysheva, M. M. (ed.) (1996) *Gendernye aspekty sotsial'noi transformatsii*, Demografiia i sotsiologiia, Moscow

Mandel, E. (1969) *Marxist Economic Theory*, London

Manser, M. & M. Brown (1980) 'Marriage and Household Decision Making: A Bargaining Analysis', *International Economic Review*, 21, pp. 31–44

Marchenko, T. & Tetrenko, E. (1994) *Zhenshchiny v perelomnyi period rossiiskoi zhizni* 'Fond Obshchestvennoe Mnenie', Moscow

Marnie, S. (1986) 'Transition from School to Work: Satisfying Pupils' Aspirations and the Needs of the Economy', in Lane (ed.) (1986)

Marnie, S. (1992) *The Soviet Labour Market in Transition*, European University Institute, Florence

Marx, K. (1976) *Capital*, Volume 1, Harmondsworth

Mashika, T. A. (1989) *Zaniatost' zhenshchin i materinstvo*, Moscow

McAuley, A. (1979) *Economic Welfare in the Soviet Union. Poverty, Living Standards and Inequality*, Madison, Wisconsin

McAuley, A. (1981) *Women's Work and Wages in the Soviet Union*, London

McCrate, E. (1988) 'Gender Difference: The Role of Endogenous Preferences and Collective Action', *American Economic Review*, 78:2, pp. 235–39

McElroy, M. and M. Horney (1981) 'Nash Bargained Household Decisions: Towards a Generalized Model', *International Economic Review*, 22, pp. 333–49

Mezentseva, E. (1994a) 'What Does the Future Hold? (Some Thoughts on the Prospects for Women's Employment)', in Posadskaya, (1994), pp. 74–84

Mezentseva, E. (1994b) 'Equal Opportunities or Protectionist Measures? The Choice Facing Women', in Posadskaya (1994), pp. 109–22

Migranova, L. A. & M. A. Mozhina (1991) 'Zarabotnaia plata i dokhody semei. Osnovnye napravleniia sovershenstvovaniia raspredelitel'nykh otnoshenii', in Rimashevskaia & Onikov (1991)

Millar, J. (ed.) (1987). *Politics, Work and Daily Life in the USSR*, Cambridge, Mass.

Mincer, J. (1974) *Schooling, Experience and Earnings*, New York

Monosouva, G. (1996) 'Gender Differentiation and Industrial Relations', in Clarke (ed.) (1996b)

Moroney, J. R. (ed.) (1979a) *Income Inequality. Trends and International Comparisons*, Lexington, Mass.

Moskoff, W. (1982) 'Part time employment in the Soviet Union', *Soviet Studies* 34:2, pp. 270–85

Mozhina, M. A., R. I. Popova & L. N. Ovcharova (1992) 'Uroven' i differentsiatsiia dokhodov', in N. M. Rimashevskaia & V. V. Patsiorkovskii (eds) (1992a)

Narodnoe Khoziaistvo SSSR 1968, TsSU, Moscow

Narodnoe Khoziaistvo SSSR 1982–1982, TsSU, Moscow

Narodnoe Khoziaistvo SSSR v 1988 g., Gokomstat, Moscow

Narodnoe Khoziaistvo SSSR v 1989 g., Goskomstat, Moscow

Narodnoe Khoziaistvo SSSR v 1990 g., Goskomstat, Moscow&

Narodnoe Obrazovanie i kul'tura v SSSR, Goskomstat, Moscow 1989

Naselenie SSSR 1988. Statisticheskii ezhegodnik, Goskomstat, Moscow

Neumark, D. (1988) 'Employers' Discriminatory Behavior and the Estimation of Wage Discrimination', *Journal of Human Resources*, 23:3, pp. 279–95

Newcity, M. A. (1986) *Taxation in the Soviet Union*, New York

Newell, A. & B. Reilly (1996) 'The Gender Wage Gap in Russia: Some Empirical Evidence', *Labour Economics*, 3, pp. 337–56

Niemi, I., Eglite, P., Mitrikas, A., Patrushev, V. D. & Pääkkönen, H. (1991) *Time Use in Finland, Latvia, Lithuania and Russia*, Central Statistical Office of Finland, Studies 182

Nilsson, A. (1988) *Strukturomvandling och arbetsmarknads-segmentering. En studie av arbetsmarknadens utveckling i Sjuhäradsbygden*. Dept. of Sociology, University of Gothenburg

Nove, A. (1977) *The Soviet Economic System*, London

Oaxaca, R. (1973) 'Male–Female Wage Differentials in Urban Labor Markets', *International Economic Review*, 14, pp. 693–709

Oaxaca, R. L. & M. R. Ransom (1994) 'On Discrimination and the Decomposition of Wage Differentials', *Journal of Econometrics* 61:1, pp. 5–21

Ofer, G. & Vinokur, A. (1981) 'Earnings Differentials by Sex in the Soviet Union: A First Look', in S. Rosefielde (ed.) *Economic Welfare and the Economics of Soviet Socialism: Essays in Honor of Abram Bergson*, Cambridge, Mass.

Ofer, G. & Vinokur, A. (1983) 'The Labor-Force Participation of Married Women in the Soviet Union: A Household Cross-Section Analysis', *Journal of Comparative Economics*, 7:2, pp. 158–76

Ofer, G. & A. Vinokur (1992) *The Soviet Household under the Old Regime. Economic Conditions and Behaviour in the 1970s*, Cambridge

Ogloblin, C. G. (1999) 'The Gender Earnings Differential in the Russian Transition Economy', *Industrial & Labor Relations Review*, 52:4, pp. 602–27

Olsson, L. (1993) 'Kvinnokraft, arbetskraft, maskinkraft', *Arbetets historia: föreläsningar i Lund*, vol. 6, pp. 47–60

O'Neill, J. (1991) 'The Wage Gap Between Men and Women in The United States', in Willborn (1991)

Onikov, L. A. (ed.) (1977) *Sem'ia, trud, dokhody, potreblenie*, Moscow

'O polozhenie semei v Rossiiskoi federatsii' (1994) Iuridicheskaya Literatura, Moscow

Ott, N. (1995) 'Fertility and Division of Work in the Family. A Game-theoretic Model of Household Decisions', in Kuiper and Sap (1995)

Ovsiannikov, A. A. (1985) 'The Interconnection Between Work and Consumption', in Yanowitch (1985)

Oxenstierna, S. (1990) *From Labour Shortage to Unemployment? The Soviet Labour Market in the 1980s*, Swedish Institute for Social Research, Stockholm

Paci, P., Joshi, H. & G. Makepeace (1995) 'Pay Gaps Facing Men and Women Born in 1958: Differences Within the Labour Market', in Humphries & Rubery (1995).

Palme, M. & R. Wright (1992) 'Gender Discrimination and Compensating Differentials in Sweden, *Applied Economics*, 24, pp. 751–9

Pavlichenko, L. D. (1992) 'Zhilishchnoe obespechenie', in N. M. Rimashevskaia & V. V. Patsiorkovskii (eds) (1992a)

Persson, I. & C. Jonung (eds) (1997) *Economics of the Family and Family Policies*, London

Persson, I. & C. Jonung, (eds) (1998) *Women's Work and Wages*, London

Petersen, T., Meyerson, E. M. & Snartland, V. (1996) 'The Within-job Gender Wage Gap: The Case of Sweden', IUI Working Paper, Stockholm

Phillips, A. & B. Taylor (1980) 'Sex and Skill: Notes towards a Feminist Economics', *Feminist Review*, 6, pp. 79–88

Pilkington, H. (ed.) (1996) *Gender, Generation and Identity in Contemporary Russia*, London

Piore, M. (1983) 'Labor Market Segmentation. To What Paradigm Does It Belong?', *American Economic Review*, 73:2 (May)

Polachek, S. (1995) 'Human Capital and the Gender Earnings Gap', in Kuiper & Sap (1995)

Posadskaia, A. (1989) 'Sotsial'no-ekonomicheskie problemy trudovoi aktivnost'i zhenshchin', PhD thesis, Moscow

Posadskaia, A. & Zakharova, N. (1992) 'Problema "sovmeshcheniia rolei": gendernyi analiz', in N. M. Rimashevskaia & V. V. Patsiorkovskii (eds) (1992a)

Posadskaia, A. (1992) 'Potentsial sotsial'noi integratsii zhenshchin i muzhchin v novye ekonomicheskie struktury', in N. M. Rimashevskaia & V. V. Patsiorkovskii (eds) (1992a)

Posadskaya, A. (ed.) (1994) *Women in Russia. A New Era in Russian Feminism*, London.

Posadskaia, A. (1996) 'Zhenskie issledovaniia v Rossii: Perspektivy novoga videniia', in Malysheva (ed.) (1996)

Pravda, A. (1982) 'Is There a Soviet Working Class?', *Problems of Communism*, 31:6, pp. 1–24

Prokofeva, L. M. (1988) 'Tendentsiia i faktory dinamiki semeinogo blagosostoianiia na razlichnykh stadiakh razvitiia sem'i', in Yu. N. Netesin (ed.) (1988) *Ekonomika i sem'i*, Riga

Prokofeva, L. M. (1991) 'Sotsial'no-ekonomicheskii status semei na otdel'nykh etapakh zhiznennogo tsikla', in Rimashevskaia and Onikov (1991)

Prokofeva, L. M. (1992) 'Naselenie goroda i sem'ia', in N. M. Rimashevskaia & V. V. Patsiorkovskii (eds) (1992a)

Psacharopoulos, G. (1981) 'Returns to Education: An Updated International Comparison', *Comparative Education*, 17:3, pp. 321–41

Ragan, J. R. & C. H. Tremblay (1988) 'Testing for Employee Discrimination by Race and Sex', *Journal of Human Resources*, 23:1, pp. 123–37

Raissi Bysiewicz, S. & L. I. Shelley (1987) 'Women in the Soviet Economy: Proclamations and Practice', in O. S. Ioffe & M. W. Janis (eds.) *Soviet Law and Economy*

Rebitzer, J. (1993) 'Radical Political Economy and Labor Markets', *Journal of Economic Literature*, 31:3, pp. 1394–1434

Redor, D. (1992) *Wage Inequalities in East and West*, Cambridge

Rees, A. (1993) 'The Role of Fairness in Wage Determination', *Journal of Labor Economics*, 11:1, pt. 1, pp. 243–52

Rimashevskaia, N. M. (ed.) (1988a) *Narodnoe blagosostoianie. Metodologiia i metodika issledovaniia*, Moscow

Rimashevskaia, N. M. (1988b) 'Current Problems of the Status of Women', *Soviet Sociology*, pp. 58–71

Rimashevskaia, N. M. (1988c) 'The Need for New Approaches', *Problems of Economics*, 30:12, pp. 59–72

Rimashevskaia, N. M. (1989) 'Public Well-Being: Myth and Reality', *Problems of Economics*, 31:1, pp. 34–49,

Rimashevskaia, N. M. (1992) 'Semeinoe blagosostoianie, usloviia, uroven', obraz i kachestvo zhizni naseleniia Rossii: Taganrogskie issledovaniia', paper, Taganrog, (May)

Rimashevskaia, N. M. (1996) 'Gender i ekonomicheskii perekhod v Rossii (na primere Taganrogskikh issledovanii)', in Malysheva (ed.) (1996)

Rimashevskaya, N. M. (1997) 'Poverty Trends in Russia: A Russian Perspective', in Klugman (ed.) (1997)

Rimashevskaia, N. M. (ed.) (1998) *Rossiia 1997. Sotsial'no-ekonomicheskaia situatsiia. VII ezhegodnyi doklad*, ISESP, Moscow

Rimashevskaia, N. M. & L. A. Onikov (eds) (1991) *Narodnoe blagosostoianie. Tendentsii perspektivy*, Moscow

Rimashevskaia , N. M. & V. V. Patsiorkovskii (eds.) (1992a) *Sotsial'no- ekonomchiskie issledovaniia blagosostoianiia, obraza i urovnia zhizni naseleniia goroda. Proekt Taganrog-III*, Moscow

Rimashevskaia, N. M. & V. V. Patsiorkovskii (1992b) 'Metodologicheskie printsipy izucheniia blagosostoianiia, obraza i urovnia zhizni naseleniia goroda', in N. M. Rimashevskaia & V. V. Patsiorkovskii (eds) (1992a)

Rimashevskaia, N. M. & Zakharova, N. (1989) 'The Diversification of Women's Training and Employment: The Case of the USSR', Training Discussion Paper No. 44, ILO

Rofe, A. I., Shunikov, A. M. & N. V. Yasakova (1991) *Organizatsiia i oplata truda na predpriiatii*, Moscow

Rosen, S. (1986) 'The Theory of Equalizing Differences', in Ashenfelter & Layard (1986)

Rosenfeld, R. A. & A. Kalleberg (1991) 'Gender Inequality in the Labor Market. A Cross-National Perspective', *Acta Sociologica*, 34, pp. 207–25

Roshin, S. & Ia. Roshina, (1994) 'Muzhchiny, zhenshchiny i predprinimatel'stvo', *Chelovek i trud*, 12

Roshin, S. (1995) 'Vtorichnaia zaniatost' zhenshchin', *Chelovek i trud*

Rossiiskii Statisticheskii Ezhegodnik, 1996 (1996) Goskomstat Rossii, Moscow

Rossiiskii Statisticheskii Ezhegodnik, 1997 (1997) Goskomstat Rossii, Moscow

Rossiiskii Statisticheskii Ezhegodnik, 1998 (1998) Goskomstat Rossii, Moscow

Rossiiskii Statisticheskii Ezhegodnik, 1999 (1999) Goskomstat Rossii, Moscow

Rubin, I. I. (1972) *Essays on Marx's Theory of Value*, Detroit

Ruble, B. (1979) 'Factory Unions and Workers' Rights', in Kahan & Ruble (1979)

Rutkevich, M. N. (1980) 'Sblizhenie rabochego klassa i inzhenerno-tekhnicheskoi intelligentsii', *Sotsiologicheskie issledovaniia*, 4, pp. 25–34

Rutkevich, M. N. (1984) 'Reforma obrazovaniia, potrebnosti obshchestva, molodezh', *Problems of Economics* 4, pp. 19–28

Rzhanitsyna, L. S. (1991) *Problems of Economics*, Moscow

Rzhanitsyna, L. (ed.) (1993) *Rabotaiushchie zhenshchiny v usloviakh perekhoda Rossii k rynku*, Moscow

Sawyer, M. (1995) 'The Operation of Labour Markets and the Economics of Equal Opportunities' in Humphries and Rubery (1995)

Schroeder, G. (1972) 'An Appraisal of Soviet Wage and Income Statistics', in V. Treml & J. Hardt (eds.), *Soviet Economic Statistics*, Durham, NC

Schwab, S. (1986) 'Is Statistical Discrimination Efficient?', *American Economic Review*, 76:1, pp. 228–34

Schwartz Rosenhan, M. (1978) 'Images of Male and Female in Children's Readers', in Atkinson et al. (1978)

SCB (1986) *Kvinno-och mansvärlden. Fakta om jämstölldheten i sverige*, Statistics Sweden, Stockholm

SCB (1992) *Tidsanvändningsundersökningen 1990/91*, Statistics Sweden, Stockholm,

Sen, A. (1984) 'Women, Technology and Sexual Divisions', *Trade and Development, an UNCTAD Review*, No. 6

Shapiro, J. (1992) 'The Industrial Labour Force', in Buckley (1992)

Sheidvasser, S. & H. Benítez-Silva (1999) 'The Educated Russian's Curse: Returns to Education in the Russian Federation', mimeo, Yale University

Shenfield, S. (1983) 'A Note on Data Quality in the Soviet Family Budget Survey', *Soviet Studies*, 35:4, pp. 561–8

Shineleva, L. (1989) 'Nuzhna gosudarstvennaia programma resheniia zhenskogo voprosa', *Sotsialisticheskii Trud*, 8

Silverman, B. & M. Yanowitch (1997) *New Rich, New Poor, New Russia. Winners and Losers on the Russian Road to Capitalism*, Armonk, NY

Sloane, P. & I. Theodossiou (1993) 'Gender and Job Tenure Effects on Earnings', *Oxford Bulletin of Economics and Statistics*, 55:4, pp. 421–37

Slottje, D. J., J. G. Hirschberg & K. J. Hayes (1994) 'A New Method for Detecting Individual and Group Labor Market Discrimination', *Journal of Econometrics*, 61:1, pp. 43–64

Smith, H. (1976) *The Russians*, New York

Smith, J. & M. Ward (1989) 'Women in the Labor Market and in the Family', *Journal of Economic Perspectives*, 3:1, pp. 9–24

Smith N. (1989) 'Kan ökonomiske teorier forklare kvinders placering på arbejdsmarkedet', *Nationalökonomisk. Tidskrift*, 127:3, pp. 321–38

Solow, R. (1990) *The Labor Market as a Social Institution*, Cambridge, Mass.

Sommestad, L. (1992) *Från mejerska till mejerist. En studie av mejeriyrkets maskuliniseringsprocess*, Lund

Sostav sem'i, dokhody i zhilishchnye usloviia (1990) Goskomstat SSSR Informatsion-no-izdatel'skii tsentr

SOU (1938) *Betänkande angående gift kvinnas förvärvsarbete*, Stockholm

Standing, G. (ed.) (1991) *In Search of Flexibility: The New Soviet Labour Market*, ILO, Geneva

Sternheimer, S. (1987) 'The Vanishing Babushka', in Herleman (1987)

Stites, R. (1978) 'Women and the Russian Intelligentsia: Three Perspectives', in Atkinson, (1978)

Strassmann, D. (1993) 'Not a Free Market: The Rethoric of Disciplinary Authority in Economics', in Ferber & Nelson (1993)

Strumilin, S. (1962) 'The Economics of Education in the USSR', *International Social Science Journal*, XIV:4, pp. 633–46

Strumilin, S. (1966) 'The Economic Significance of National Education', in E. Robinson & J. Vaizey, *The Economics of Education*, London (Russian original published in Ekonomika Truda, 1925)

Svensson, L. (1995) *Closing the Gender Gap. Determinants of Change in the Female-to-Male Blue-Collar Wage Ratio in Swedish Manufacturing 1913–1990*, Kristianstad

Swafford, M. (1978) 'Sex Diffences in Soviet Earnings', *American Sociological Review*, 43, pp. 657–73

Swafford, M. (1979) 'The Socialization and Training of Soviet Industrial Workers', in Kahan & Ruble (eds) (1979)

Terebilova V. I. (ed.) (1981) *Kommentarii k zakonodatel'stvu o trude*, Moscow,

The 1989 USSR Census, Microfiche, East View Publications, Minneapolis

Ticktin, H. H. (1973) 'Towards a Political Economy of the USSR', *Critique*, No. 1, pp. 20–41

Ticktin, H. H. (1992): *Origins of the Crisis in the USSR*, New York

Trotsky, L. D. (1973) *Revolution Betrayed*, London (originally published 1936 as *Chto takoe SSSR i kuda on idet*)

Trud v SSSR (1988) Goskomstat SSSR Informatsionno-izdatel'skii tsentr, Moscow

Trud i zaniatost' v Rossii (1995) Goskomstat Rossii, Moscow

Trud i zaniatost' v Rossii (1996) Goskomstat Rossii, Moscow

Trud i zaniatost' v Rossii (1999) Goskomstat Rossii, Moscow

Veretennikov, V (1991) 'Wage Differentials: The Trade Union View', in Standing (1991)

Vlasova, N., M. Kocheetkova & T. Prokhortseva (1994) 'Zhenskaia bezrabotitsa v Rossii', *Chelovek i trud*, 3

Walby, S. (ed.) (1988) *Gender Segregation at Work*, Milton Keynes

Waters, E. (1993) 'Finding a Voice: The Emergence of a Women's Movement', in Funk & Mueller (eds) (1993)

Watts, M. and Rich, J (1993) 'Occupational Sex Segregation in Britain, 1979–1989: The Persistence of Sexual Stereotyping', *Cambridge Journal of Economics*, 17, pp. 159–77

White, H. (1980) 'A Heteroskedasticity-consistent Covariance Matrix Estimator and a Direct Test for Heteroskedasticity', *Econometrica*, 48:4, pp. 817–38

Willborn, S. L. (ed.) (1991) 'Women's Wages: Stability and Change in Six Industrialised Countries', *International Review of Comparative Public Policy*, vol. 3

Willis, R. J. (1986) 'Wage Determinants: A Survey and Reinterpretation of Human Capital Earnings Functions', in Ashenfelter & Layard (1986)

Winter-Ebmer, R. & J. Zweimüller (1997) 'Unequal Assignnment and Unequal Promotion in Job Ladders', *Journal of Labor Economics*, 15:1, pp. 43–71

Witz, A. (1988) 'Patriarchal Relations and Patterns of Sex Segregation in the Medical Division of Labour', in Walby (1988)

Yanowitch, M. & N. Dodge (1969) 'The Social Evaluation of Occupations in the USSR', *Slavic Review*, 20:1, pp. 619–43

Yanowitch, M. (1985) *The Social Structure of the USSR*, New York

Zakharova, N., Posadskaia , A., Rimashevskaia, N. (1989) 'Kak my reshaem zhenskii vopros', *Kommunist*, 4, pp. 56–65

Zhenshchiny v SSSR 1989, (1989) Finansy i statistika, Goskomstat, Moscow

Zhenshchiny v SSSR 1990, (1990) Finansy i statistika, Goskomstat, Moscow

Zhenshchiny v SSSR 1991, (1991) Finansy i statistika, Goskomstat, Moscow

Zhenschiny i muzhchiny Rossii 97, (1997) Goskomstat, Moscow

Zhenschiny i muzhchiny Rossii 99, (1999) Goskomstat, Moscow

Index

Absenteeism, 75
Agricultural labour, female labour force participation, 99
Akerlof, G.,17, 18, 35, 36
Anti-discrimination measures, 24
  see also discrimination; labour legislation
Attestat (secondary school diploma), 183
  and see education, complete secondary

Basic pay, 57, 61
Becker, G., 20, 250 n.13, 252, n.34
Benefits, non-monetary, 5, 62–3
  see also child-care; consumer goods, enterprise-provided; fringe benefits; holidays; housing
Birth rate
  and education, 103
  fall in, 91–2, 101–2, 214–15
  see also working mothers
Blue-collar industrial workers, 60–6
  overqualified, 192–6
  status of, 61, 81
  working conditions of, 61–3
Bonuses, Bonus system, 49, 53, 56, 64–5, 70, 155–7
  as percentage of wage, 68
Bribery, 77

Career
  break, 22, 23, 24; *see also* maternity leave
  and education, 16, 89
Certification committees, 51
  child-care, 101
  effect on career, 20
  public, 93, 102, 104
  subsidised, 71, 73
Clarke, S., 265, n. 15
Class conflict, 63
Collective bargaining, absence of, 51
Commodity fetishism, 17

Company stores, 74
  see also benefits, non-monetary; consumer goods, access to
Comparable worth, 34
Compensating differentials, 75–6, 78, 181–4, 243–4
Complete secondary education, 87, 162, 188–9, nn. 4 *and* 6
  universal achievement of, 189
  vocational school with, 87, 182, 188
  and see generally education
Consumer goods
  access to, 5
  scarcity of, 5, 78
  supplied by enterprise, 73
  supply of, 60
Corruption, 77–8
Crowding effect, 19, 101
  and see occupational segregation

Dacha, 72
  and see fringe benefits
Demographic question, 84–5, 91–2, 101–2, 214
  and see birth rate; mortality, male
Deskilling, 34
Disaffection, 18, 184, 197
Discrimination, 19, 23, 28–37, 244–5
  hiring practices, 30–1
  quantifying, 38–46
  by sector, 70
  statistical, 29
Dismissals, 51–2
Domestic work, 15
  see also housework
Drunkenness, at work, 75, 85
  see also dismissals
Dual labour market theory, 36, 37

Earnings
  differential, inter-industrial, 57
  dispersion, 59
  potential of women, 91

Strikes, 51, 52
Strumilin, S., 165
Sturmovshchina *see* storming
Subsistence gardening, 72, 256, n. 38
  see also fringe benefits
Surplus labour and wage depression, 19
Swafford, M., 8
Sweden, female/male wage ratios 13

Taganrog
  age distribution, 117
  average wage, 83, 110–11, 112, 113,
    114, 119
  earnings dispersion, 54
  education, 83, 90, 111, 118
  employment rates, 94
  heavy industry sector, 83
  household surveys, 3, 82, 84–6, 207–9
  housework, 105–9
  housing, 73
  post-USSR, 202–31
  poverty, 208
  relative wages, 163–4
  turnover rates, 125
  working hours, average, 96–7, 123
  working mothers, 103–5
Take-home wage, 110
Tarifnaia stavka see basic pay
Tarifnaia setka see skill scale
Taxation, 76
Tenure, returns to, 24, 53
Theft, workplace, 77
Time-rates, 55, 56
  cf. piece rates
Trade unions, role of, 51
  distribution of fringe benefits by, 73
Turnover rates, 125
  see also quits

UK female/male wage ratios, 13
Underqualification, 192
Unemployment, 202, 219–23
  duration of, 221
  hidden, 221–3
  of women, 219–20
Union membership, effect on wages, 32
United States, female/male wage ratios,
  13
Unpaid leave, 223–4

Uravnilovka see wage-levelling
USSR
  collapse of, 1, 2
  dysfunctional, 5
  social structure, 4–5
Utility function, 20, 41
Utility maximisation, individual, 15

Victimisation, 51
Vocational-technical schools, 62, 87
  bias against girls, 88–9
  recruitment to, 188
VUZ *see* higher education

Wage
  -age profile, 128
  arrears, 223–4
  -bargaining, 49
  centrally determined, 49, 53
  compression, 161
  decomposition of differentials,
    39–43, 139–43
  default, 202
  differentials, 110, 161, 162, 240–3
  discrimination, 5
  dispersion, 54
  drift, 57, 65, 197
  equilibrium, 16, 35
  expectations, 18, 93
  formation, post-Soviet, 55–60
  formation, Soviet, 49–55
  incentives, 193
  inflation, 53
  labour, 5
  market-clearing, 18
  minimum, 58–9
  modelling, 37–46
  non-payment of, 223–4
  policy, 50, 184–7
  post-Soviet system, 55
  rates, 122–33, 135–9
  reforms, 56–60
  reservation, 16
  scales, industrial, 55–6
  starting, 23
  structure, 5
  supplements, 53
  take-home, 110
Wage Fund, 59, 60, 67, 165